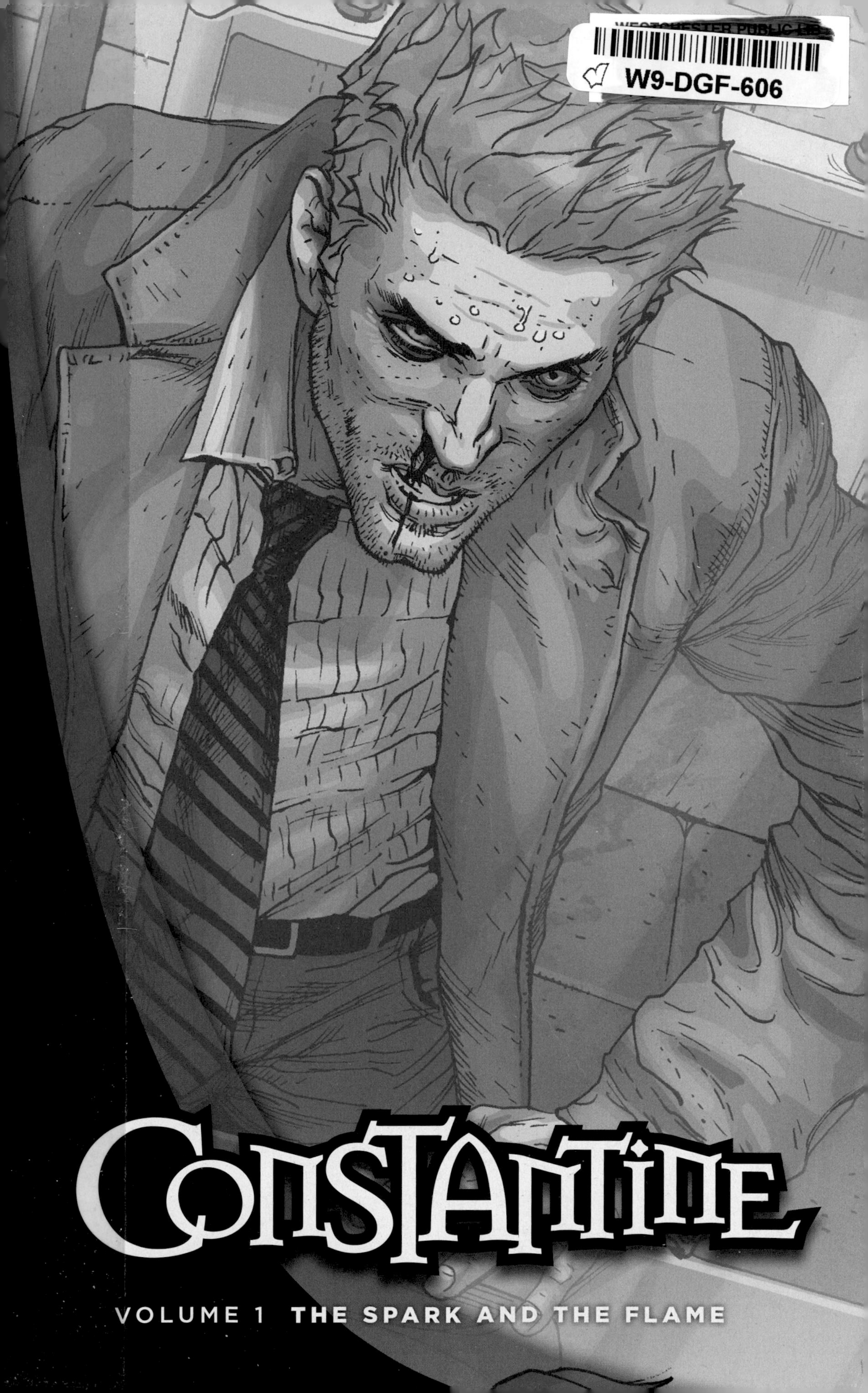

CONSTANTINE

VOLUME 1 THE SPARK AND THE FLAME

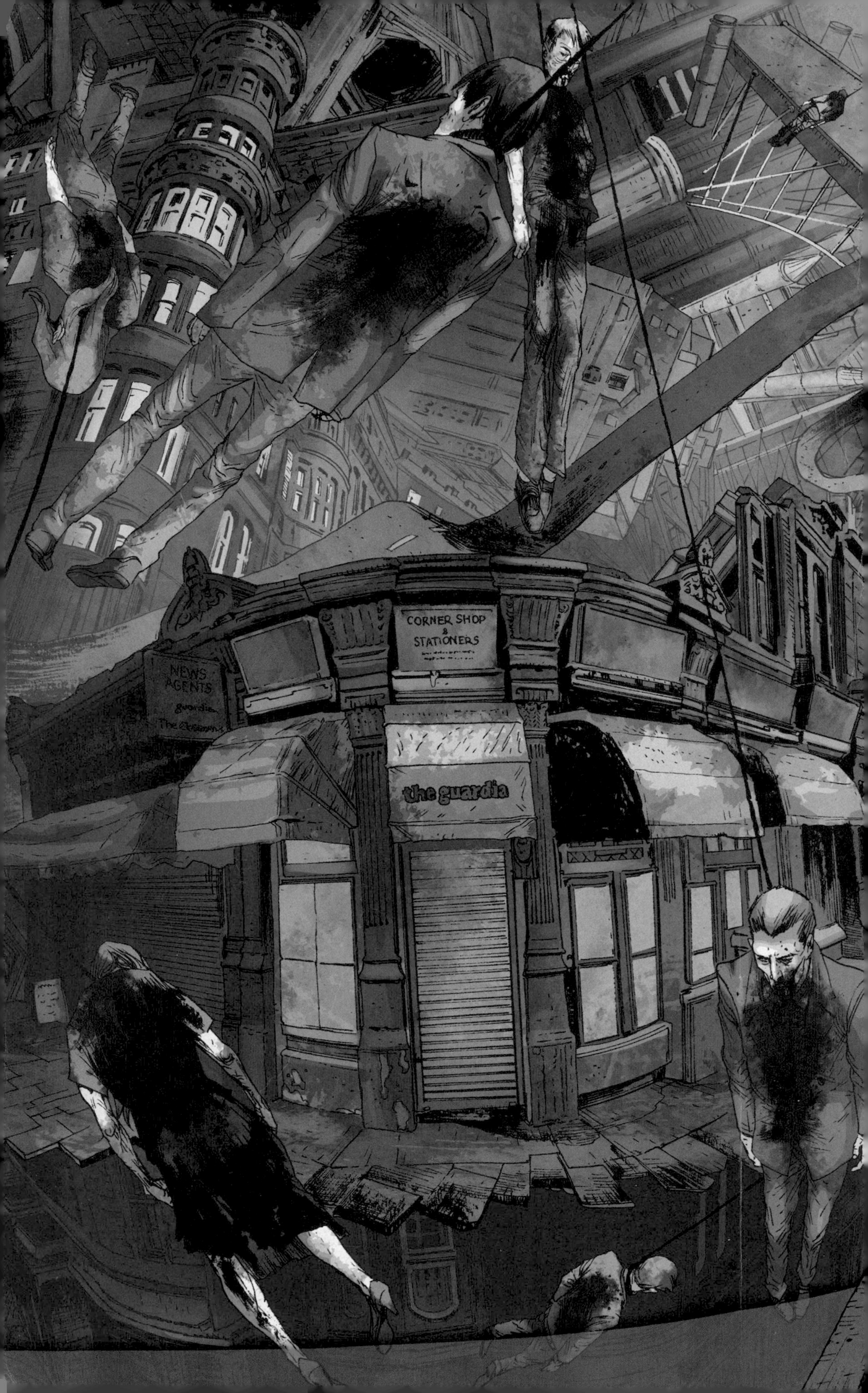
NEWS AGENTS
guardian
CORNER SHOP & STATIONERS
the guardia

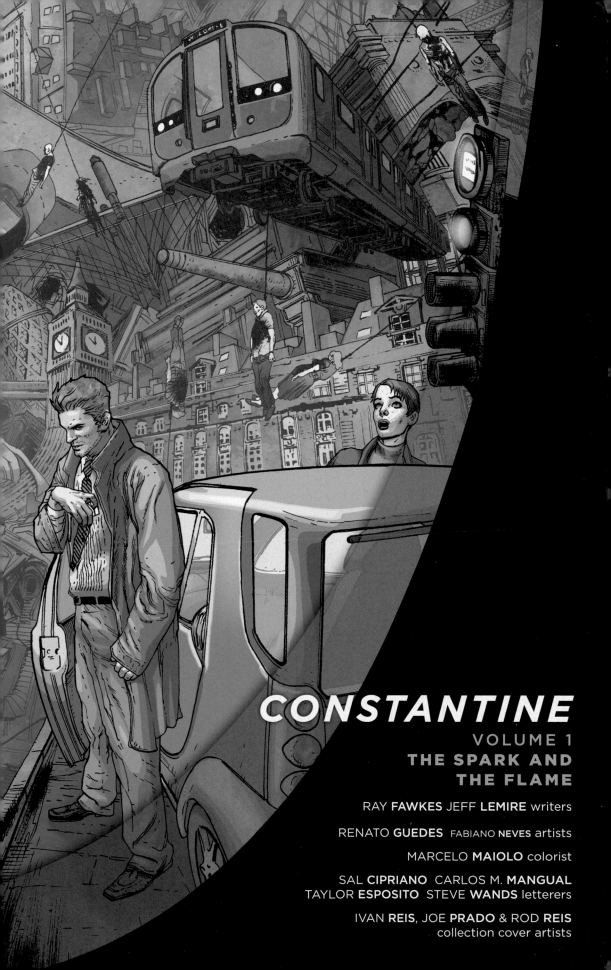

CONSTANTINE

VOLUME 1
THE SPARK AND
THE FLAME

RAY **FAWKES** JEFF **LEMIRE** writers

RENATO **GUEDES** FABIANO **NEVES** artists

MARCELO **MAIOLO** colorist

SAL **CIPRIANO** CARLOS M. **MANGUAL**
TAYLOR **ESPOSITO** STEVE **WANDS** letterers

IVAN **REIS**, JOE **PRADO** & ROD **REIS**
collection cover artists

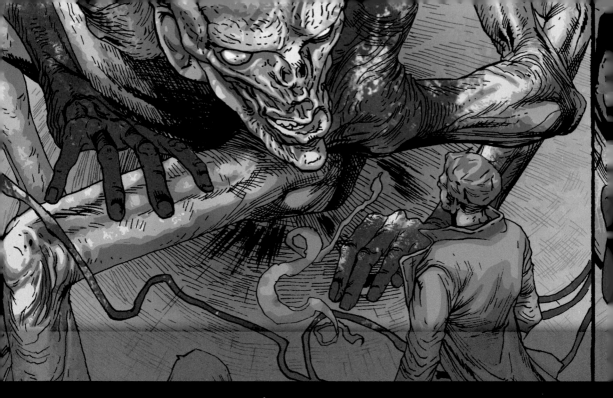

BRIAN CUNNINGHAM Editor – Original Series KATIE KUBERT Associate Editor – Original Series
KATE STEWART Assistant Editor – Original Series ROWENA YOW Editor
ROBBIN BROSTERMAN Design Director – Books ROBBIE BIEDERMAN Publication Design

BOB HARRAS Senior VP – Editor-in-Chief, DC Comics

DIANE NELSON President DAN DIDIO and JIM LEE Co-Publishers GEOFF JOHNS Chief Creative Officer
AMIT DESAI Senior VP – Marketing & Franchise Management AMY GENKINS Senior VP – Business & Legal Affairs
NAIRI GARDINER Senior VP – Finance JEFF BOISON VP – Publishing Planning MARK CHIARELLO VP – Art Direction & Design
JOHN CUNNINGHAM VP – Marketing TERRI CUNNINGHAM VP – Editorial Administration LARRY GANEM VP – Talent Relations & Services
ALISON GILL Senior VP – Manufacturing & Operations HANK KANALZ Senior VP – Vertigo & Integrated Publishing
JAY KOGAN VP – Business & Legal Affairs, Publishing JACK MAHAN VP – Business Affairs, Talent
NICK NAPOLITANO VP – Manufacturing Administration SUE POHJA VP – Book Sales
Fred Ruiz VP – Manufacturing Administration COURTNEY SIMMONS Senior VP – Publicity
BOB WAYNE Senior VP – Sales

CONSTANTINE VOLUME 1: THE SPARK AND THE FLAME

DC Comics, 4000 Warner Blvd., Burbank, CA 91522.
A Warner Bros. Entertainment Company.
Printed by Solisco Printers, Scott, QC, Canada. 5/27/15. Third Printing.
ISBN: 978-1-4012-4323-4

Library of Congress Cataloging-in-Publication Data

Lemire, Jeff.
Constantine. Volume 1, The Spark and the Flame / Jeff Lemire, Ray Fawkes ; [illustrated by] Renato Guedes.
pages cm.
Summary: "The star of JUSTICE LEAGUE DARK and HELLBLAZER—the longest-running Vertigo series—is unleashed in his own DCU title! Liar, cheater, manipulator...John Constantine is all of these, and yet he uses these skills and more to protect the world from the darkest corners of the DC Universe. Collects Constantine #1-6"— Provided by publisher.
ISBN 978-1-4012-4323-4 (pbk.)
1. Graphic novels. I. Fawkes, Ray, author. II. Guedes, Renato, illustrator. III. Title. IV. Title: Spark and the Flame.
PN6727.C675L46 2014
741.5'973—dc23
2013039608

SUSTAINABLE FORESTRY INITIATIVE
Certified Chain of Custody
Promoting Sustainable Forestry
www.sfiprogram.org
SFI-01368
This Label only applies to the text section

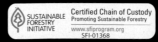

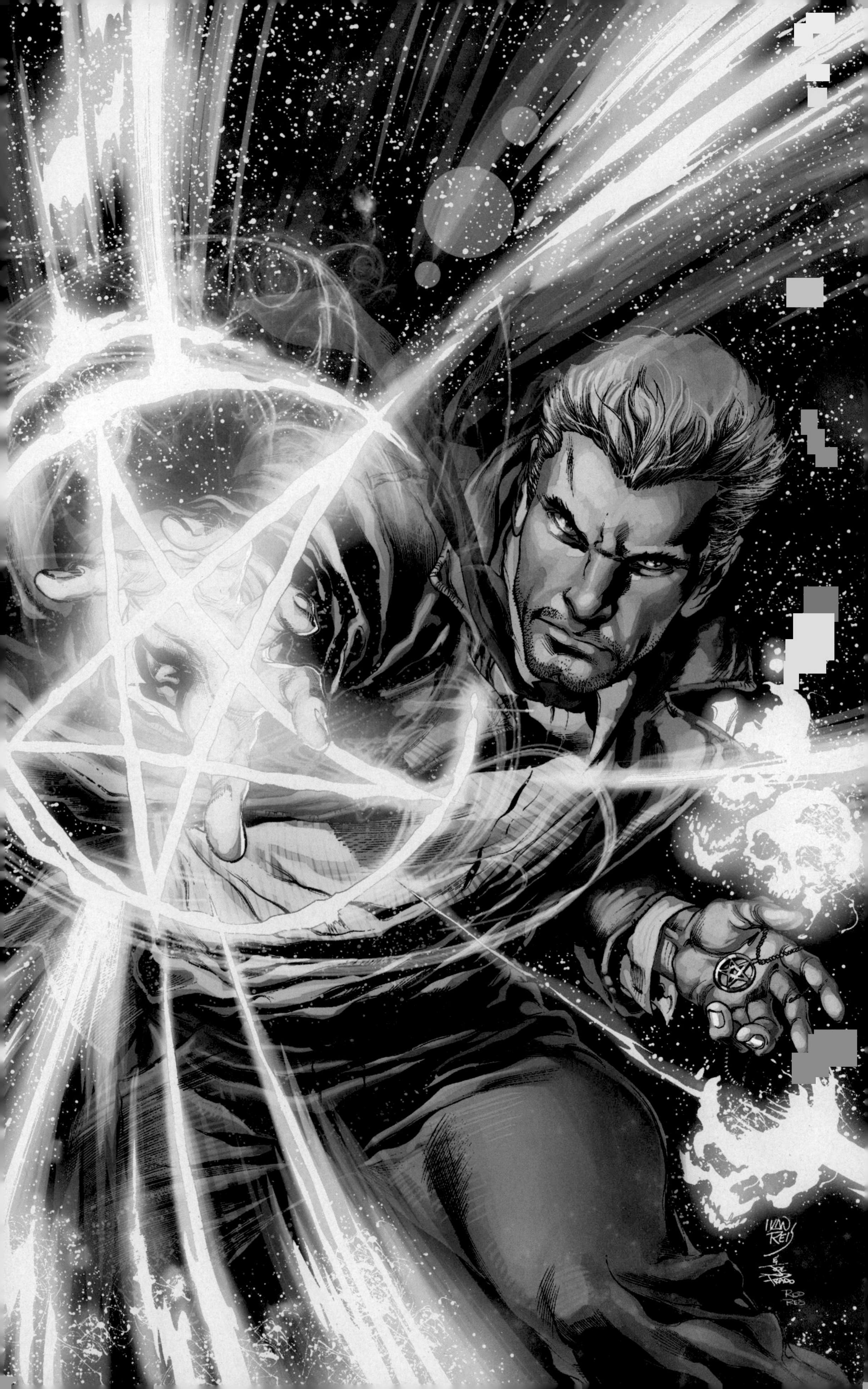

THE SPARK AND THE FLAME PART 1: THE PRICE WE PAY

JEFF LEMIRE & RAY FAWKES writers **RENATO GUEDES** artist cover art by **IVAN REIS, JOE PRADO & ROD REIS**

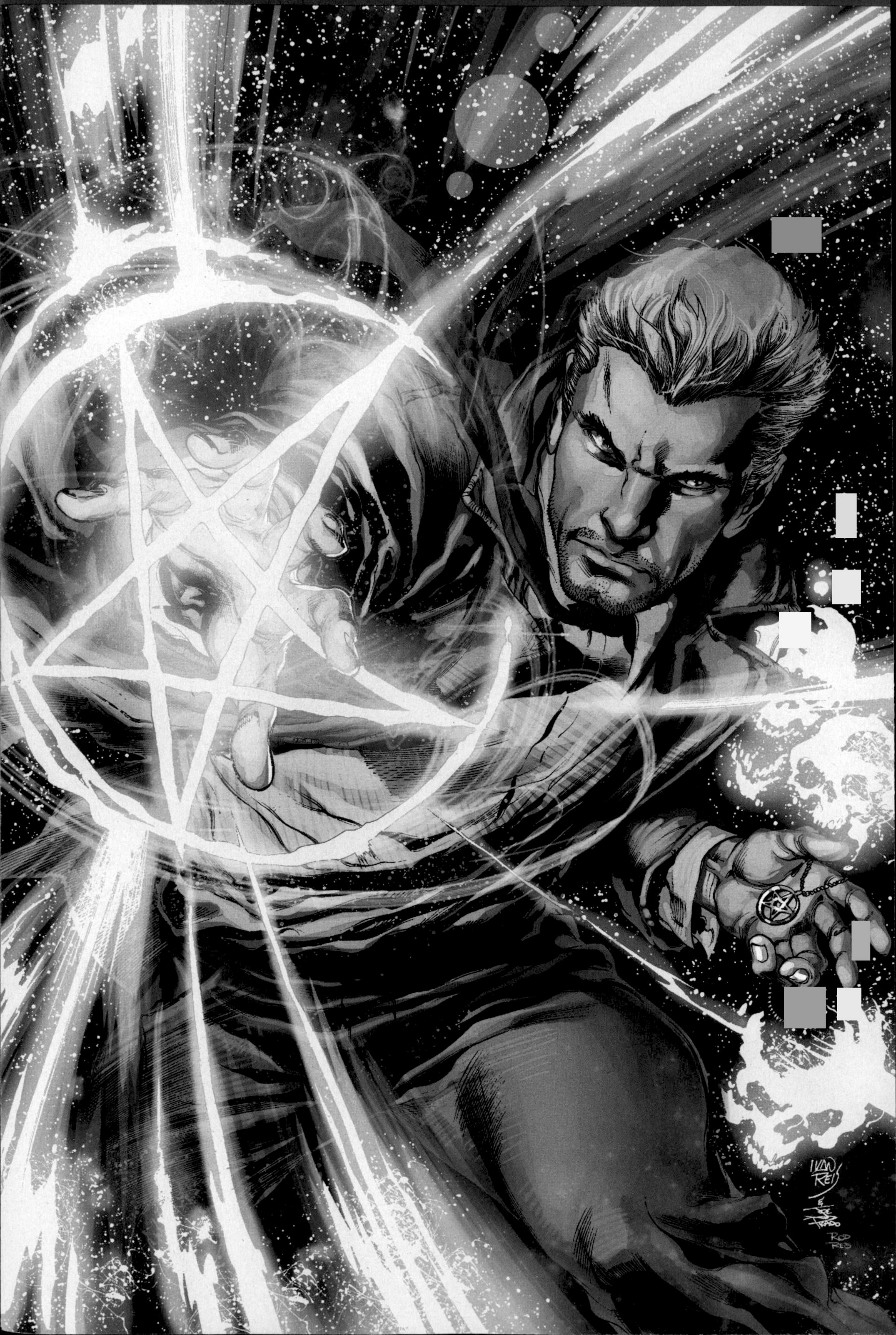

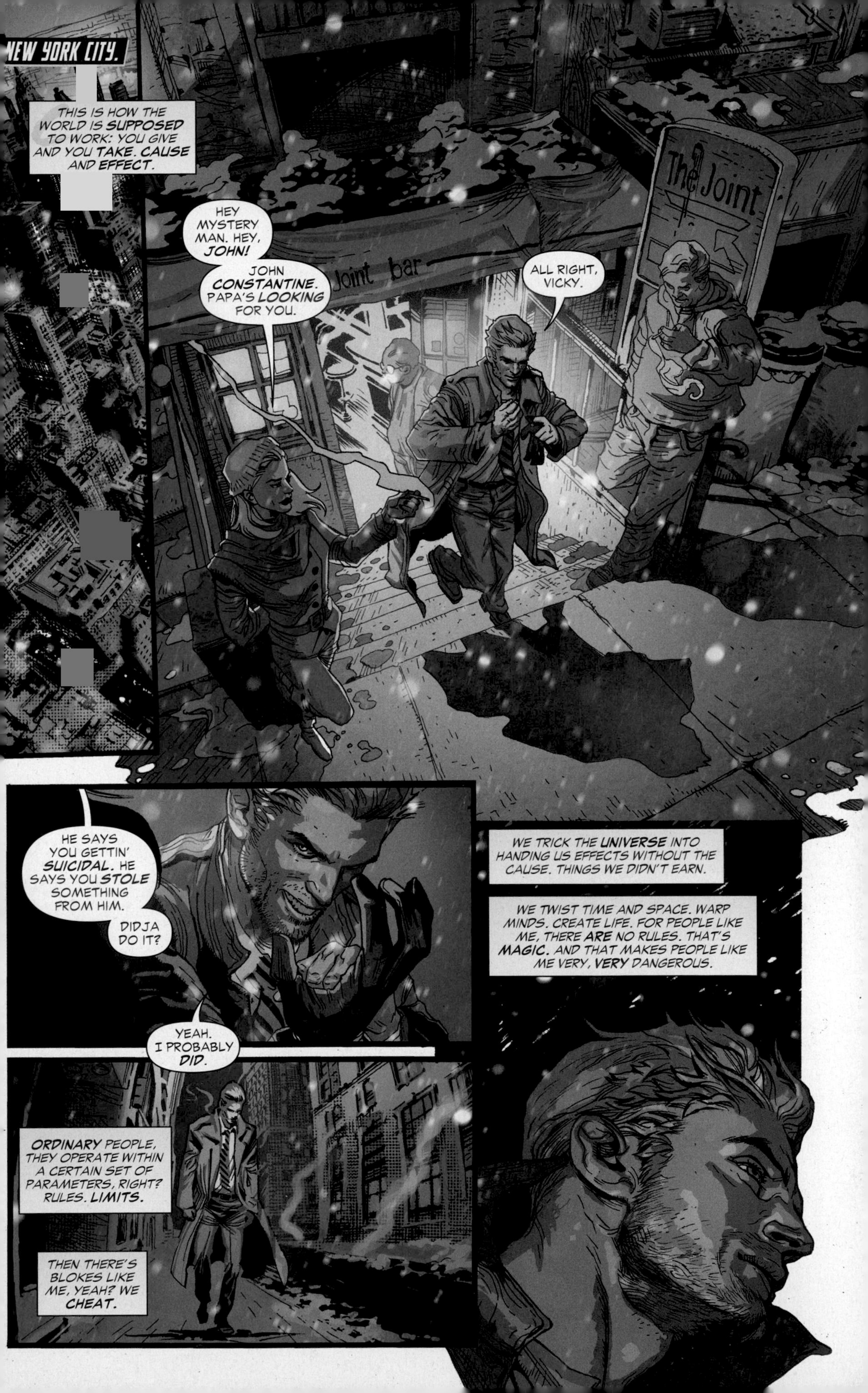

NEW YORK CITY.
THIS IS HOW THE WORLD IS SUPPOSED TO WORK: YOU GIVE AND YOU TAKE. CAUSE AND EFFECT.
HEY MYSTERY MAN. HEY, JOHN!
JOHN CONSTANTINE. PAPA'S LOOKING FOR YOU.
ALL RIGHT, VICKY.
The Joint
Joint bar
HE SAYS YOU GETTIN' SUICIDAL. HE SAYS YOU STOLE SOMETHING FROM HIM.
DIDJA DO IT?
YEAH. I PROBABLY DID.
ORDINARY PEOPLE, THEY OPERATE WITHIN A CERTAIN SET OF PARAMETERS, RIGHT? RULES. LIMITS.
THEN THERE'S BLOKES LIKE ME, YEAH? WE CHEAT.
WE TRICK THE UNIVERSE INTO HANDING US EFFECTS WITHOUT THE CAUSE. THINGS WE DIDN'T EARN.
WE TWIST TIME AND SPACE. WARP MINDS. CREATE LIFE. FOR PEOPLE LIKE ME, THERE ARE NO RULES. THAT'S MAGIC. AND THAT MAKES PEOPLE LIKE ME VERY, VERY DANGEROUS.

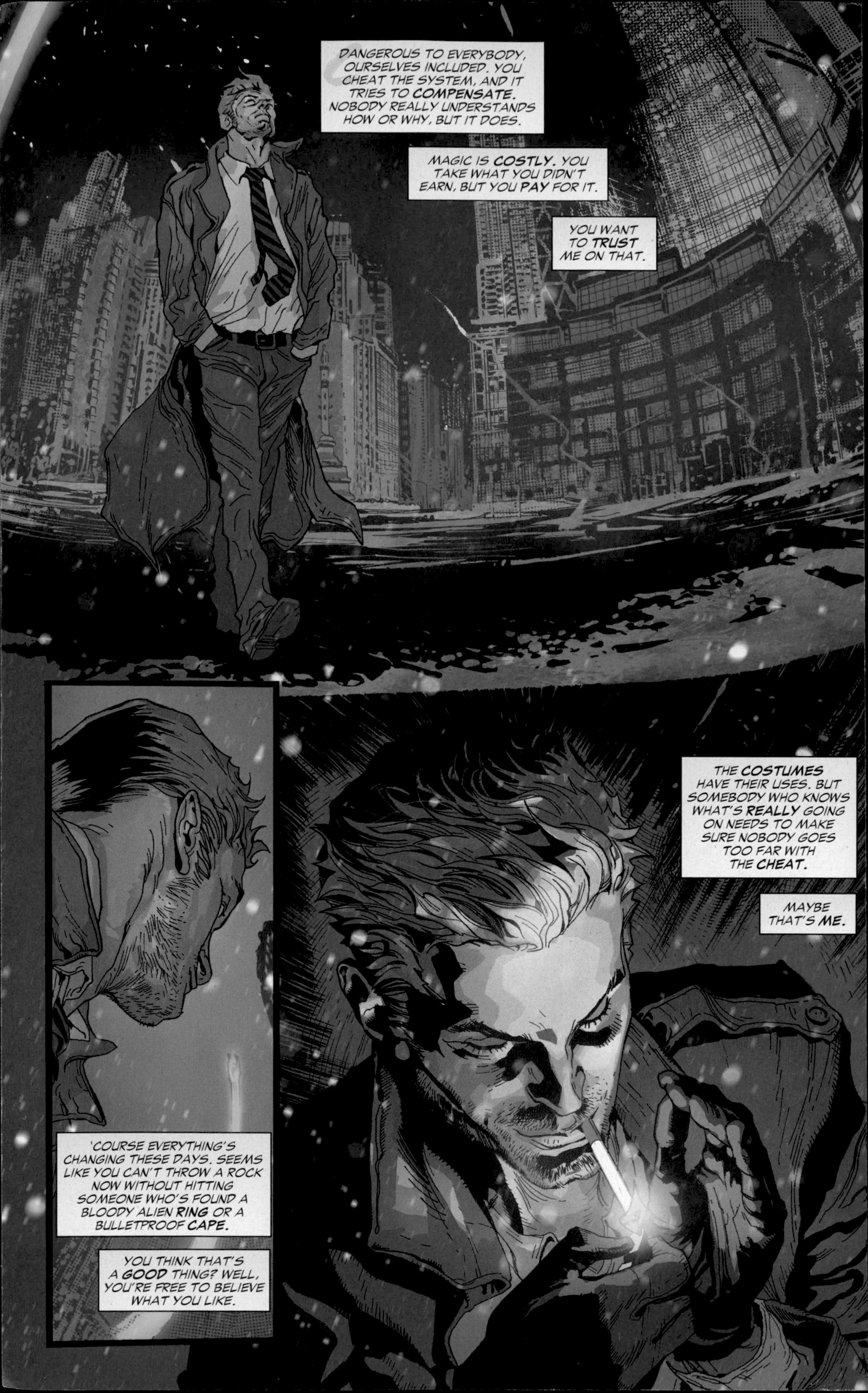
DANGEROUS TO EVERYBODY, OURSELVES INCLUDED. YOU CHEAT THE SYSTEM, AND IT TRIES TO COMPENSATE. NOBODY REALLY UNDERSTANDS HOW OR WHY, BUT IT DOES.
MAGIC IS COSTLY. YOU TAKE WHAT YOU DIDN'T EARN, BUT YOU PAY FOR IT.
YOU WANT TO TRUST ME ON THAT.
'COURSE EVERYTHING'S CHANGING THESE DAYS. SEEMS LIKE YOU CAN'T THROW A ROCK NOW WITHOUT HITTING SOMEONE WHO'S FOUND A BLOODY ALIEN RING OR A BULLETPROOF CAPE.
YOU THINK THAT'S A GOOD THING? WELL, YOU'RE FREE TO BELIEVE WHAT YOU LIKE.
THE COSTUMES HAVE THEIR USES. BUT SOMEBODY WHO KNOWS WHAT'S REALLY GOING ON NEEDS TO MAKE SURE NOBODY GOES TOO FAR WITH THE CHEAT.
MAYBE THAT'S ME.

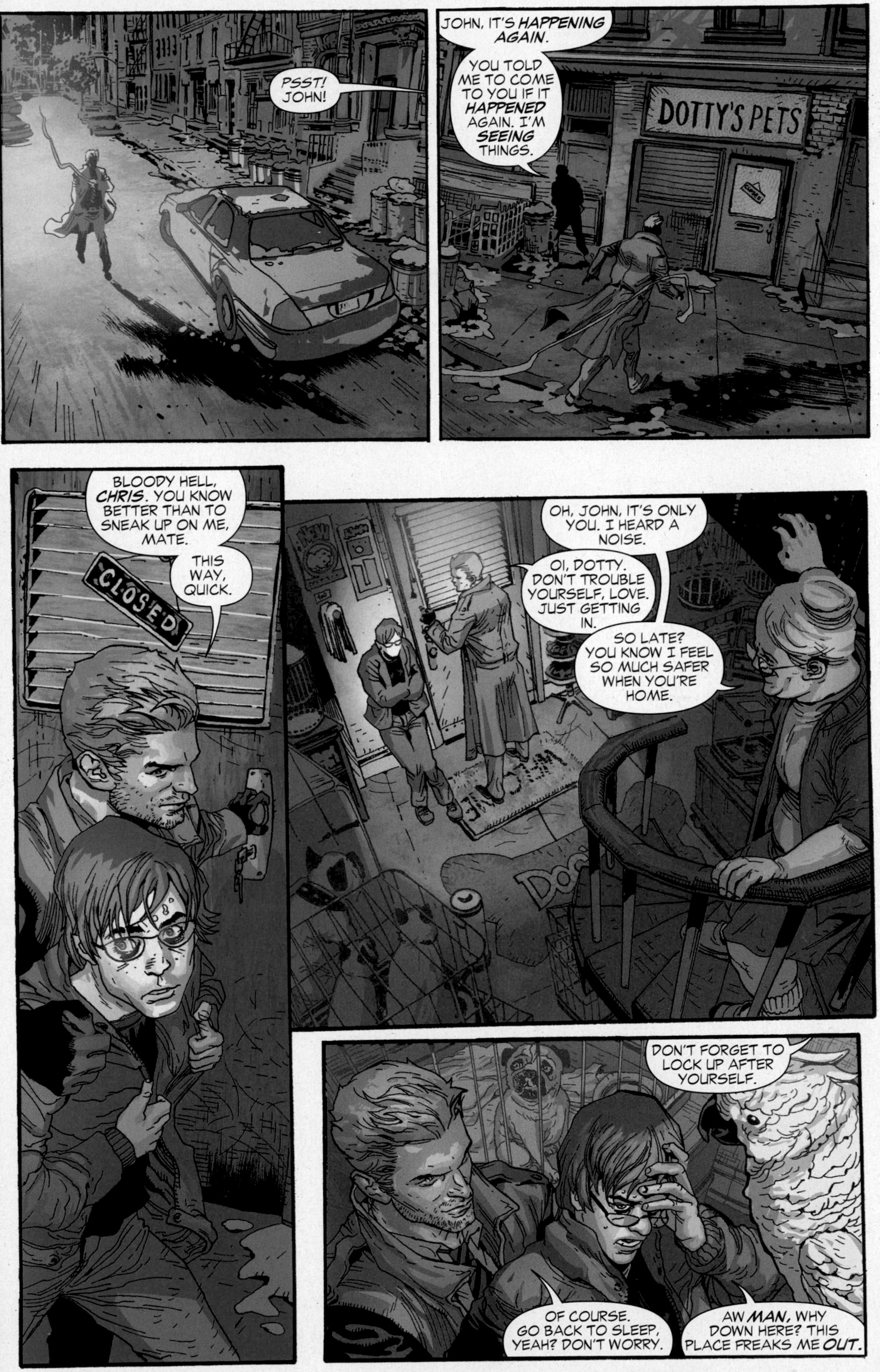

PSST! JOHN!
JOHN, IT'S HAPPENING AGAIN.
YOU TOLD ME TO COME TO YOU IF IT HAPPENED AGAIN. I'M SEEING THINGS.
DOTTY'S PETS
BLOODY HELL, CHRIS. YOU KNOW BETTER THAN TO SNEAK UP ON ME, MATE.
THIS WAY, QUICK.
CLOSED
OH, JOHN, IT'S ONLY YOU. I HEARD A NOISE.
OI, DOTTY. DON'T TROUBLE YOURSELF, LOVE. JUST GETTING IN.
SO LATE? YOU KNOW I FEEL SO MUCH SAFER WHEN YOU'RE HOME.
DON'T FORGET TO LOCK UP AFTER YOURSELF.
OF COURSE. GO BACK TO SLEEP, YEAH? DON'T WORRY.
AW MAN, WHY DOWN HERE? THIS PLACE FREAKS ME OUT.

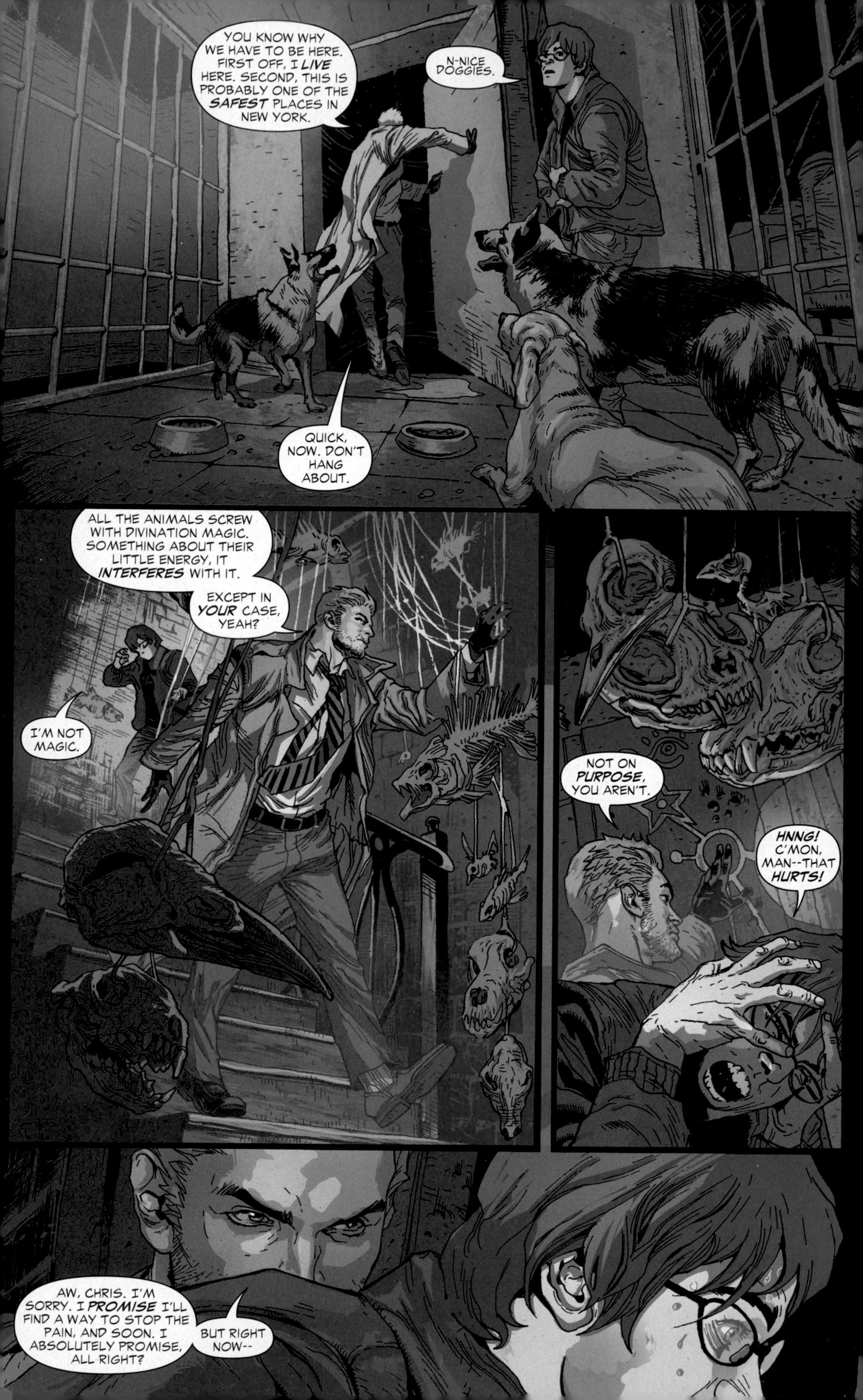

YOU KNOW WHY WE HAVE TO BE HERE. FIRST OFF, I *LIVE* HERE. SECOND, THIS IS PROBABLY ONE OF THE *SAFEST* PLACES IN NEW YORK.
N-NICE DOGGIES.
QUICK, NOW. DON'T HANG ABOUT.
ALL THE ANIMALS SCREW WITH DIVINATION MAGIC. SOMETHING ABOUT THEIR LITTLE ENERGY, IT *INTERFERES* WITH IT.
EXCEPT IN *YOUR* CASE, YEAH?
I'M NOT MAGIC.
NOT ON *PURPOSE*, YOU AREN'T.
HNNG! C'MON, MAN--THAT *HURTS!*
AW, CHRIS. I'M SORRY. I *PROMISE* I'LL FIND A WAY TO STOP THE PAIN, AND SOON. I ABSOLUTELY PROMISE, ALL RIGHT?
BUT RIGHT NOW--

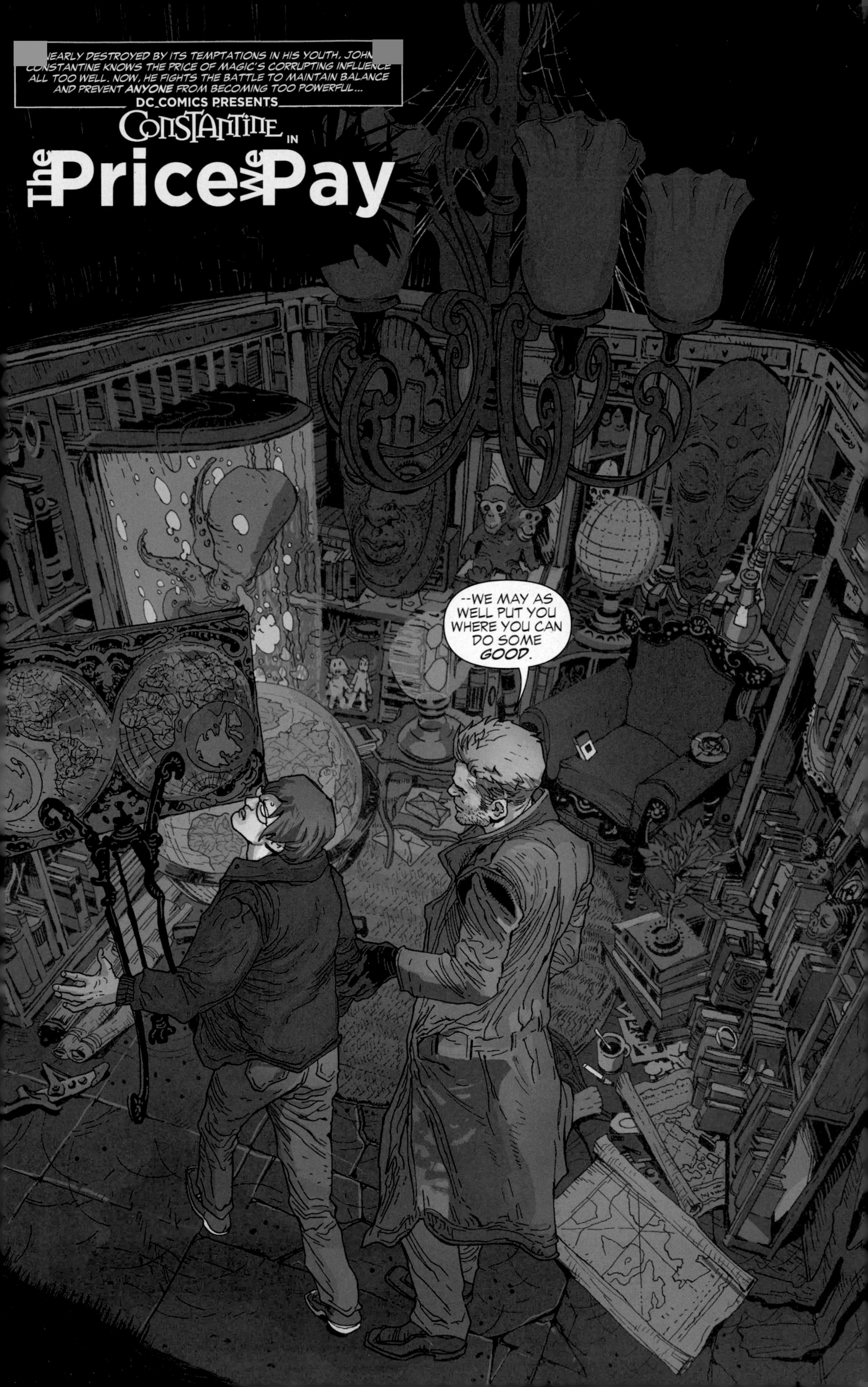
NEARLY DESTROYED BY ITS TEMPTATIONS IN HIS YOUTH, JOHN CONSTANTINE KNOWS THE PRICE OF MAGIC'S CORRUPTING INFLUENCE ALL TOO WELL. NOW, HE FIGHTS THE BATTLE TO MAINTAIN BALANCE AND PREVENT ANYONE FROM BECOMING TOO POWERFUL...
DC COMICS PRESENTS
CONSTANTINE IN
The Price We Pay
--WE MAY AS WELL PUT YOU WHERE YOU CAN DO SOME GOOD.

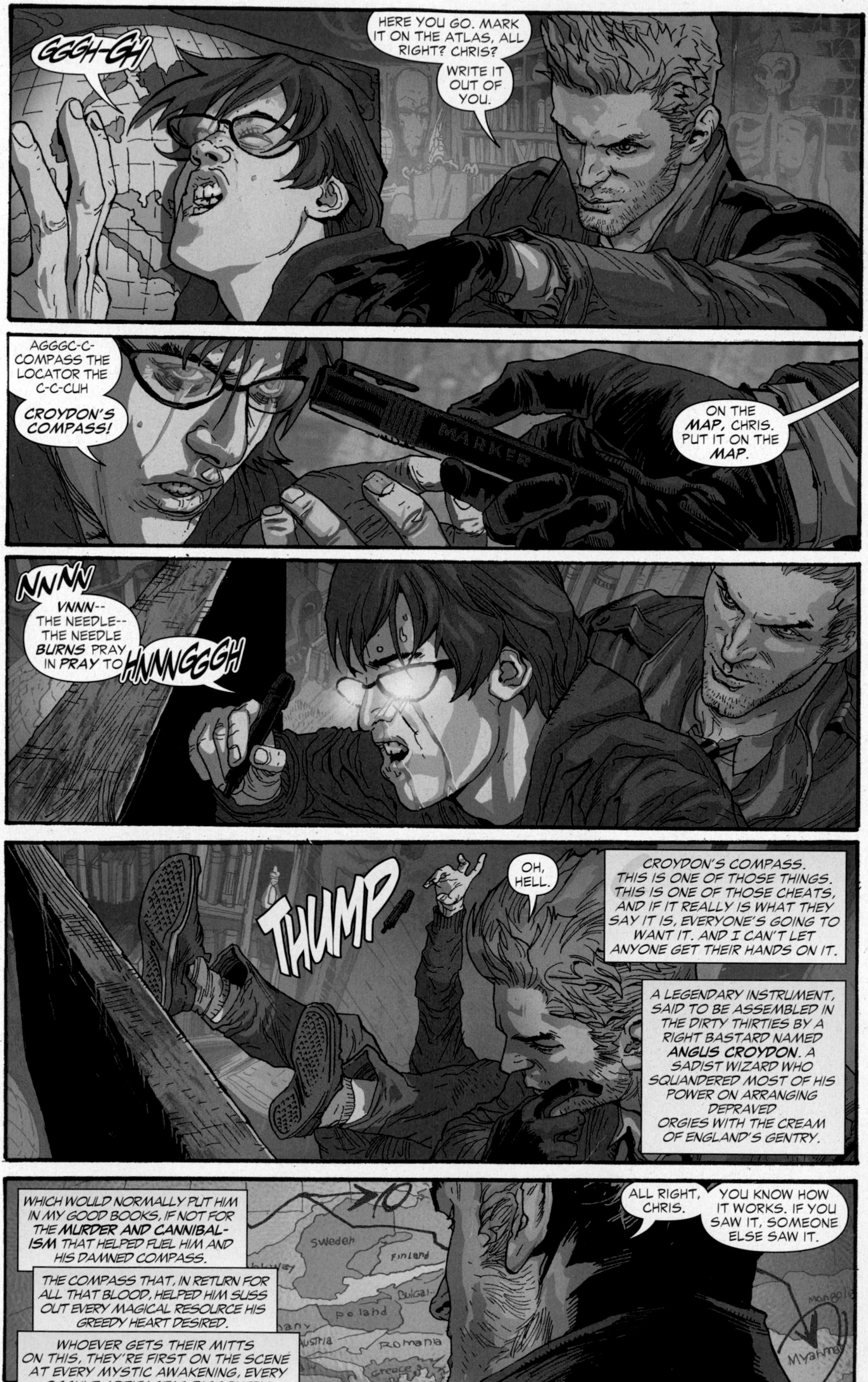
GGGH-GH
HERE YOU GO. MARK IT ON THE ATLAS, ALL RIGHT? CHRIS?
WRITE IT OUT OF YOU.
AGGGC-C-COMPASS THE LOCATOR THE C-C-CUH **CROYDON'S COMPASS!**
MARKER
ON THE **MAP,** CHRIS. PUT IT ON THE **MAP**.
NNNN
VNNN-- THE NEEDLE-- THE NEEDLE **BURNS** PRAY IN **PRAY** TO HNNNGGGH
THUMP
OH, HELL.
CROYDON'S COMPASS. THIS IS ONE OF THOSE THINGS. THIS IS ONE OF THOSE CHEATS, AND IF IT REALLY IS WHAT THEY SAY IT IS, EVERYONE'S GOING TO WANT IT. AND I CAN'T LET ANYONE GET THEIR HANDS ON IT.
A LEGENDARY INSTRUMENT, SAID TO BE ASSEMBLED IN THE DIRTY THIRTIES BY A RIGHT BASTARD NAMED **ANGUS CROYDON**. A SADIST WIZARD WHO SQUANDERED MOST OF HIS POWER ON ARRANGING DEPRAVED ORGIES WITH THE CREAM OF ENGLAND'S GENTRY.
WHICH WOULD NORMALLY PUT HIM IN MY GOOD BOOKS, IF NOT FOR THE **MURDER AND CANNIBALISM** THAT HELPED FUEL HIM AND HIS DAMNED COMPASS.
THE COMPASS THAT, IN RETURN FOR ALL THAT BLOOD, HELPED HIM SUSS OUT EVERY MAGICAL RESOURCE HIS GREEDY HEART DESIRED.
WHOEVER GETS THEIR MITTS ON THIS, THEY'RE FIRST ON THE SCENE AT EVERY MYSTIC AWAKENING, EVERY OCCULT ARTIFACT'S DISCOVERY.
ALL RIGHT, CHRIS.
YOU KNOW HOW IT WORKS. IF YOU SAW IT, SOMEONE ELSE SAW IT.
Sweden
Finland
Poland
Romania
Greece

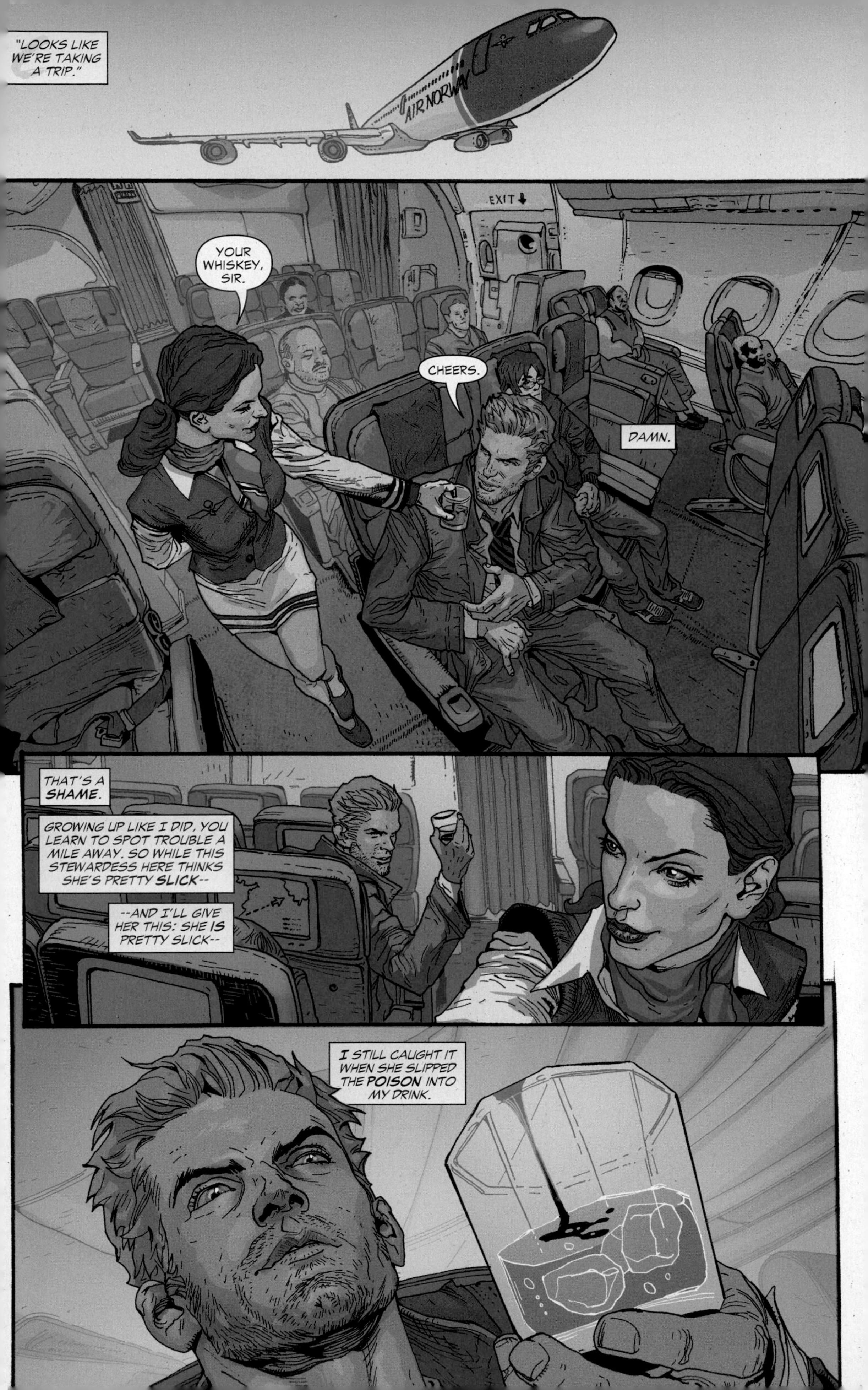
"LOOKS LIKE WE'RE TAKING A TRIP."
AIR NORWAY
EXIT
YOUR WHISKEY, SIR.
CHEERS.
DAMN.
THAT'S A SHAME.
GROWING UP LIKE I DID, YOU LEARN TO SPOT TROUBLE A MILE AWAY. SO WHILE THIS STEWARDESS HERE THINKS SHE'S PRETTY SLICK--
--AND I'LL GIVE HER THIS: SHE IS PRETTY SLICK--
I STILL CAUGHT IT WHEN SHE SLIPPED THE POISON INTO MY DRINK.

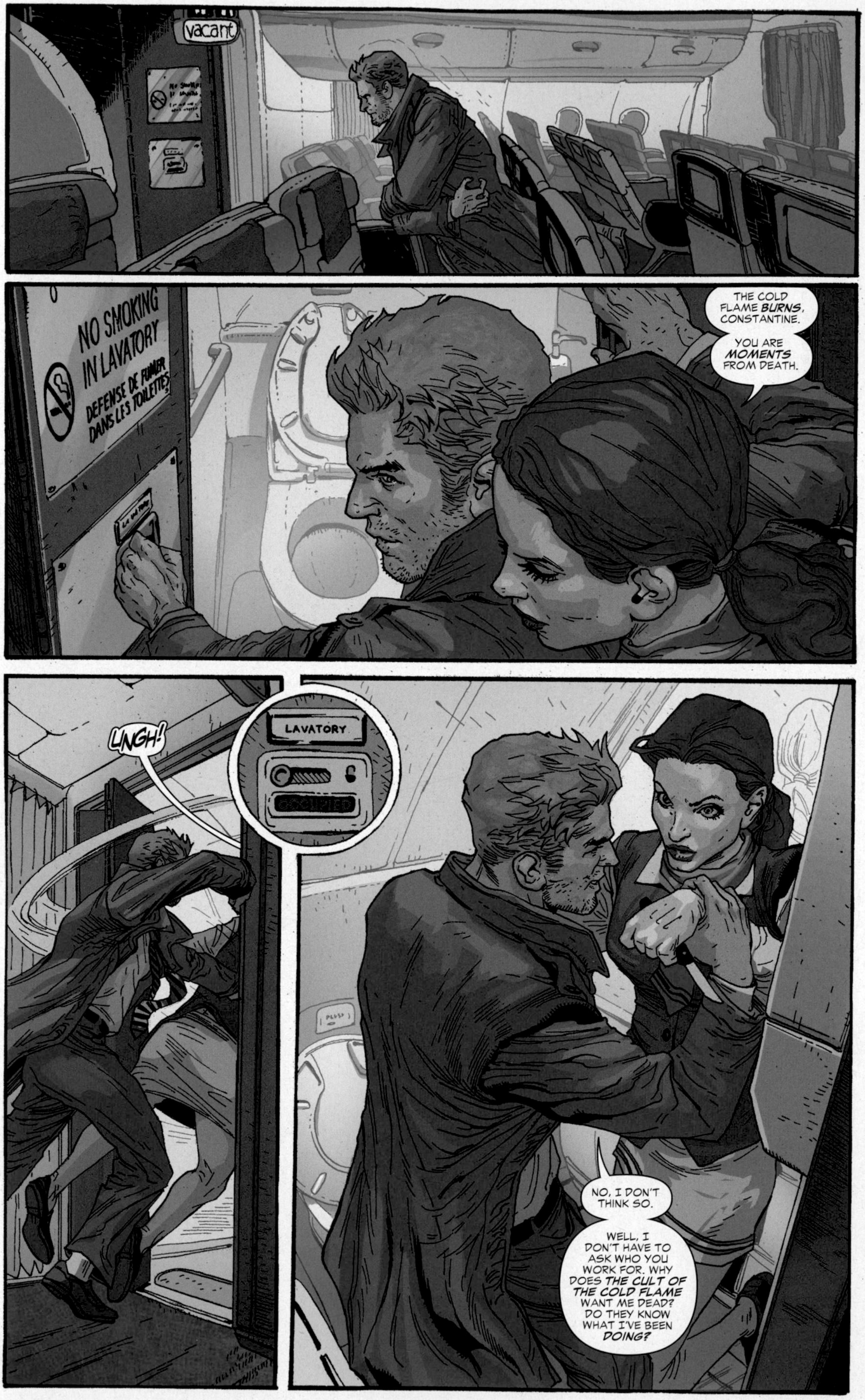
vacant
NO SMOKING IN LAVATORY
DEFENSE DE FUMER DANS LES TOILETTES
THE COLD FLAME BURNS, CONSTANTINE.
YOU ARE MOMENTS FROM DEATH.
UNGH!
LAVATORY
NO, I DON'T THINK SO.
WELL, I DON'T HAVE TO ASK WHO YOU WORK FOR. WHY DOES THE CULT OF THE COLD FLAME WANT ME DEAD? DO THEY KNOW WHAT I'VE BEEN DOING?

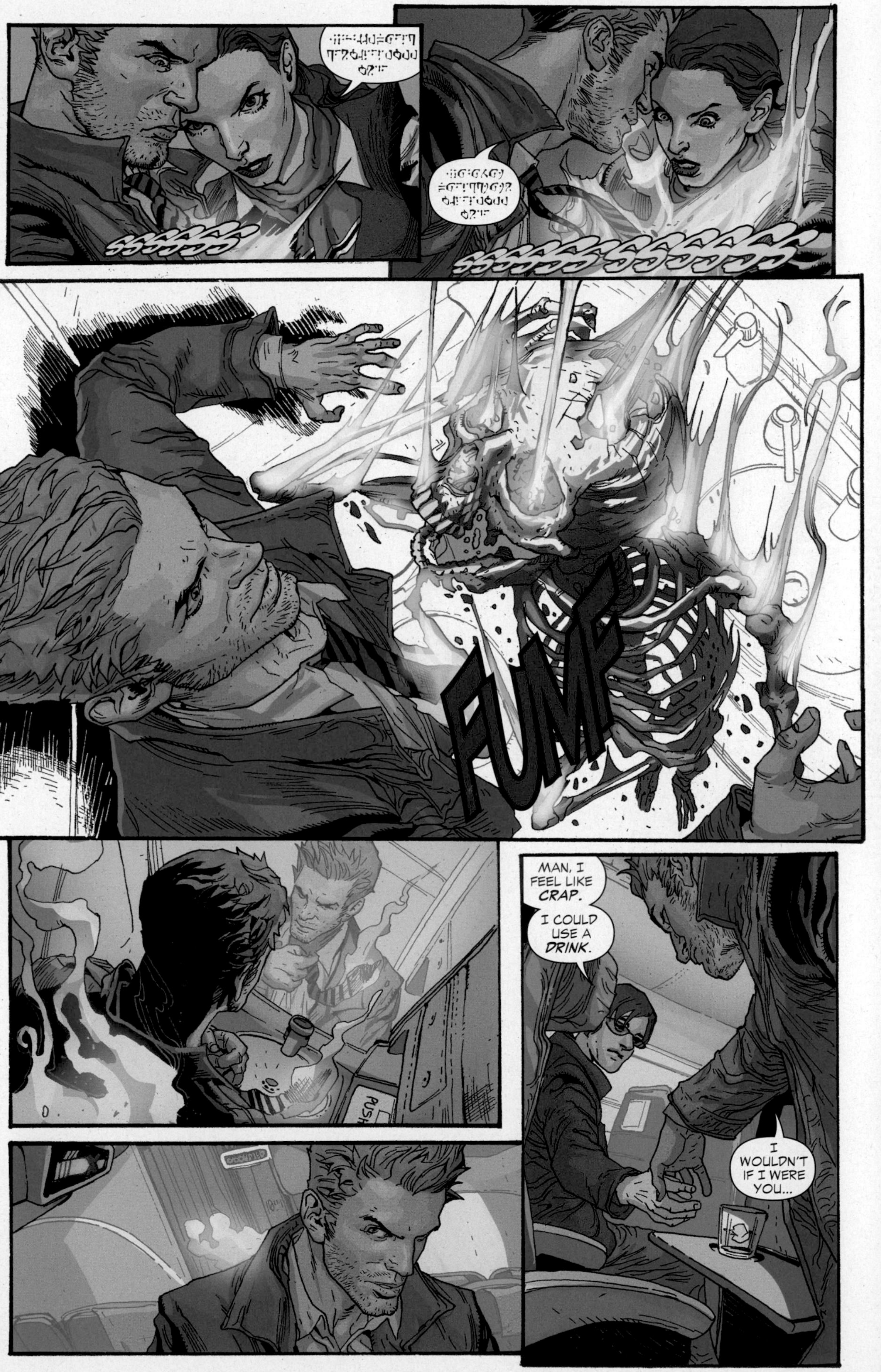
SSSSSS
SSSSSSSSSSSS
FUMP
PUSH
MAN, I FEEL LIKE CRAP.
I COULD USE A DRINK.
I WOULDN'T IF I WERE YOU...

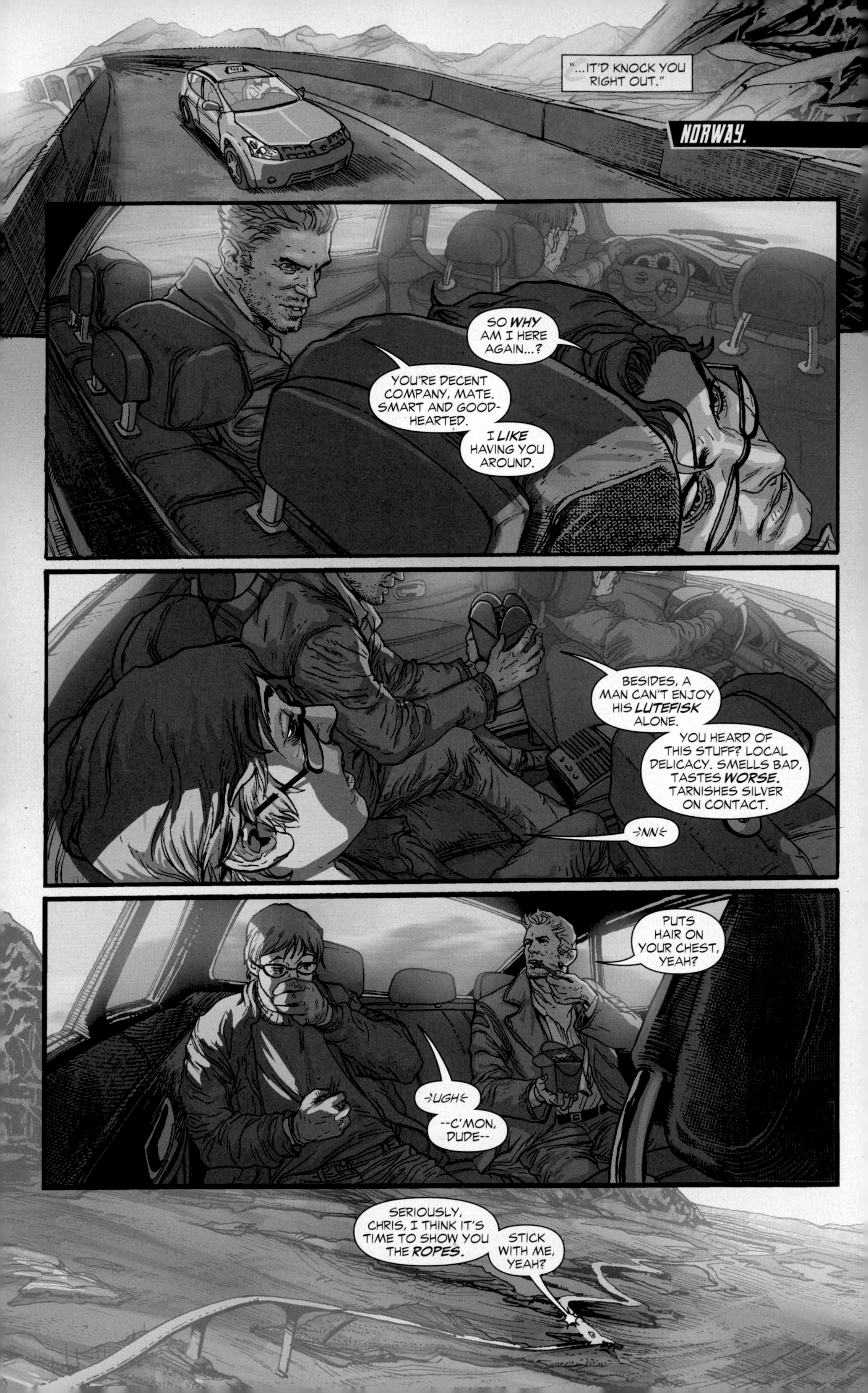

"...IT'D KNOCK YOU RIGHT OUT."
NORWAY.
SO WHY AM I HERE AGAIN...?
YOU'RE DECENT COMPANY, MATE. SMART AND GOOD-HEARTED.
I LIKE HAVING YOU AROUND.
BESIDES, A MAN CAN'T ENJOY HIS LUTEFISK ALONE.
YOU HEARD OF THIS STUFF? LOCAL DELICACY. SMELLS BAD, TASTES WORSE. TARNISHES SILVER ON CONTACT.
NN
PUTS HAIR ON YOUR CHEST, YEAH?
UGH
--C'MON, DUDE--
SERIOUSLY, CHRIS, I THINK IT'S TIME TO SHOW YOU THE ROPES.
STICK WITH ME, YEAH?

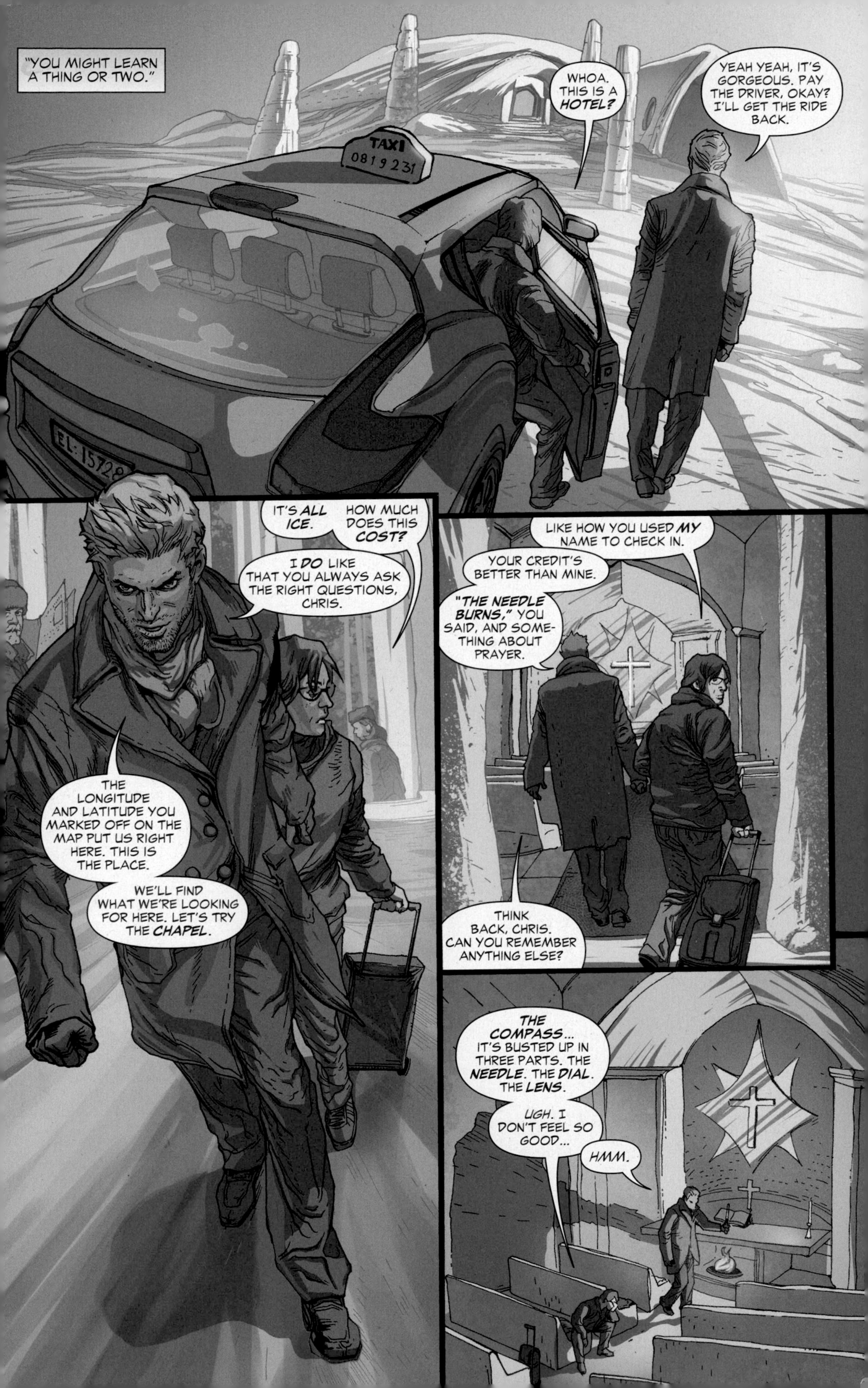
"YOU MIGHT LEARN A THING OR TWO."
WHOA. THIS IS A HOTEL?
YEAH YEAH, IT'S GORGEOUS. PAY THE DRIVER, OKAY? I'LL GET THE RIDE BACK.
TAXI 0819231
EL 15728
IT'S ALL ICE.
HOW MUCH DOES THIS COST?
I DO LIKE THAT YOU ALWAYS ASK THE RIGHT QUESTIONS, CHRIS.
THE LONGITUDE AND LATITUDE YOU MARKED OFF ON THE MAP PUT US RIGHT HERE. THIS IS THE PLACE.
WE'LL FIND WHAT WE'RE LOOKING FOR HERE. LET'S TRY THE CHAPEL.
LIKE HOW YOU USED MY NAME TO CHECK IN.
YOUR CREDIT'S BETTER THAN MINE.
"THE NEEDLE BURNS," YOU SAID, AND SOMETHING ABOUT PRAYER.
THINK BACK, CHRIS. CAN YOU REMEMBER ANYTHING ELSE?
THE COMPASS... IT'S BUSTED UP IN THREE PARTS. THE NEEDLE. THE DIAL. THE LENS.
UGH. I DON'T FEEL SO GOOD...
HMM.

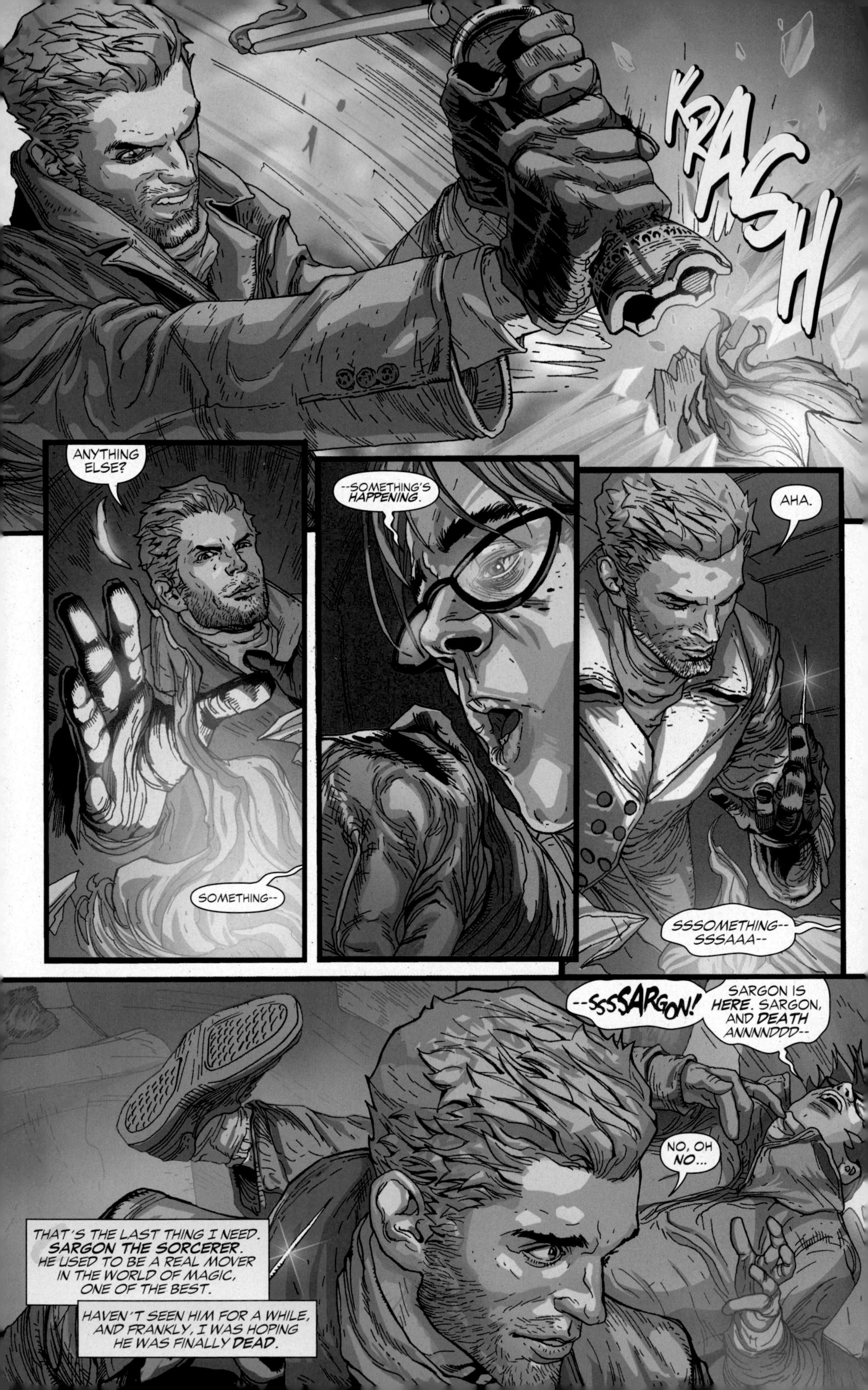
KRASH
ANYTHING ELSE?
SOMETHING--
--SOMETHING'S HAPPENING.
AHA.
SSSOMETHING-- SSSAAA--
--SSSSARGON!
SARGON IS HERE. SARGON, AND DEATH ANNNNDDD--
NO, OH NO...
THAT'S THE LAST THING I NEED. SARGON THE SORCERER. HE USED TO BE A REAL MOVER IN THE WORLD OF MAGIC, ONE OF THE BEST.
HAVEN'T SEEN HIM FOR A WHILE, AND FRANKLY, I WAS HOPING HE WAS FINALLY DEAD.

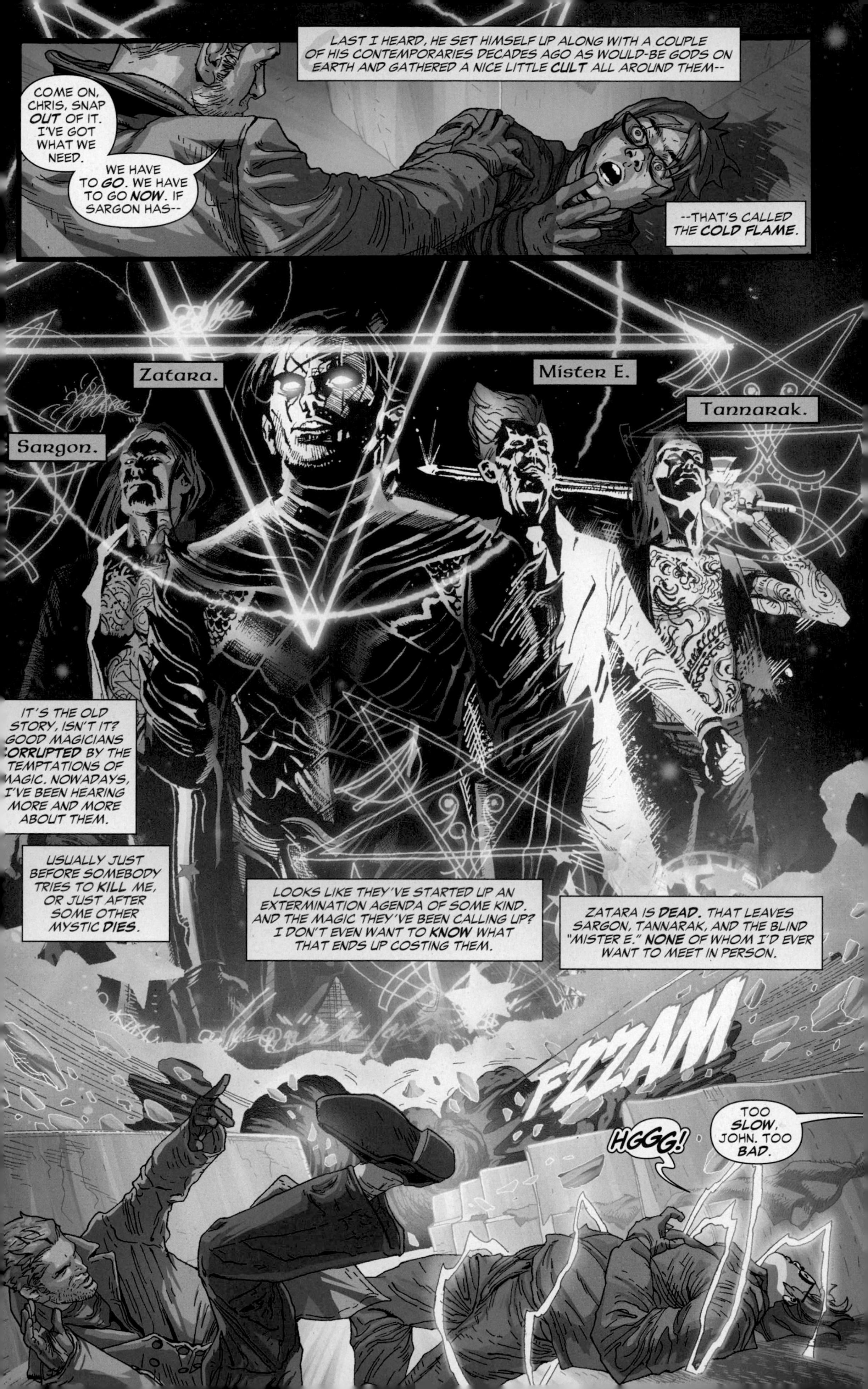
LAST I HEARD, HE SET HIMSELF UP ALONG WITH A COUPLE OF HIS CONTEMPORARIES DECADES AGO AS WOULD-BE GODS ON EARTH AND GATHERED A NICE LITTLE CULT ALL AROUND THEM--
COME ON, CHRIS, SNAP OUT OF IT. I'VE GOT WHAT WE NEED.
WE HAVE TO GO. WE HAVE TO GO NOW. IF SARGON HAS--
--THAT'S CALLED THE COLD FLAME.
Zatara.
Mister E.
Tannarak.
Sargon.
IT'S THE OLD STORY, ISN'T IT? GOOD MAGICIANS CORRUPTED BY THE TEMPTATIONS OF MAGIC. NOWADAYS, I'VE BEEN HEARING MORE AND MORE ABOUT THEM.
USUALLY JUST BEFORE SOMEBODY TRIES TO KILL ME, OR JUST AFTER SOME OTHER MYSTIC DIES.
LOOKS LIKE THEY'VE STARTED UP AN EXTERMINATION AGENDA OF SOME KIND. AND THE MAGIC THEY'VE BEEN CALLING UP? I DON'T EVEN WANT TO KNOW WHAT THAT ENDS UP COSTING THEM.
ZATARA IS DEAD. THAT LEAVES SARGON, TANNARAK, AND THE BLIND "MISTER E." NONE OF WHOM I'D EVER WANT TO MEET IN PERSON.
FZZZAM
HGGG!
TOO SLOW, JOHN. TOO BAD.

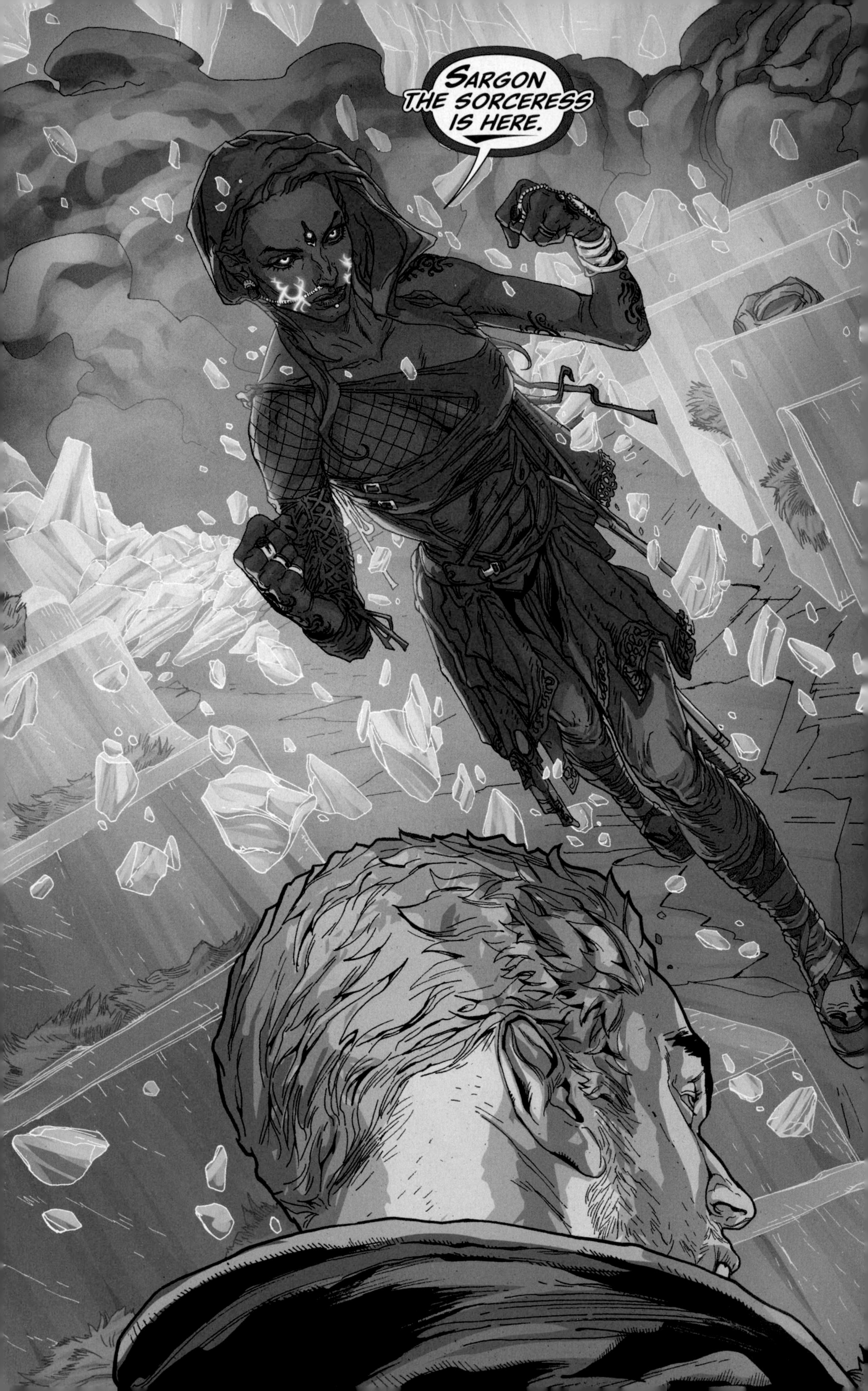
SARGON THE SORCERESS IS HERE.

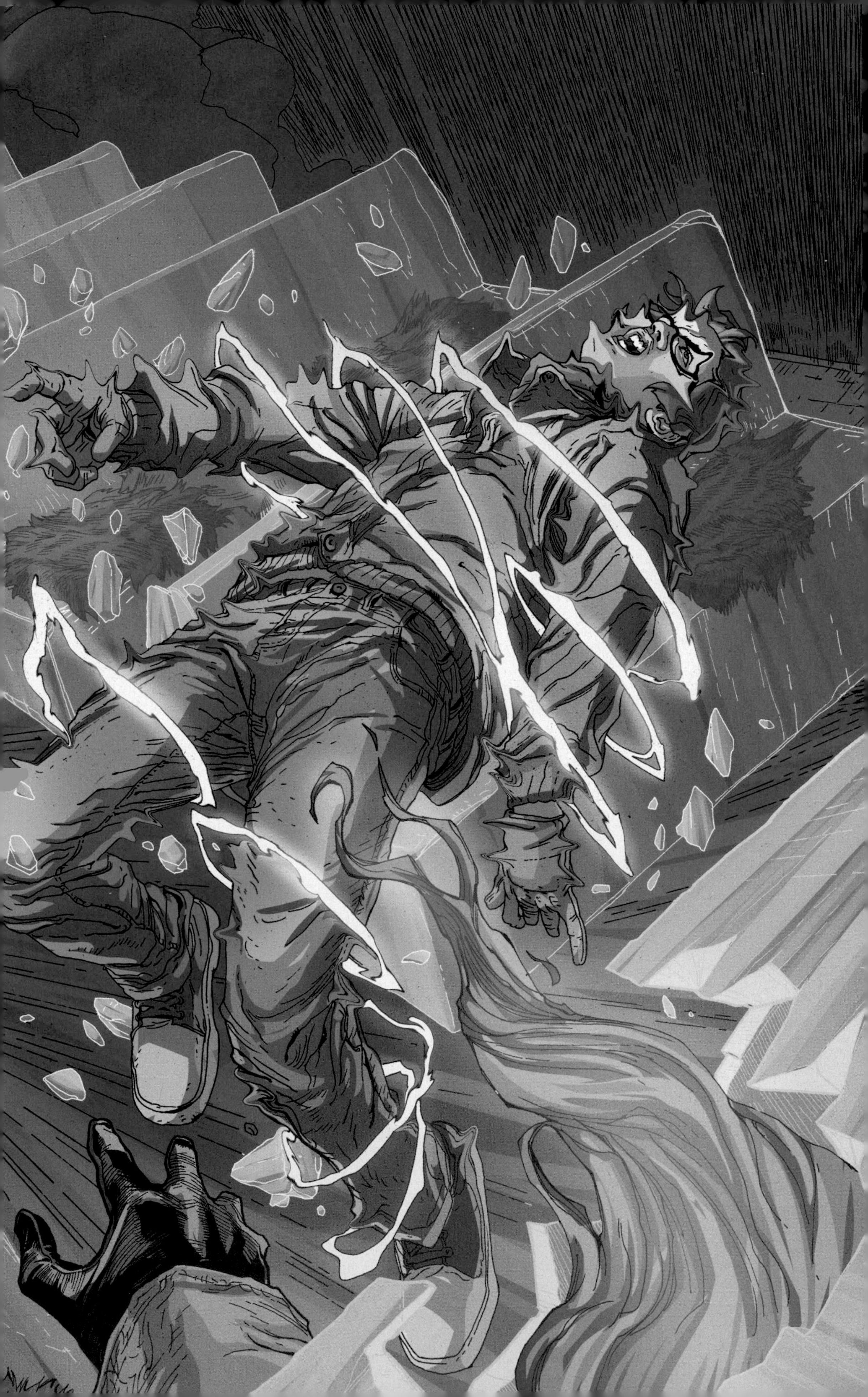

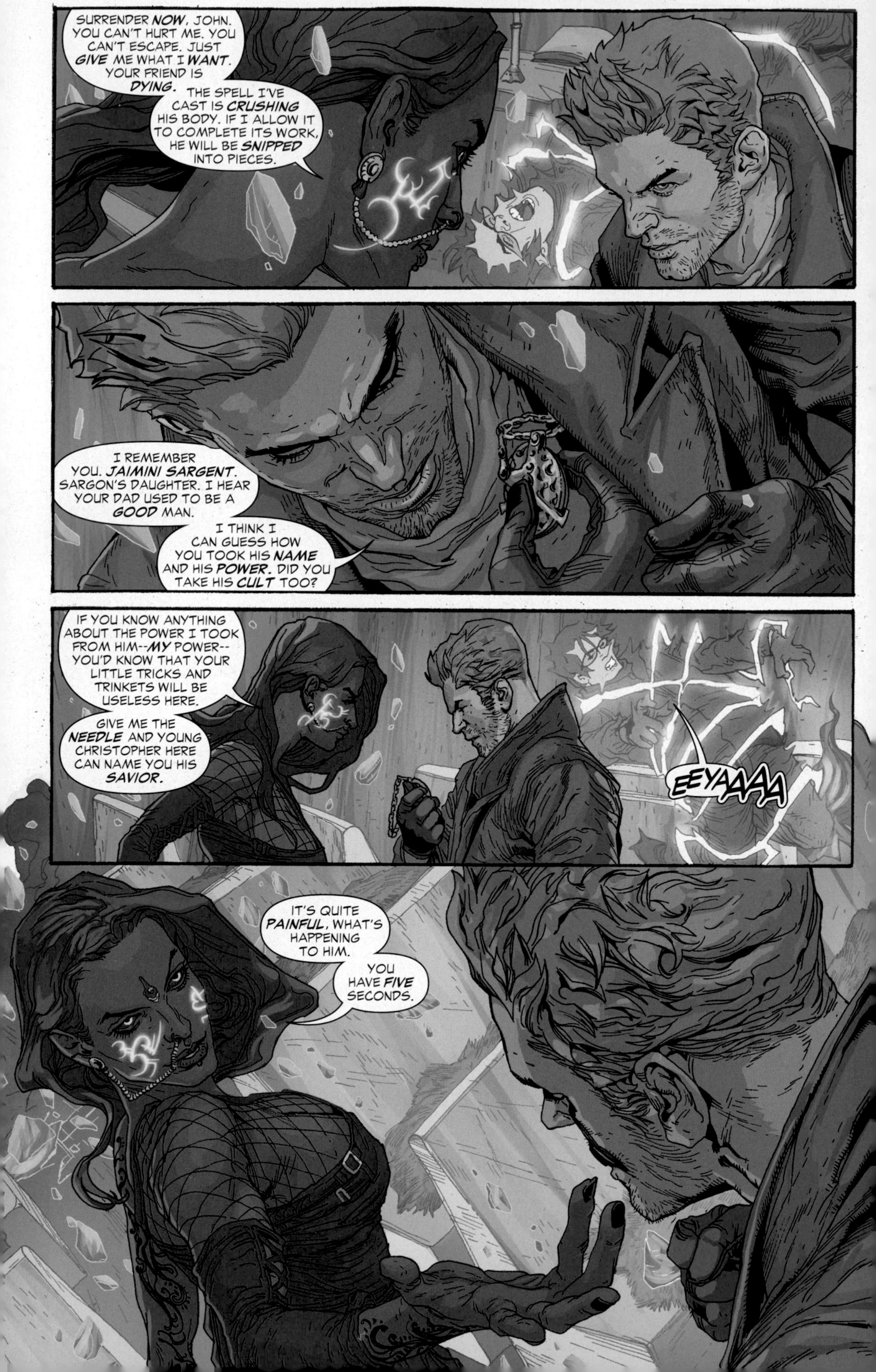
SURRENDER NOW, JOHN. YOU CAN'T HURT ME. YOU CAN'T ESCAPE. JUST GIVE ME WHAT I WANT. YOUR FRIEND IS DYING.
THE SPELL I'VE CAST IS CRUSHING HIS BODY. IF I ALLOW IT TO COMPLETE ITS WORK, HE WILL BE SNIPPED INTO PIECES.
I REMEMBER YOU. JAIMINI SARGENT. SARGON'S DAUGHTER. I HEAR YOUR DAD USED TO BE A GOOD MAN.
I THINK I CAN GUESS HOW YOU TOOK HIS NAME AND HIS POWER. DID YOU TAKE HIS CULT TOO?
IF YOU KNOW ANYTHING ABOUT THE POWER I TOOK FROM HIM--MY POWER--YOU'D KNOW THAT YOUR LITTLE TRICKS AND TRINKETS WILL BE USELESS HERE.
GIVE ME THE NEEDLE AND YOUNG CHRISTOPHER HERE CAN NAME YOU HIS SAVIOR.
EEYAAAAA
IT'S QUITE PAINFUL, WHAT'S HAPPENING TO HIM.
YOU HAVE FIVE SECONDS.

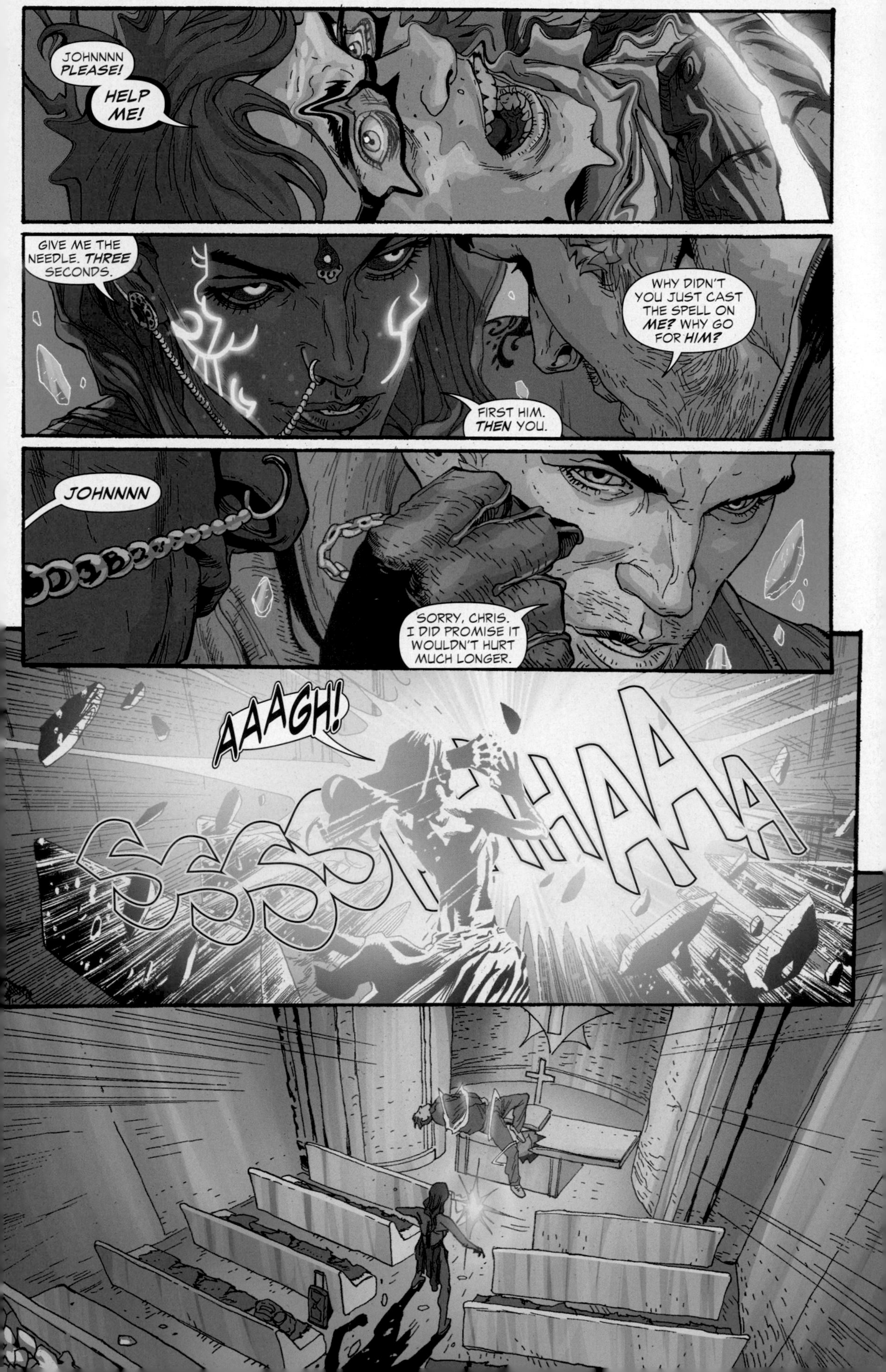
JOHNNNN PLEASE!
HELP ME!
GIVE ME THE NEEDLE. THREE SECONDS.
WHY DIDN'T YOU JUST CAST THE SPELL ON ME? WHY GO FOR HIM?
FIRST HIM. THEN YOU.
JOHNNNN
SORRY, CHRIS. I DID PROMISE IT WOULDN'T HURT MUCH LONGER.
AAAGH!
SSSHHAAAA

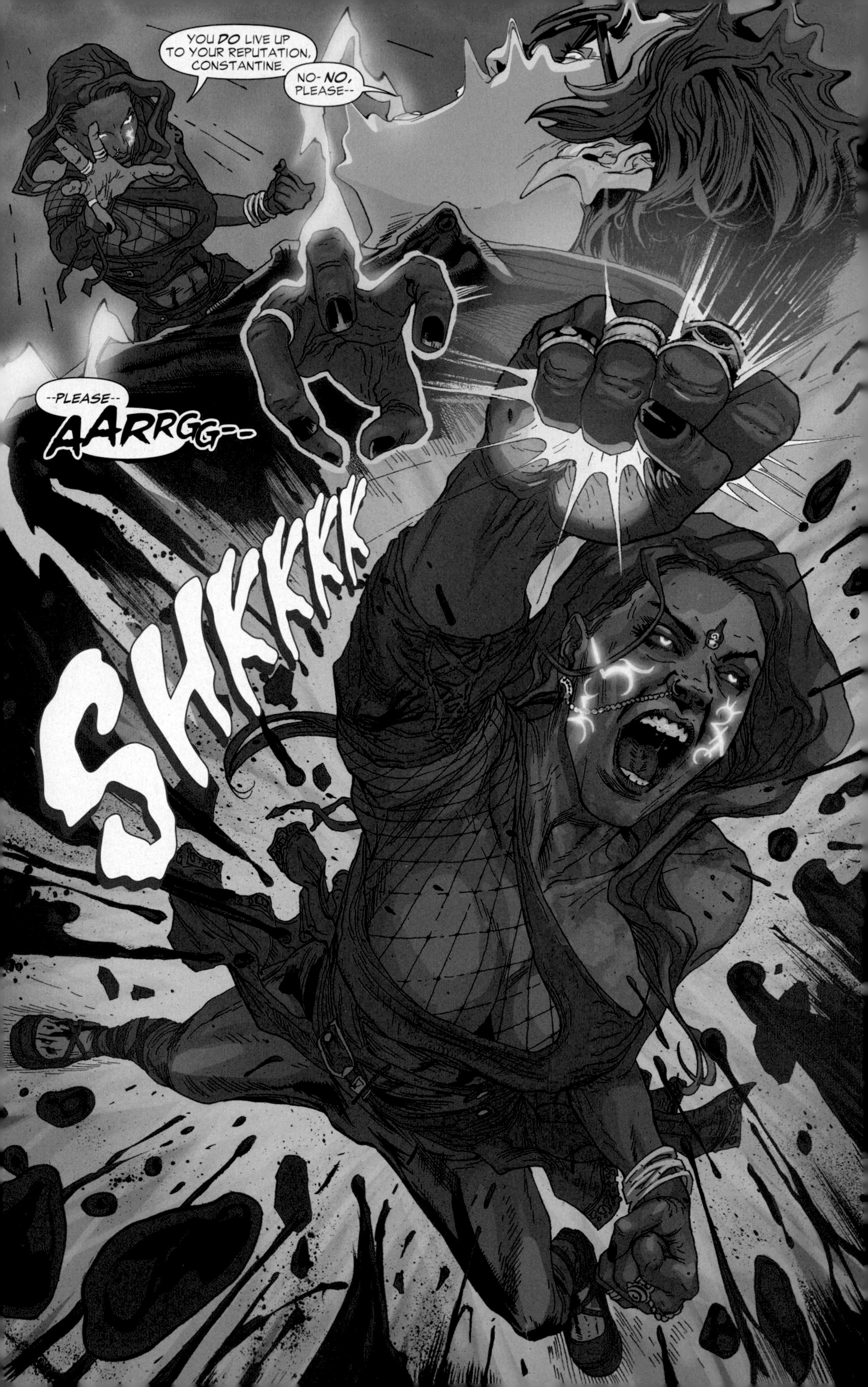
YOU DO LIVE UP TO YOUR REPUTATION, CONSTANTINE.
NO-NO, PLEASE--
--PLEASE-- AARRGG--
SHKKKK

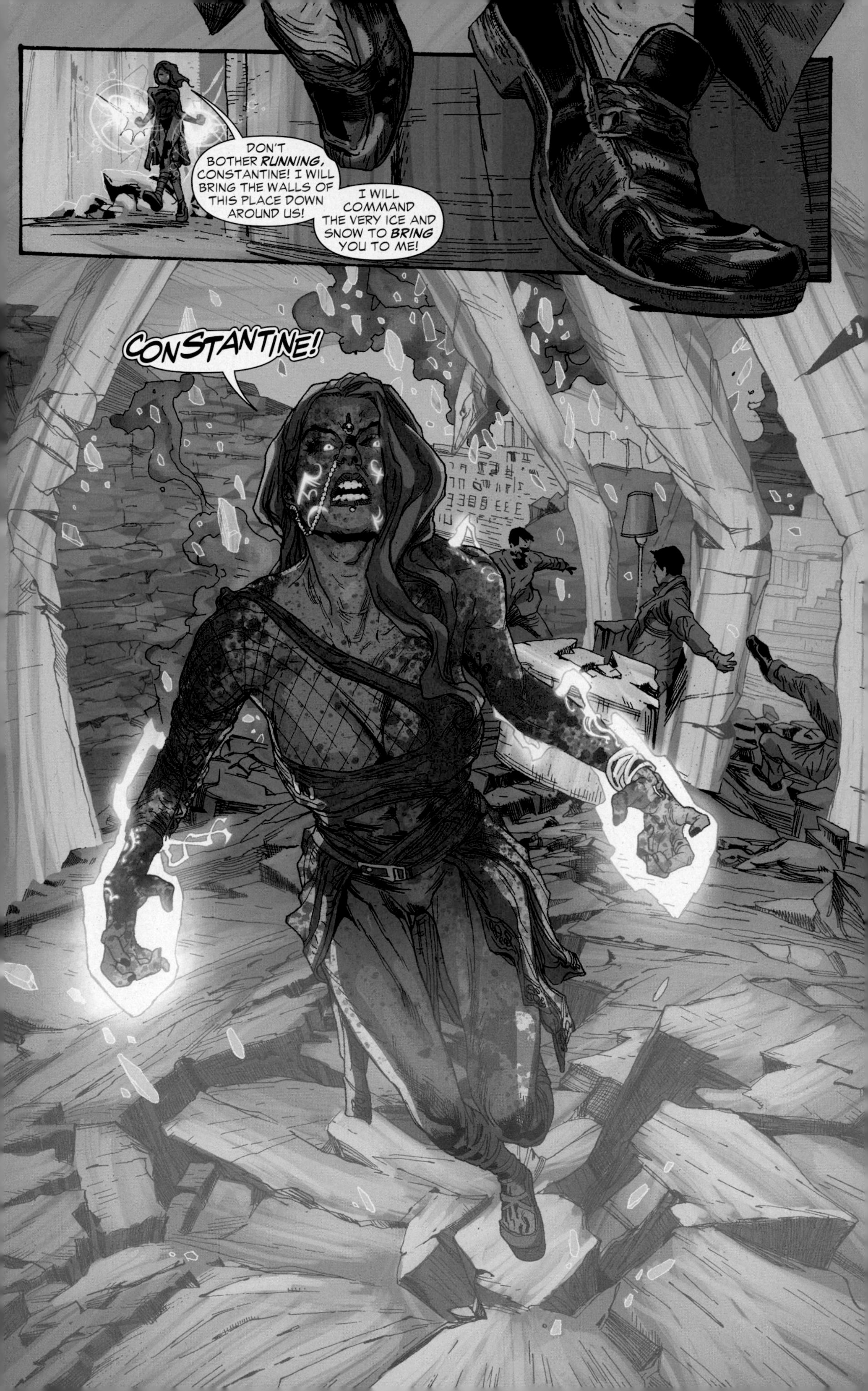
DON'T BOTHER *RUNNING*, CONSTANTINE! I WILL BRING THE WALLS OF THIS PLACE DOWN AROUND US!
I WILL COMMAND THE VERY ICE AND SNOW TO *BRING* YOU TO ME!
CONSTANTINE!

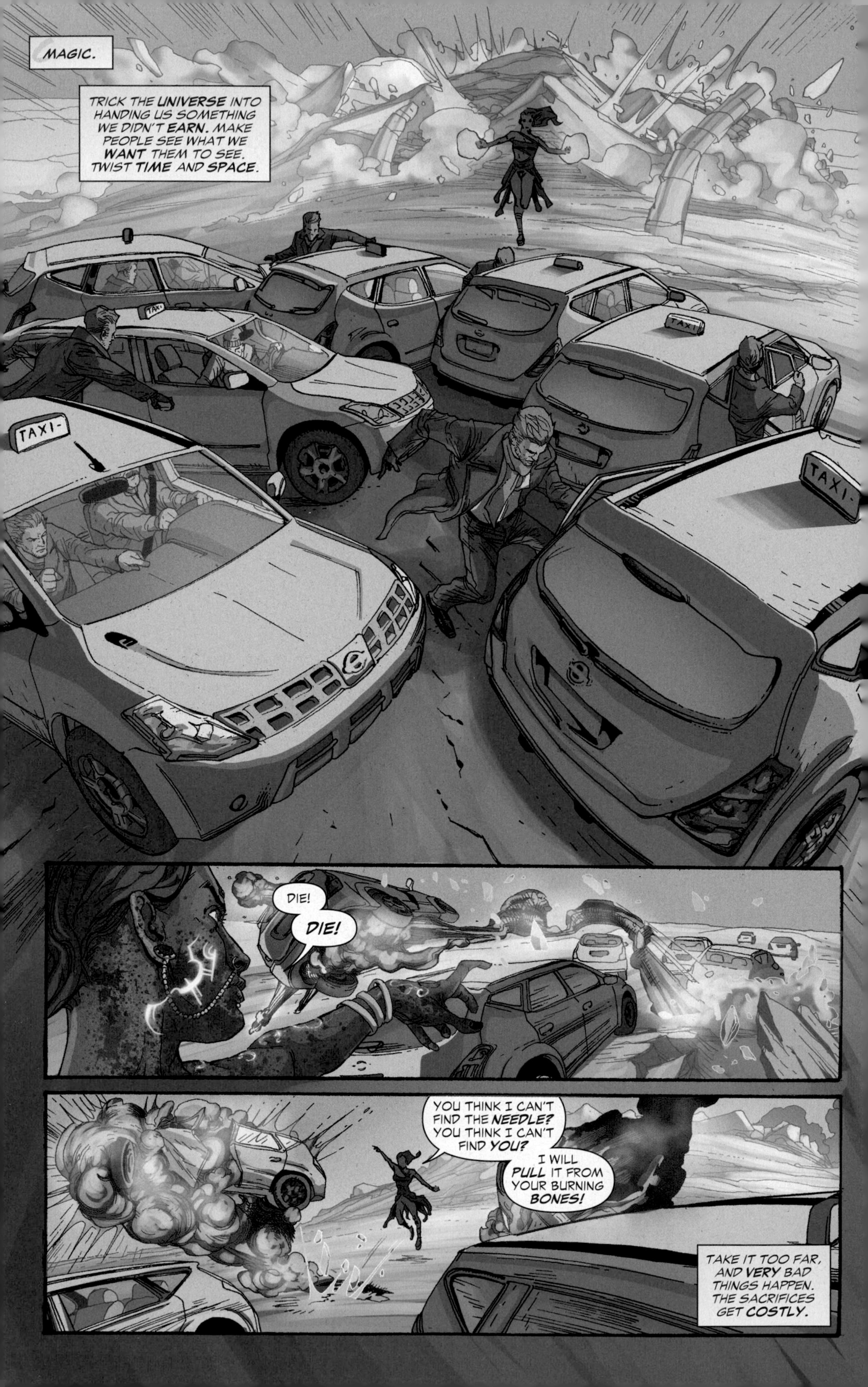
MAGIC.
TRICK THE UNIVERSE INTO HANDING US SOMETHING WE DIDN'T EARN. MAKE PEOPLE SEE WHAT WE WANT THEM TO SEE. TWIST TIME AND SPACE.
TAXI
TAXI
TAXI
TAXI
DIE!
DIE!
YOU THINK I CAN'T FIND THE NEEDLE? YOU THINK I CAN'T FIND YOU?
I WILL PULL IT FROM YOUR BURNING BONES!
TAKE IT TOO FAR, AND VERY BAD THINGS HAPPEN. THE SACRIFICES GET COSTLY.

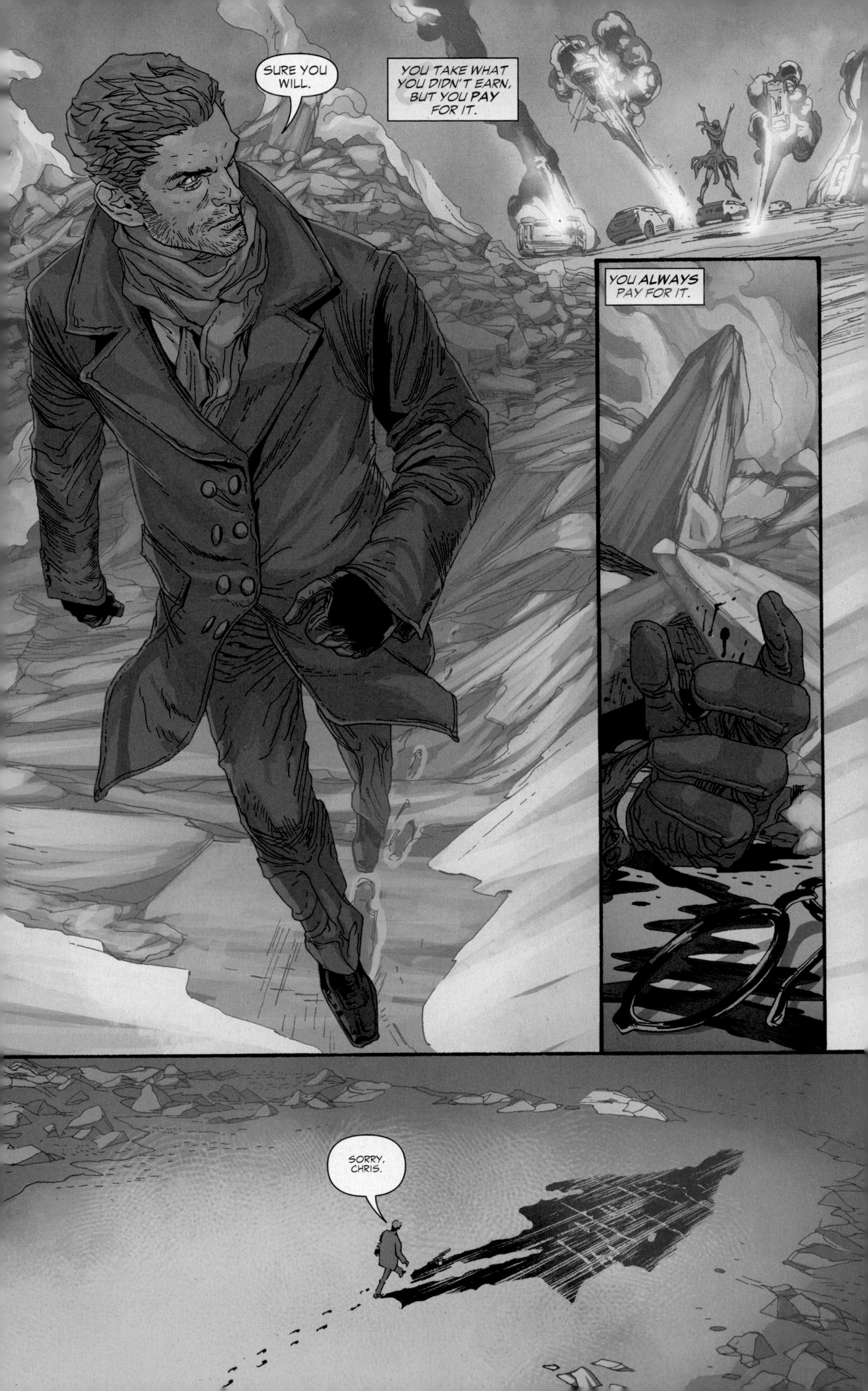
SURE YOU WILL.
YOU TAKE WHAT YOU DIDN'T EARN, BUT YOU PAY FOR IT.
YOU ALWAYS PAY FOR IT.
SORRY, CHRIS.

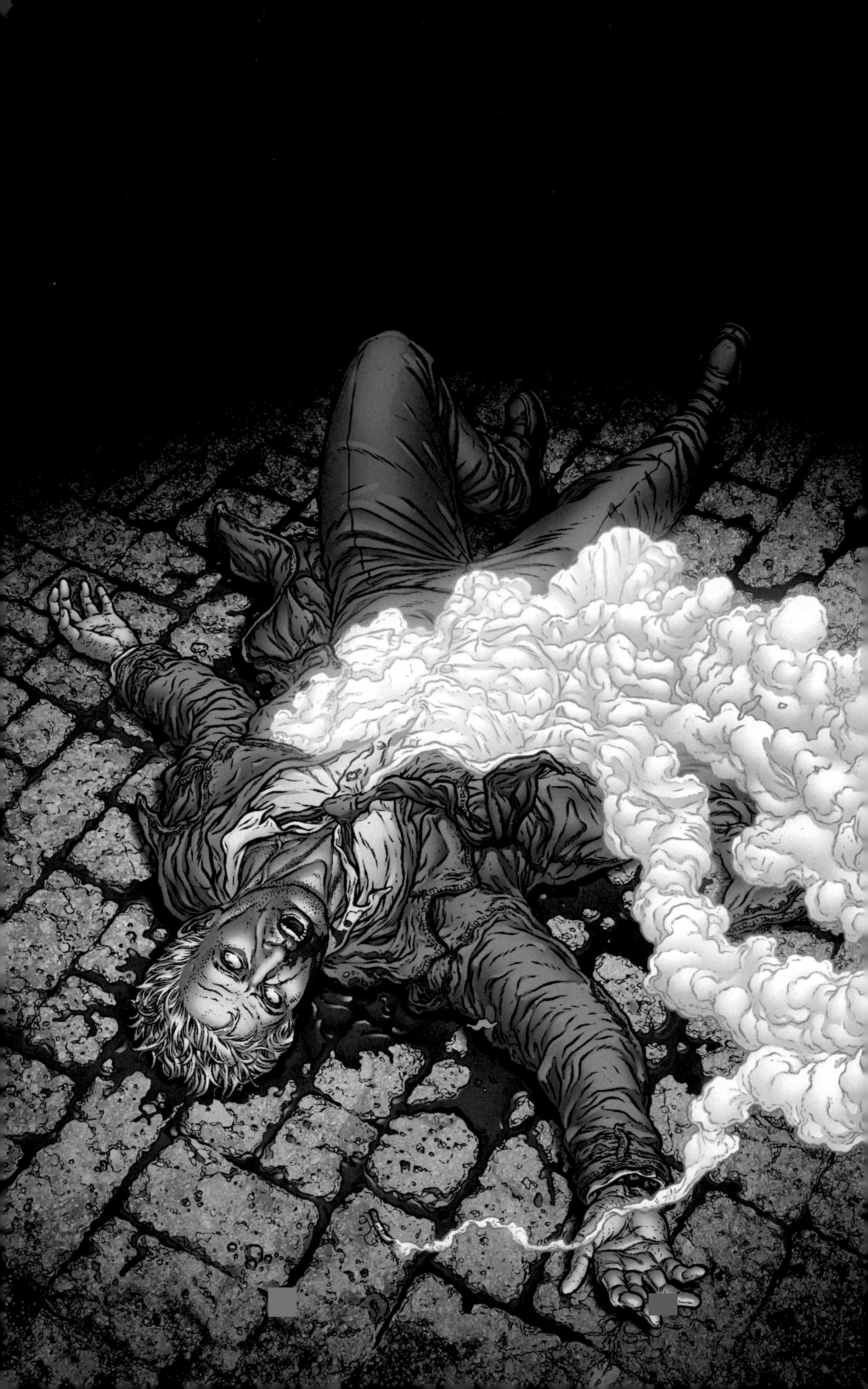

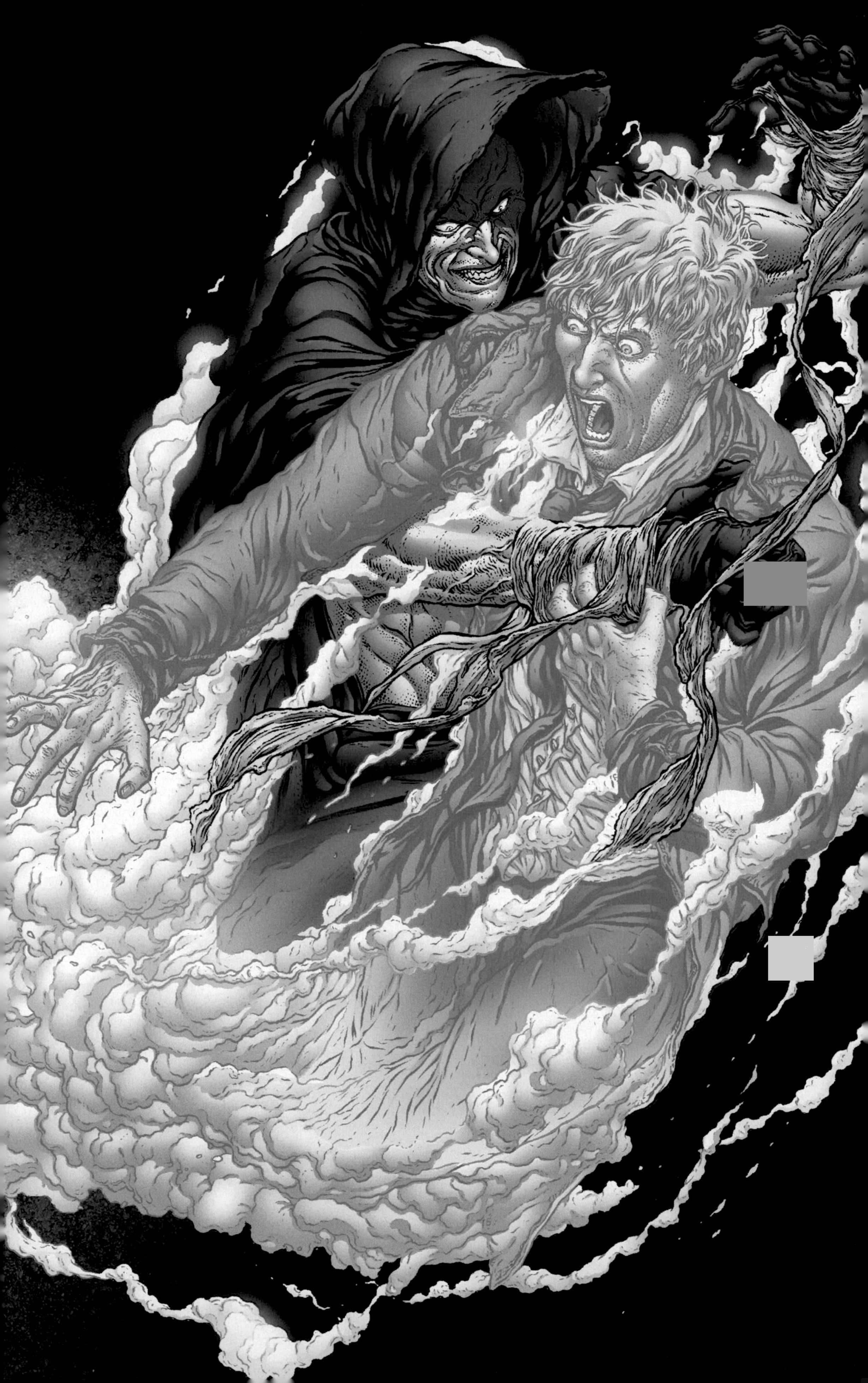

THE SPARK AND THE FLAME PART 2: THE BLIND MAN

JEFF LEMIRE & RAY FAWKES writers **RENATO GUEDES** artist cover art by **JUAN JOSE RYP & BRETT SMITH**

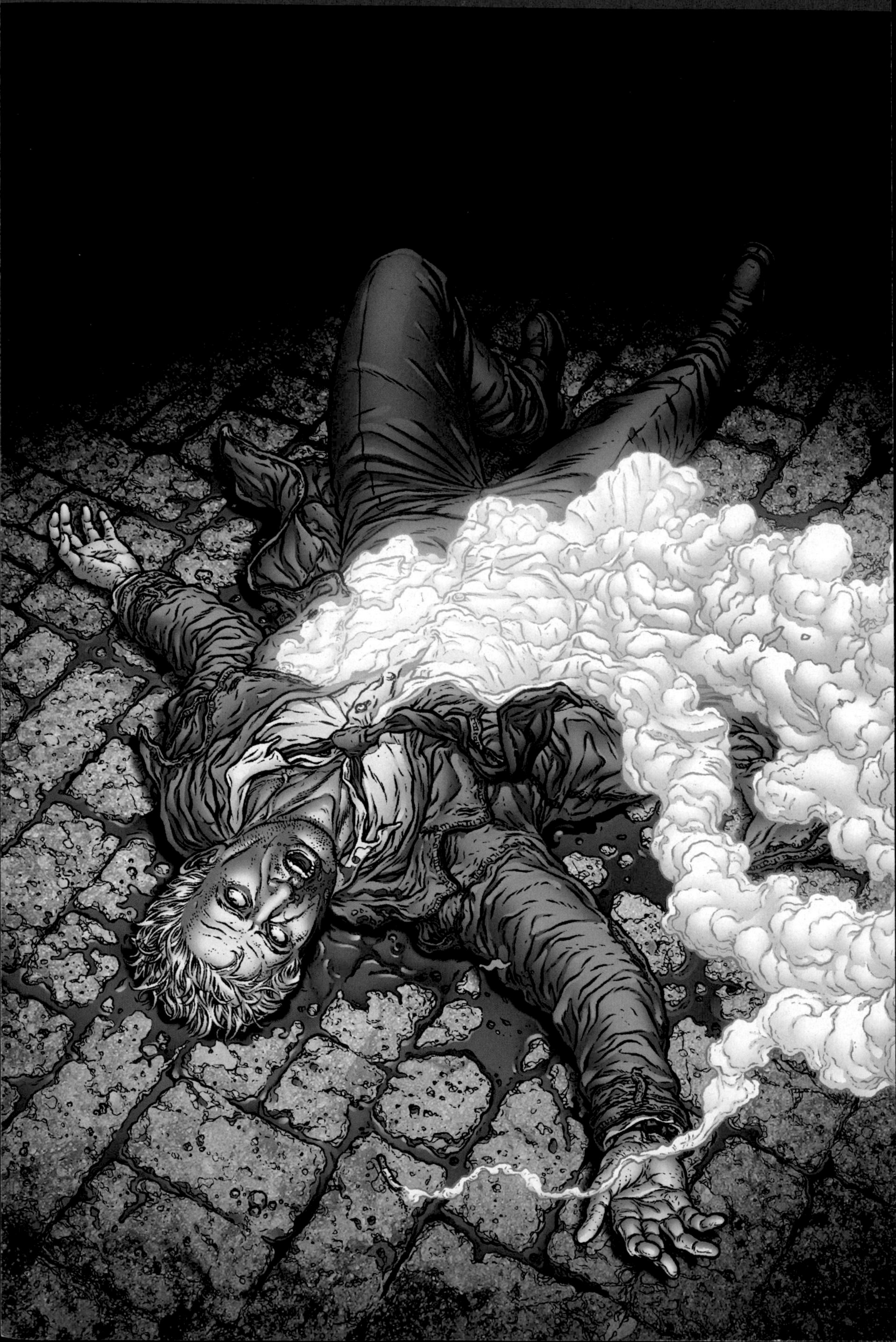

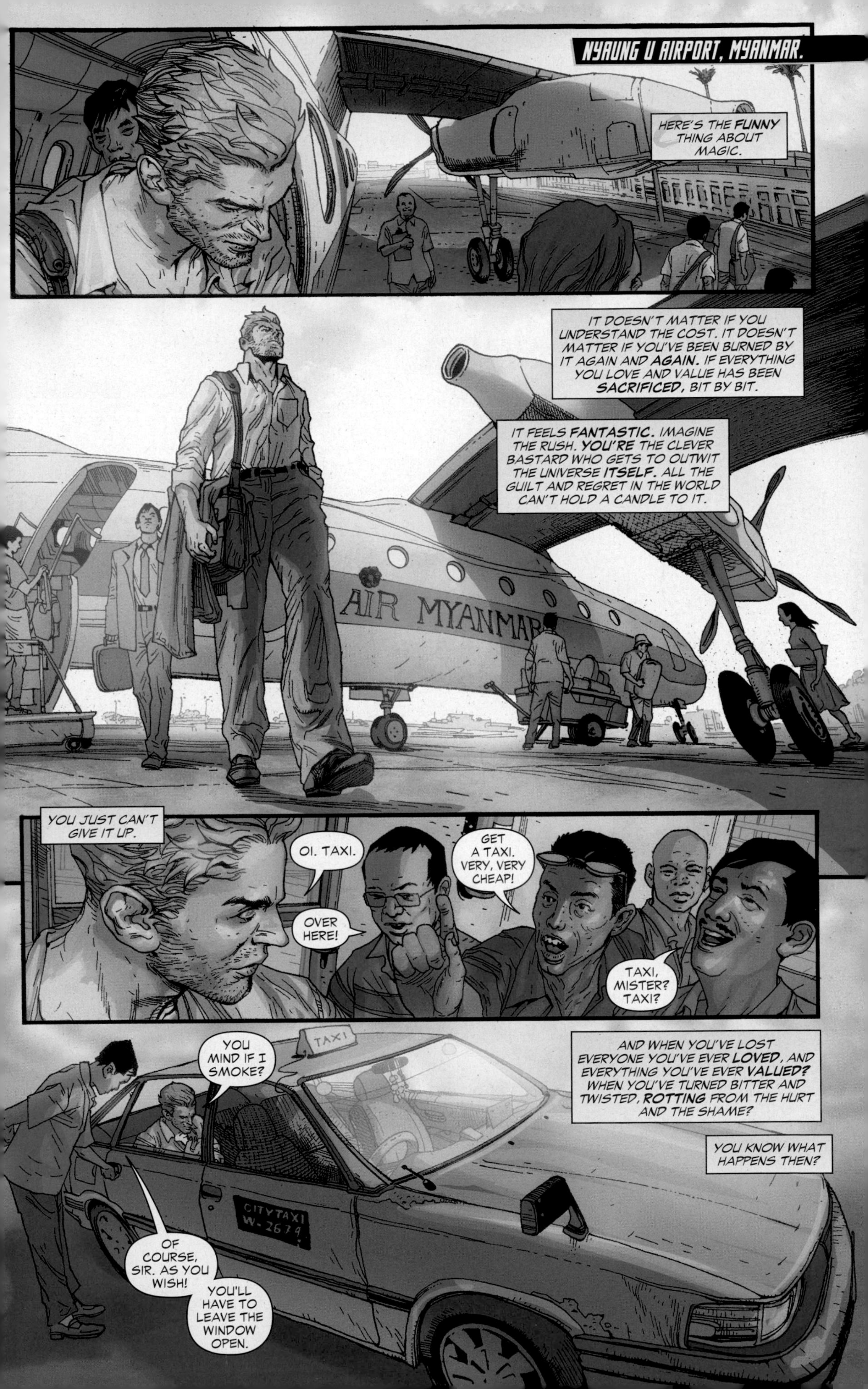
NYAUNG U AIRPORT, MYANMAR.
HERE'S THE FUNNY THING ABOUT MAGIC.
IT DOESN'T MATTER IF YOU UNDERSTAND THE COST. IT DOESN'T MATTER IF YOU'VE BEEN BURNED BY IT AGAIN AND AGAIN. IF EVERYTHING YOU LOVE AND VALUE HAS BEEN SACRIFICED, BIT BY BIT.
IT FEELS FANTASTIC. IMAGINE THE RUSH. YOU'RE THE CLEVER BASTARD WHO GETS TO OUTWIT THE UNIVERSE ITSELF. ALL THE GUILT AND REGRET IN THE WORLD CAN'T HOLD A CANDLE TO IT.
AIR MYANMAR
YOU JUST CAN'T GIVE IT UP.
OI. TAXI.
OVER HERE!
GET A TAXI. VERY, VERY CHEAP!
TAXI, MISTER? TAXI?
TAXI
YOU MIND IF I SMOKE?
AND WHEN YOU'VE LOST EVERYONE YOU'VE EVER LOVED, AND EVERYTHING YOU'VE EVER VALUED? WHEN YOU'VE TURNED BITTER AND TWISTED, ROTTING FROM THE HURT AND THE SHAME?
YOU KNOW WHAT HAPPENS THEN?
CITY TAXI W-2679
OF COURSE, SIR. AS YOU WISH!
YOU'LL HAVE TO LEAVE THE WINDOW OPEN.

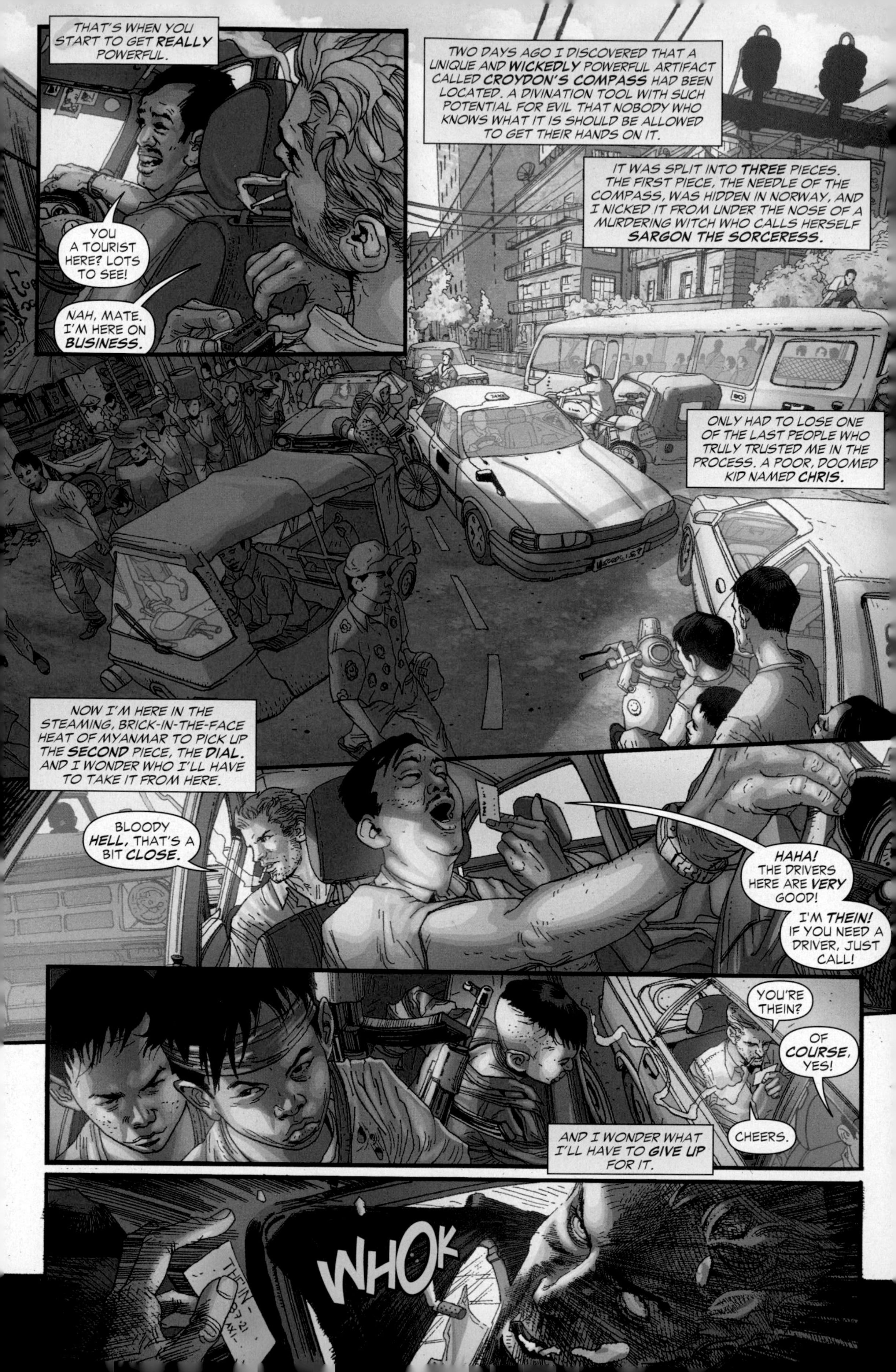
THAT'S WHEN YOU START TO GET REALLY POWERFUL.
YOU A TOURIST HERE? LOTS TO SEE!
NAH, MATE. I'M HERE ON BUSINESS.
TWO DAYS AGO I DISCOVERED THAT A UNIQUE AND WICKEDLY POWERFUL ARTIFACT CALLED CROYDON'S COMPASS HAD BEEN LOCATED. A DIVINATION TOOL WITH SUCH POTENTIAL FOR EVIL THAT NOBODY WHO KNOWS WHAT IT IS SHOULD BE ALLOWED TO GET THEIR HANDS ON IT.
IT WAS SPLIT INTO THREE PIECES. THE FIRST PIECE, THE NEEDLE OF THE COMPASS, WAS HIDDEN IN NORWAY, AND I NICKED IT FROM UNDER THE NOSE OF A MURDERING WITCH WHO CALLS HERSELF SARGON THE SORCERESS.
ONLY HAD TO LOSE ONE OF THE LAST PEOPLE WHO TRULY TRUSTED ME IN THE PROCESS. A POOR, DOOMED KID NAMED CHRIS.
NOW I'M HERE IN THE STEAMING, BRICK-IN-THE-FACE HEAT OF MYANMAR TO PICK UP THE SECOND PIECE, THE DIAL. AND I WONDER WHO I'LL HAVE TO TAKE IT FROM HERE.
BLOODY HELL, THAT'S A BIT CLOSE.
HAHA! THE DRIVERS HERE ARE VERY GOOD!
I'M THEIN! IF YOU NEED A DRIVER, JUST CALL!
YOU'RE THEIN?
OF COURSE, YES!
CHEERS.
AND I WONDER WHAT I'LL HAVE TO GIVE UP FOR IT.
WHOK
THEIN

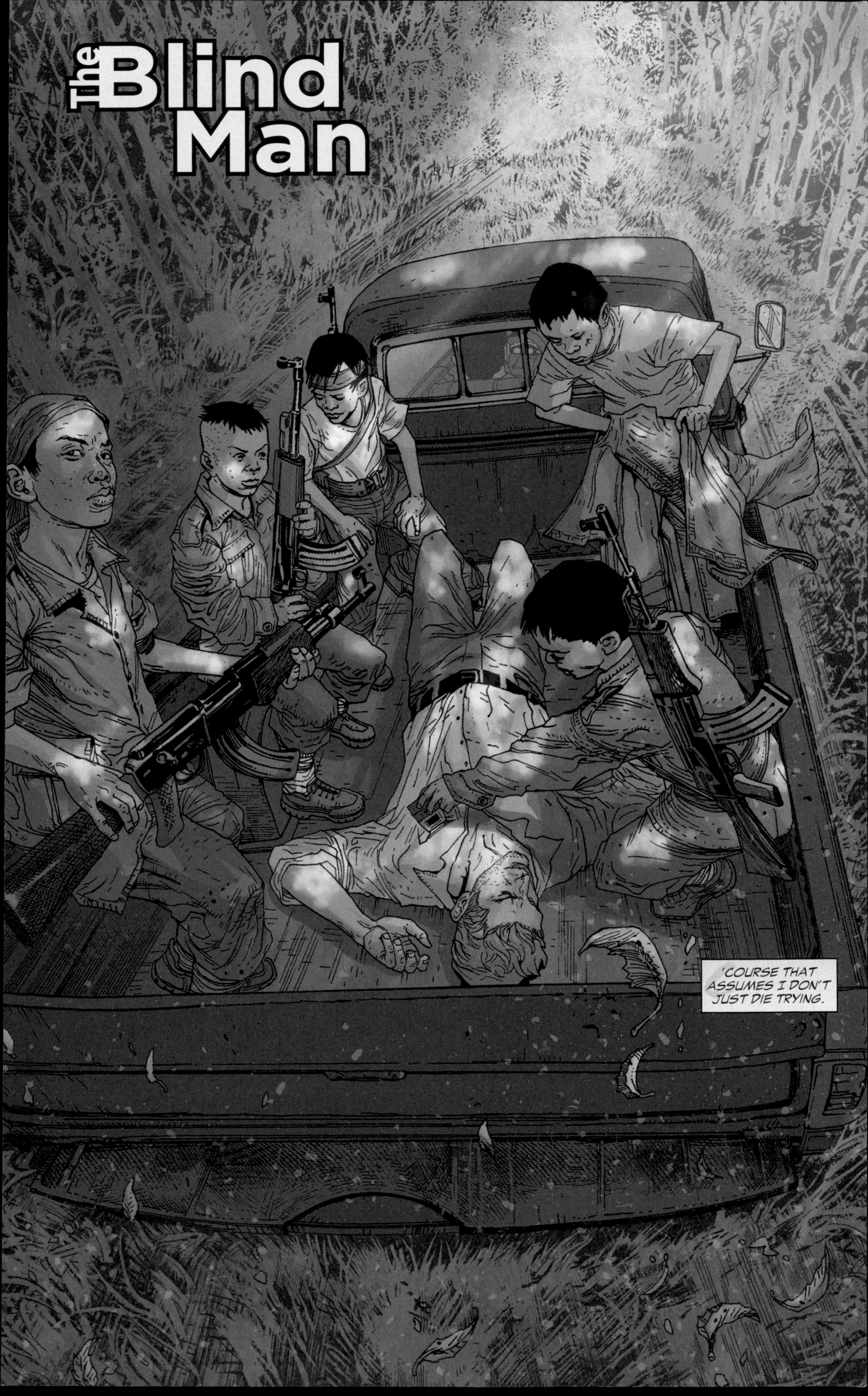
The Blind Man
'COURSE THAT ASSUMES I DON'T JUST DIE TRYING.

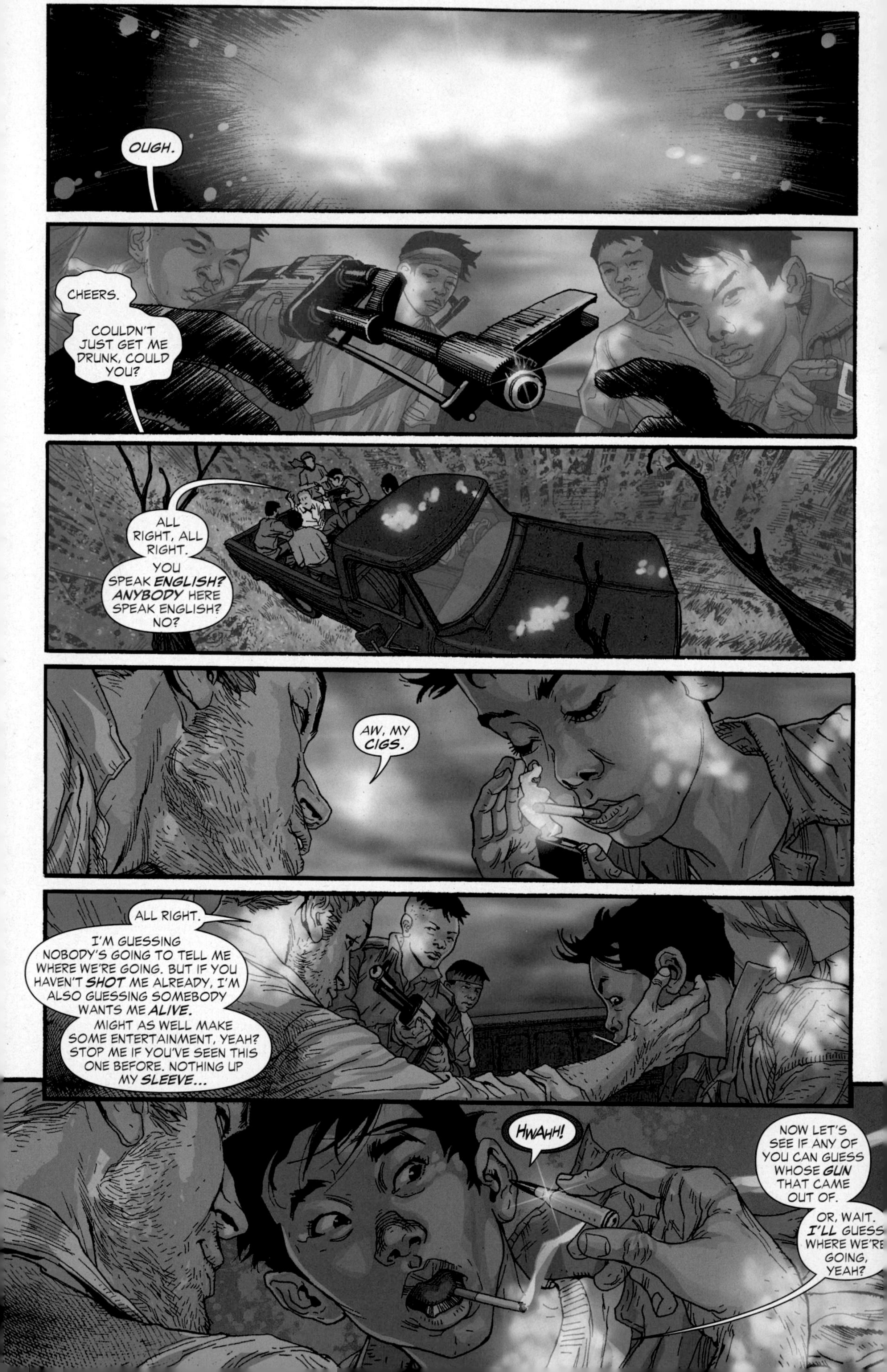
OUGH.
CHEERS.
COULDN'T JUST GET ME DRUNK, COULD YOU?
ALL RIGHT, ALL RIGHT. YOU SPEAK ENGLISH? ANYBODY HERE SPEAK ENGLISH? NO?
AW, MY CIGS.
ALL RIGHT.
I'M GUESSING NOBODY'S GOING TO TELL ME WHERE WE'RE GOING. BUT IF YOU HAVEN'T SHOT ME ALREADY, I'M ALSO GUESSING SOMEBODY WANTS ME ALIVE.
MIGHT AS WELL MAKE SOME ENTERTAINMENT, YEAH? STOP ME IF YOU'VE SEEN THIS ONE BEFORE. NOTHING UP MY SLEEVE...
HWAHH!
NOW LET'S SEE IF ANY OF YOU CAN GUESS WHOSE GUN THAT CAME OUT OF.
OR, WAIT. I'LL GUESS WHERE WE'RE GOING, YEAH?

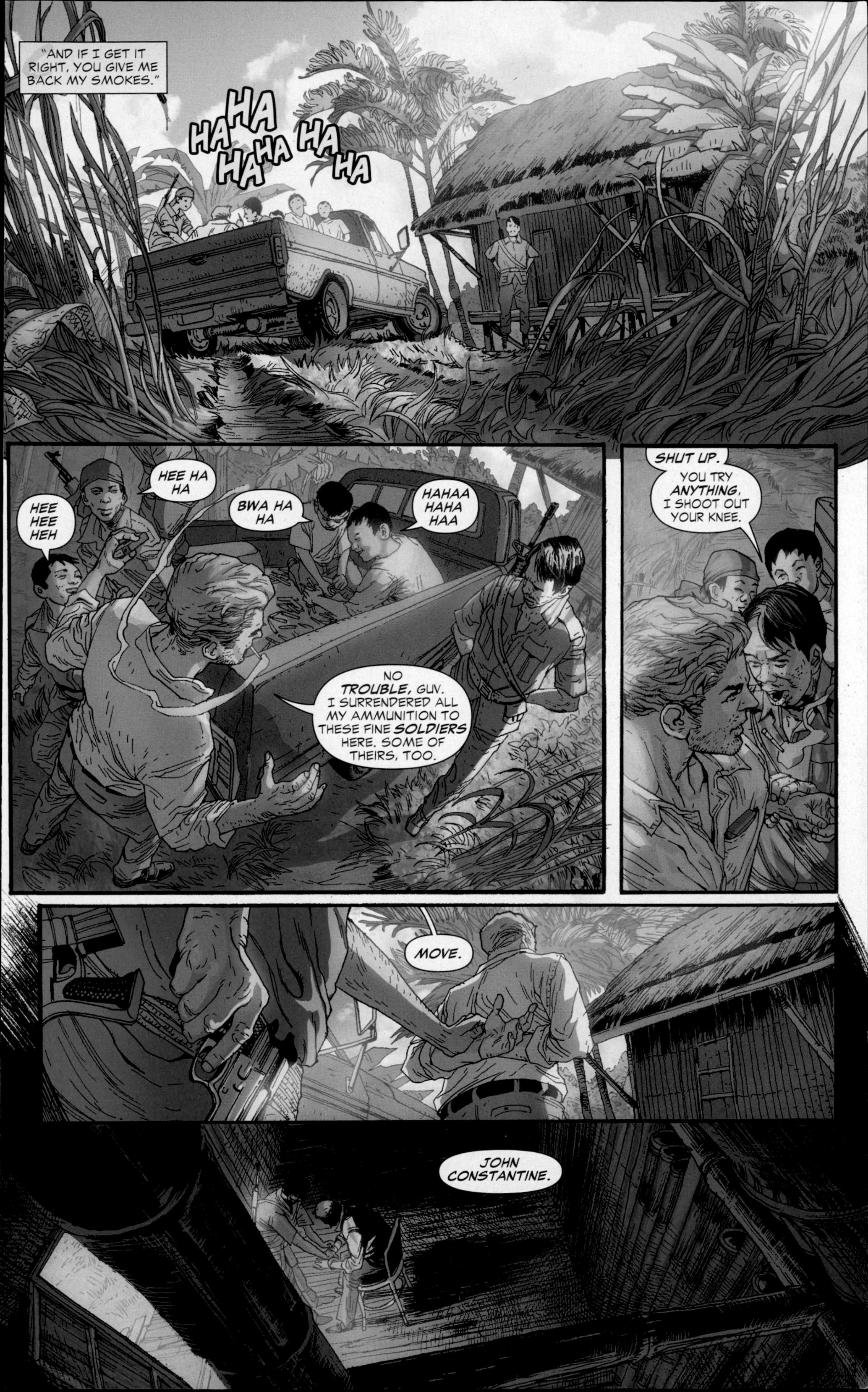
"AND IF I GET IT RIGHT, YOU GIVE ME BACK MY SMOKES."
HA HA HA HA HA HA HA
HEE HEE HEH
HEE HA HA
BWA HA HA
HAHAA HAHA HAA
NO TROUBLE, GUV. I SURRENDERED ALL MY AMMUNITION TO THESE FINE SOLDIERS HERE. SOME OF THEIRS, TOO.
SHUT UP.
YOU TRY ANYTHING, I SHOOT OUT YOUR KNEE.
MOVE.
JOHN CONSTANTINE.

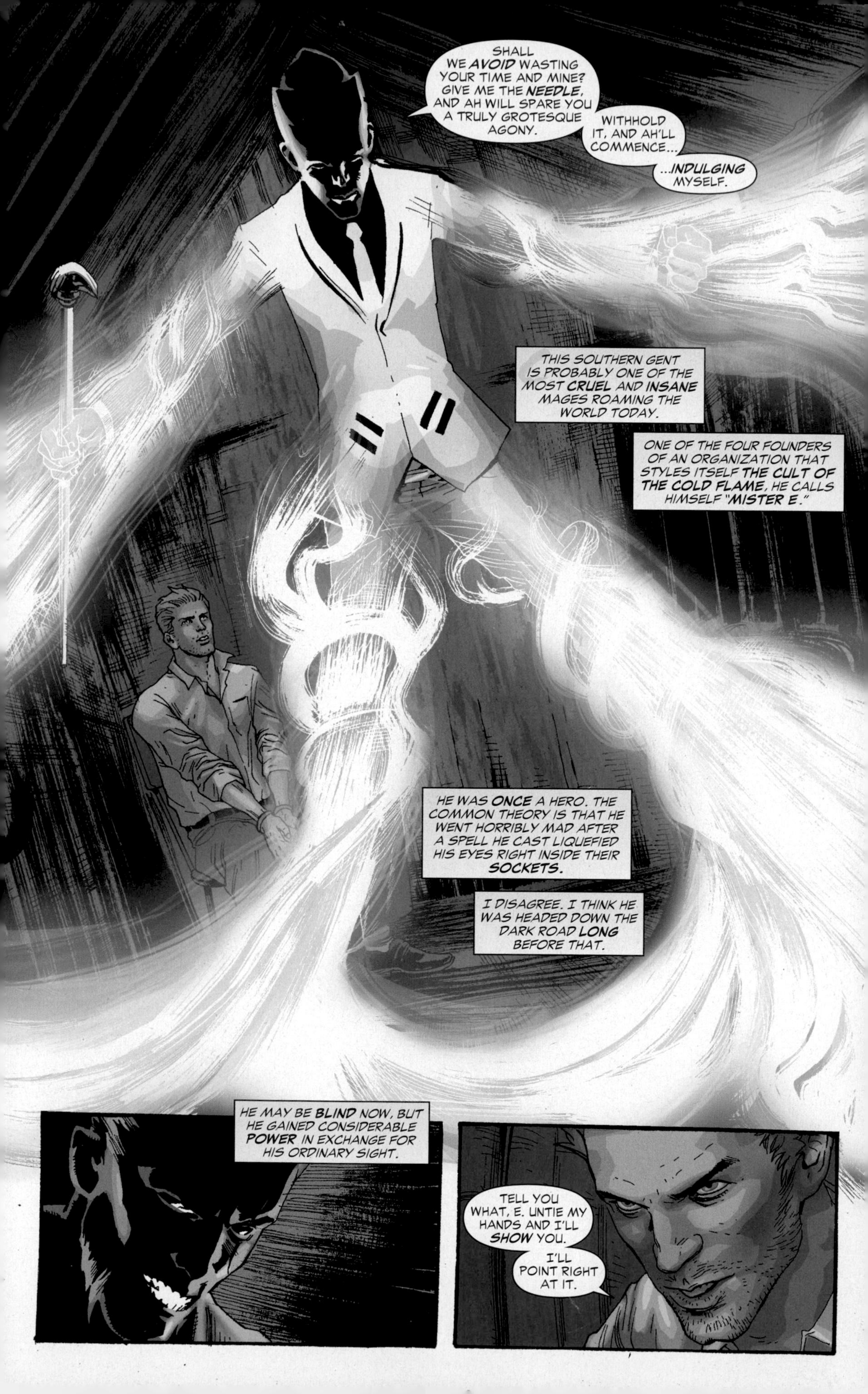
SHALL WE *AVOID* WASTING YOUR TIME AND MINE? GIVE ME THE *NEEDLE*, AND AH WILL SPARE YOU A TRULY GROTESQUE AGONY.
WITHHOLD IT, AND AH'LL COMMENCE...
...*INDULGING* MYSELF.
THIS SOUTHERN GENT IS PROBABLY ONE OF THE MOST **CRUEL** AND **INSANE** MAGES ROAMING THE WORLD TODAY.
ONE OF THE FOUR FOUNDERS OF AN ORGANIZATION THAT STYLES ITSELF **THE CULT OF THE COLD FLAME**, HE CALLS HIMSELF "**MISTER E**."
HE WAS **ONCE** A HERO. THE COMMON THEORY IS THAT HE WENT HORRIBLY MAD AFTER A SPELL HE CAST LIQUEFIED HIS EYES RIGHT INSIDE THEIR **SOCKETS**.
I DISAGREE. I THINK HE WAS HEADED DOWN THE DARK ROAD **LONG** BEFORE THAT.
HE MAY BE **BLIND** NOW, BUT HE GAINED CONSIDERABLE **POWER** IN EXCHANGE FOR HIS ORDINARY SIGHT.
TELL YOU WHAT, E. UNTIE MY HANDS AND I'LL *SHOW* YOU.
I'LL POINT RIGHT AT IT.

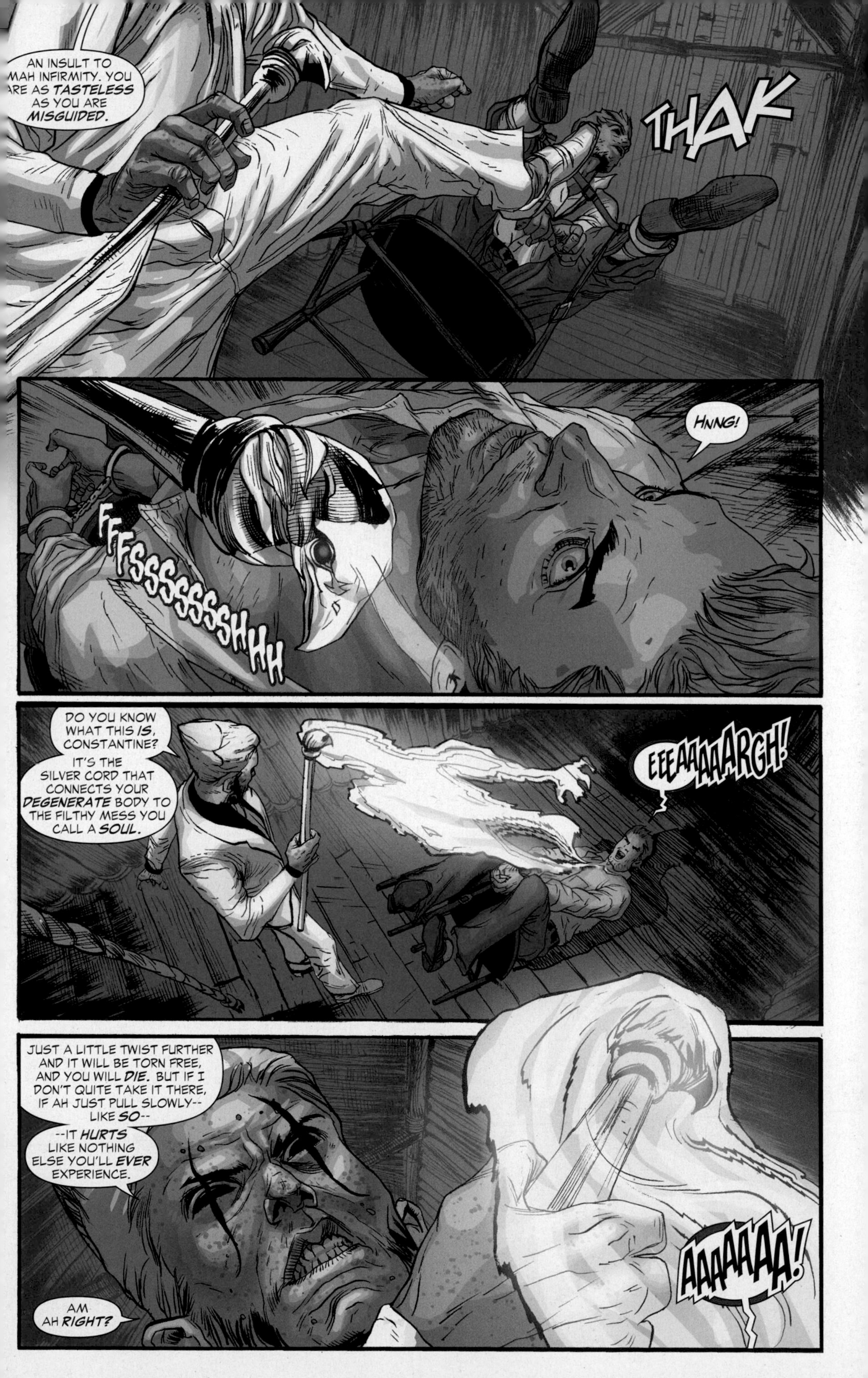
AN INSULT TO MAH INFIRMITY. YOU ARE AS TASTELESS AS YOU ARE MISGUIDED.
THAK
HNNG!
FFFSSSSSSSHHHH
DO YOU KNOW WHAT THIS IS, CONSTANTINE?
IT'S THE SILVER CORD THAT CONNECTS YOUR DEGENERATE BODY TO THE FILTHY MESS YOU CALL A SOUL.
EEEAAAAARGH!
JUST A LITTLE TWIST FURTHER AND IT WILL BE TORN FREE, AND YOU WILL DIE. BUT IF I DON'T QUITE TAKE IT THERE, IF AH JUST PULL SLOWLY-- LIKE SO--
--IT HURTS LIKE NOTHING ELSE YOU'LL EVER EXPERIENCE.
AAAAAAA!
AM AH RIGHT?

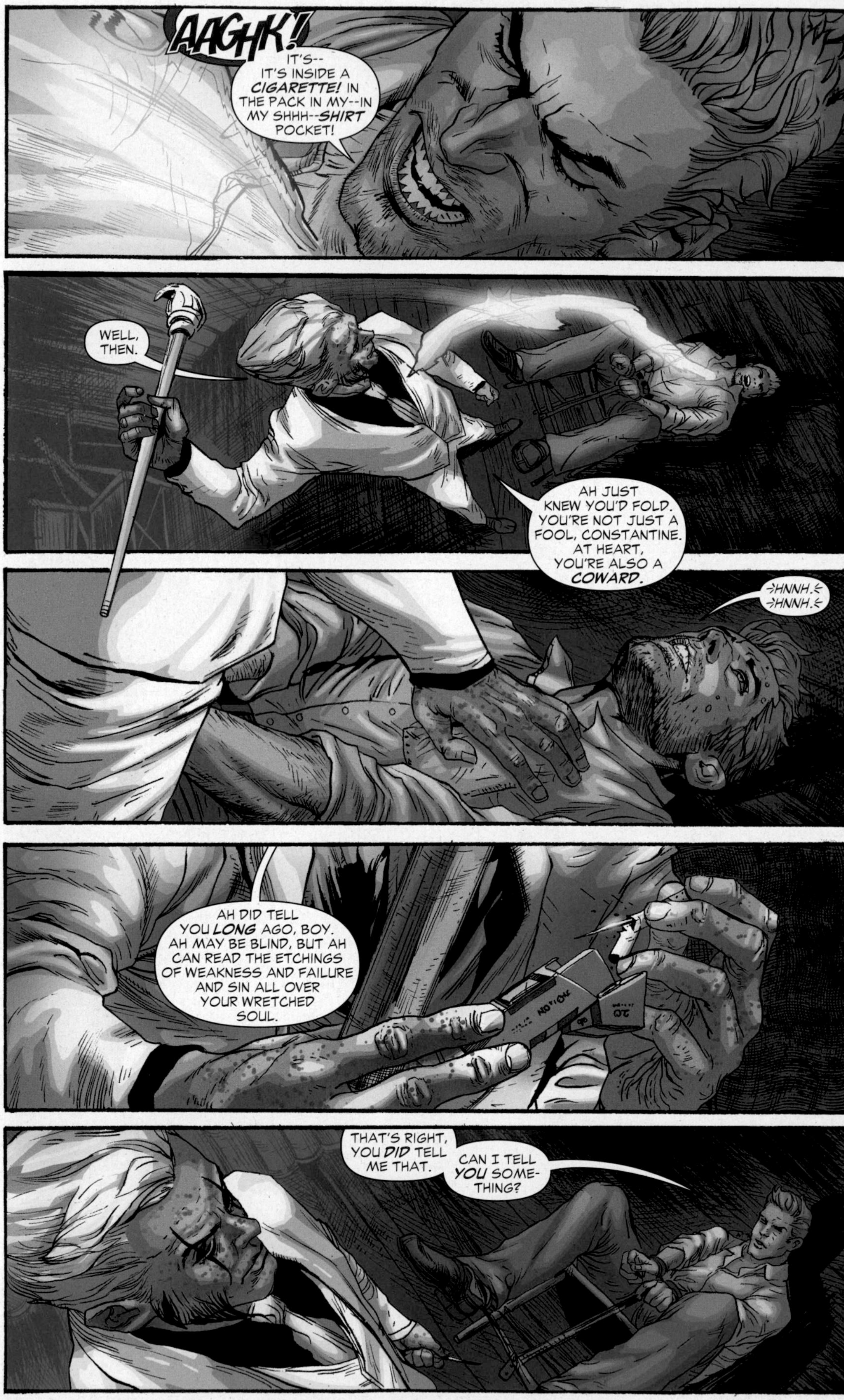
AAGHK!
IT'S-- IT'S INSIDE A CIGARETTE! IN THE PACK IN MY--IN MY SHHH--SHIRT POCKET!
WELL, THEN.
AH JUST KNEW YOU'D FOLD. YOU'RE NOT JUST A FOOL, CONSTANTINE. AT HEART, YOU'RE ALSO A COWARD.
HNNH. HNNH.
AH DID TELL YOU LONG AGO, BOY. AH MAY BE BLIND, BUT AH CAN READ THE ETCHINGS OF WEAKNESS AND FAILURE AND SIN ALL OVER YOUR WRETCHED SOUL.
THAT'S RIGHT, YOU DID TELL ME THAT.
CAN I TELL YOU SOME-THING?

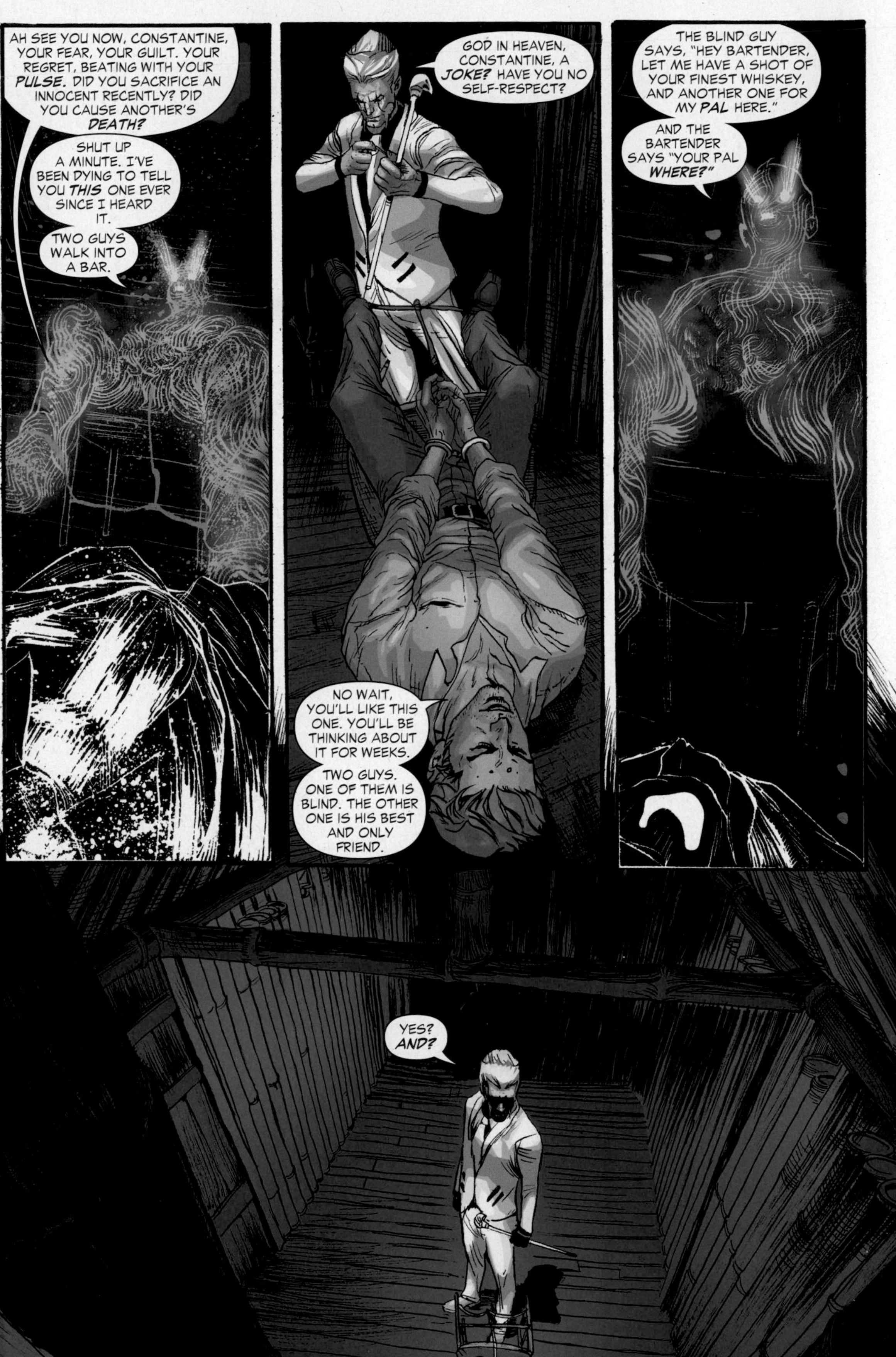
AH SEE YOU NOW, CONSTANTINE, YOUR FEAR, YOUR GUILT. YOUR REGRET, BEATING WITH YOUR PULSE. DID YOU SACRIFICE AN INNOCENT RECENTLY? DID YOU CAUSE ANOTHER'S DEATH?
SHUT UP A MINUTE. I'VE BEEN DYING TO TELL YOU THIS ONE EVER SINCE I HEARD IT.
TWO GUYS WALK INTO A BAR.
GOD IN HEAVEN, CONSTANTINE, A JOKE? HAVE YOU NO SELF-RESPECT?
NO WAIT, YOU'LL LIKE THIS ONE. YOU'LL BE THINKING ABOUT IT FOR WEEKS.
TWO GUYS. ONE OF THEM IS BLIND. THE OTHER ONE IS HIS BEST AND ONLY FRIEND.
THE BLIND GUY SAYS, "HEY BARTENDER, LET ME HAVE A SHOT OF YOUR FINEST WHISKEY, AND ANOTHER ONE FOR MY PAL HERE."
AND THE BARTENDER SAYS "YOUR PAL WHERE?"
YES? AND?

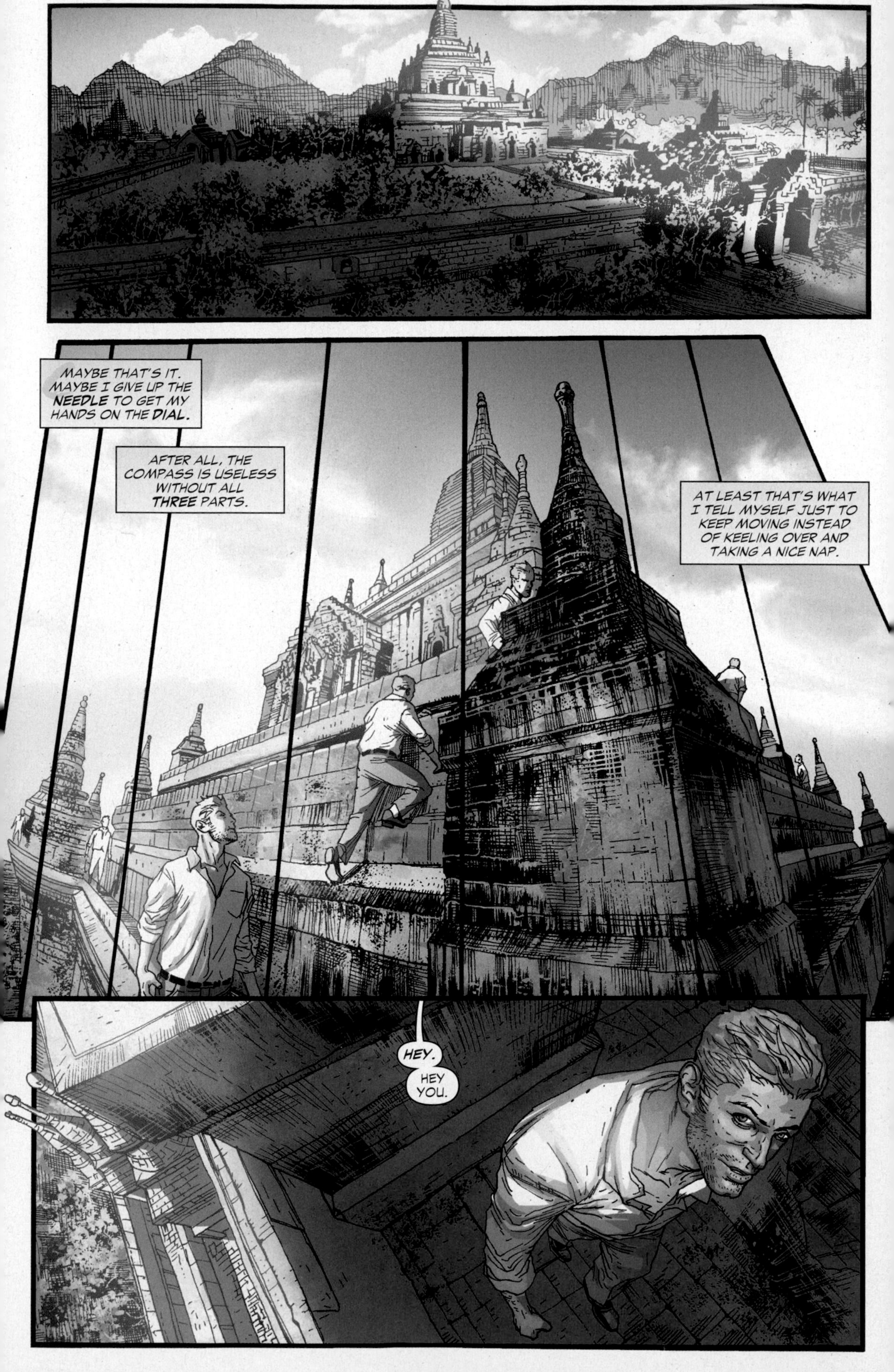
MAYBE THAT'S IT. MAYBE I GIVE UP THE NEEDLE TO GET MY HANDS ON THE DIAL.
AFTER ALL, THE COMPASS IS USELESS WITHOUT ALL THREE PARTS.
AT LEAST THAT'S WHAT I TELL MYSELF JUST TO KEEP MOVING INSTEAD OF KEELING OVER AND TAKING A NICE NAP.
HEY.
HEY YOU.

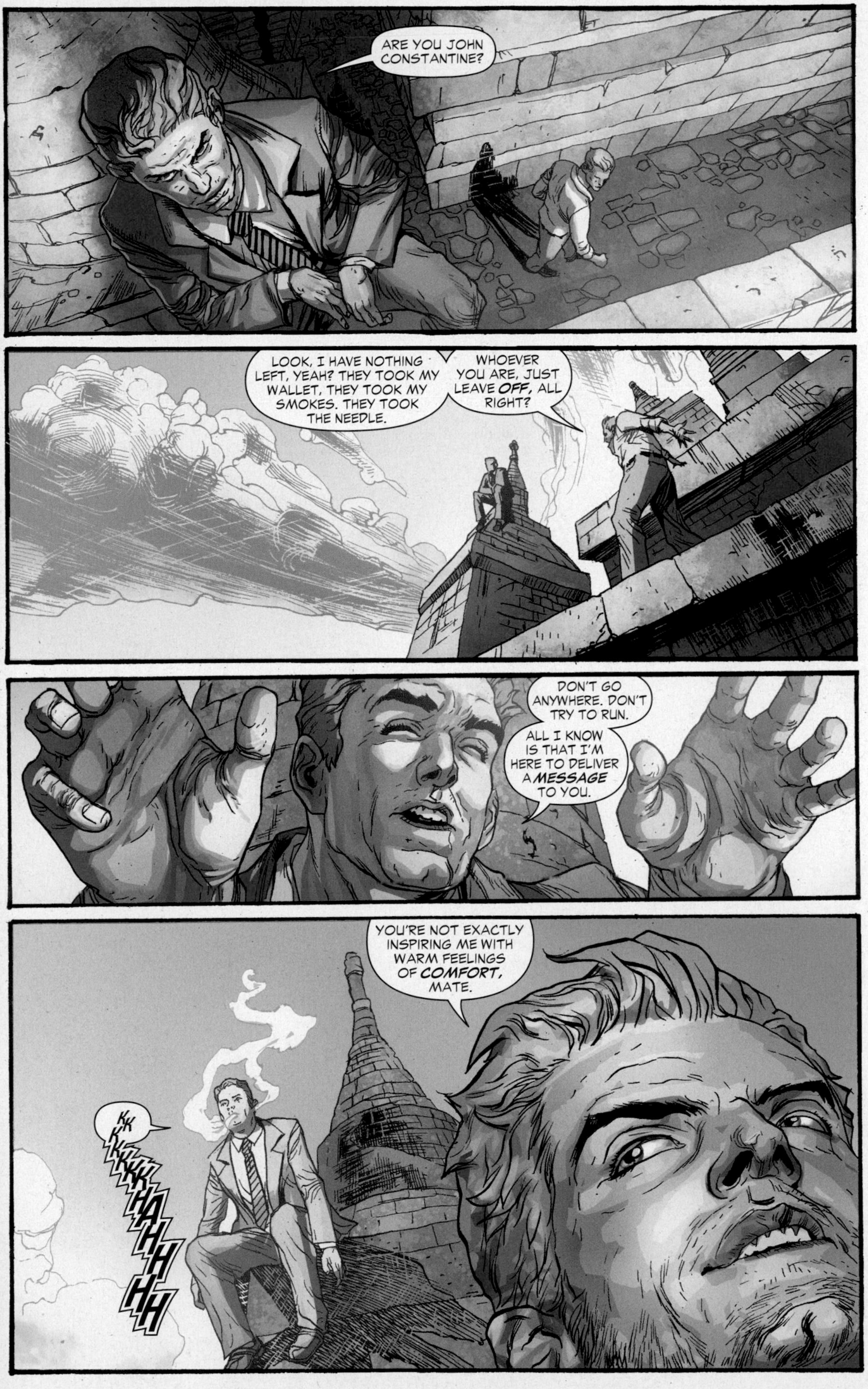
ARE YOU JOHN CONSTANTINE?
LOOK, I HAVE NOTHING LEFT, YEAH? THEY TOOK MY WALLET, THEY TOOK MY SMOKES. THEY TOOK THE NEEDLE.
WHOEVER YOU ARE, JUST LEAVE OFF, ALL RIGHT?
DON'T GO ANYWHERE. DON'T TRY TO RUN.
ALL I KNOW IS THAT I'M HERE TO DELIVER A MESSAGE TO YOU.
YOU'RE NOT EXACTLY INSPIRING ME WITH WARM FEELINGS OF COMFORT, MATE.
KKKKKKKHAHHHHHH

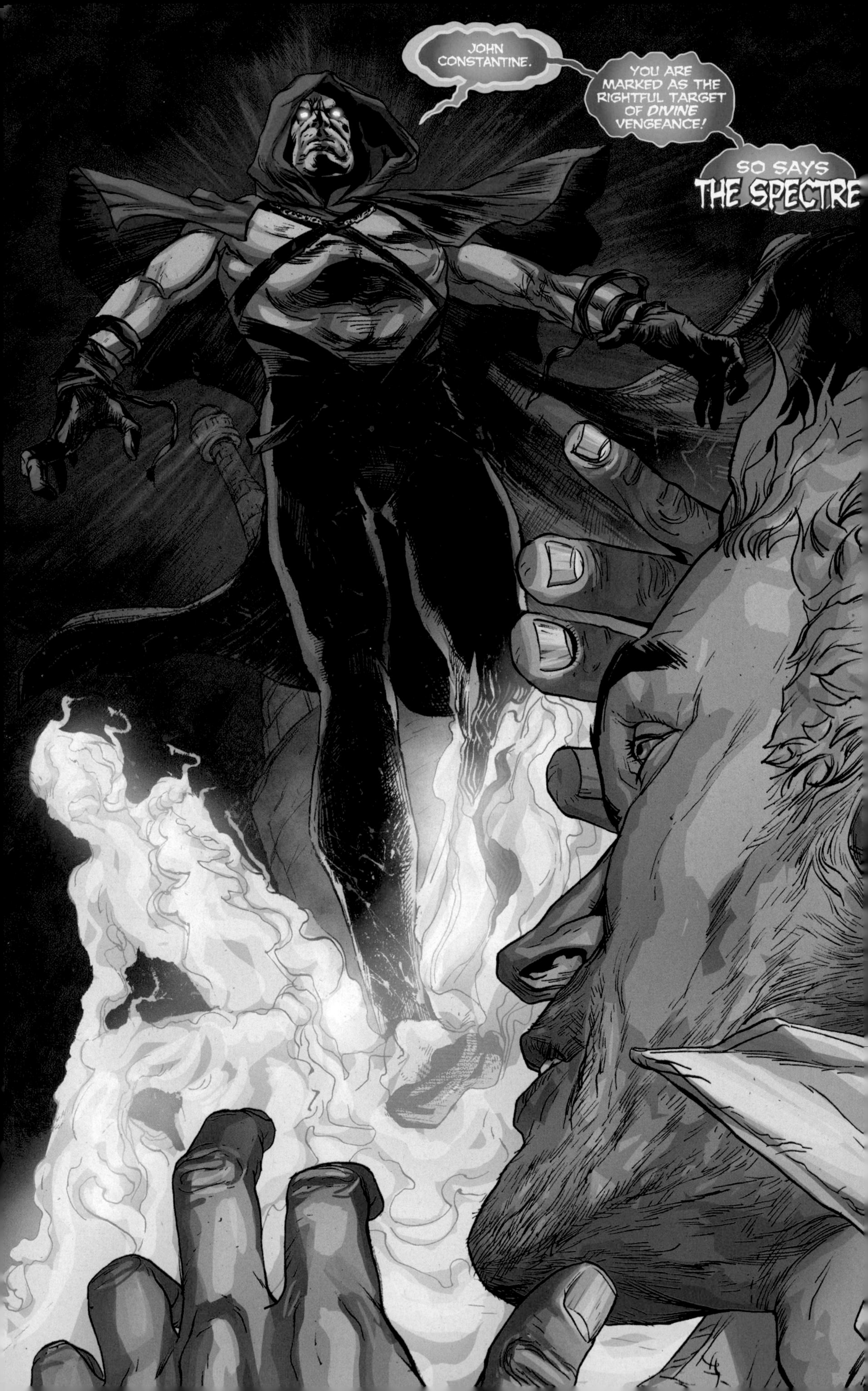
JOHN CONSTANTINE.
YOU ARE MARKED AS THE RIGHTFUL TARGET OF DIVINE VENGEANCE!
SO SAYS THE SPECTRE

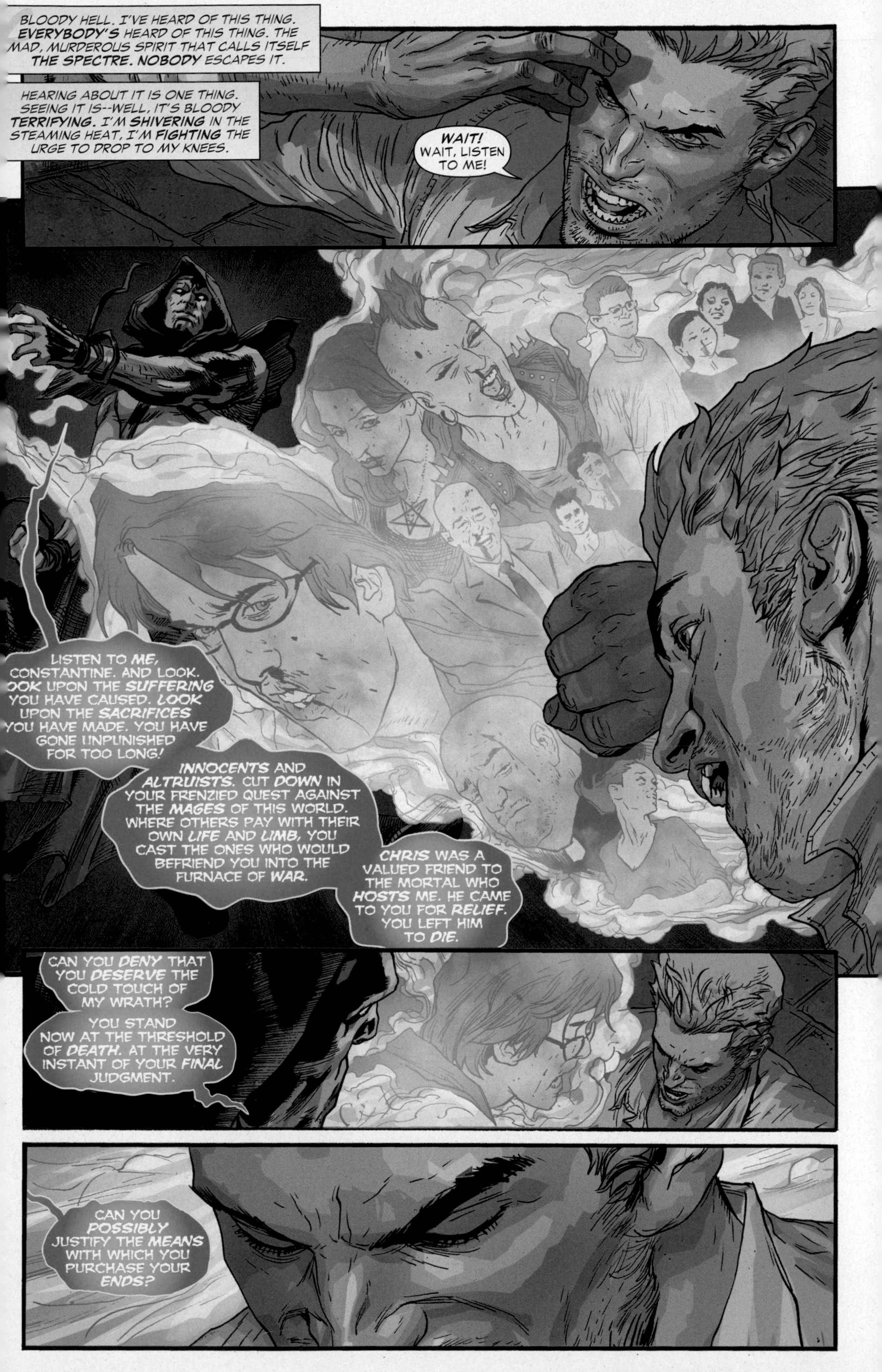
BLOODY HELL. I'VE HEARD OF THIS THING. EVERYBODY'S HEARD OF THIS THING. THE MAD, MURDEROUS SPIRIT THAT CALLS ITSELF THE SPECTRE. NOBODY ESCAPES IT.
HEARING ABOUT IT IS ONE THING. SEEING IT IS--WELL, IT'S BLOODY TERRIFYING. I'M SHIVERING IN THE STEAMING HEAT, I'M FIGHTING THE URGE TO DROP TO MY KNEES.
WAIT! WAIT, LISTEN TO ME!
LISTEN TO ME, CONSTANTINE. AND LOOK. LOOK UPON THE SUFFERING YOU HAVE CAUSED. LOOK UPON THE SACRIFICES YOU HAVE MADE. YOU HAVE GONE UNPUNISHED FOR TOO LONG!
INNOCENTS AND ALTRUISTS. CUT DOWN IN YOUR FRENZIED QUEST AGAINST THE MAGES OF THIS WORLD. WHERE OTHERS PAY WITH THEIR OWN LIFE AND LIMB, YOU CAST THE ONES WHO WOULD BEFRIEND YOU INTO THE FURNACE OF WAR.
CHRIS WAS A VALUED FRIEND TO THE MORTAL WHO HOSTS ME. HE CAME TO YOU FOR RELIEF. YOU LEFT HIM TO DIE.
CAN YOU DENY THAT YOU DESERVE THE COLD TOUCH OF MY WRATH?
YOU STAND NOW AT THE THRESHOLD OF DEATH. AT THE VERY INSTANT OF YOUR FINAL JUDGMENT.
CAN YOU POSSIBLY JUSTIFY THE MEANS WITH WHICH YOU PURCHASE YOUR ENDS?

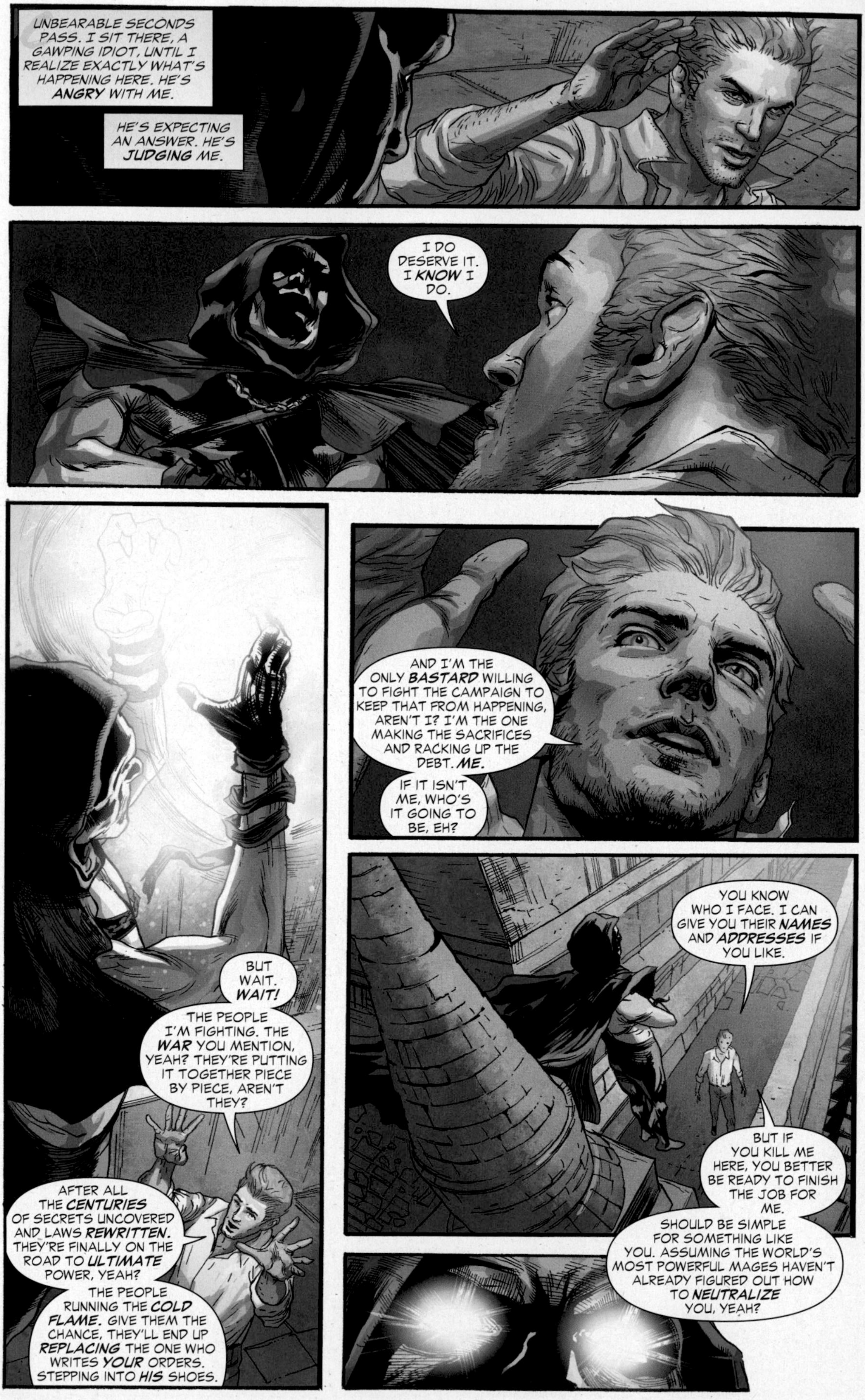
UNBEARABLE SECONDS PASS. I SIT THERE, A GAWPING IDIOT, UNTIL I REALIZE EXACTLY WHAT'S HAPPENING HERE. HE'S ANGRY WITH ME.
HE'S EXPECTING AN ANSWER. HE'S JUDGING ME.
I DO DESERVE IT. I KNOW I DO.
BUT WAIT. WAIT!
THE PEOPLE I'M FIGHTING. THE WAR YOU MENTION, YEAH? THEY'RE PUTTING IT TOGETHER PIECE BY PIECE, AREN'T THEY?
AFTER ALL THE CENTURIES OF SECRETS UNCOVERED AND LAWS REWRITTEN. THEY'RE FINALLY ON THE ROAD TO ULTIMATE POWER, YEAH?
THE PEOPLE RUNNING THE COLD FLAME. GIVE THEM THE CHANCE, THEY'LL END UP REPLACING THE ONE WHO WRITES YOUR ORDERS. STEPPING INTO HIS SHOES.
AND I'M THE ONLY BASTARD WILLING TO FIGHT THE CAMPAIGN TO KEEP THAT FROM HAPPENING, AREN'T I? I'M THE ONE MAKING THE SACRIFICES AND RACKING UP THE DEBT. ME.
IF IT ISN'T ME, WHO'S IT GOING TO BE, EH?
YOU KNOW WHO I FACE. I CAN GIVE YOU THEIR NAMES AND ADDRESSES IF YOU LIKE.
BUT IF YOU KILL ME HERE, YOU BETTER BE READY TO FINISH THE JOB FOR ME.
SHOULD BE SIMPLE FOR SOMETHING LIKE YOU. ASSUMING THE WORLD'S MOST POWERFUL MAGES HAVEN'T ALREADY FIGURED OUT HOW TO NEUTRALIZE YOU, YEAH?

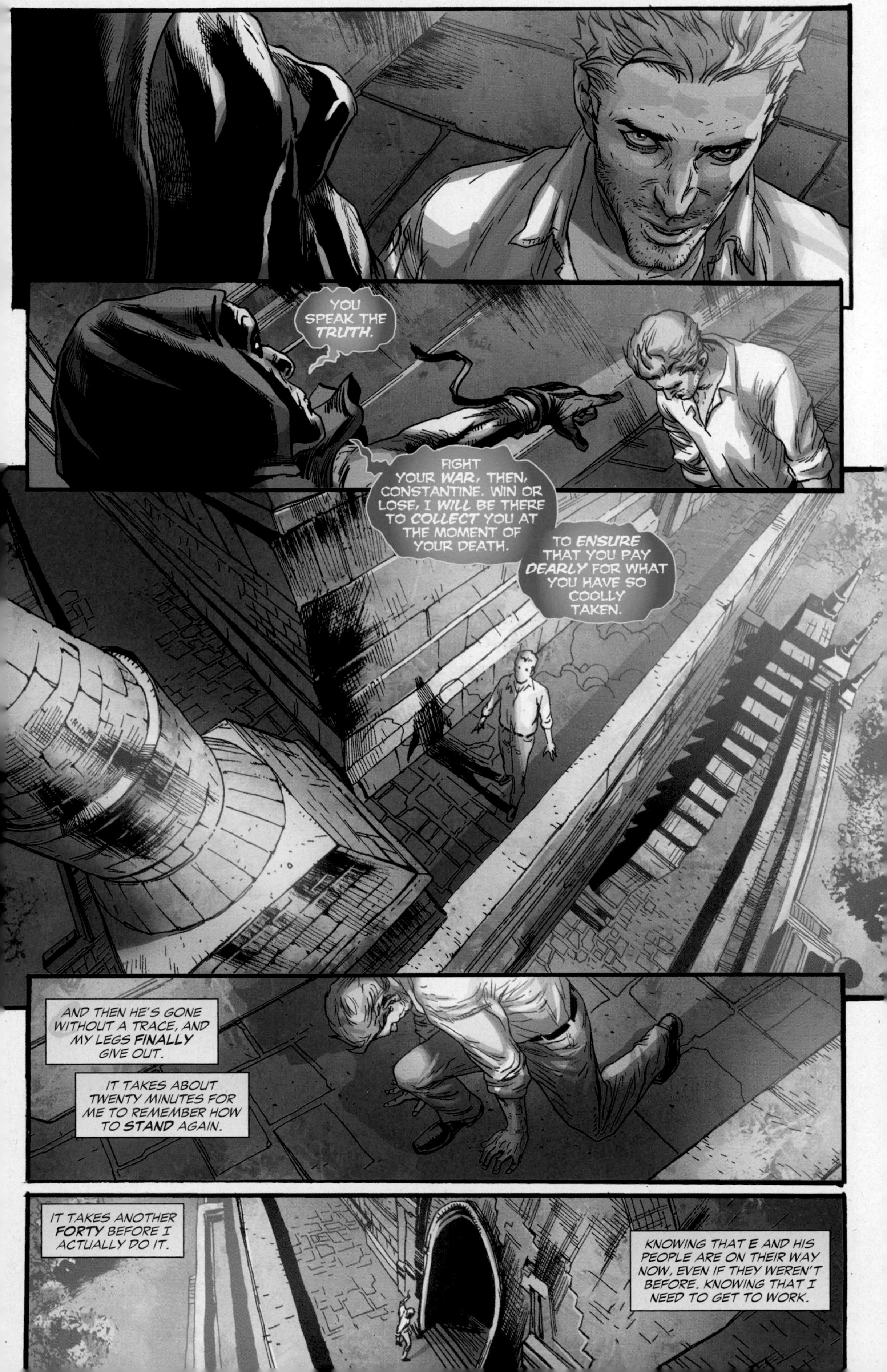
YOU SPEAK THE TRUTH.
FIGHT YOUR WAR, THEN, CONSTANTINE. WIN OR LOSE, I WILL BE THERE TO COLLECT YOU AT THE MOMENT OF YOUR DEATH.
TO ENSURE THAT YOU PAY DEARLY FOR WHAT YOU HAVE SO COOLLY TAKEN.
AND THEN HE'S GONE WITHOUT A TRACE, AND MY LEGS FINALLY GIVE OUT.
IT TAKES ABOUT TWENTY MINUTES FOR ME TO REMEMBER HOW TO STAND AGAIN.
IT TAKES ANOTHER FORTY BEFORE I ACTUALLY DO IT.
KNOWING THAT E AND HIS PEOPLE ARE ON THEIR WAY NOW, EVEN IF THEY WEREN'T BEFORE. KNOWING THAT I NEED TO GET TO WORK.

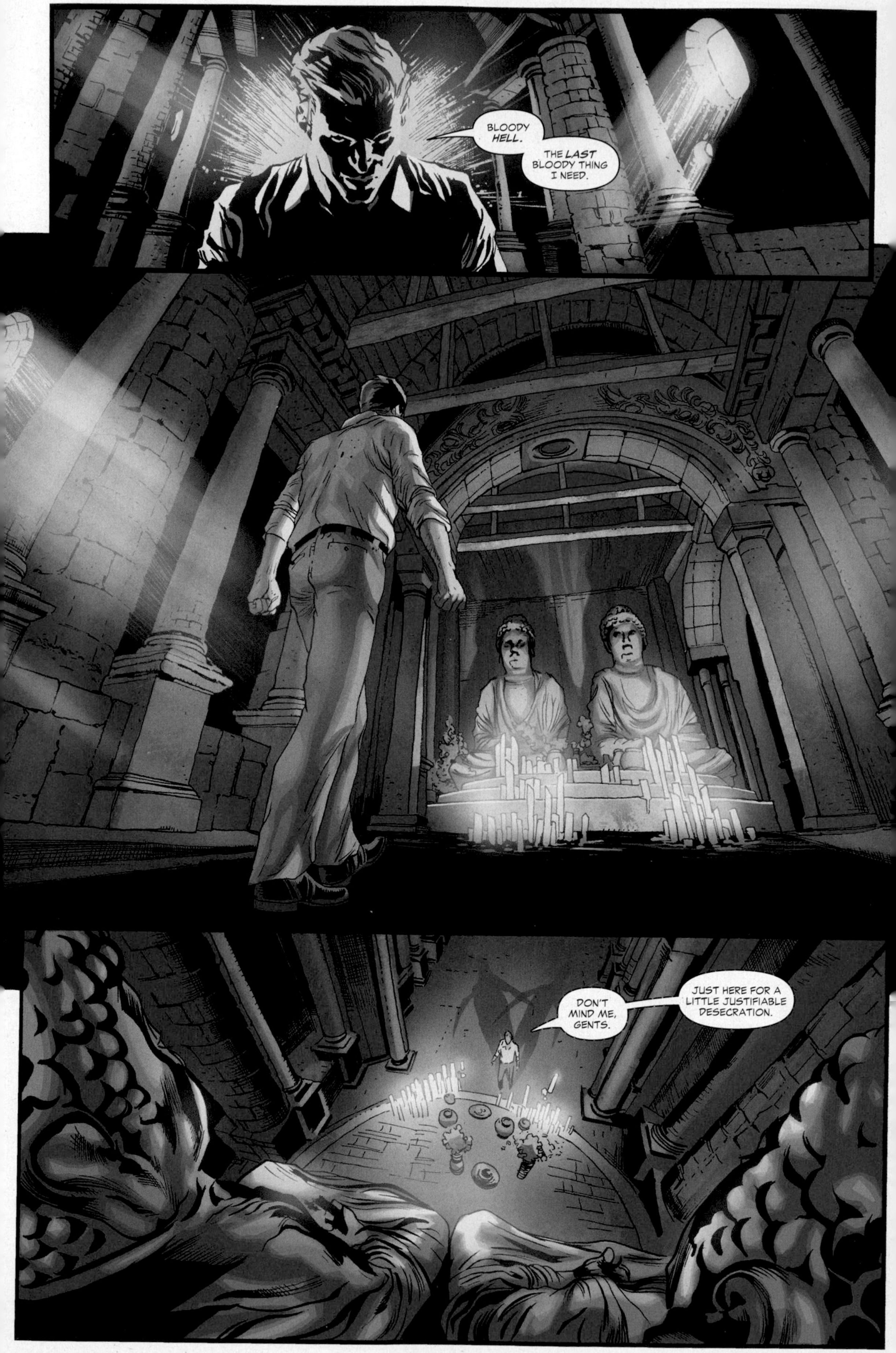
BLOODY HELL.
THE LAST BLOODY THING I NEED.
DON'T MIND ME, GENTS.
JUST HERE FOR A LITTLE JUSTIFIABLE DESECRATION.

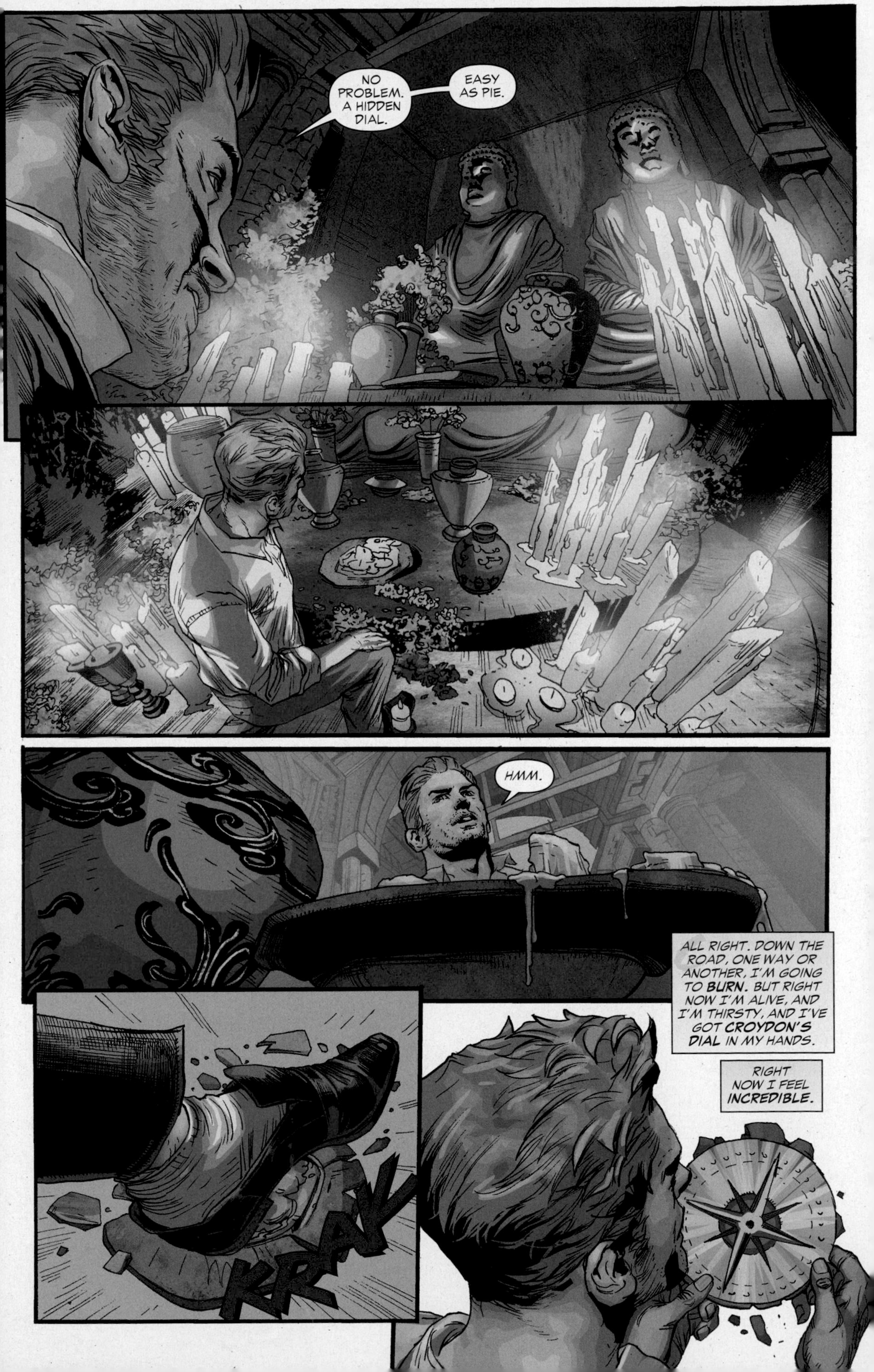
NO PROBLEM. A HIDDEN DIAL.
EASY AS PIE.
HMM.
ALL RIGHT. DOWN THE ROAD, ONE WAY OR ANOTHER, I'M GOING TO **BURN**. BUT RIGHT NOW I'M ALIVE, AND I'M THIRSTY, AND I'VE GOT **CROYDON'S DIAL** IN MY HANDS.
RIGHT NOW I FEEL **INCREDIBLE**.
KRAK

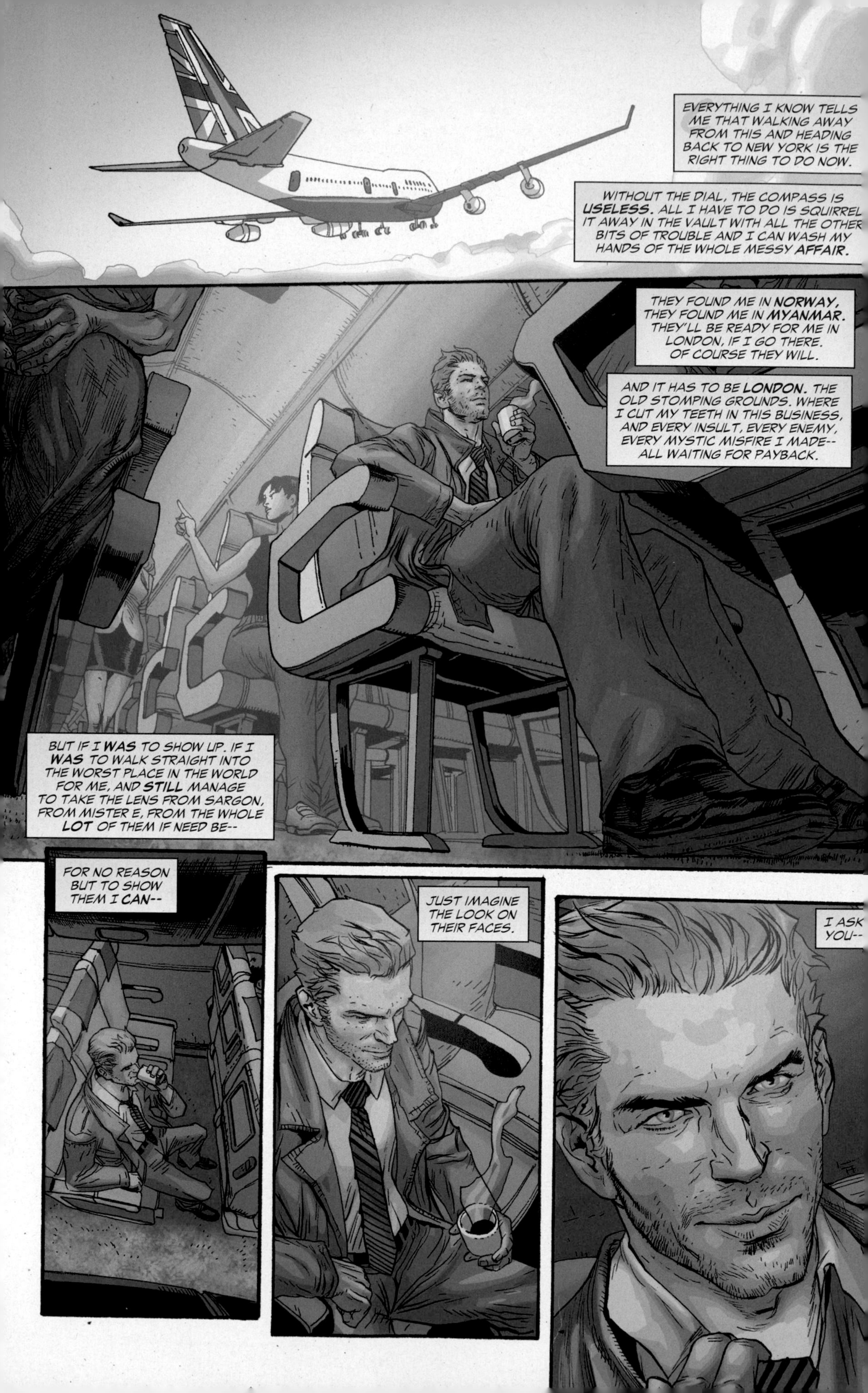
EVERYTHING I KNOW TELLS ME THAT WALKING AWAY FROM THIS AND HEADING BACK TO NEW YORK IS THE RIGHT THING TO DO NOW.
WITHOUT THE DIAL, THE COMPASS IS USELESS. ALL I HAVE TO DO IS SQUIRREL IT AWAY IN THE VAULT WITH ALL THE OTHER BITS OF TROUBLE AND I CAN WASH MY HANDS OF THE WHOLE MESSY AFFAIR.
THEY FOUND ME IN NORWAY, THEY FOUND ME IN MYANMAR. THEY'LL BE READY FOR ME IN LONDON, IF I GO THERE. OF COURSE THEY WILL.
AND IT HAS TO BE LONDON. THE OLD STOMPING GROUNDS. WHERE I CUT MY TEETH IN THIS BUSINESS, AND EVERY INSULT, EVERY ENEMY, EVERY MYSTIC MISFIRE I MADE-- ALL WAITING FOR PAYBACK.
BUT IF I WAS TO SHOW UP. IF I WAS TO WALK STRAIGHT INTO THE WORST PLACE IN THE WORLD FOR ME, AND STILL MANAGE TO TAKE THE LENS FROM SARGON, FROM MISTER E, FROM THE WHOLE LOT OF THEM IF NEED BE--
FOR NO REASON BUT TO SHOW THEM I CAN--
JUST IMAGINE THE LOOK ON THEIR FACES.
I ASK YOU--

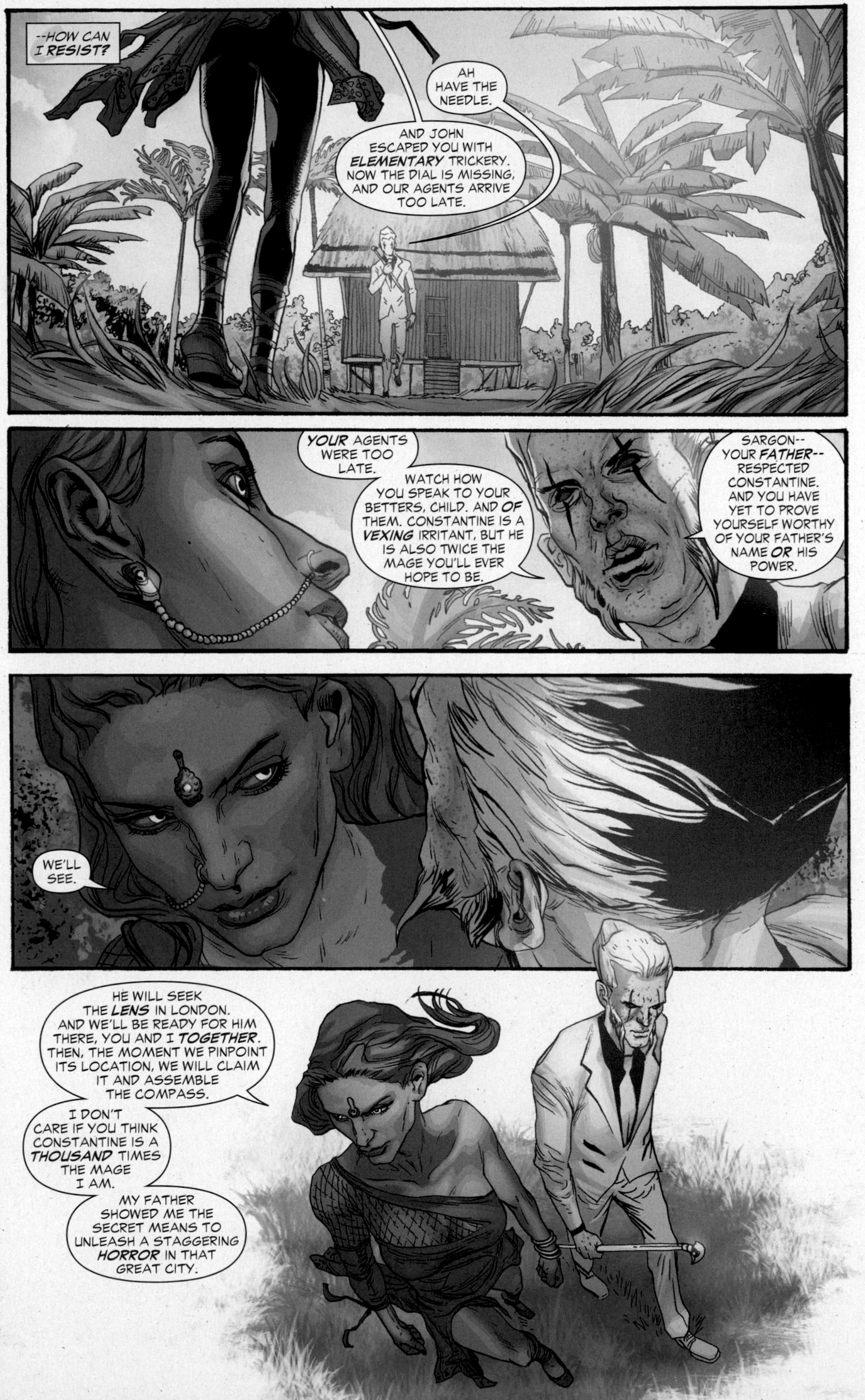
--HOW CAN I RESIST?
AH HAVE THE NEEDLE.
AND JOHN ESCAPED YOU WITH ELEMENTARY TRICKERY. NOW THE DIAL IS MISSING, AND OUR AGENTS ARRIVE TOO LATE.
YOUR AGENTS WERE TOO LATE.
WATCH HOW YOU SPEAK TO YOUR BETTERS, CHILD. AND OF THEM. CONSTANTINE IS A VEXING IRRITANT, BUT HE IS ALSO TWICE THE MAGE YOU'LL EVER HOPE TO BE.
SARGON-- YOUR FATHER-- RESPECTED CONSTANTINE. AND YOU HAVE YET TO PROVE YOURSELF WORTHY OF YOUR FATHER'S NAME OR HIS POWER.
WE'LL SEE.
HE WILL SEEK THE LENS IN LONDON. AND WE'LL BE READY FOR HIM THERE, YOU AND I TOGETHER. THEN, THE MOMENT WE PINPOINT ITS LOCATION, WE WILL CLAIM IT AND ASSEMBLE THE COMPASS.
I DON'T CARE IF YOU THINK CONSTANTINE IS A THOUSAND TIMES THE MAGE I AM.
MY FATHER SHOWED ME THE SECRET MEANS TO UNLEASH A STAGGERING HORROR IN THAT GREAT CITY.

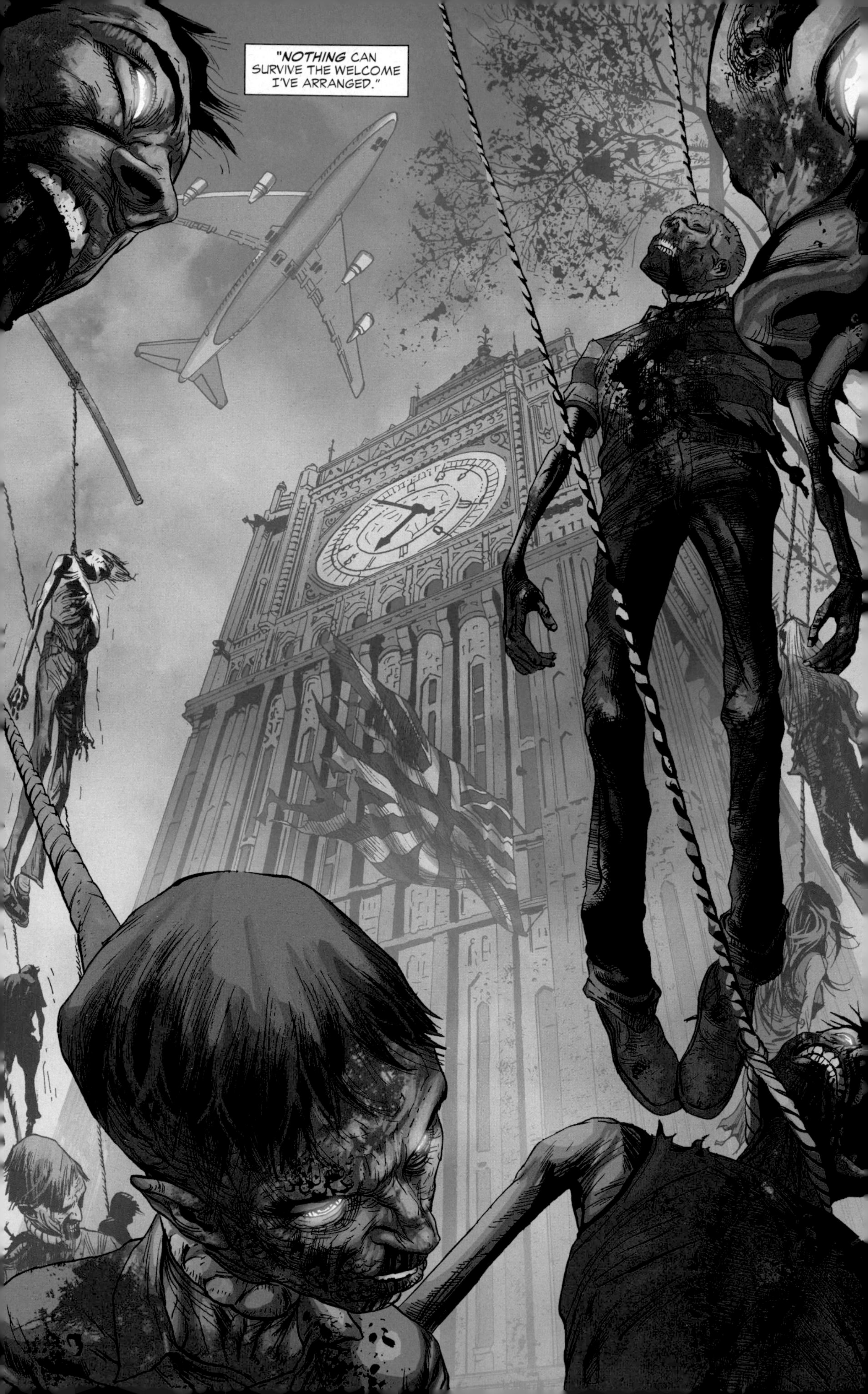
"NOTHING CAN SURVIVE THE WELCOME I'VE ARRANGED."

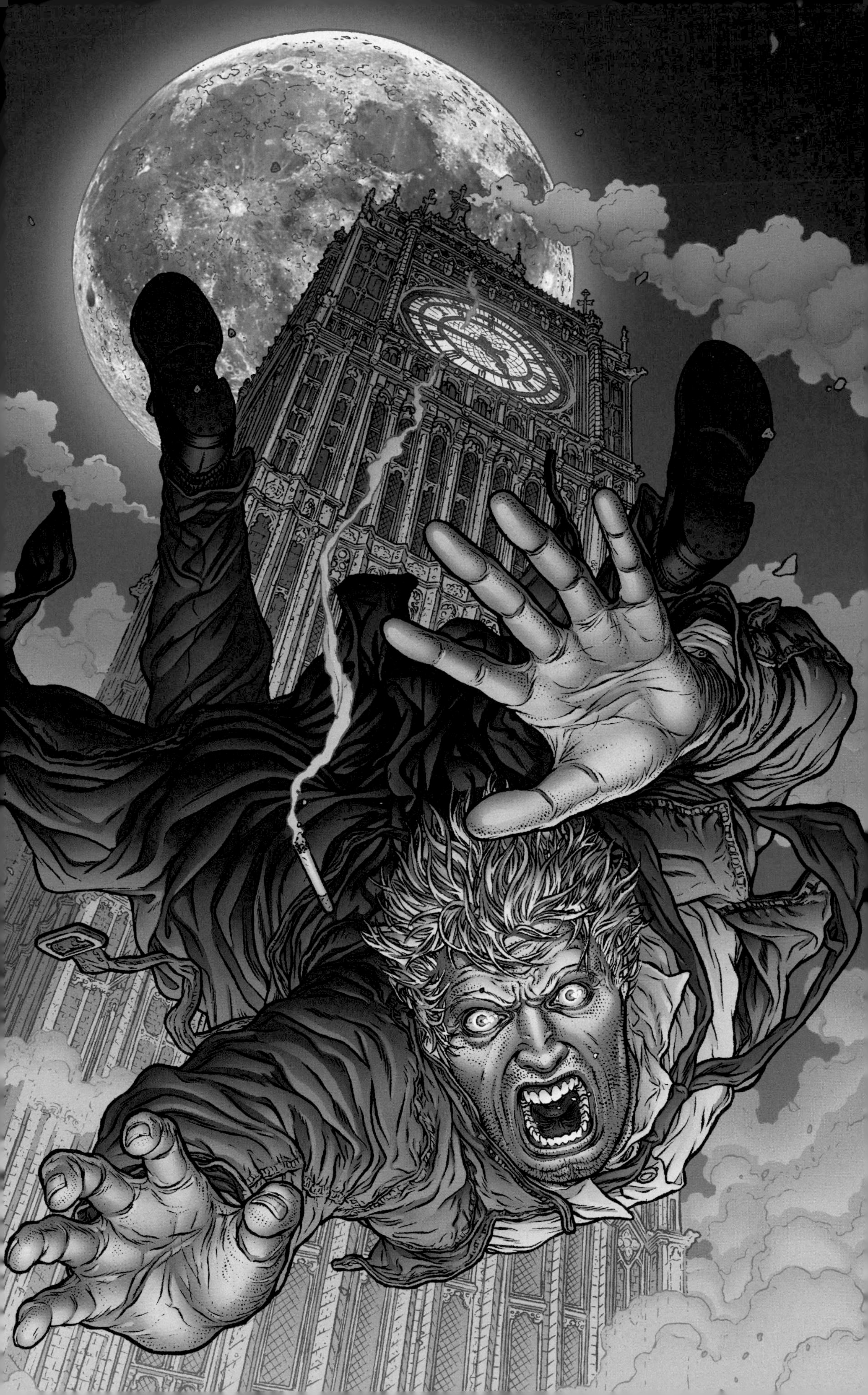

THE SPARK AND THE FLAME PART 3: THE BIG SMOKE

JEFF LEMIRE & RAY FAWKES writers RENATO GUEDES artist cover art by JUAN JOSE RYP & BRETT SMITH

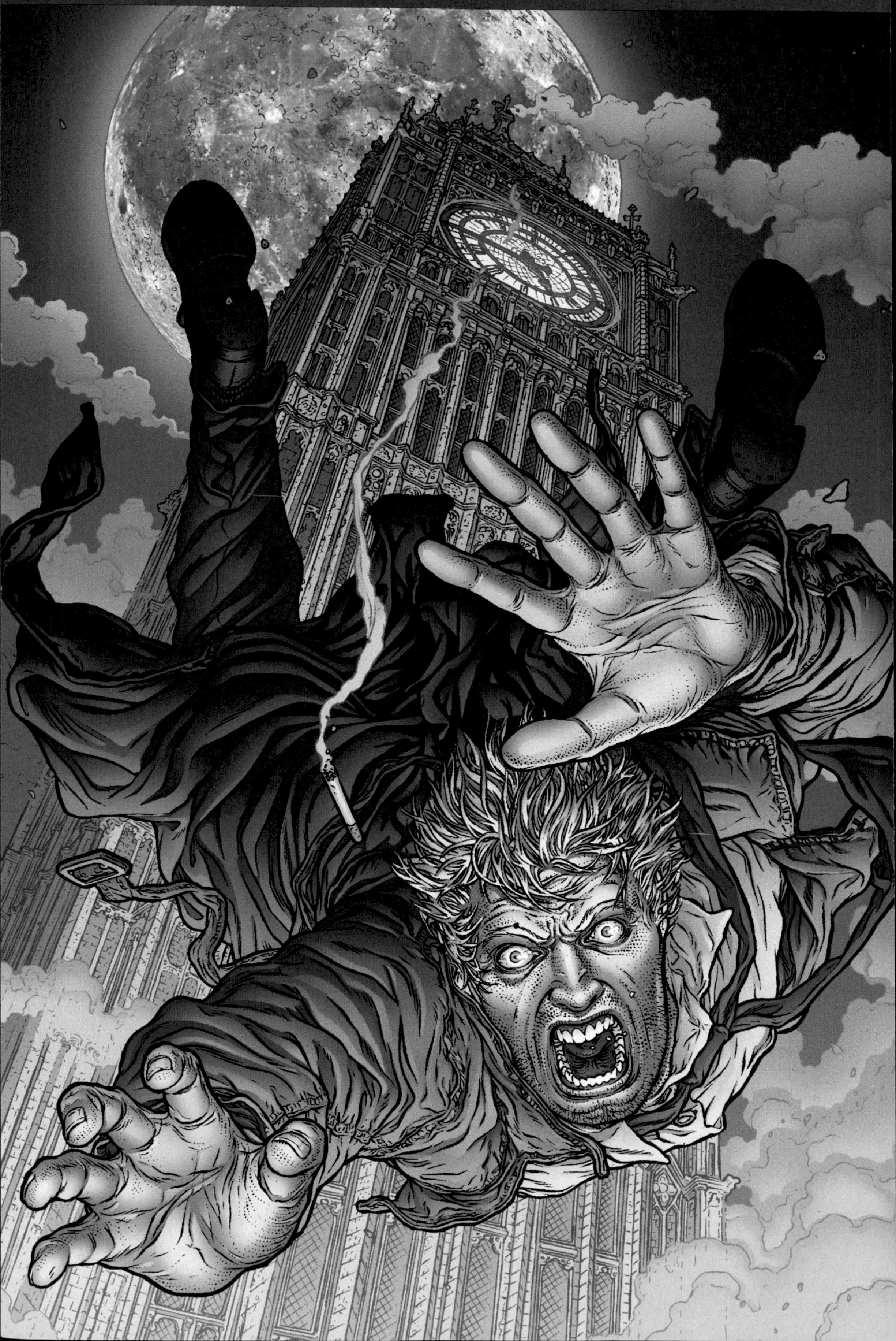

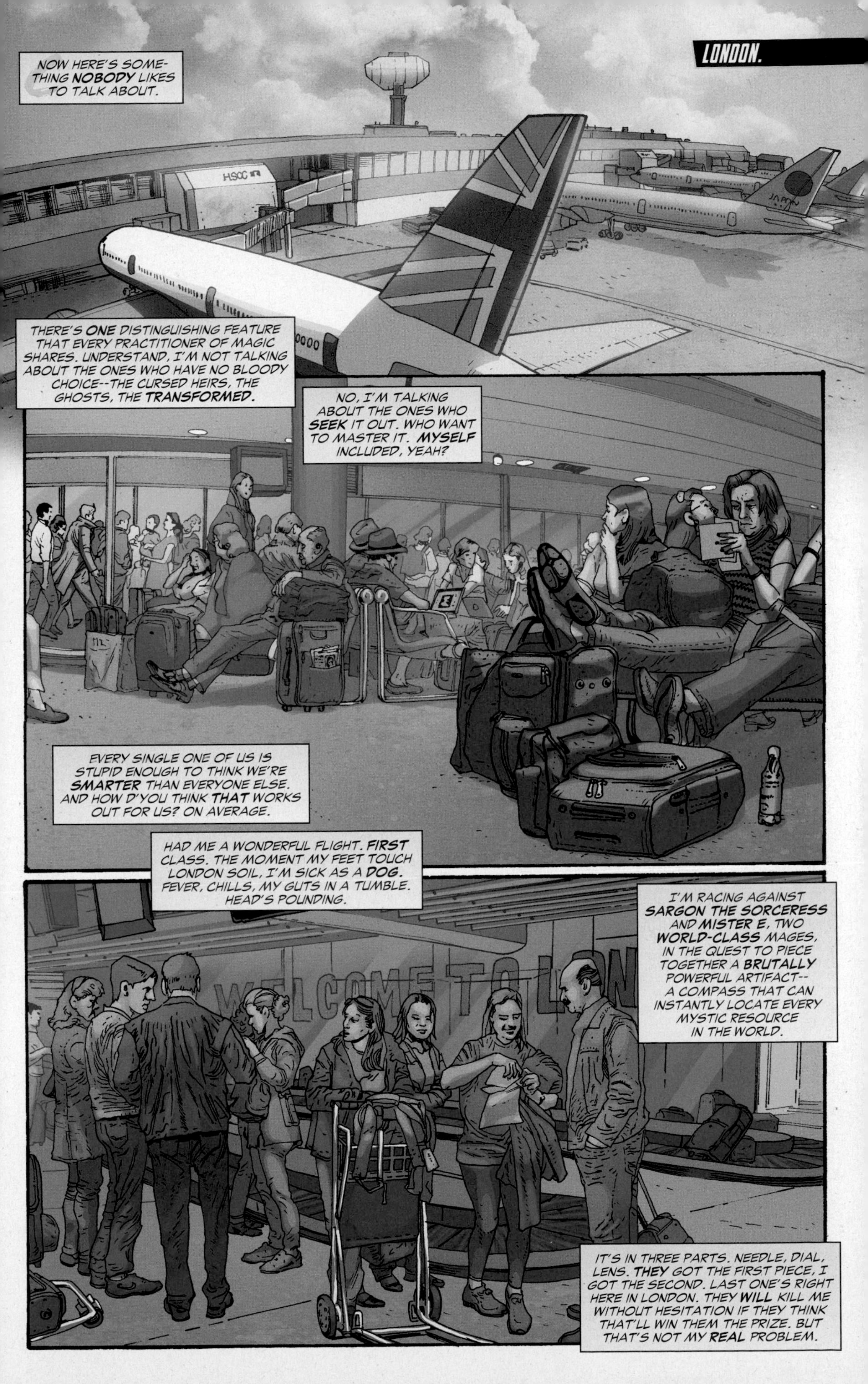
LONDON.
NOW HERE'S SOMETHING NOBODY LIKES TO TALK ABOUT.
THERE'S ONE DISTINGUISHING FEATURE THAT EVERY PRACTITIONER OF MAGIC SHARES. UNDERSTAND, I'M NOT TALKING ABOUT THE ONES WHO HAVE NO BLOODY CHOICE--THE CURSED HEIRS, THE GHOSTS, THE TRANSFORMED.
NO, I'M TALKING ABOUT THE ONES WHO SEEK IT OUT. WHO WANT TO MASTER IT. MYSELF INCLUDED, YEAH?
EVERY SINGLE ONE OF US IS STUPID ENOUGH TO THINK WE'RE SMARTER THAN EVERYONE ELSE. AND HOW D'YOU THINK THAT WORKS OUT FOR US? ON AVERAGE.
HAD ME A WONDERFUL FLIGHT. FIRST CLASS. THE MOMENT MY FEET TOUCH LONDON SOIL, I'M SICK AS A DOG. FEVER, CHILLS, MY GUTS IN A TUMBLE. HEAD'S POUNDING.
I'M RACING AGAINST SARGON THE SORCERESS AND MISTER E, TWO WORLD-CLASS MAGES, IN THE QUEST TO PIECE TOGETHER A BRUTALLY POWERFUL ARTIFACT-- A COMPASS THAT CAN INSTANTLY LOCATE EVERY MYSTIC RESOURCE IN THE WORLD.
WELCOME TO LON
IT'S IN THREE PARTS. NEEDLE, DIAL, LENS. THEY GOT THE FIRST PIECE, I GOT THE SECOND. LAST ONE'S RIGHT HERE IN LONDON. THEY WILL KILL ME WITHOUT HESITATION IF THEY THINK THAT'LL WIN THEM THE PRIZE. BUT THAT'S NOT MY REAL PROBLEM.

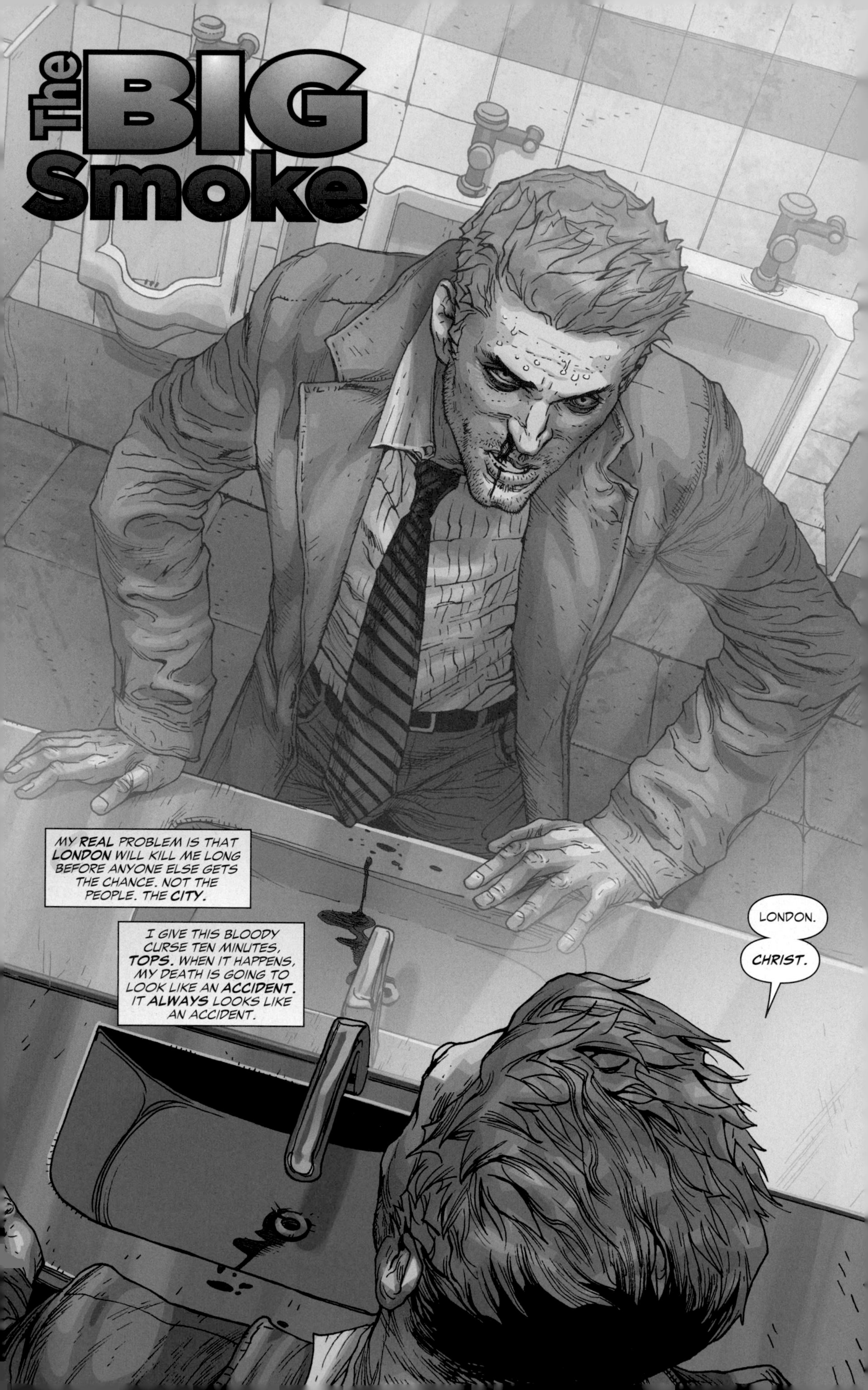
The BIG Smoke
MY REAL PROBLEM IS THAT LONDON WILL KILL ME LONG BEFORE ANYONE ELSE GETS THE CHANCE. NOT THE PEOPLE. THE CITY.
I GIVE THIS BLOODY CURSE TEN MINUTES, TOPS. WHEN IT HAPPENS, MY DEATH IS GOING TO LOOK LIKE AN ACCIDENT. IT ALWAYS LOOKS LIKE AN ACCIDENT.
LONDON.
CHRIST.

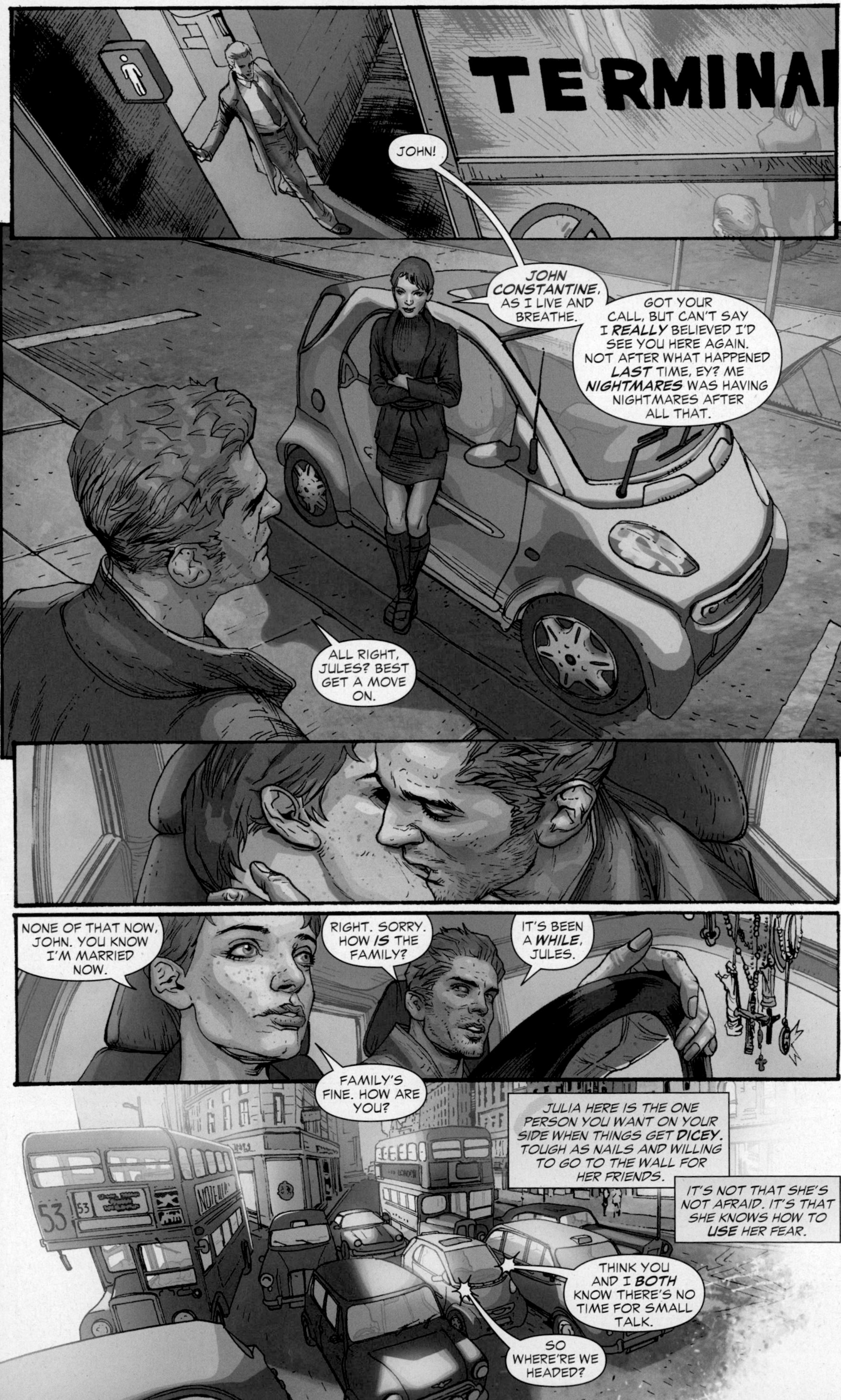
TERMINAL
JOHN!
JOHN CONSTANTINE, AS I LIVE AND BREATHE.
GOT YOUR CALL, BUT CAN'T SAY I REALLY BELIEVED I'D SEE YOU HERE AGAIN. NOT AFTER WHAT HAPPENED LAST TIME, EY? ME NIGHTMARES WAS HAVING NIGHTMARES AFTER ALL THAT.
ALL RIGHT, JULES? BEST GET A MOVE ON.
NONE OF THAT NOW, JOHN. YOU KNOW I'M MARRIED NOW.
RIGHT. SORRY. HOW IS THE FAMILY?
IT'S BEEN A WHILE, JULES.
FAMILY'S FINE. HOW ARE YOU?
JULIA HERE IS THE ONE PERSON YOU WANT ON YOUR SIDE WHEN THINGS GET DICEY. TOUGH AS NAILS AND WILLING TO GO TO THE WALL FOR HER FRIENDS.
IT'S NOT THAT SHE'S NOT AFRAID. IT'S THAT SHE KNOWS HOW TO USE HER FEAR.
THINK YOU AND I BOTH KNOW THERE'S NO TIME FOR SMALL TALK.
SO WHERE'RE WE HEADED?

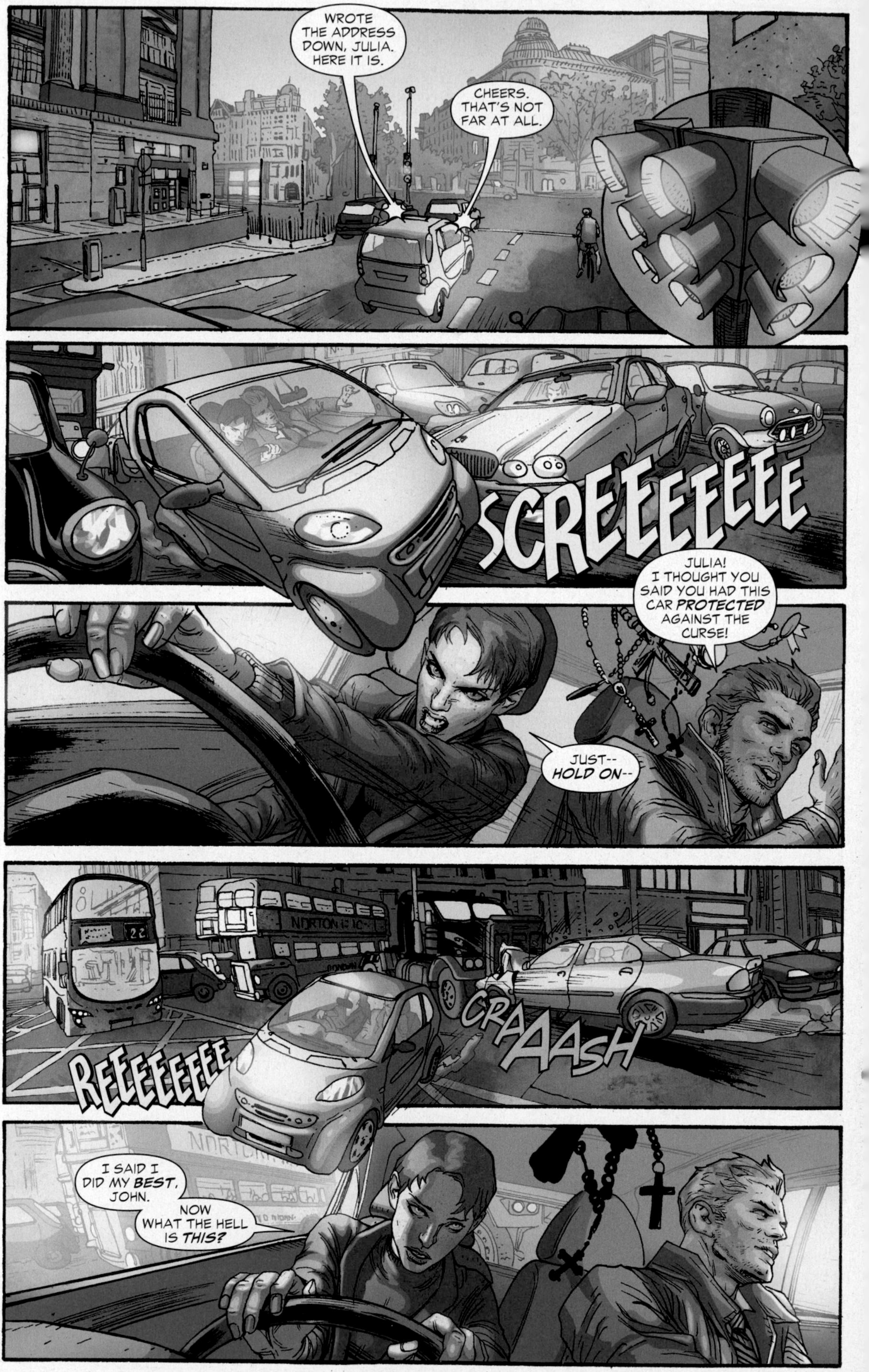

WROTE THE ADDRESS DOWN, JULIA. HERE IT IS.
CHEERS. THAT'S NOT FAR AT ALL.
SCREEEEEEE
JULIA! I THOUGHT YOU SAID YOU HAD THIS CAR PROTECTED AGAINST THE CURSE!
JUST-- HOLD ON--
NORTON
REEEEEEEE
CRAAASH
I SAID I DID MY BEST, JOHN.
NOW WHAT THE HELL IS THIS?

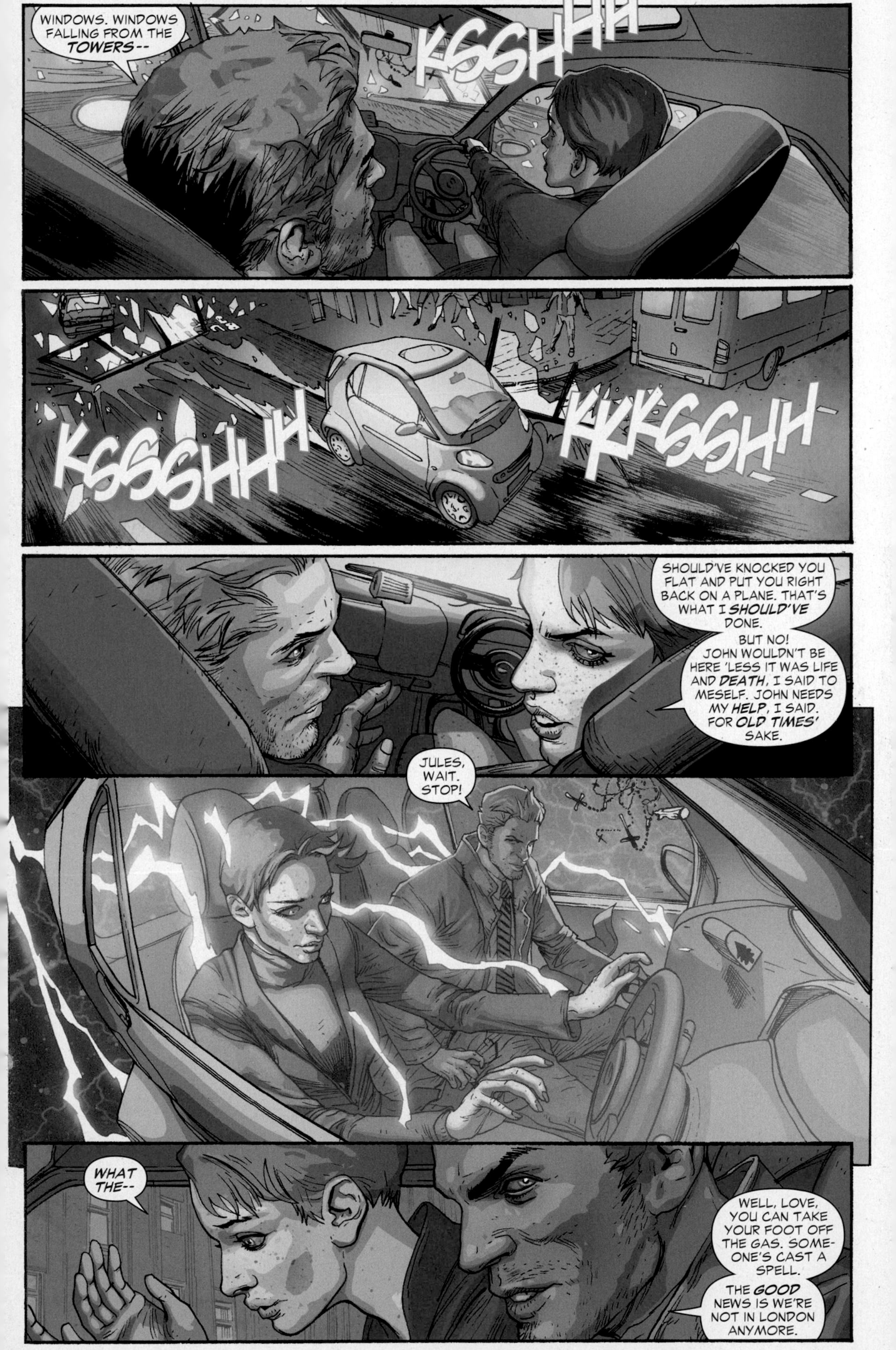
WINDOWS. WINDOWS FALLING FROM THE *TOWERS*--
KSSHHH
KSSSHHH
KKKSSHH
SHOULD'VE KNOCKED YOU FLAT AND PUT YOU RIGHT BACK ON A PLANE. THAT'S WHAT I *SHOULD'VE* DONE.
BUT NO! JOHN WOULDN'T BE HERE 'LESS IT WAS LIFE AND *DEATH*, I SAID TO MESELF. JOHN NEEDS MY *HELP*, I SAID. FOR *OLD TIMES'* SAKE.
JULES, WAIT. STOP!
WHAT THE--
WELL, LOVE, YOU CAN TAKE YOUR FOOT OFF THE GAS. SOME-ONE'S CAST A SPELL.
THE *GOOD* NEWS IS WE'RE NOT IN LONDON ANYMORE.

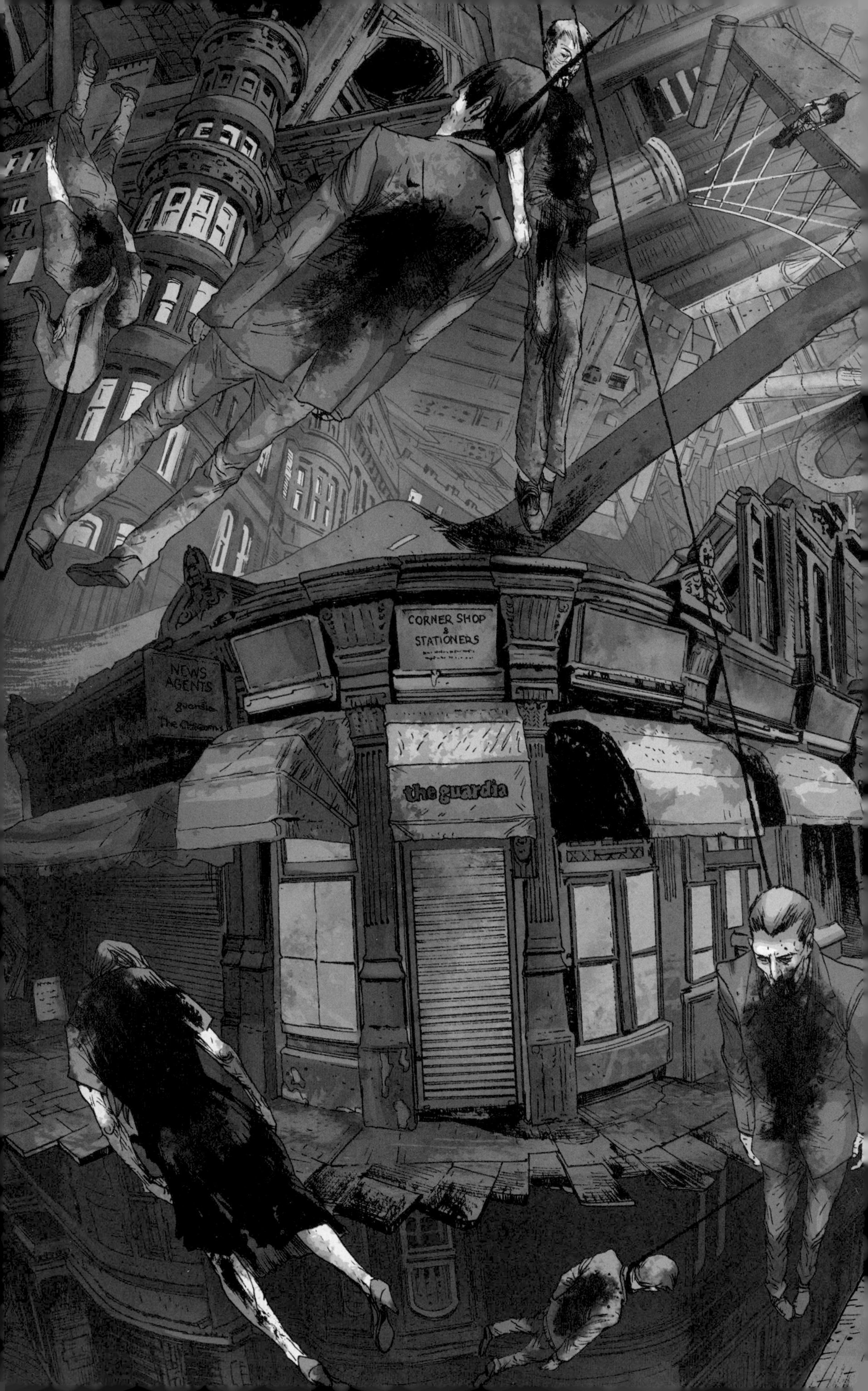
NEWS AGENTS
CORNER SHOP & STATIONERS
the guardia

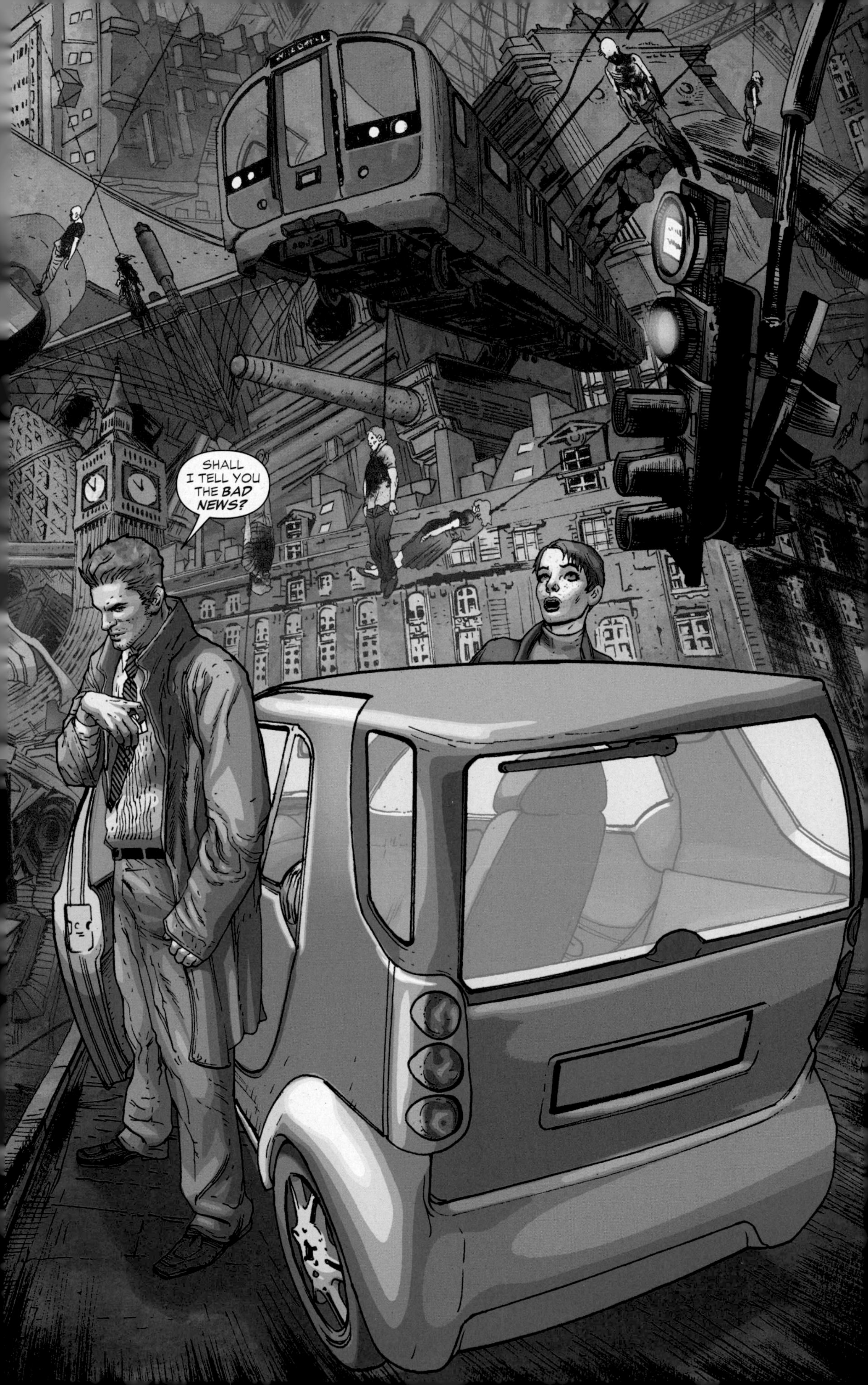
SHALL I TELL YOU THE BAD NEWS?

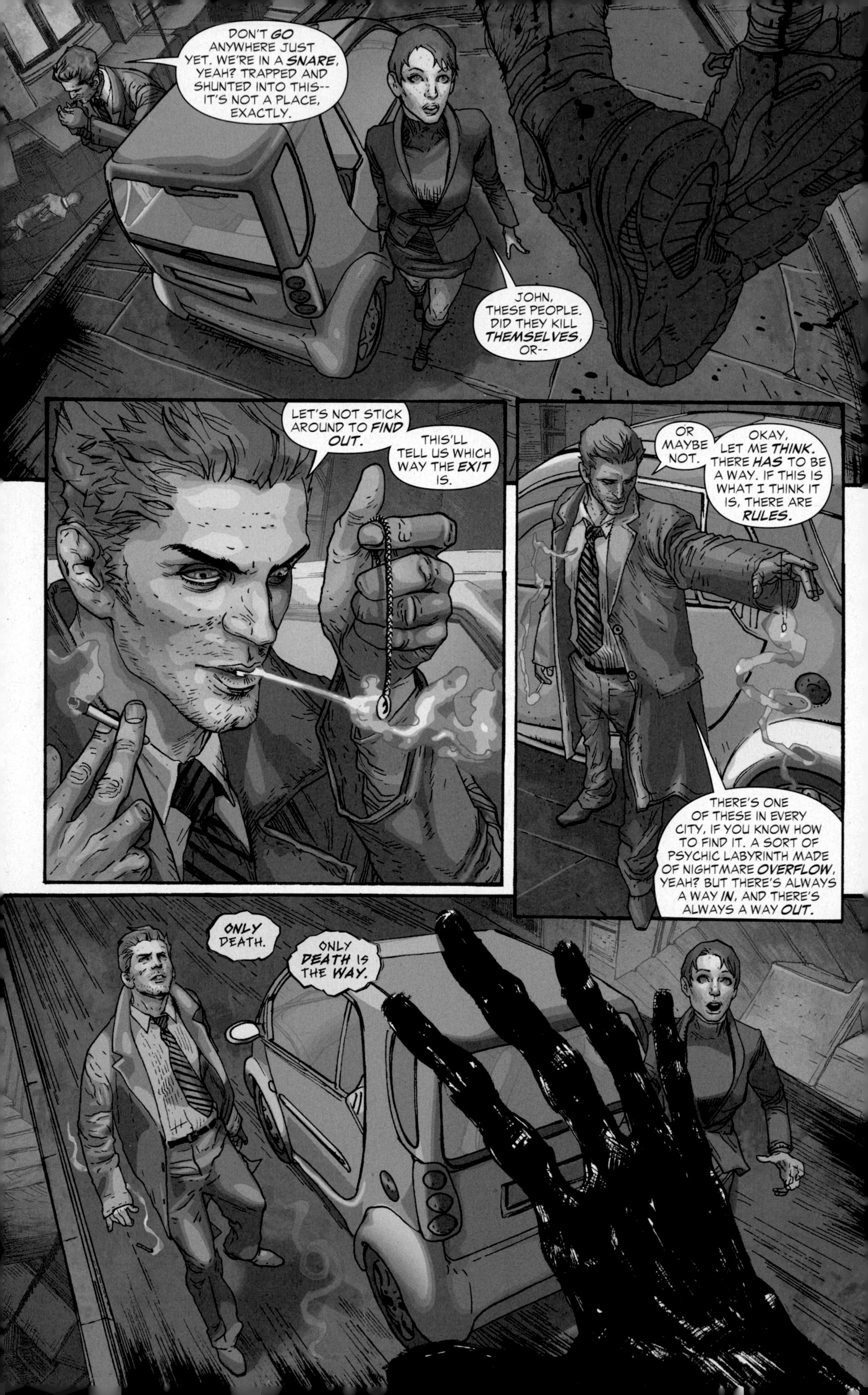
DON'T GO ANYWHERE JUST YET. WE'RE IN A SNARE, YEAH? TRAPPED AND SHUNTED INTO THIS-- IT'S NOT A PLACE, EXACTLY.
JOHN, THESE PEOPLE. DID THEY KILL THEMSELVES, OR--
LET'S NOT STICK AROUND TO FIND OUT.
THIS'LL TELL US WHICH WAY THE EXIT IS.
OR MAYBE NOT.
OKAY, LET ME THINK. THERE HAS TO BE A WAY. IF THIS IS WHAT I THINK IT IS, THERE ARE RULES.
THERE'S ONE OF THESE IN EVERY CITY, IF YOU KNOW HOW TO FIND IT. A SORT OF PSYCHIC LABYRINTH MADE OF NIGHTMARE OVERFLOW, YEAH? BUT THERE'S ALWAYS A WAY IN, AND THERE'S ALWAYS A WAY OUT.
ONLY DEATH.
ONLY DEATH IS THE WAY.

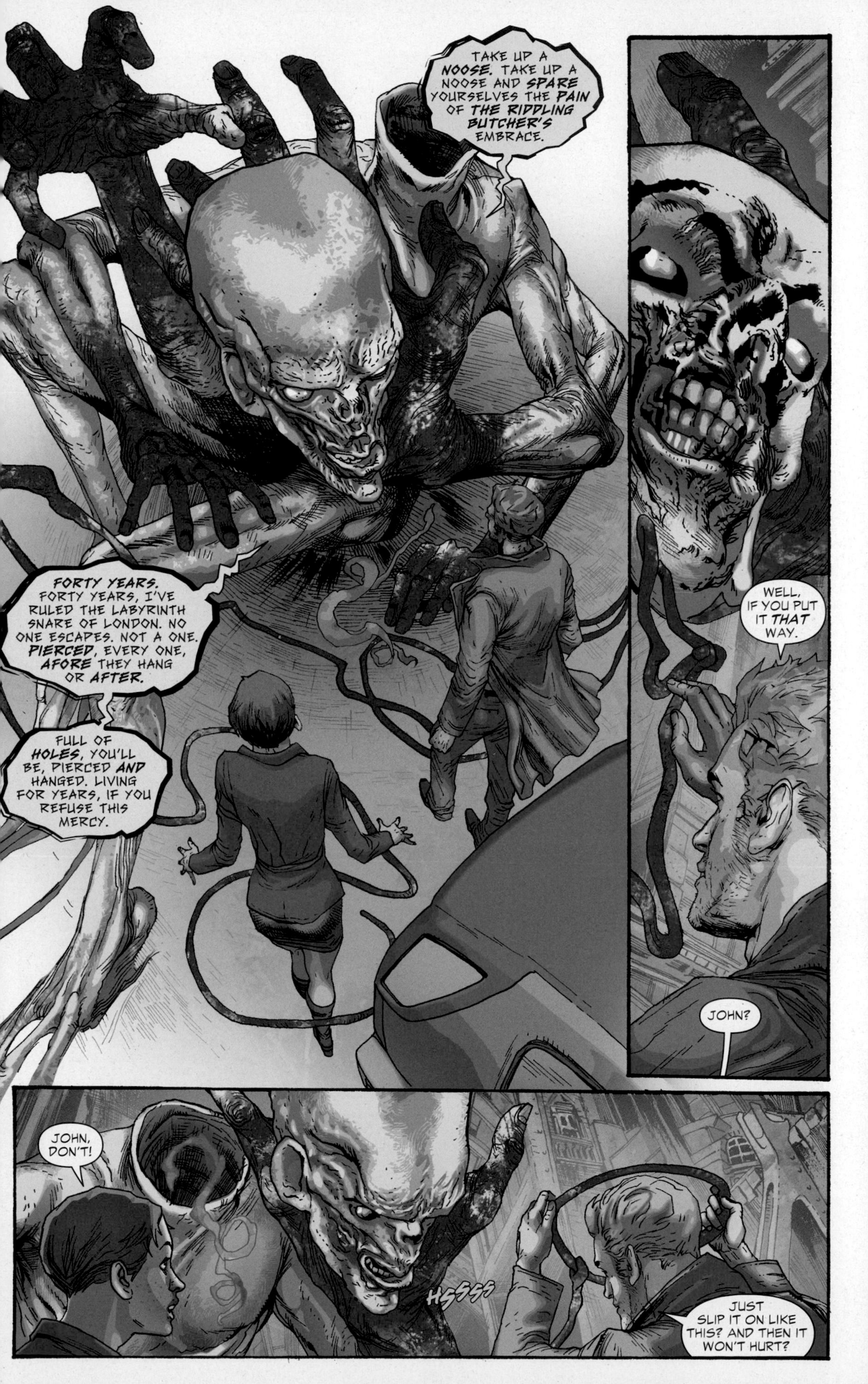
TAKE UP A NOOSE. TAKE UP A NOOSE AND SPARE YOURSELVES THE PAIN OF THE RIDDLING BUTCHER'S EMBRACE.
FORTY YEARS. FORTY YEARS, I'VE RULED THE LABYRINTH SNARE OF LONDON. NO ONE ESCAPES. NOT A ONE. PIERCED, EVERY ONE, AFORE THEY HANG OR AFTER.
FULL OF HOLES, YOU'LL BE, PIERCED AND HANGED. LIVING FOR YEARS, IF YOU REFUSE THIS MERCY.
WELL, IF YOU PUT IT THAT WAY.
JOHN?
JOHN, DON'T!
HSSSS
JUST SLIP IT ON LIKE THIS? AND THEN IT WON'T HURT?

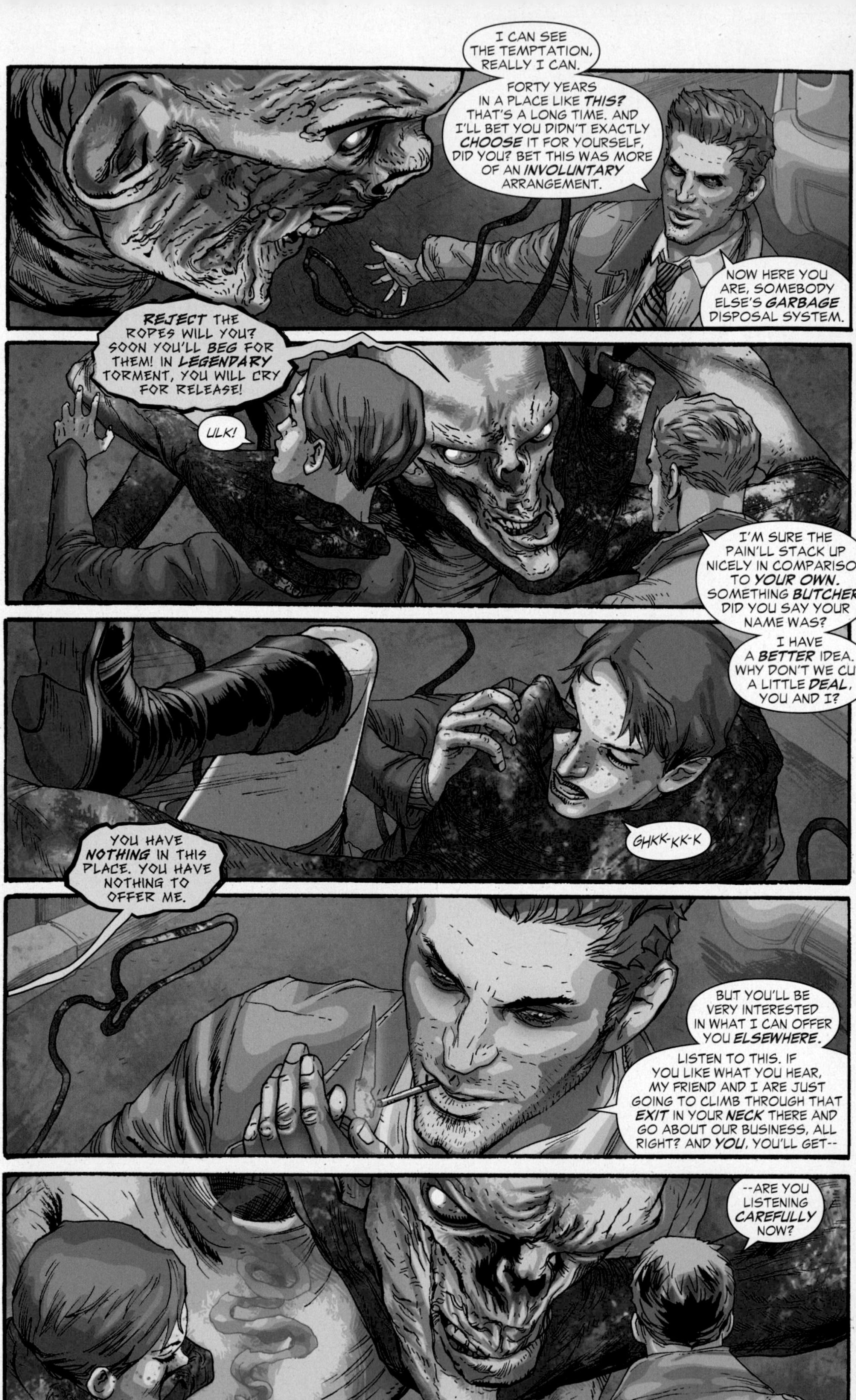

I CAN SEE THE TEMPTATION, REALLY I CAN.
FORTY YEARS IN A PLACE LIKE THIS? THAT'S A LONG TIME. AND I'LL BET YOU DIDN'T EXACTLY CHOOSE IT FOR YOURSELF, DID YOU? BET THIS WAS MORE OF AN INVOLUNTARY ARRANGEMENT.
NOW HERE YOU ARE, SOMEBODY ELSE'S GARBAGE DISPOSAL SYSTEM.
REJECT THE ROPES WILL YOU? SOON YOU'LL BEG FOR THEM! IN LEGENDARY TORMENT, YOU WILL CRY FOR RELEASE!
ULK!
I'M SURE THE PAIN'LL STACK UP NICELY IN COMPARISON TO YOUR OWN. SOMETHING BUTCHER, DID YOU SAY YOUR NAME WAS?
I HAVE A BETTER IDEA. WHY DON'T WE CUT A LITTLE DEAL, YOU AND I?
YOU HAVE NOTHING IN THIS PLACE. YOU HAVE NOTHING TO OFFER ME.
GHKK-KK-K
BUT YOU'LL BE VERY INTERESTED IN WHAT I CAN OFFER YOU ELSEWHERE.
LISTEN TO THIS. IF YOU LIKE WHAT YOU HEAR, MY FRIEND AND I ARE JUST GOING TO CLIMB THROUGH THAT EXIT IN YOUR NECK THERE AND GO ABOUT OUR BUSINESS, ALL RIGHT? AND YOU, YOU'LL GET--
--ARE YOU LISTENING CAREFULLY NOW?

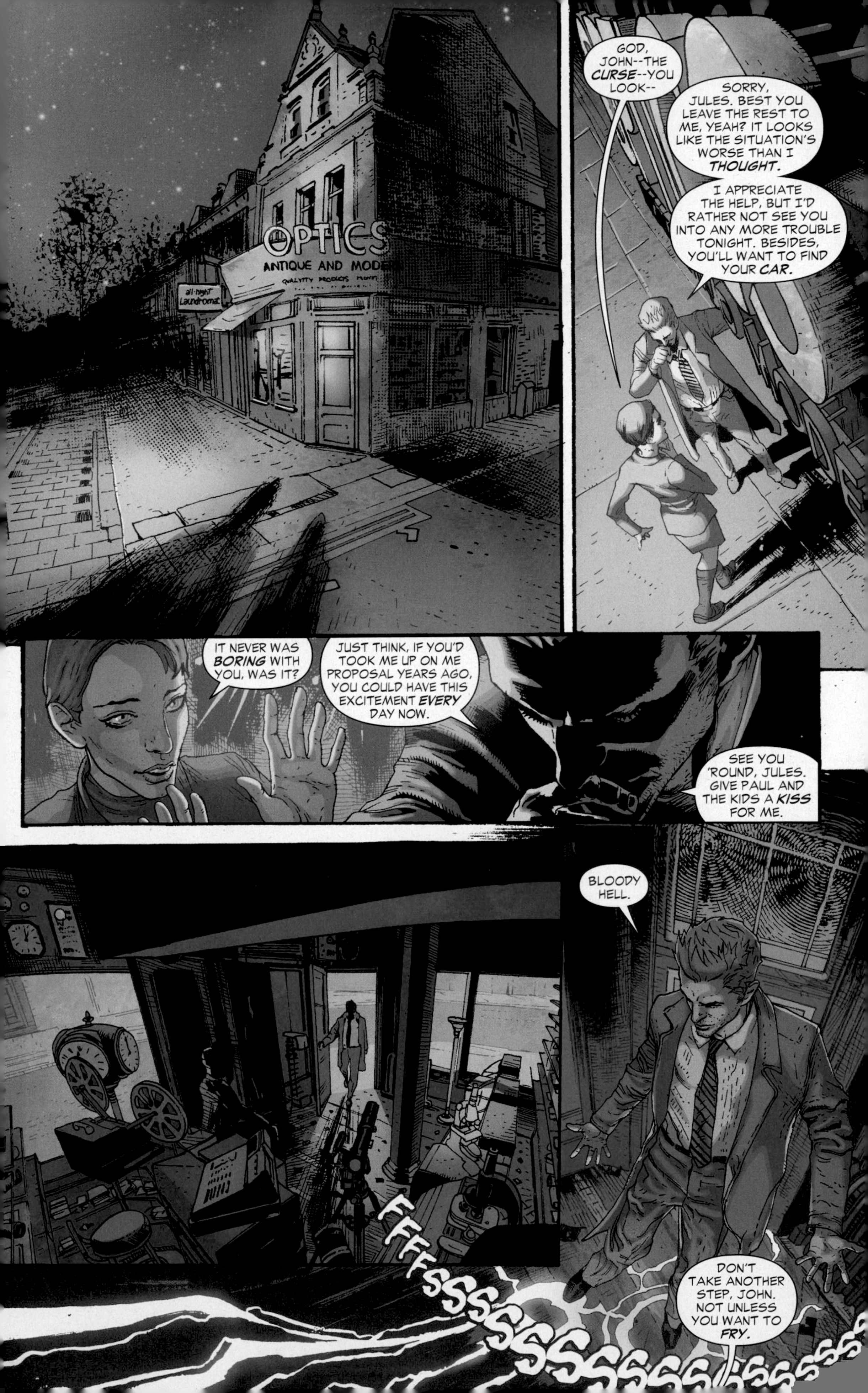
OPTICS
ANTIQUE AND MODER
all-night Laundromat
GOD, JOHN--THE CURSE--YOU LOOK--
SORRY, JULES. BEST YOU LEAVE THE REST TO ME, YEAH? IT LOOKS LIKE THE SITUATION'S WORSE THAN I THOUGHT.
I APPRECIATE THE HELP, BUT I'D RATHER NOT SEE YOU INTO ANY MORE TROUBLE TONIGHT. BESIDES, YOU'LL WANT TO FIND YOUR CAR.
IT NEVER WAS BORING WITH YOU, WAS IT?
JUST THINK, IF YOU'D TOOK ME UP ON ME PROPOSAL YEARS AGO, YOU COULD HAVE THIS EXCITEMENT EVERY DAY NOW.
SEE YOU 'ROUND, JULES. GIVE PAUL AND THE KIDS A KISS FOR ME.
BLOODY HELL.
FFFSSSSSSSSSSSSSSSSS
DON'T TAKE ANOTHER STEP, JOHN. NOT UNLESS YOU WANT TO FRY.

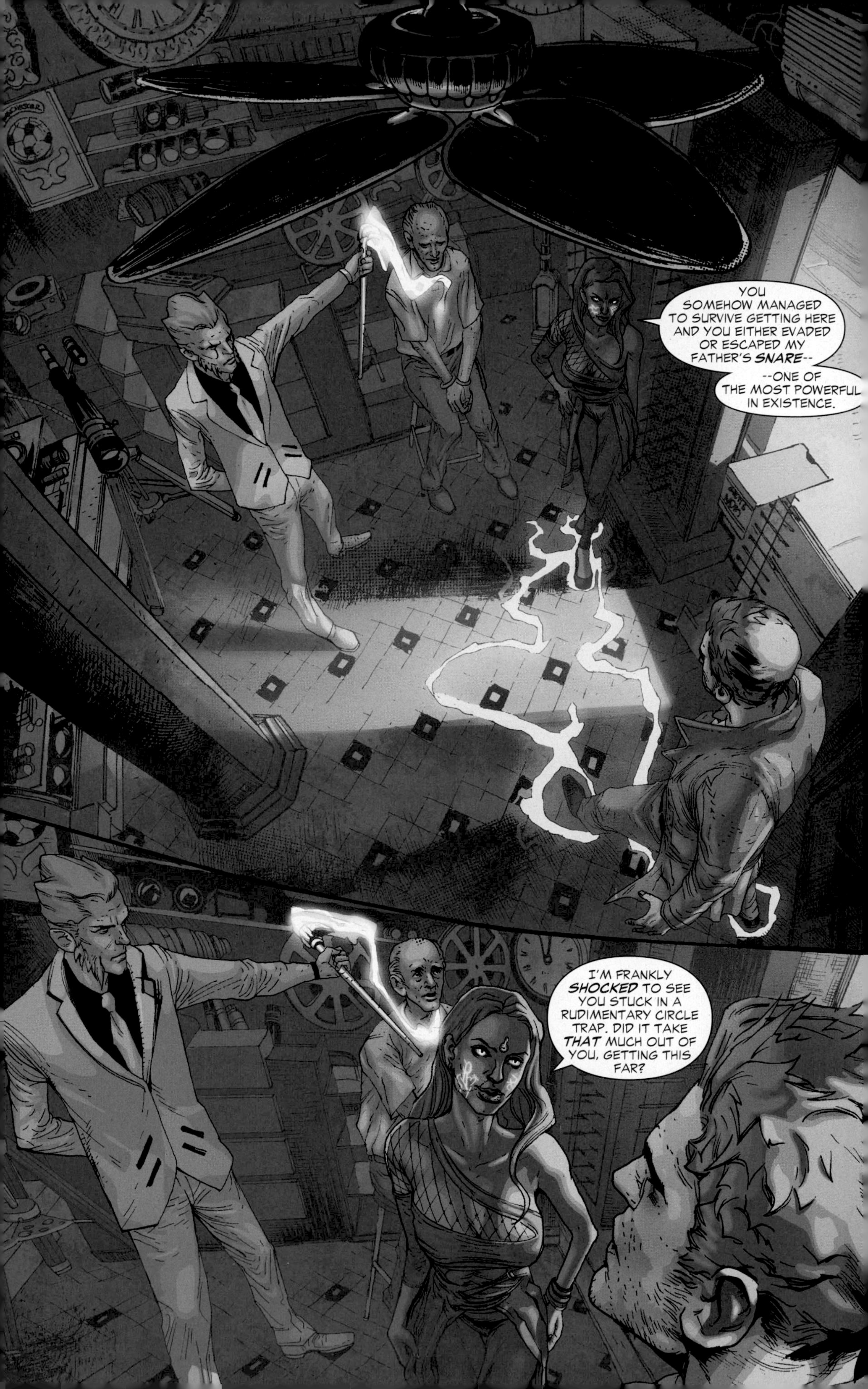
YOU SOMEHOW MANAGED TO SURVIVE GETTING HERE AND YOU EITHER EVADED OR ESCAPED MY FATHER'S SNARE--
--ONE OF THE MOST POWERFUL IN EXISTENCE.
I'M FRANKLY SHOCKED TO SEE YOU STUCK IN A RUDIMENTARY CIRCLE TRAP. DID IT TAKE THAT MUCH OUT OF YOU, GETTING THIS FAR?

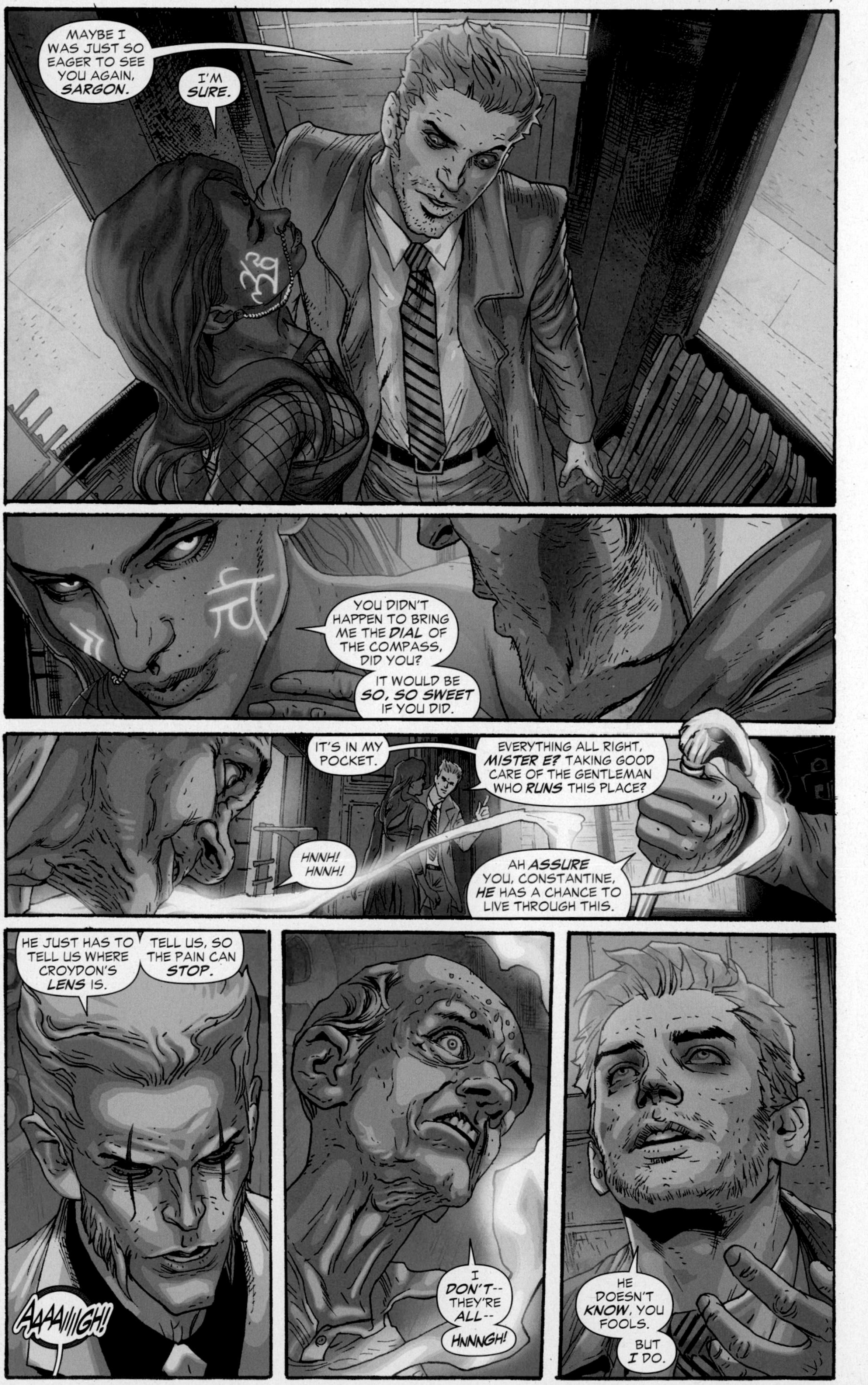

MAYBE I WAS JUST SO EAGER TO SEE YOU AGAIN, SARGON.
I'M SURE.
YOU DIDN'T HAPPEN TO BRING ME THE DIAL OF THE COMPASS, DID YOU?
IT WOULD BE SO, SO SWEET IF YOU DID.
IT'S IN MY POCKET.
EVERYTHING ALL RIGHT, MISTER E? TAKING GOOD CARE OF THE GENTLEMAN WHO RUNS THIS PLACE?
HNNH! HNNH!
AH ASSURE YOU, CONSTANTINE, HE HAS A CHANCE TO LIVE THROUGH THIS.
HE JUST HAS TO TELL US WHERE CROYDON'S LENS IS.
TELL US, SO THE PAIN CAN STOP.
AAAAIIIGH!
I DON'T-- THEY'RE ALL--
HNNNGH!
HE DOESN'T KNOW, YOU FOOLS.
BUT I DO.

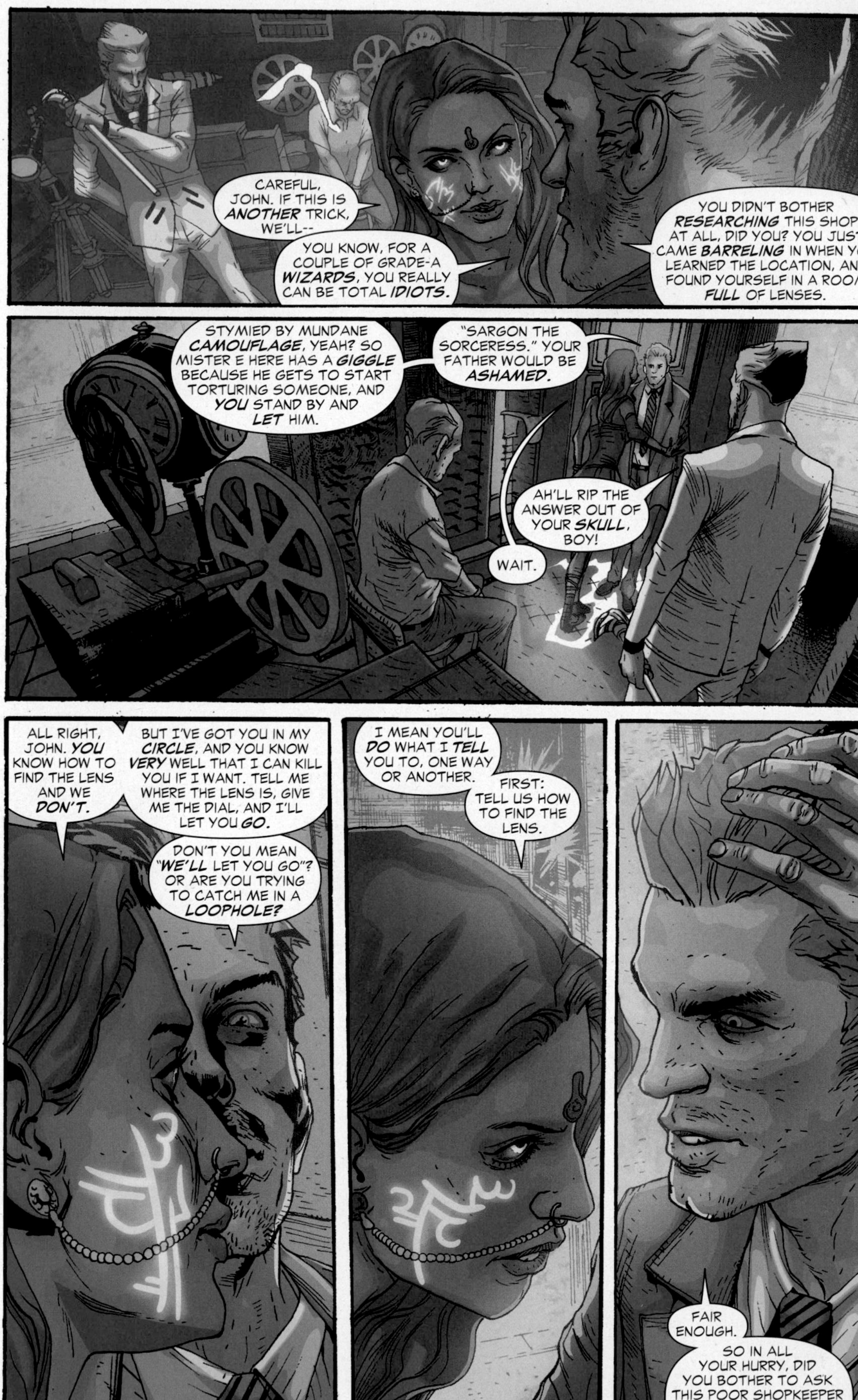
CAREFUL, JOHN. IF THIS IS ANOTHER TRICK, WE'LL--
YOU KNOW, FOR A COUPLE OF GRADE-A WIZARDS, YOU REALLY CAN BE TOTAL IDIOTS.
YOU DIDN'T BOTHER RESEARCHING THIS SHOP AT ALL, DID YOU? YOU JUST CAME BARRELING IN WHEN YOU LEARNED THE LOCATION, AND FOUND YOURSELF IN A ROOM FULL OF LENSES.
STYMIED BY MUNDANE CAMOUFLAGE, YEAH? SO MISTER E HERE HAS A GIGGLE BECAUSE HE GETS TO START TORTURING SOMEONE, AND YOU STAND BY AND LET HIM.
"SARGON THE SORCERESS." YOUR FATHER WOULD BE ASHAMED.
AH'LL RIP THE ANSWER OUT OF YOUR SKULL, BOY!
WAIT.
ALL RIGHT, JOHN. YOU KNOW HOW TO FIND THE LENS AND WE DON'T.
BUT I'VE GOT YOU IN MY CIRCLE, AND YOU KNOW VERY WELL THAT I CAN KILL YOU IF I WANT. TELL ME WHERE THE LENS IS, GIVE ME THE DIAL, AND I'LL LET YOU GO.
DON'T YOU MEAN "WE'LL LET YOU GO"? OR ARE YOU TRYING TO CATCH ME IN A LOOPHOLE?
I MEAN YOU'LL DO WHAT I TELL YOU TO, ONE WAY OR ANOTHER.
FIRST: TELL US HOW TO FIND THE LENS.
FAIR ENOUGH.
SO IN ALL YOUR HURRY, DID YOU BOTHER TO ASK THIS POOR SHOPKEEPER WHAT HIS NAME IS?

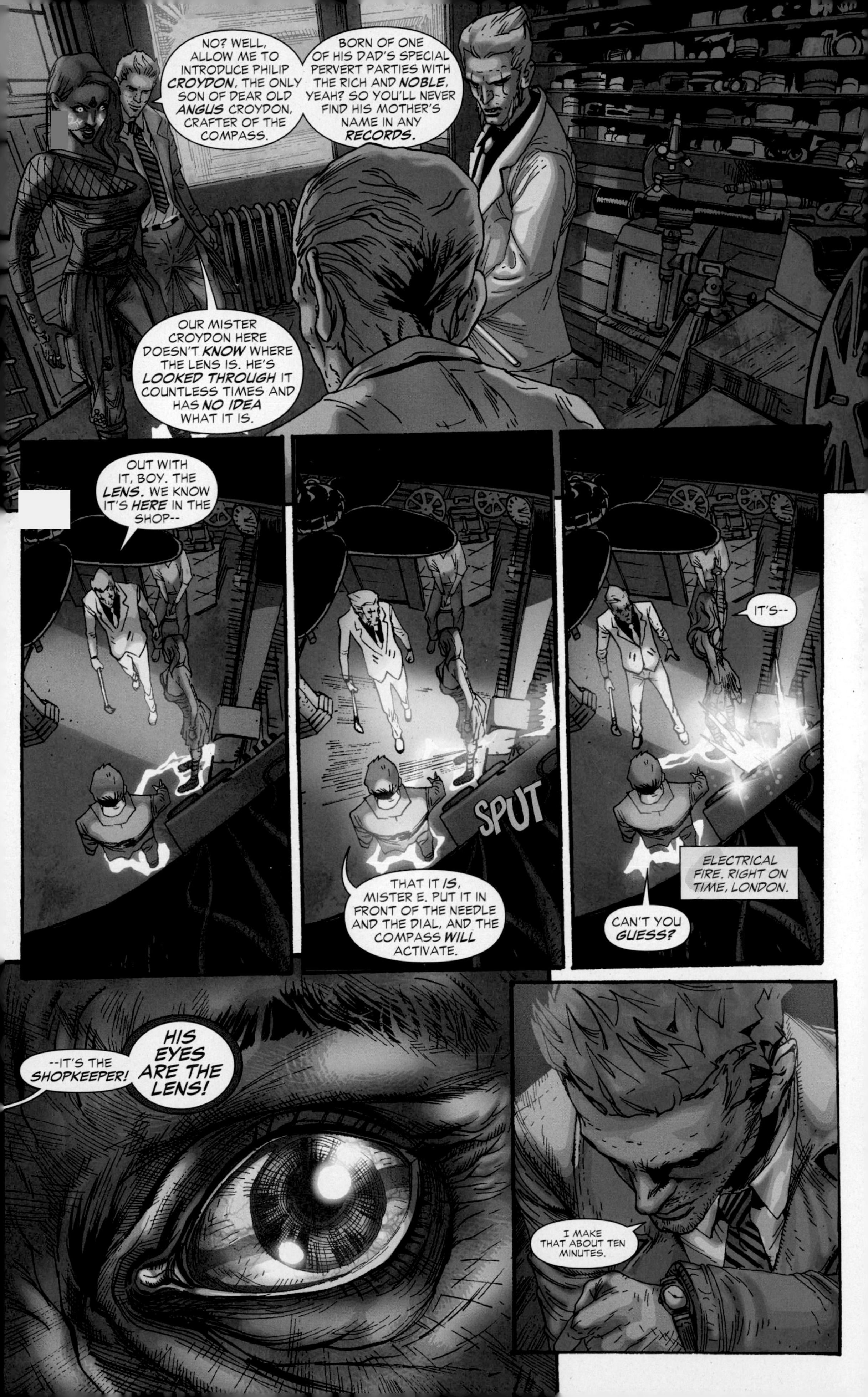
NO? WELL, ALLOW ME TO INTRODUCE PHILIP CROYDON, THE ONLY SON OF DEAR OLD ANGUS CROYDON, CRAFTER OF THE COMPASS.
BORN OF ONE OF HIS DAD'S SPECIAL PERVERT PARTIES WITH THE RICH AND NOBLE, YEAH? SO YOU'LL NEVER FIND HIS MOTHER'S NAME IN ANY RECORDS.
OUR MISTER CROYDON HERE DOESN'T KNOW WHERE THE LENS IS. HE'S LOOKED THROUGH IT COUNTLESS TIMES AND HAS NO IDEA WHAT IT IS.
OUT WITH IT, BOY. THE LENS. WE KNOW IT'S HERE IN THE SHOP--
SPUT
THAT IT IS, MISTER E. PUT IT IN FRONT OF THE NEEDLE AND THE DIAL, AND THE COMPASS WILL ACTIVATE.
IT'S--
ELECTRICAL FIRE. RIGHT ON TIME, LONDON.
CAN'T YOU GUESS?
--IT'S THE SHOPKEEPER!
HIS EYES ARE THE LENS!
I MAKE THAT ABOUT TEN MINUTES.

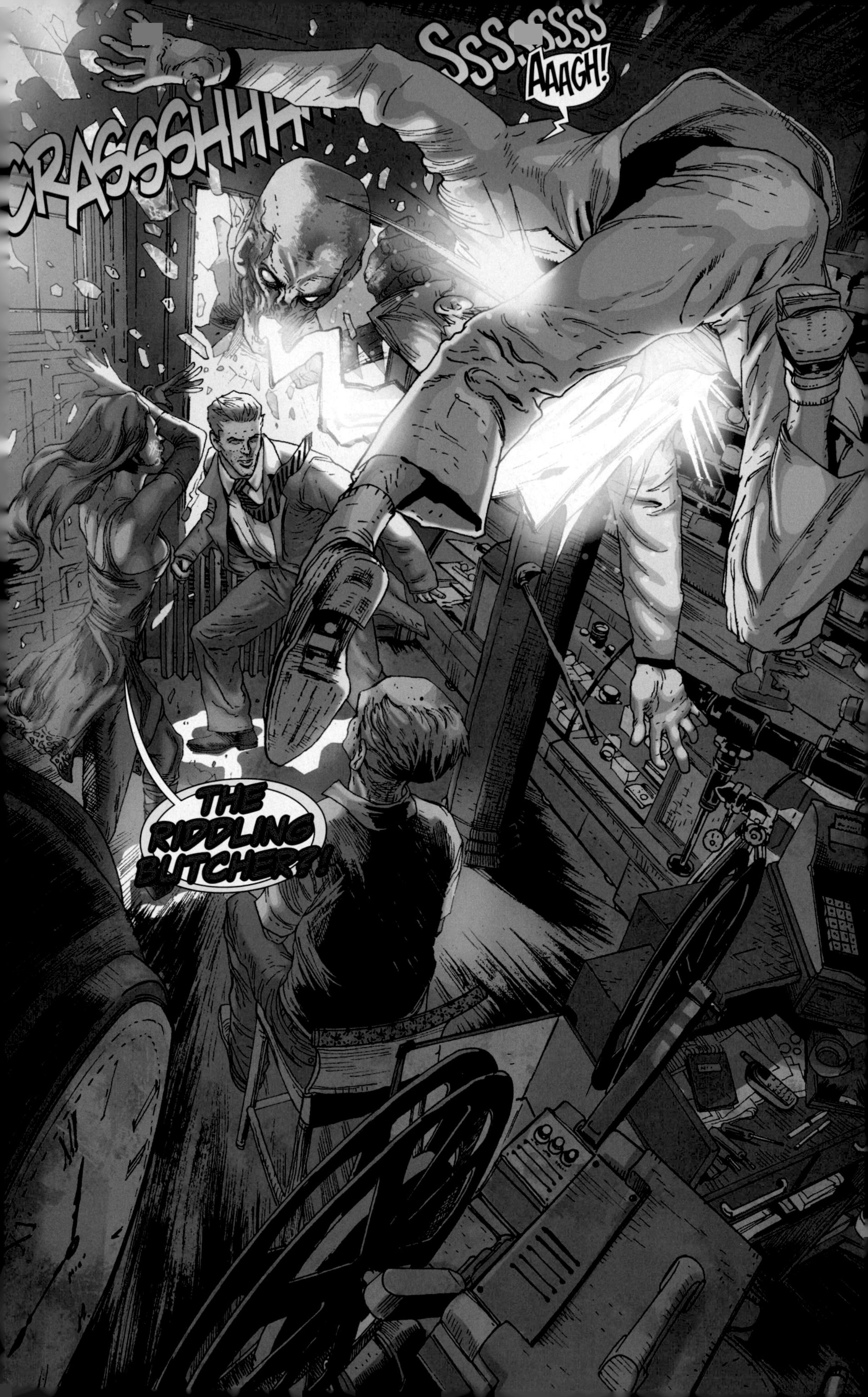
CRASSSHHH
AAAGH!
THE RIDDLING BUTCHER?!

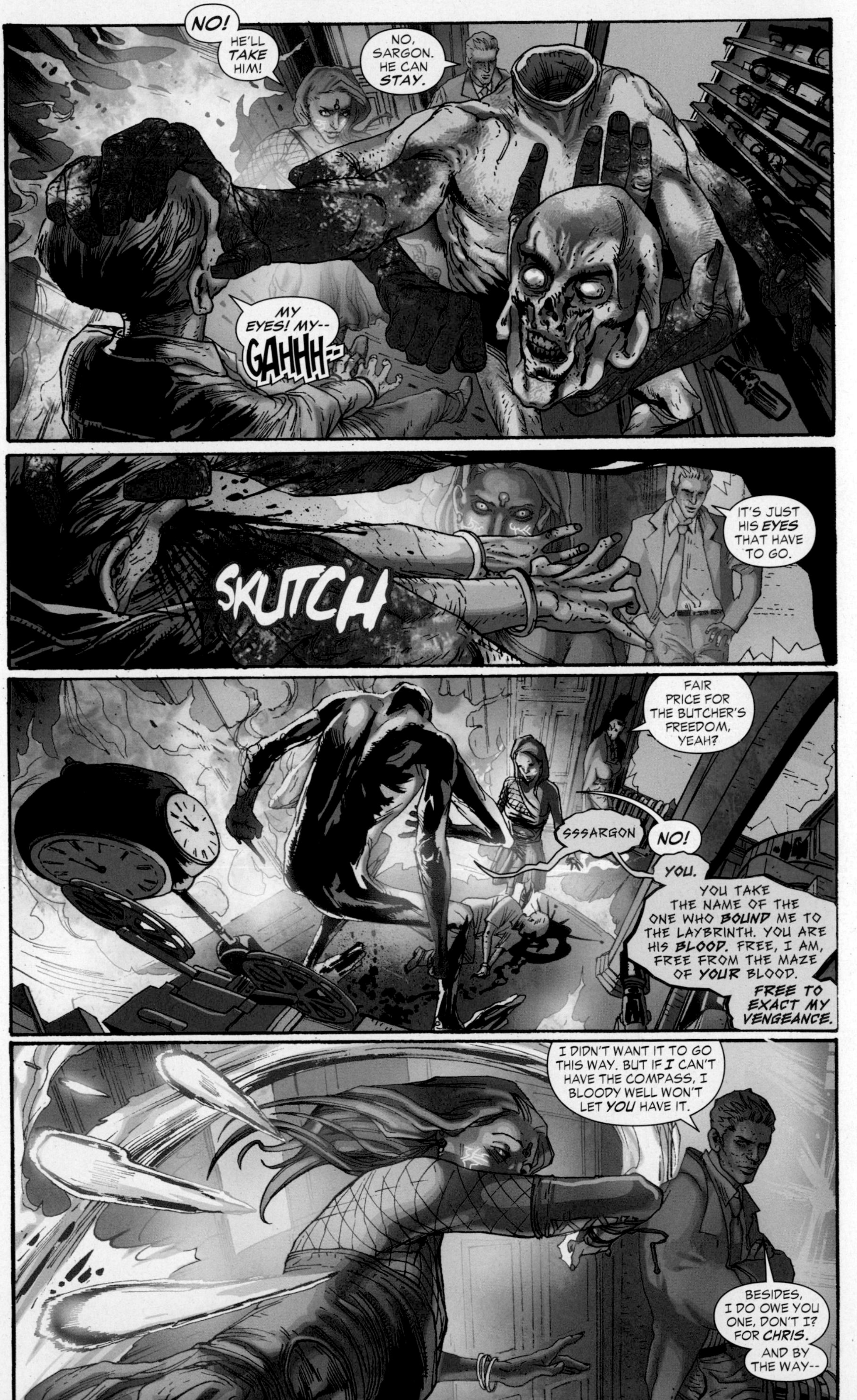

NO!
HE'LL TAKE HIM!
NO, SARGON. HE CAN STAY.
MY EYES! MY--
GAHHH--
SKUTCH
IT'S JUST HIS EYES THAT HAVE TO GO.
FAIR PRICE FOR THE BUTCHER'S FREEDOM, YEAH?
SSSARGON
NO!
YOU.
YOU TAKE THE NAME OF THE ONE WHO BOUND ME TO THE LAYBRINTH. YOU ARE HIS BLOOD. FREE, I AM, FREE FROM THE MAZE OF YOUR BLOOD.
FREE TO EXACT MY VENGEANCE.
I DIDN'T WANT IT TO GO THIS WAY. BUT IF I CAN'T HAVE THE COMPASS, I BLOODY WELL WON'T LET YOU HAVE IT.
BESIDES, I DO OWE YOU ONE, DON'T I? FOR CHRIS.
AND BY THE WAY--

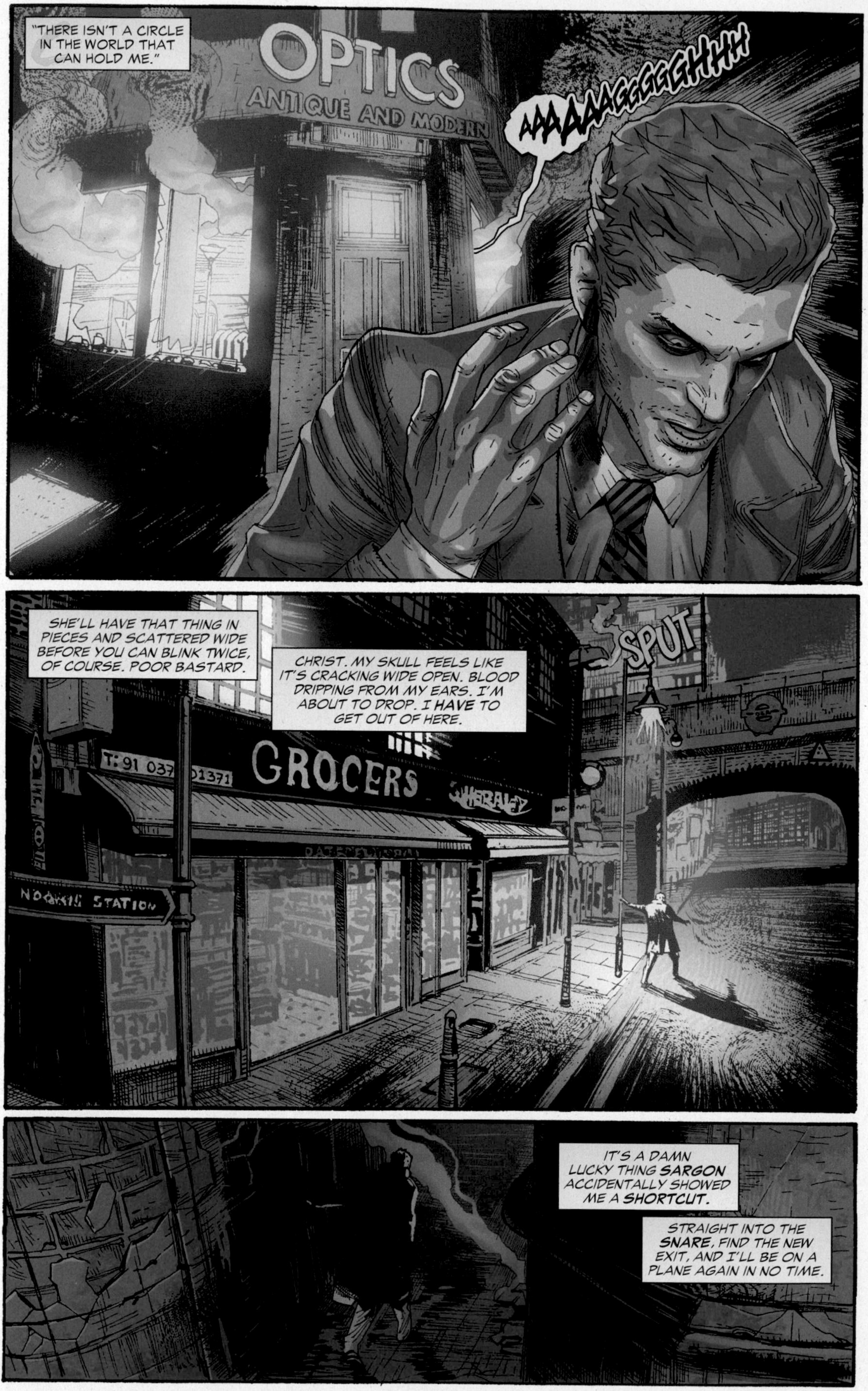
"THERE ISN'T A CIRCLE IN THE WORLD THAT CAN HOLD ME."
OPTICS
ANTIQUE AND MODERN
AAAAAAGGGGHHHH
SHE'LL HAVE THAT THING IN PIECES AND SCATTERED WIDE BEFORE YOU CAN BLINK TWICE, OF COURSE. POOR BASTARD.
CHRIST. MY SKULL FEELS LIKE IT'S CRACKING WIDE OPEN. BLOOD DRIPPING FROM MY EARS. I'M ABOUT TO DROP. I HAVE TO GET OUT OF HERE.
SPUT
GROCERS
IT'S A DAMN LUCKY THING SARGON ACCIDENTALLY SHOWED ME A SHORTCUT.
STRAIGHT INTO THE SNARE, FIND THE NEW EXIT, AND I'LL BE ON A PLANE AGAIN IN NO TIME.

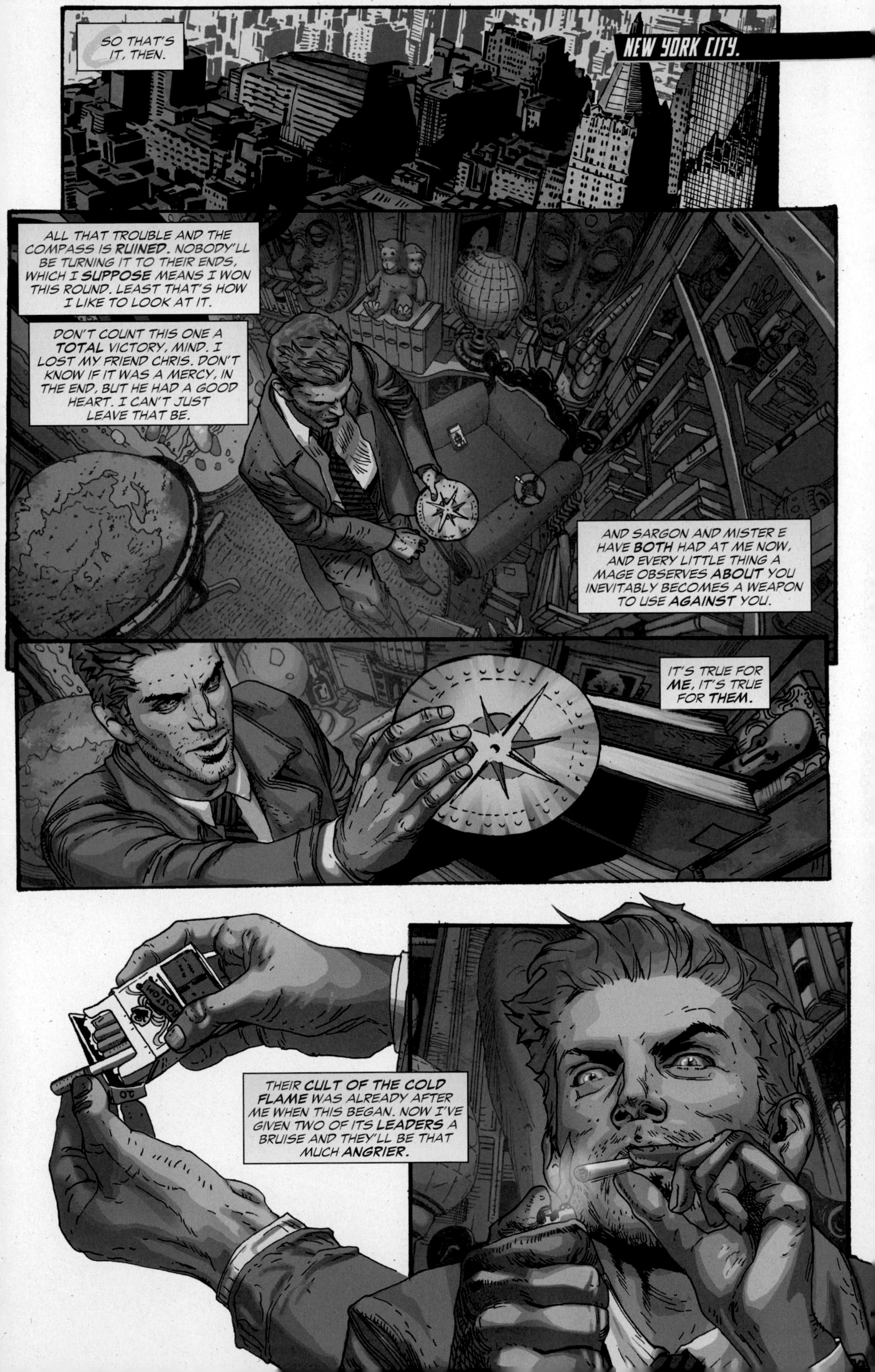
SO THAT'S IT, THEN.
NEW YORK CITY.
ALL THAT TROUBLE AND THE COMPASS IS RUINED. NOBODY'LL BE TURNING IT TO THEIR ENDS, WHICH I SUPPOSE MEANS I WON THIS ROUND. LEAST THAT'S HOW I LIKE TO LOOK AT IT.
DON'T COUNT THIS ONE A TOTAL VICTORY, MIND. I LOST MY FRIEND CHRIS. DON'T KNOW IF IT WAS A MERCY, IN THE END, BUT HE HAD A GOOD HEART. I CAN'T JUST LEAVE THAT BE.
AND SARGON AND MISTER E HAVE BOTH HAD AT ME NOW, AND EVERY LITTLE THING A MAGE OBSERVES ABOUT YOU INEVITABLY BECOMES A WEAPON TO USE AGAINST YOU.
IT'S TRUE FOR ME, IT'S TRUE FOR THEM.
THEIR CULT OF THE COLD FLAME WAS ALREADY AFTER ME WHEN THIS BEGAN. NOW I'VE GIVEN TWO OF ITS LEADERS A BRUISE AND THEY'LL BE THAT MUCH ANGRIER.

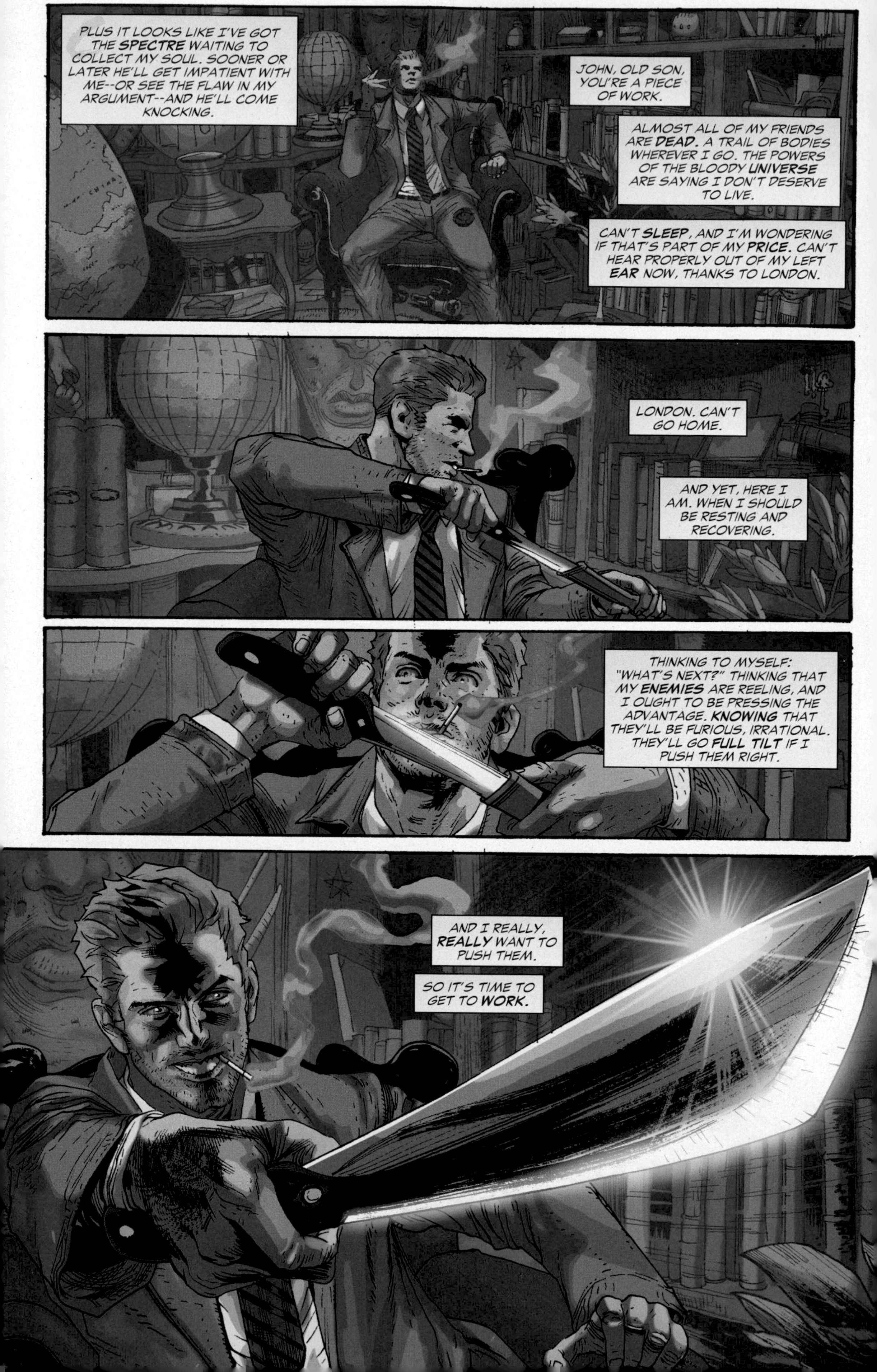
PLUS IT LOOKS LIKE I'VE GOT THE SPECTRE WAITING TO COLLECT MY SOUL. SOONER OR LATER HE'LL GET IMPATIENT WITH ME--OR SEE THE FLAW IN MY ARGUMENT--AND HE'LL COME KNOCKING.
JOHN, OLD SON, YOU'RE A PIECE OF WORK.
ALMOST ALL OF MY FRIENDS ARE DEAD. A TRAIL OF BODIES WHEREVER I GO. THE POWERS OF THE BLOODY UNIVERSE ARE SAYING I DON'T DESERVE TO LIVE.
CAN'T SLEEP, AND I'M WONDERING IF THAT'S PART OF MY PRICE. CAN'T HEAR PROPERLY OUT OF MY LEFT EAR NOW, THANKS TO LONDON.
LONDON. CAN'T GO HOME.
AND YET, HERE I AM. WHEN I SHOULD BE RESTING AND RECOVERING.
THINKING TO MYSELF: "WHAT'S NEXT?" THINKING THAT MY ENEMIES ARE REELING, AND I OUGHT TO BE PRESSING THE ADVANTAGE. KNOWING THAT THEY'LL BE FURIOUS, IRRATIONAL. THEY'LL GO FULL TILT IF I PUSH THEM RIGHT.
AND I REALLY, REALLY WANT TO PUSH THEM.
SO IT'S TIME TO GET TO WORK.

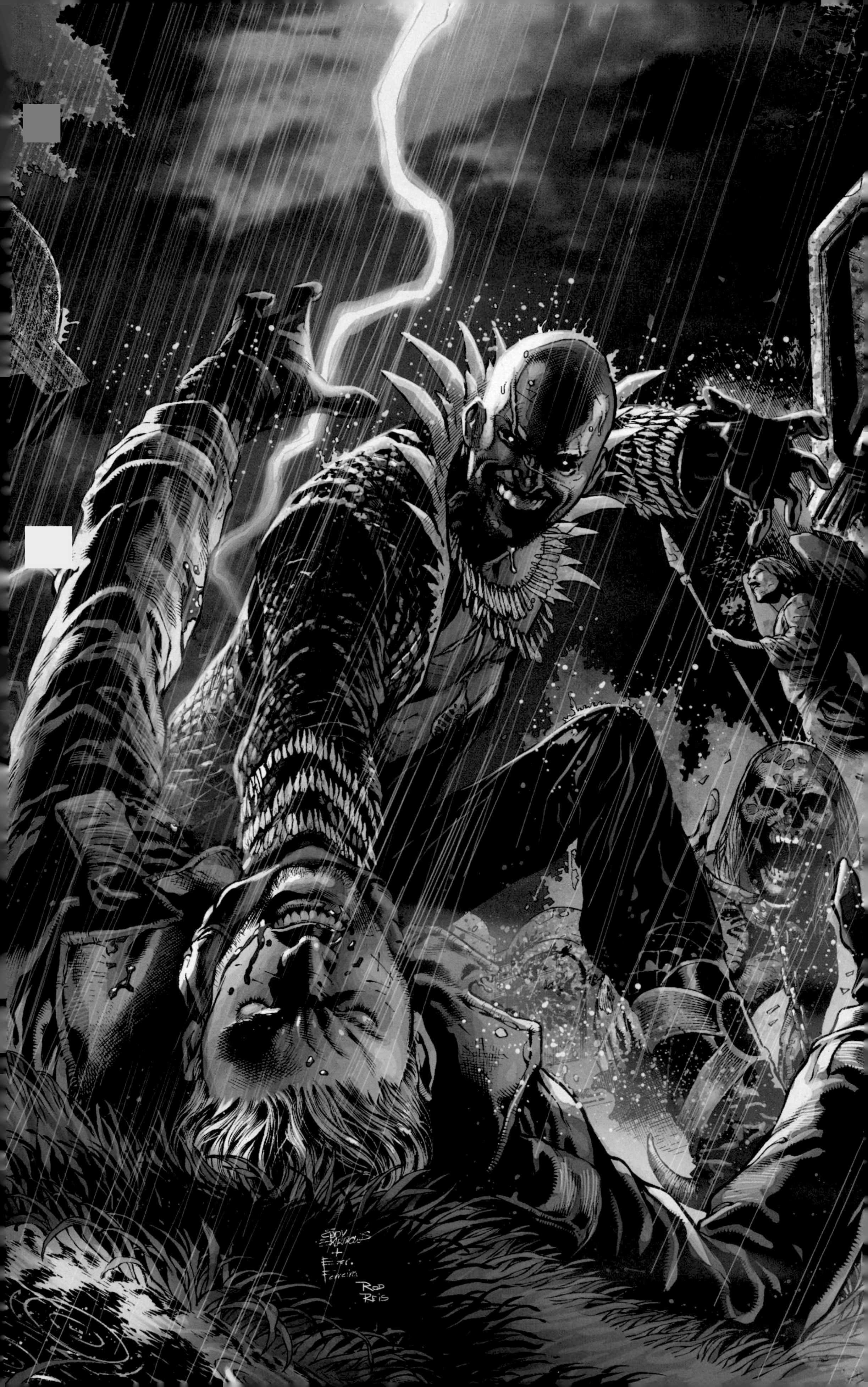
ROD REIS

ALL MY FRIENDS

JEFF LEMIRE & RAY FAWKES writers **FABIANO NEVES** artist cover art by **EDDY BARROWS, EBER FERREIRA & ROD REIS**

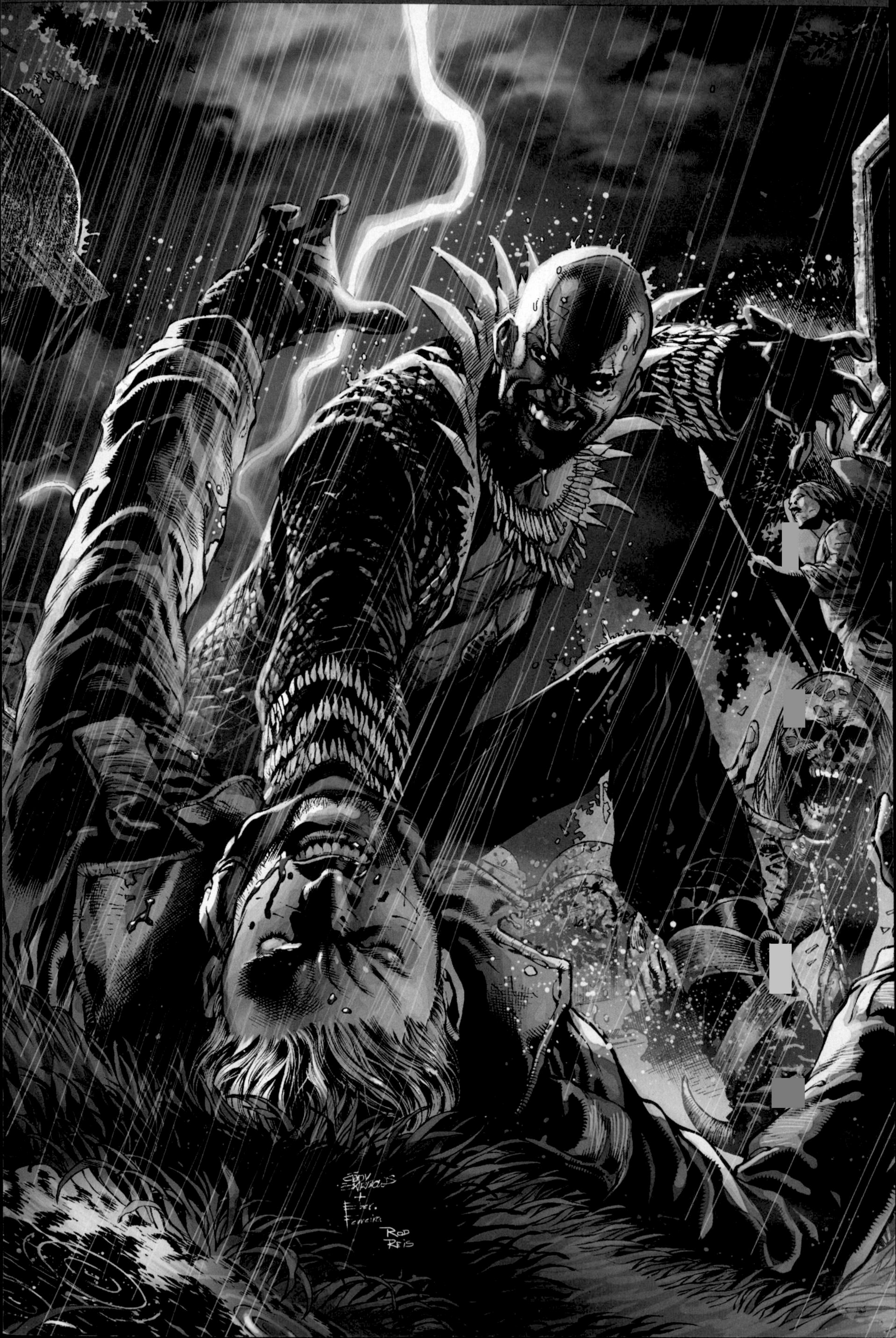

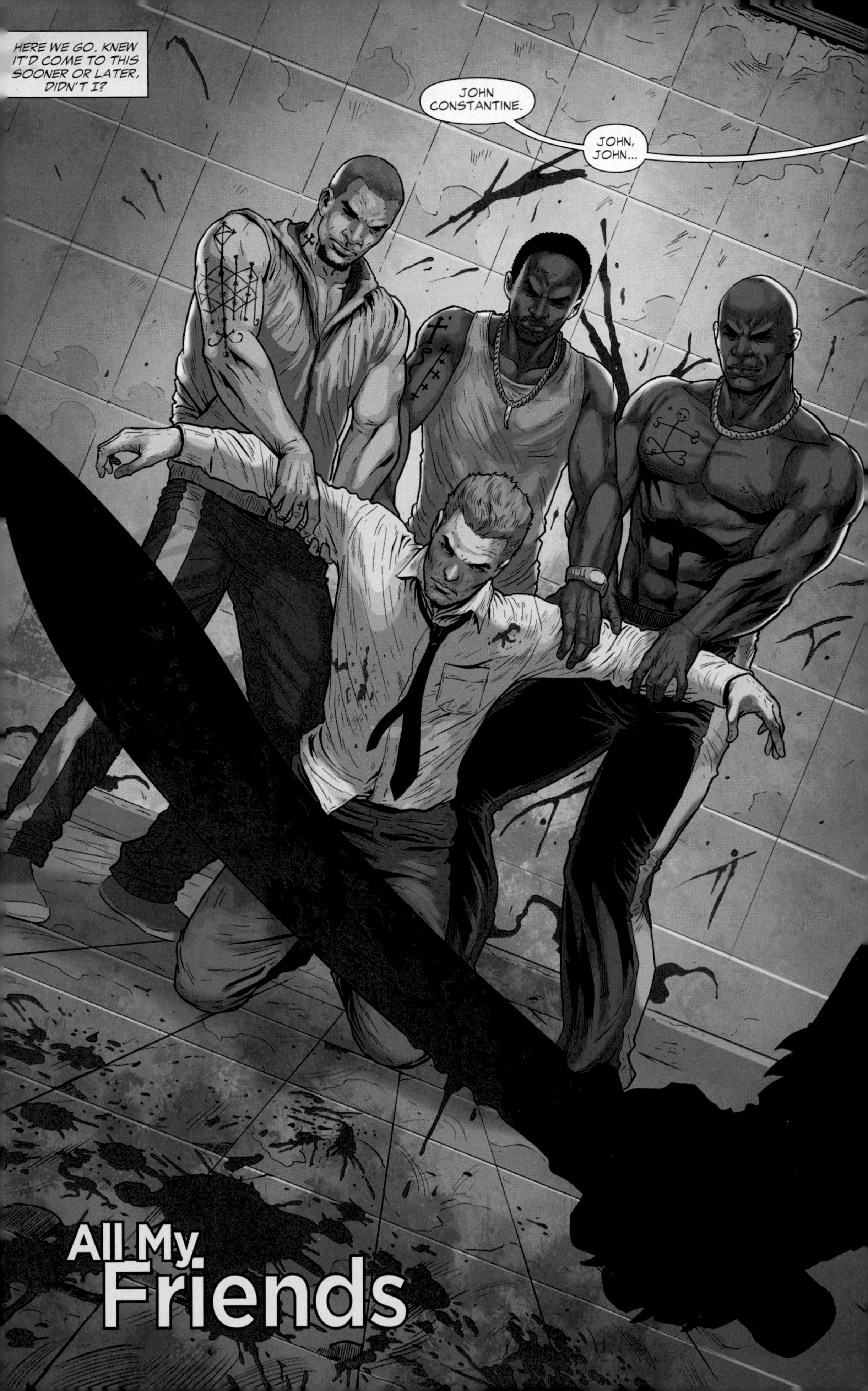
HERE WE GO. KNEW IT'D COME TO THIS SOONER OR LATER, DIDN'T I?
JOHN CONSTANTINE.
JOHN, JOHN...
All My Friends

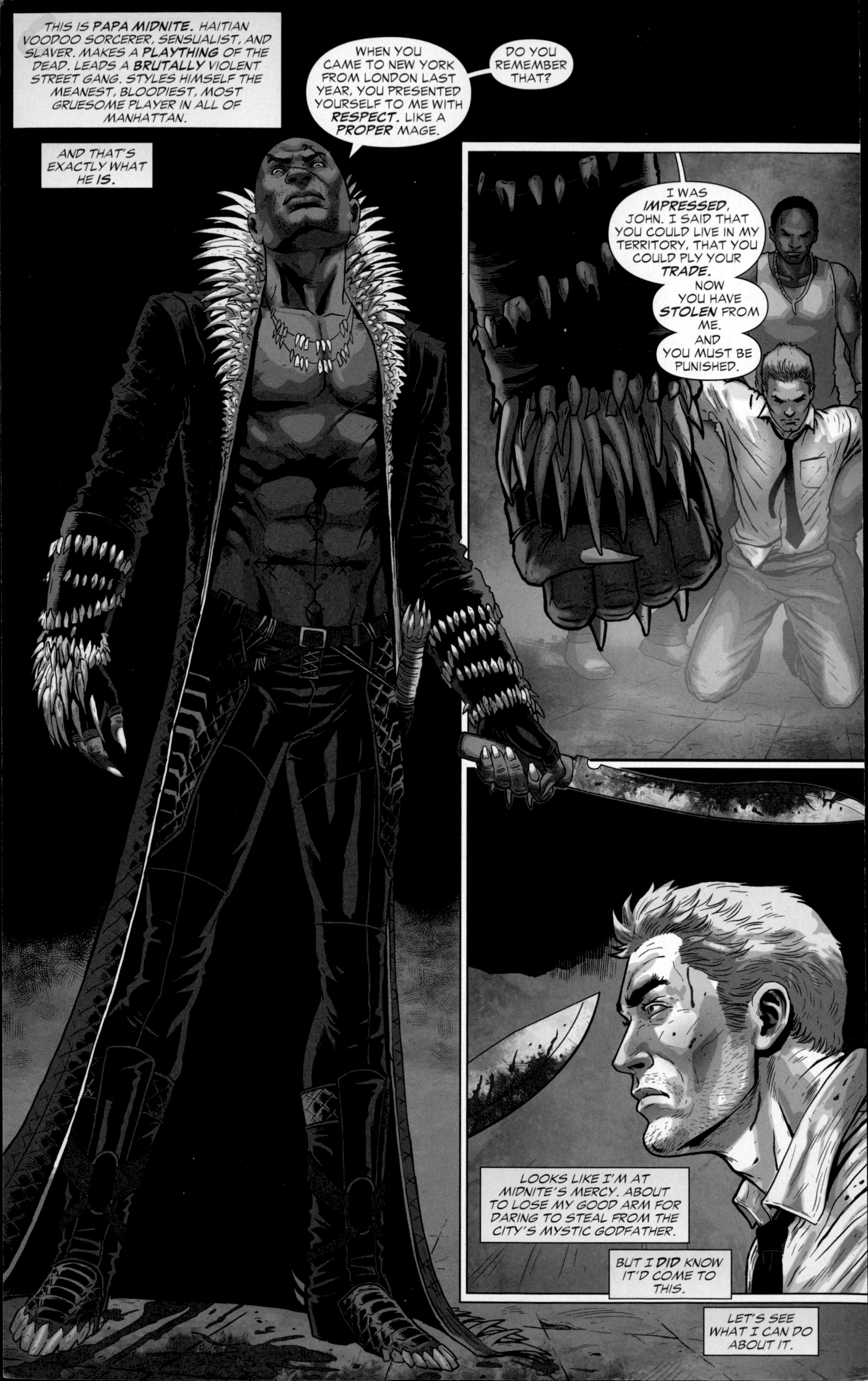
THIS IS PAPA MIDNITE. HAITIAN VOODOO SORCERER, SENSUALIST, AND SLAVER. MAKES A PLAYTHING OF THE DEAD. LEADS A BRUTALLY VIOLENT STREET GANG. STYLES HIMSELF THE MEANEST, BLOODIEST, MOST GRUESOME PLAYER IN ALL OF MANHATTAN.
AND THAT'S EXACTLY WHAT HE IS.
WHEN YOU CAME TO NEW YORK FROM LONDON LAST YEAR, YOU PRESENTED YOURSELF TO ME WITH RESPECT. LIKE A PROPER MAGE.
DO YOU REMEMBER THAT?
I WAS IMPRESSED, JOHN. I SAID THAT YOU COULD LIVE IN MY TERRITORY, THAT YOU COULD PLY YOUR TRADE.
NOW YOU HAVE STOLEN FROM ME.
AND YOU MUST BE PUNISHED.
LOOKS LIKE I'M AT MIDNITE'S MERCY. ABOUT TO LOSE MY GOOD ARM FOR DARING TO STEAL FROM THE CITY'S MYSTIC GODFATHER.
BUT I DID KNOW IT'D COME TO THIS.
LET'S SEE WHAT I CAN DO ABOUT IT.

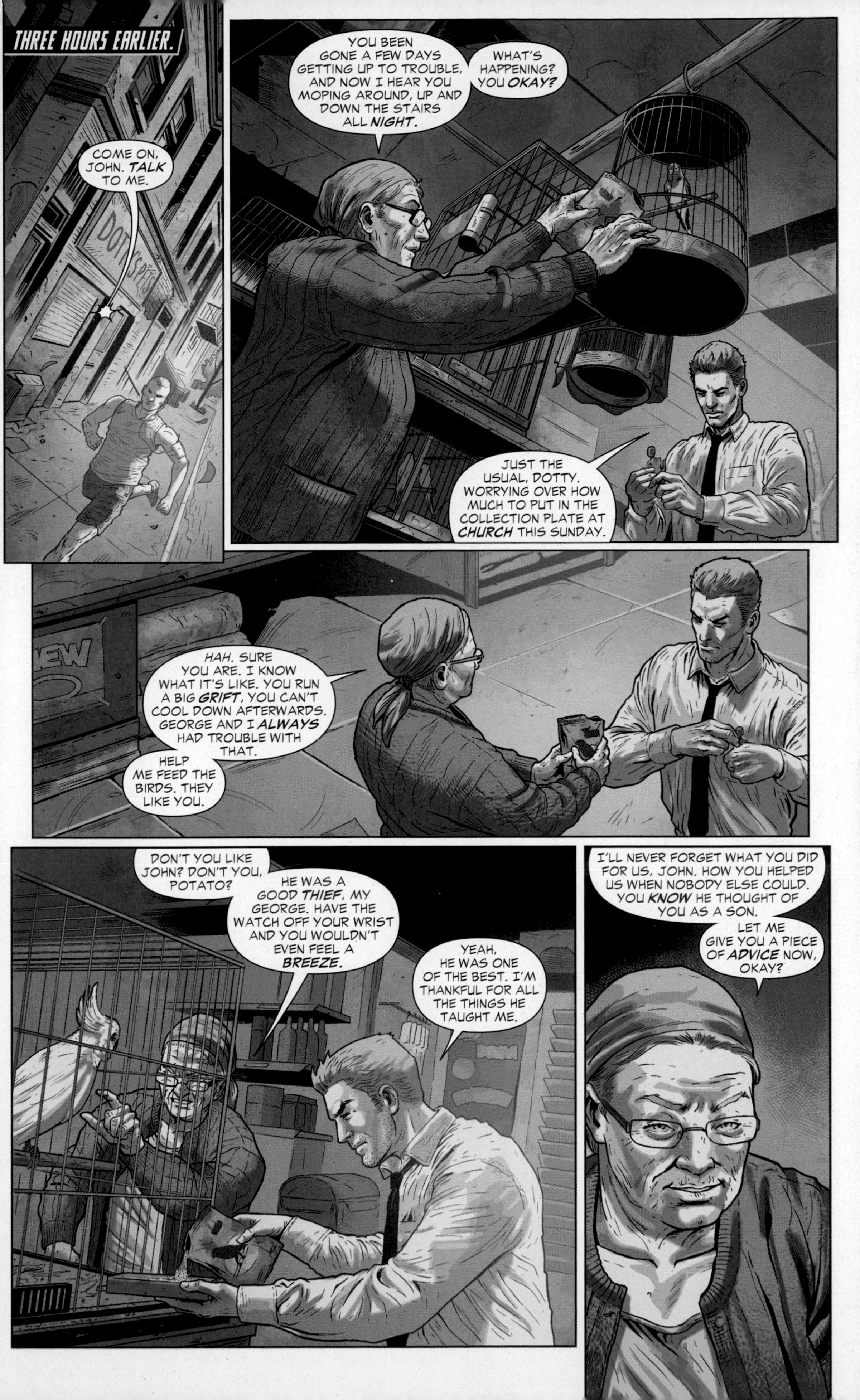
THREE HOURS EARLIER.
COME ON, JOHN. TALK TO ME.
DOTTY'S PETS
YOU BEEN GONE A FEW DAYS GETTING UP TO TROUBLE, AND NOW I HEAR YOU MOPING AROUND, UP AND DOWN THE STAIRS ALL NIGHT.
WHAT'S HAPPENING? YOU OKAY?
JUST THE USUAL, DOTTY. WORRYING OVER HOW MUCH TO PUT IN THE COLLECTION PLATE AT CHURCH THIS SUNDAY.
HAH. SURE YOU ARE. I KNOW WHAT IT'S LIKE. YOU RUN A BIG GRIFT, YOU CAN'T COOL DOWN AFTERWARDS. GEORGE AND I ALWAYS HAD TROUBLE WITH THAT.
HELP ME FEED THE BIRDS. THEY LIKE YOU.
DON'T YOU LIKE JOHN? DON'T YOU, POTATO?
HE WAS A GOOD THIEF, MY GEORGE. HAVE THE WATCH OFF YOUR WRIST AND YOU WOULDN'T EVEN FEEL A BREEZE.
YEAH, HE WAS ONE OF THE BEST. I'M THANKFUL FOR ALL THE THINGS HE TAUGHT ME.
I'LL NEVER FORGET WHAT YOU DID FOR US, JOHN. HOW YOU HELPED US WHEN NOBODY ELSE COULD. YOU KNOW HE THOUGHT OF YOU AS A SON.
LET ME GIVE YOU A PIECE OF ADVICE NOW, OKAY?

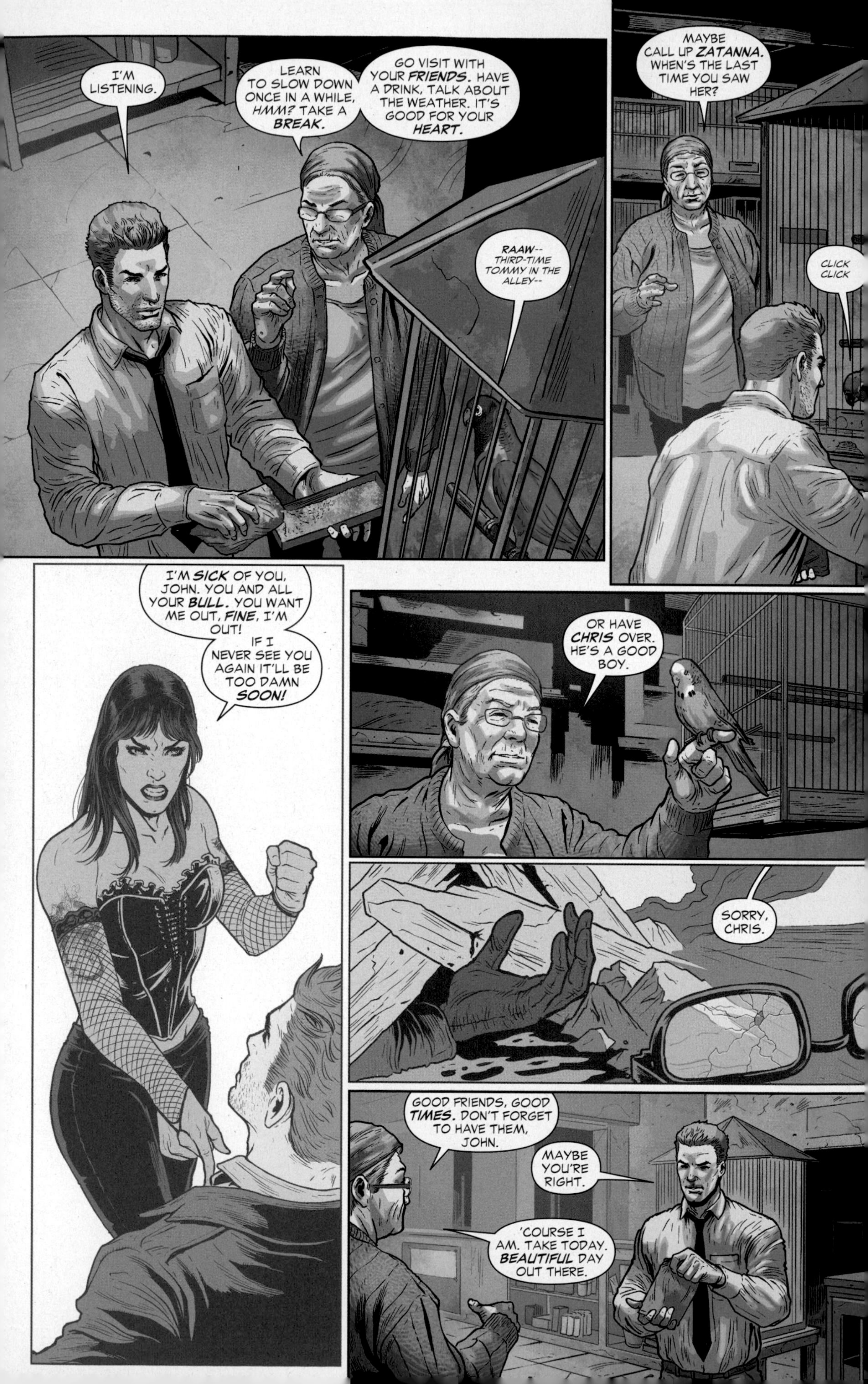

I'M LISTENING.
LEARN TO SLOW DOWN ONCE IN A WHILE, HMM? TAKE A BREAK.
GO VISIT WITH YOUR FRIENDS. HAVE A DRINK, TALK ABOUT THE WEATHER. IT'S GOOD FOR YOUR HEART.
RAAW-- THIRD-TIME TOMMY IN THE ALLEY--
MAYBE CALL UP ZATANNA. WHEN'S THE LAST TIME YOU SAW HER?
CLICK CLICK
I'M SICK OF YOU, JOHN. YOU AND ALL YOUR BULL. YOU WANT ME OUT, FINE, I'M OUT!
IF I NEVER SEE YOU AGAIN IT'LL BE TOO DAMN SOON!
OR HAVE CHRIS OVER. HE'S A GOOD BOY.
SORRY, CHRIS.
GOOD FRIENDS, GOOD TIMES. DON'T FORGET TO HAVE THEM, JOHN.
MAYBE YOU'RE RIGHT.
'COURSE I AM. TAKE TODAY. BEAUTIFUL DAY OUT THERE.

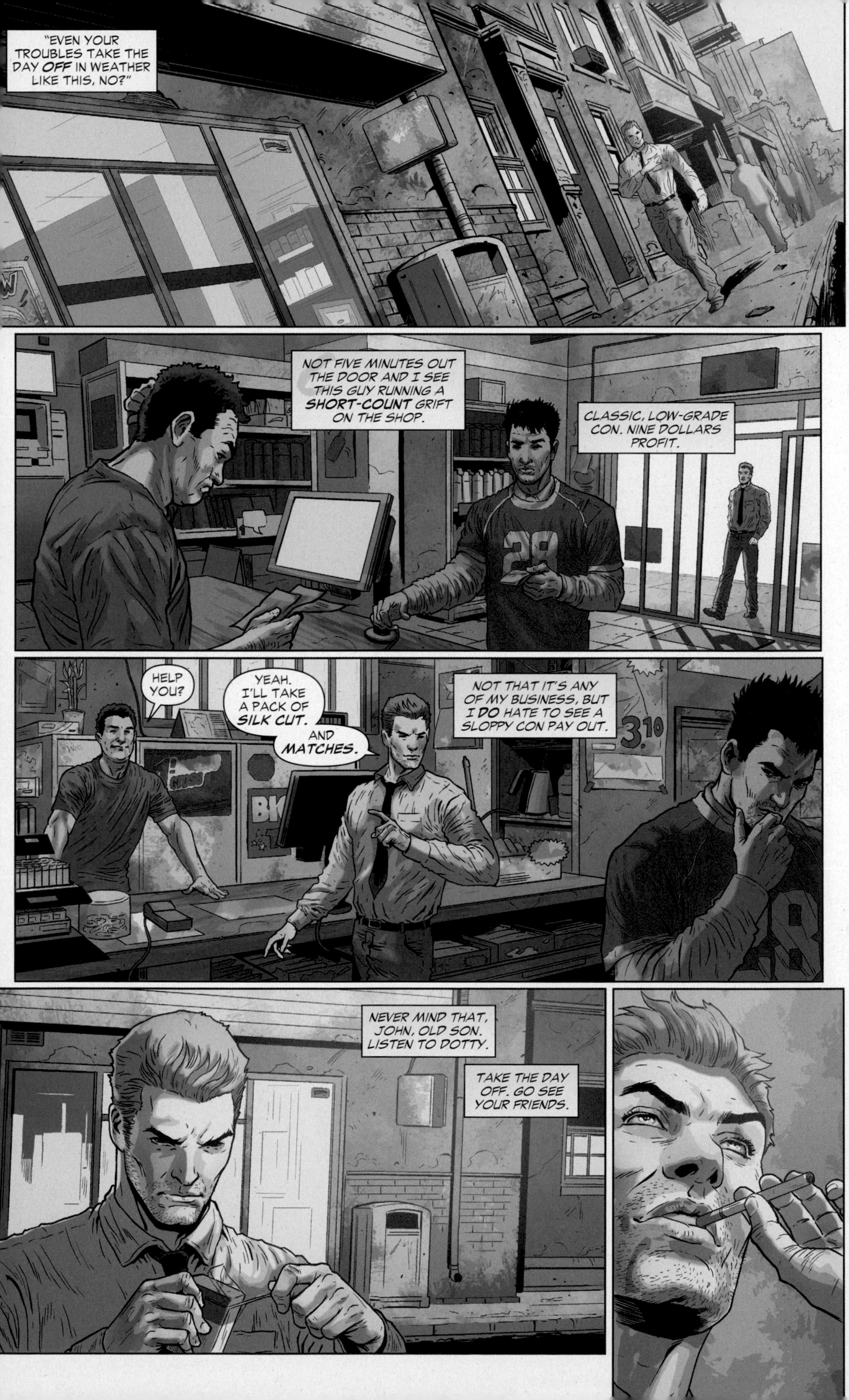
"EVEN YOUR TROUBLES TAKE THE DAY OFF IN WEATHER LIKE THIS, NO?"
NOT FIVE MINUTES OUT THE DOOR AND I SEE THIS GUY RUNNING A SHORT-COUNT GRIFT ON THE SHOP.
CLASSIC, LOW-GRADE CON. NINE DOLLARS PROFIT.
HELP YOU?
YEAH. I'LL TAKE A PACK OF SILK CUT.
AND MATCHES.
NOT THAT IT'S ANY OF MY BUSINESS, BUT I DO HATE TO SEE A SLOPPY CON PAY OUT.
3.10
NEVER MIND THAT, JOHN, OLD SON. LISTEN TO DOTTY.
TAKE THE DAY OFF. GO SEE YOUR FRIENDS.

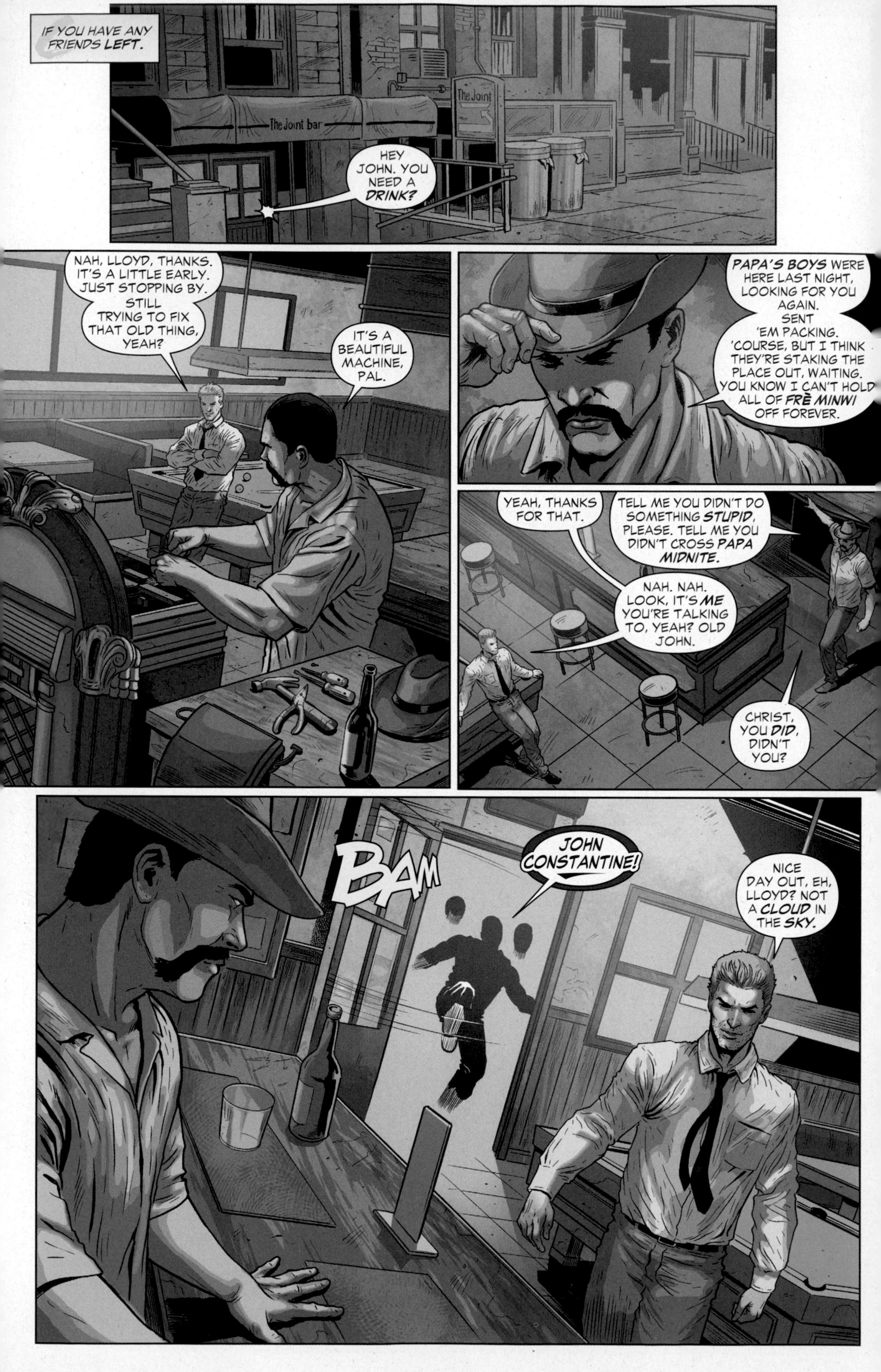
IF YOU HAVE ANY FRIENDS LEFT.
The Joint bar
The Joint
HEY JOHN. YOU NEED A DRINK?
NAH, LLOYD, THANKS. IT'S A LITTLE EARLY. JUST STOPPING BY. STILL TRYING TO FIX THAT OLD THING, YEAH?
IT'S A BEAUTIFUL MACHINE, PAL.
PAPA'S BOYS WERE HERE LAST NIGHT, LOOKING FOR YOU AGAIN. SENT 'EM PACKING. 'COURSE, BUT I THINK THEY'RE STAKING THE PLACE OUT, WAITING. YOU KNOW I CAN'T HOLD ALL OF FRÈ MINWI OFF FOREVER.
YEAH, THANKS FOR THAT.
TELL ME YOU DIDN'T DO SOMETHING STUPID, PLEASE. TELL ME YOU DIDN'T CROSS PAPA MIDNITE.
NAH. NAH. LOOK, IT'S ME YOU'RE TALKING TO, YEAH? OLD JOHN.
CHRIST, YOU DID, DIDN'T YOU?
BAM
JOHN CONSTANTINE!
NICE DAY OUT, EH, LLOYD? NOT A CLOUD IN THE SKY.

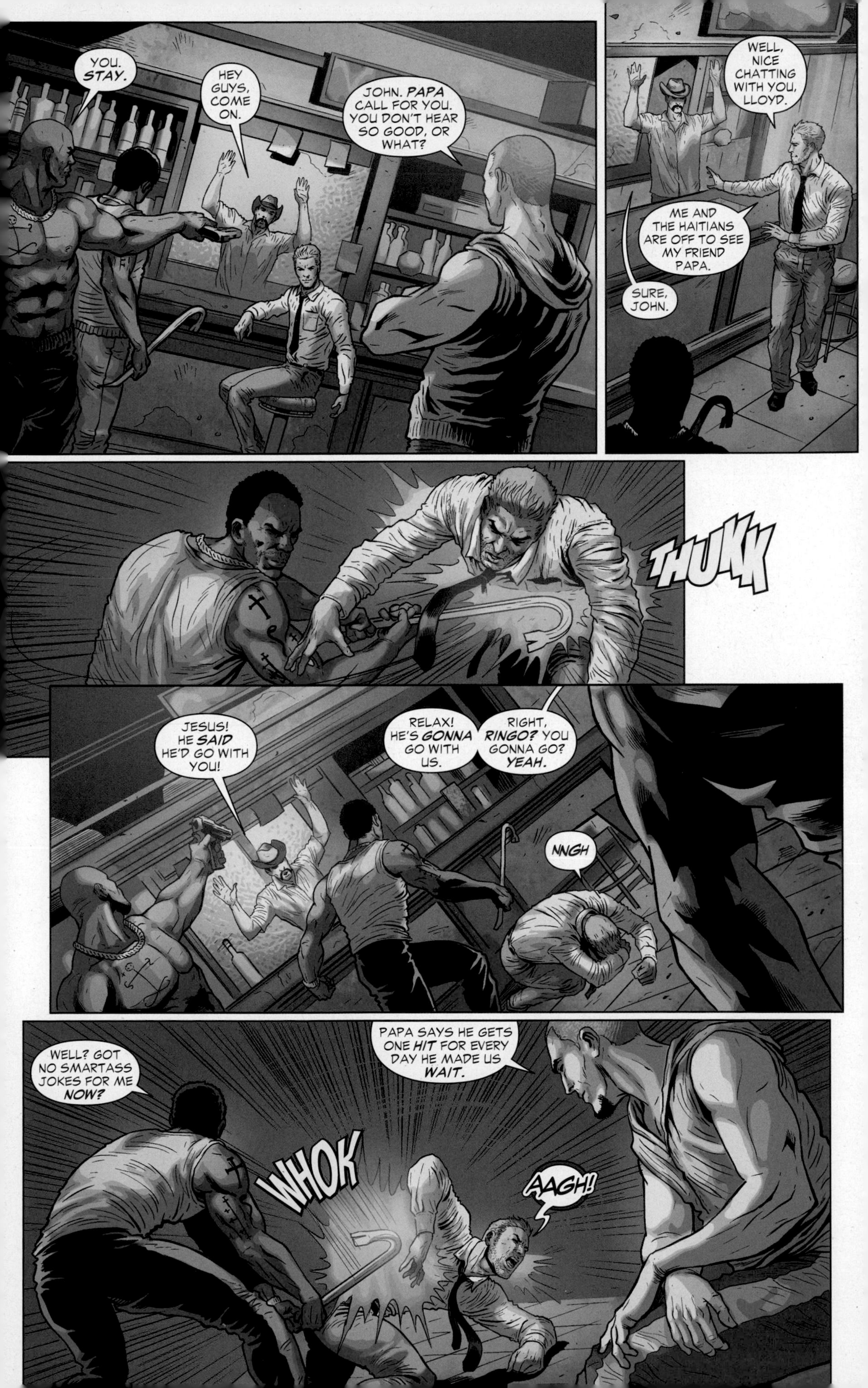
YOU. STAY.
HEY GUYS, COME ON.
JOHN. PAPA CALL FOR YOU. YOU DON'T HEAR SO GOOD, OR WHAT?
WELL, NICE CHATTING WITH YOU, LLOYD.
ME AND THE HAITIANS ARE OFF TO SEE MY FRIEND PAPA.
SURE, JOHN.
THUKK
JESUS! HE SAID HE'D GO WITH YOU!
RELAX! HE'S GONNA GO WITH US.
RIGHT, RINGO? YOU GONNA GO? YEAH.
NNGH
WELL? GOT NO SMARTASS JOKES FOR ME NOW?
PAPA SAYS HE GETS ONE HIT FOR EVERY DAY HE MADE US WAIT.
WHOK
AAGH!

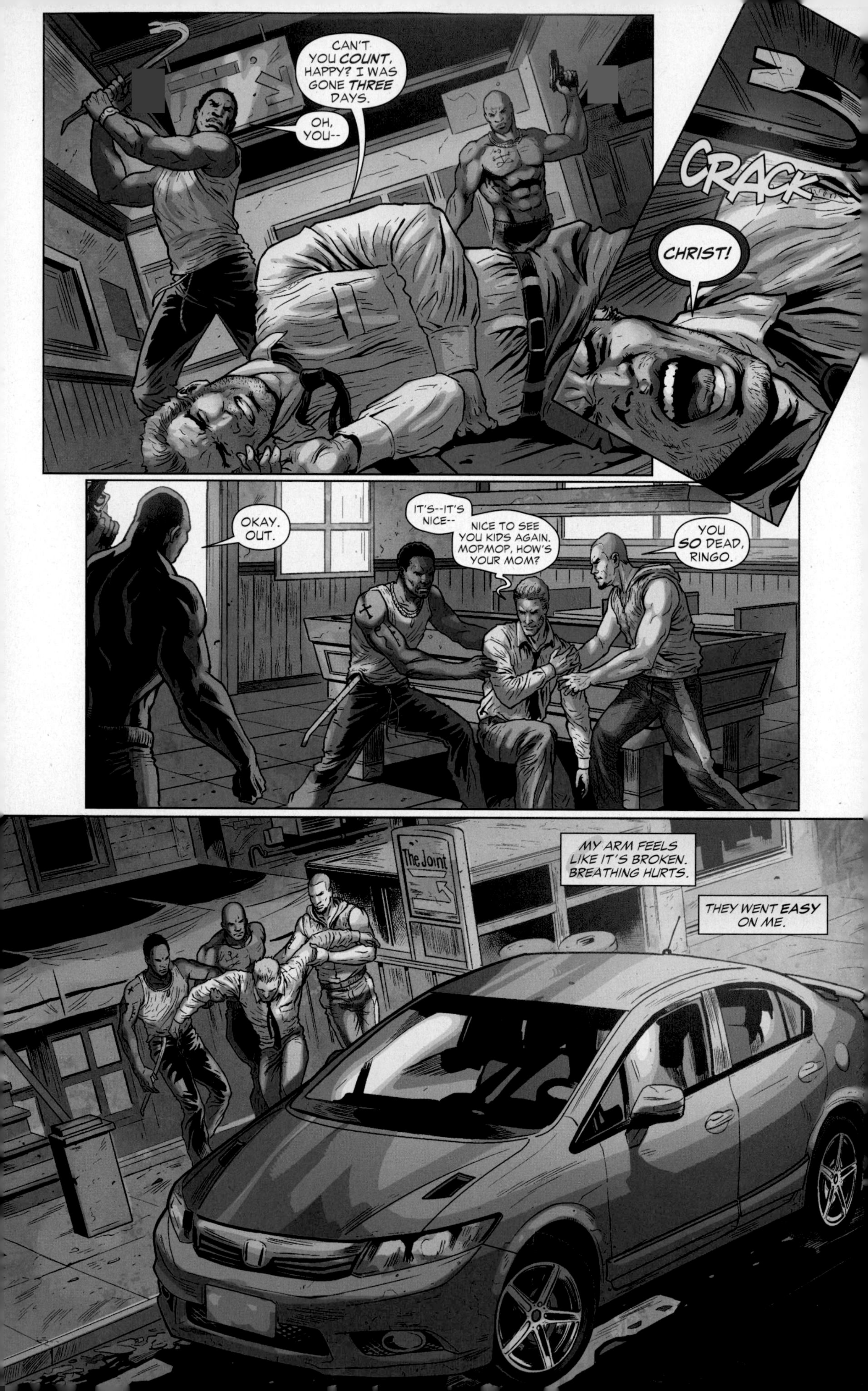
CAN'T YOU COUNT, HAPPY? I WAS GONE THREE DAYS.
OH, YOU--
CRACK
CHRIST!
OKAY. OUT.
IT'S--IT'S NICE--
NICE TO SEE YOU KIDS AGAIN. MOPMOP, HOW'S YOUR MOM?
YOU SO DEAD, RINGO.
The Joint
MY ARM FEELS LIKE IT'S BROKEN. BREATHING HURTS.
THEY WENT EASY ON ME.

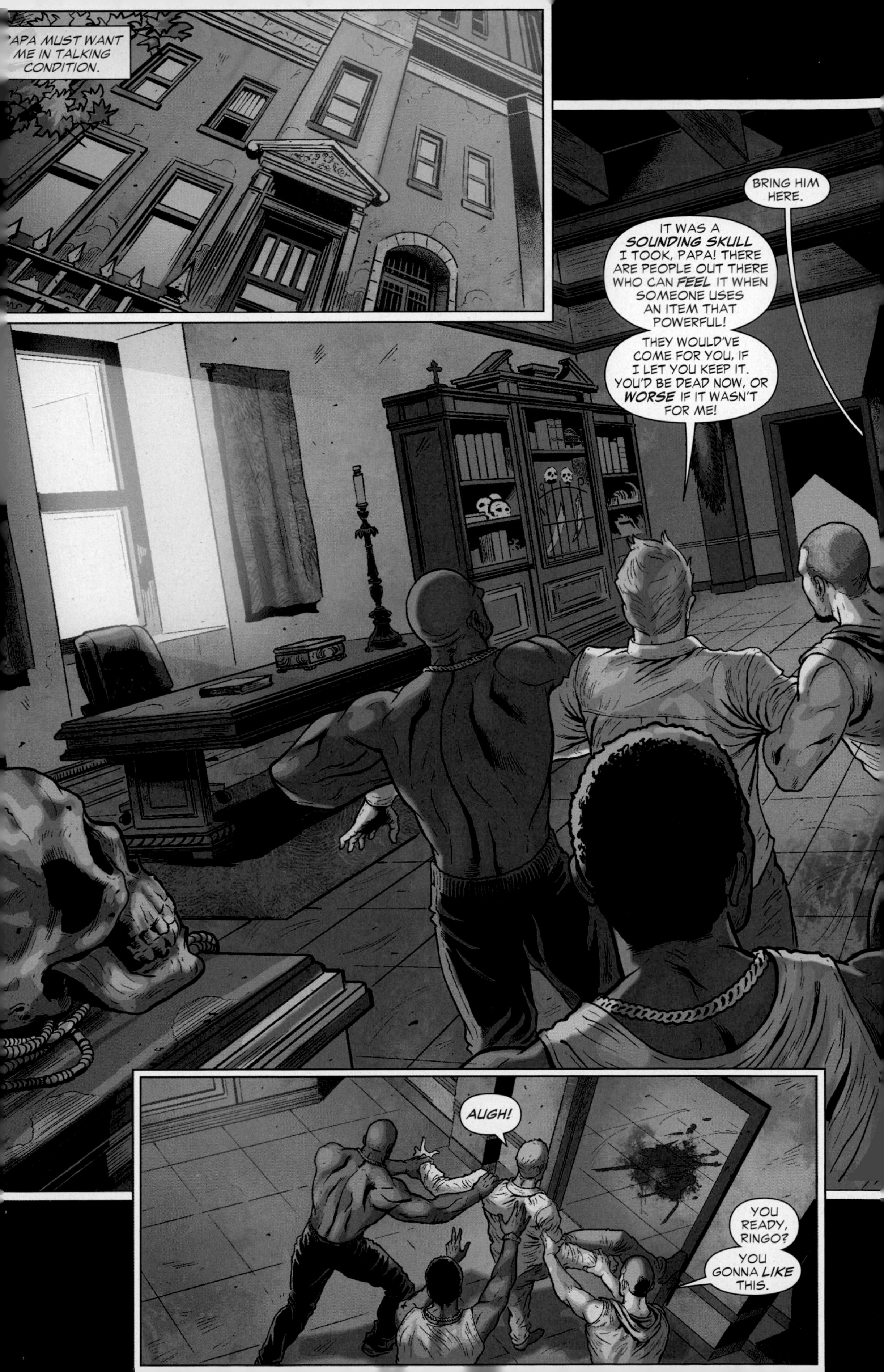
PAPA MUST WANT ME IN TALKING CONDITION.
BRING HIM HERE.
IT WAS A SOUNDING SKULL I TOOK, PAPA! THERE ARE PEOPLE OUT THERE WHO CAN FEEL IT WHEN SOMEONE USES AN ITEM THAT POWERFUL!
THEY WOULD'VE COME FOR YOU, IF I LET YOU KEEP IT. YOU'D BE DEAD NOW, OR WORSE IF IT WASN'T FOR ME!
AUGH!
YOU READY, RINGO?
YOU GONNA LIKE THIS.

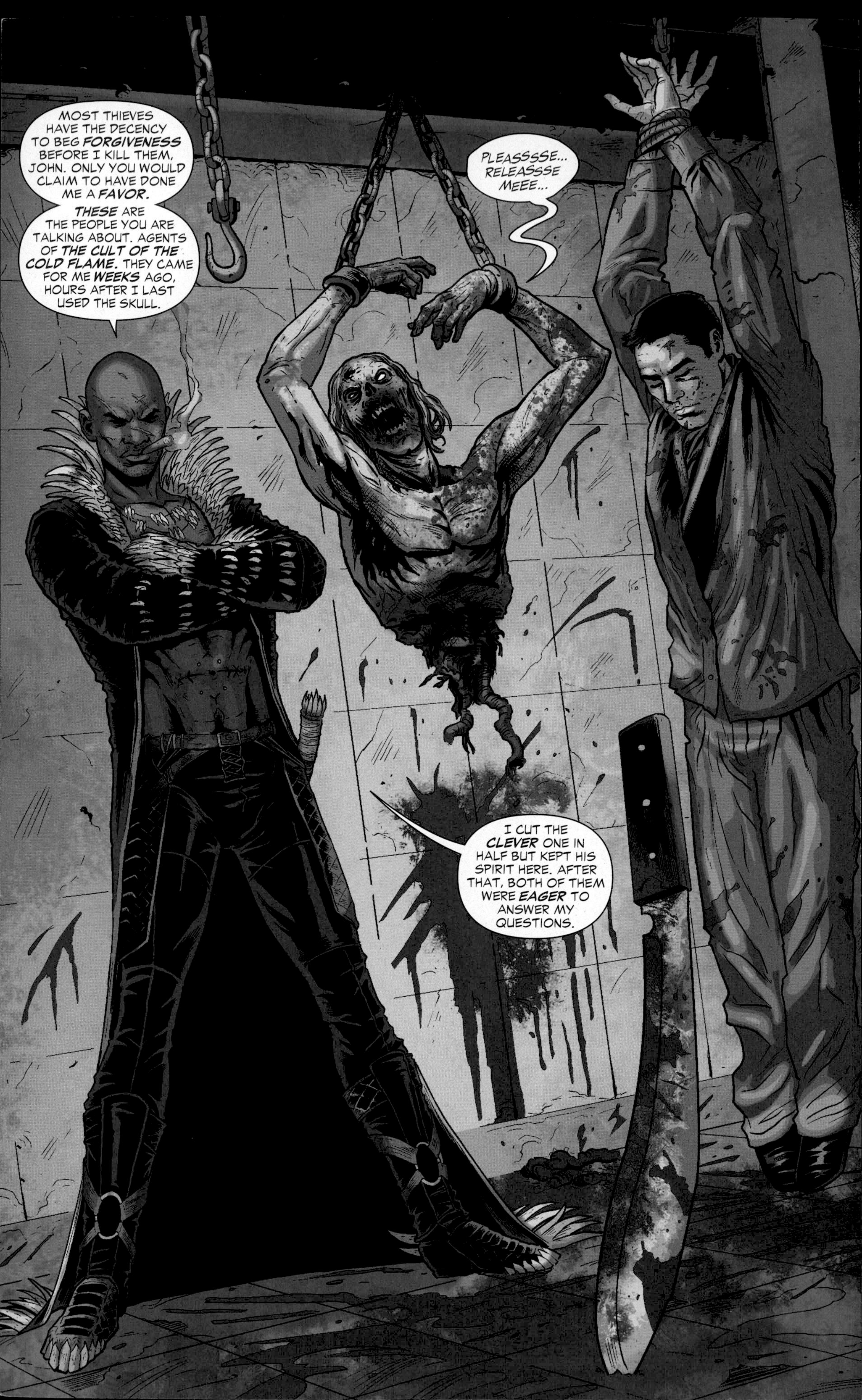

MOST THIEVES HAVE THE DECENCY TO BEG FORGIVENESS BEFORE I KILL THEM, JOHN. ONLY YOU WOULD CLAIM TO HAVE DONE ME A FAVOR.
THESE ARE THE PEOPLE YOU ARE TALKING ABOUT. AGENTS OF THE CULT OF THE COLD FLAME. THEY CAME FOR ME WEEKS AGO, HOURS AFTER I LAST USED THE SKULL.
PLEASSSSE... RELEASSSE MEEE...
I CUT THE CLEVER ONE IN HALF BUT KEPT HIS SPIRIT HERE. AFTER THAT, BOTH OF THEM WERE EAGER TO ANSWER MY QUESTIONS.

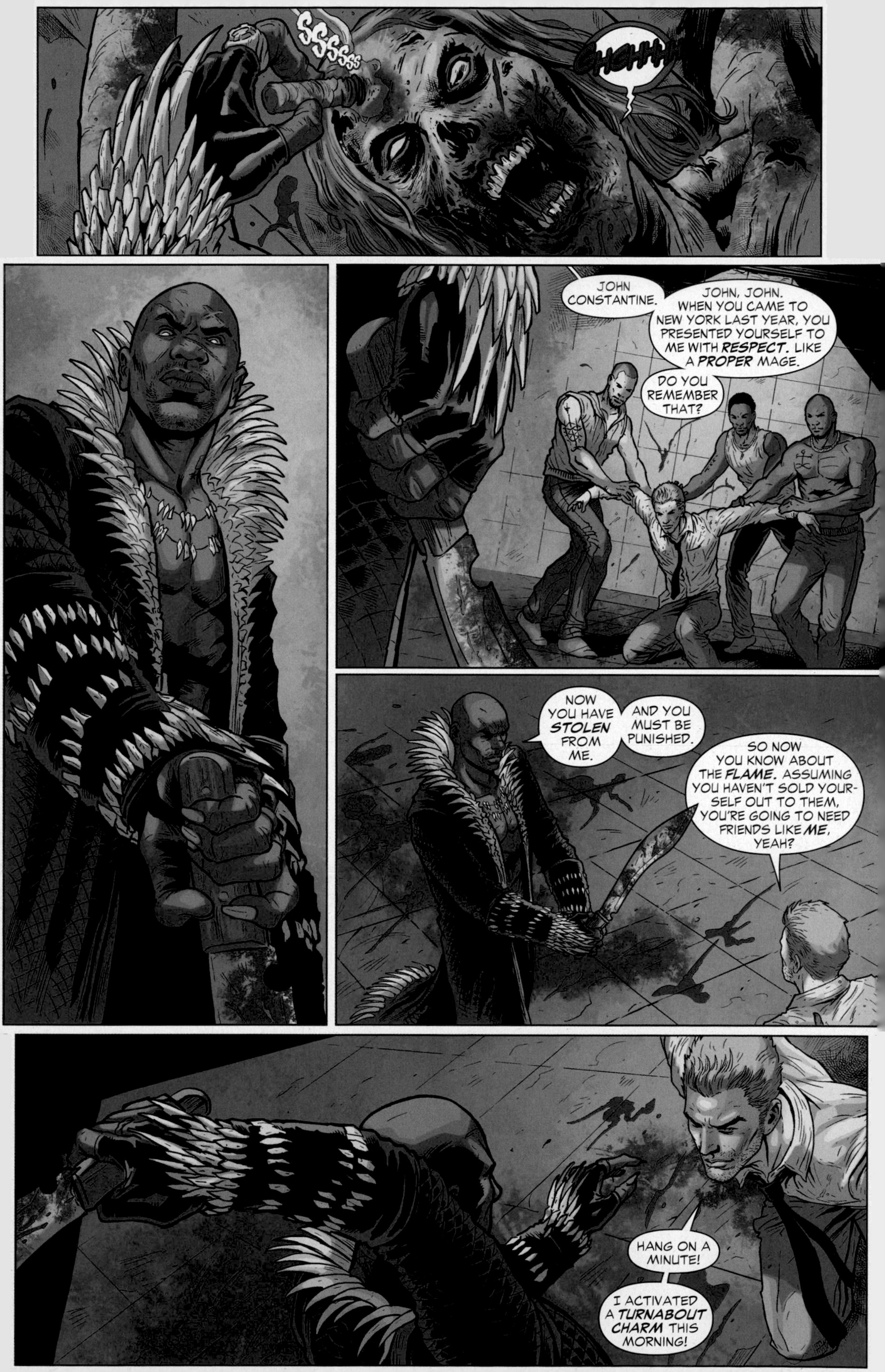
SSSSSS
GHGHHH
JOHN CONSTANTINE.
JOHN, JOHN. WHEN YOU CAME TO NEW YORK LAST YEAR, YOU PRESENTED YOURSELF TO ME WITH RESPECT. LIKE A PROPER MAGE.
DO YOU REMEMBER THAT?
NOW YOU HAVE STOLEN FROM ME.
AND YOU MUST BE PUNISHED.
SO NOW YOU KNOW ABOUT THE FLAME. ASSUMING YOU HAVEN'T SOLD YOURSELF OUT TO THEM, YOU'RE GOING TO NEED FRIENDS LIKE ME, YEAH?
HANG ON A MINUTE!
I ACTIVATED A TURNABOUT CHARM THIS MORNING!

WELL, AT LEAST HE KNOWS WHAT A *TURNABOUT* IS. HE'S SMART ENOUGH TO LOWER THE BLADE.

IT'S COMPLICATED AND QUITE PAINFUL TO *PREPARE*, BUT THE RESULT IS SIMPLE. ANY INJURY I SUFFER TODAY WILL RETURN TO THE PERSON WHO INFLICTED IT BEFORE SUNDOWN.

YOU DIDN'T *SEARCH* HIM FIRST?

LEFT FRONT POCKET, BOSS.

OF COURSE THE OTHERS ARE STILL GOING THROUGH THE *MOTIONS*. THEY HAVE *NO* IDEA WHAT IT MEANS.

YOU DIDN'T *SEARCH* HIM?

GUESS I SHOULD HAVE *WARNED* YOU, EH, HAPPY?

THUKK

WHOK

NICE TIMING. WHAT WAS IT HE SAID? ONE SHOT FOR EACH *DAY* I MADE PAPA WAIT.

ONE, TWO--

THREE.

CAAGH

I ALSO CAST A *SHIVERING WARD* ON MYSELF EARLIER. WOULD YOU LIKE TO FIND OUT HOW TO TRIGGER IT? IT'S A HELL OF A *RIDE*.

CRACK

I STILL RESPECT YOU, PAPA. AND I *WAS* HELPING YOU BY TAKING THAT SKULL. BUT YOU'VE GONE AND BUGGERED THAT, HAVEN'T YOU? WITH YOUR BLOODY *INTERROGATION* ACT.

TIME COMES, WE CAN STAND TOGETHER IN BATTLE AGAINST *OUR* ENEMIES--OR WE CAN FALL ALONE.

I *DO* WANT TO TALK MORE ABOUT THAT, BUT I'M GOING TO WANT TO DO THAT ON *NEUTRAL* GROUND.

BESIDES, THIS ISN'T THE DAY FOR IT.

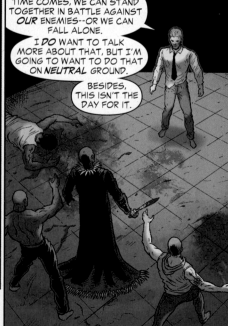

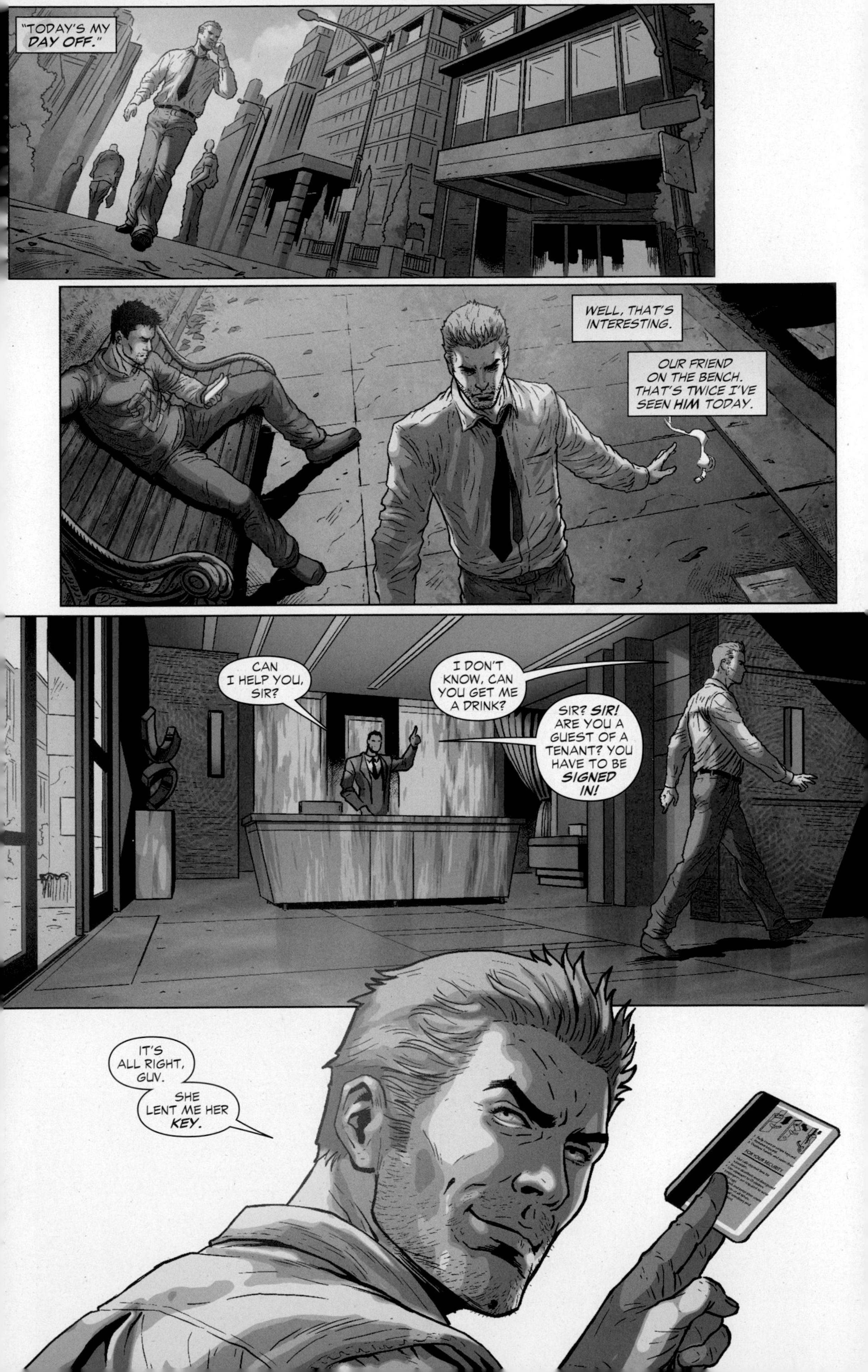
"TODAY'S MY DAY OFF."
WELL, THAT'S INTERESTING.
OUR FRIEND ON THE BENCH. THAT'S TWICE I'VE SEEN HIM TODAY.
CAN I HELP YOU, SIR?
I DON'T KNOW, CAN YOU GET ME A DRINK?
SIR? SIR! ARE YOU A GUEST OF A TENANT? YOU HAVE TO BE SIGNED IN!
IT'S ALL RIGHT, GUV.
SHE LENT ME HER KEY.
FOR YOUR SECURITY

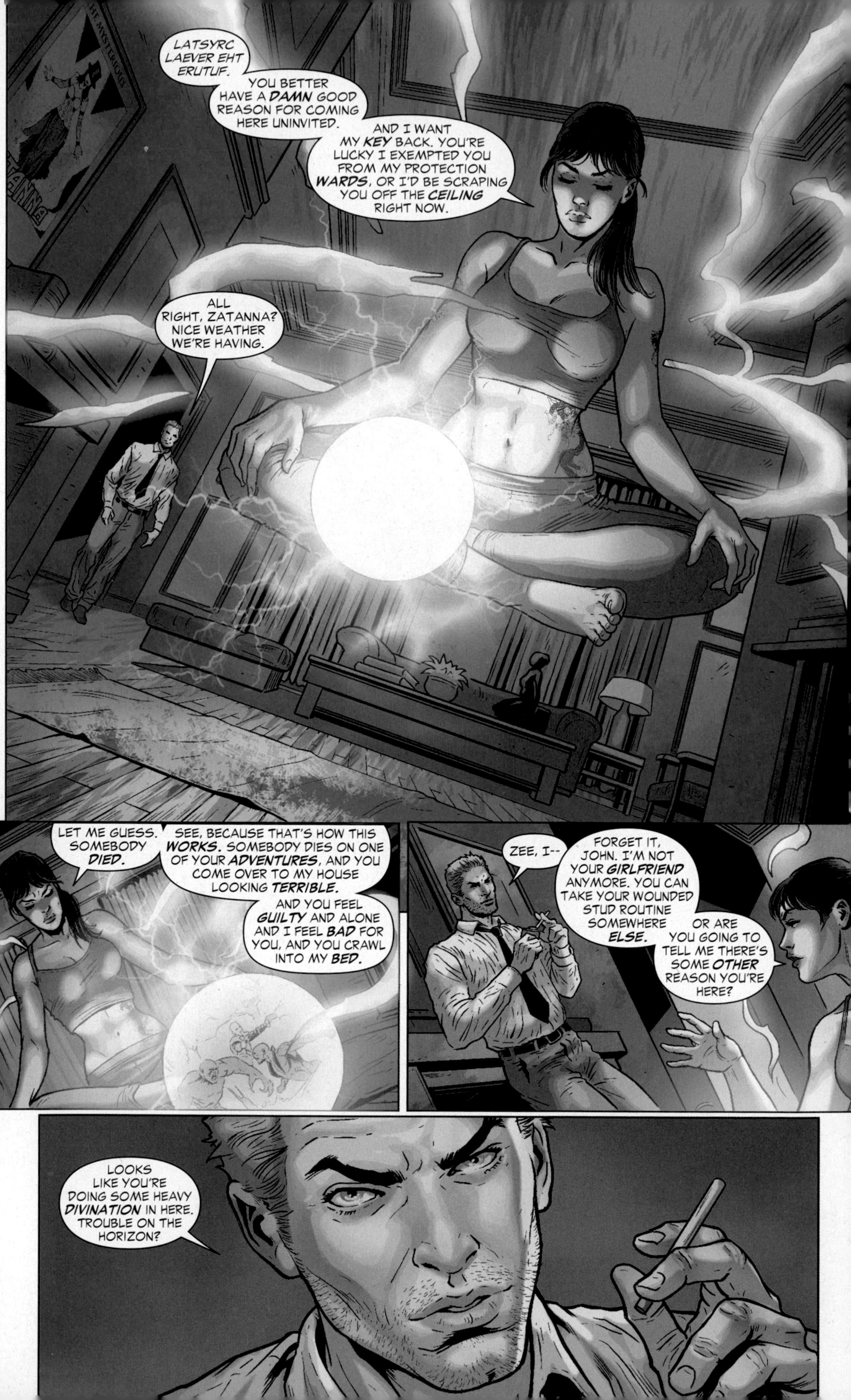
LATSYRC LAEVER EHT ERUTUF.
YOU BETTER HAVE A DAMN GOOD REASON FOR COMING HERE UNINVITED.
AND I WANT MY KEY BACK. YOU'RE LUCKY I EXEMPTED YOU FROM MY PROTECTION WARDS, OR I'D BE SCRAPING YOU OFF THE CEILING RIGHT NOW.
ALL RIGHT, ZATANNA? NICE WEATHER WE'RE HAVING.
LET ME GUESS. SOMEBODY DIED.
SEE, BECAUSE THAT'S HOW THIS WORKS. SOMEBODY DIES ON ONE OF YOUR ADVENTURES, AND YOU COME OVER TO MY HOUSE LOOKING TERRIBLE.
AND YOU FEEL GUILTY AND ALONE AND I FEEL BAD FOR YOU, AND YOU CRAWL INTO MY BED.
ZEE, I--
FORGET IT, JOHN. I'M NOT YOUR GIRLFRIEND ANYMORE. YOU CAN TAKE YOUR WOUNDED STUD ROUTINE SOMEWHERE ELSE.
OR ARE YOU GOING TO TELL ME THERE'S SOME OTHER REASON YOU'RE HERE?
LOOKS LIKE YOU'RE DOING SOME HEAVY DIVINATION IN HERE. TROUBLE ON THE HORIZON?

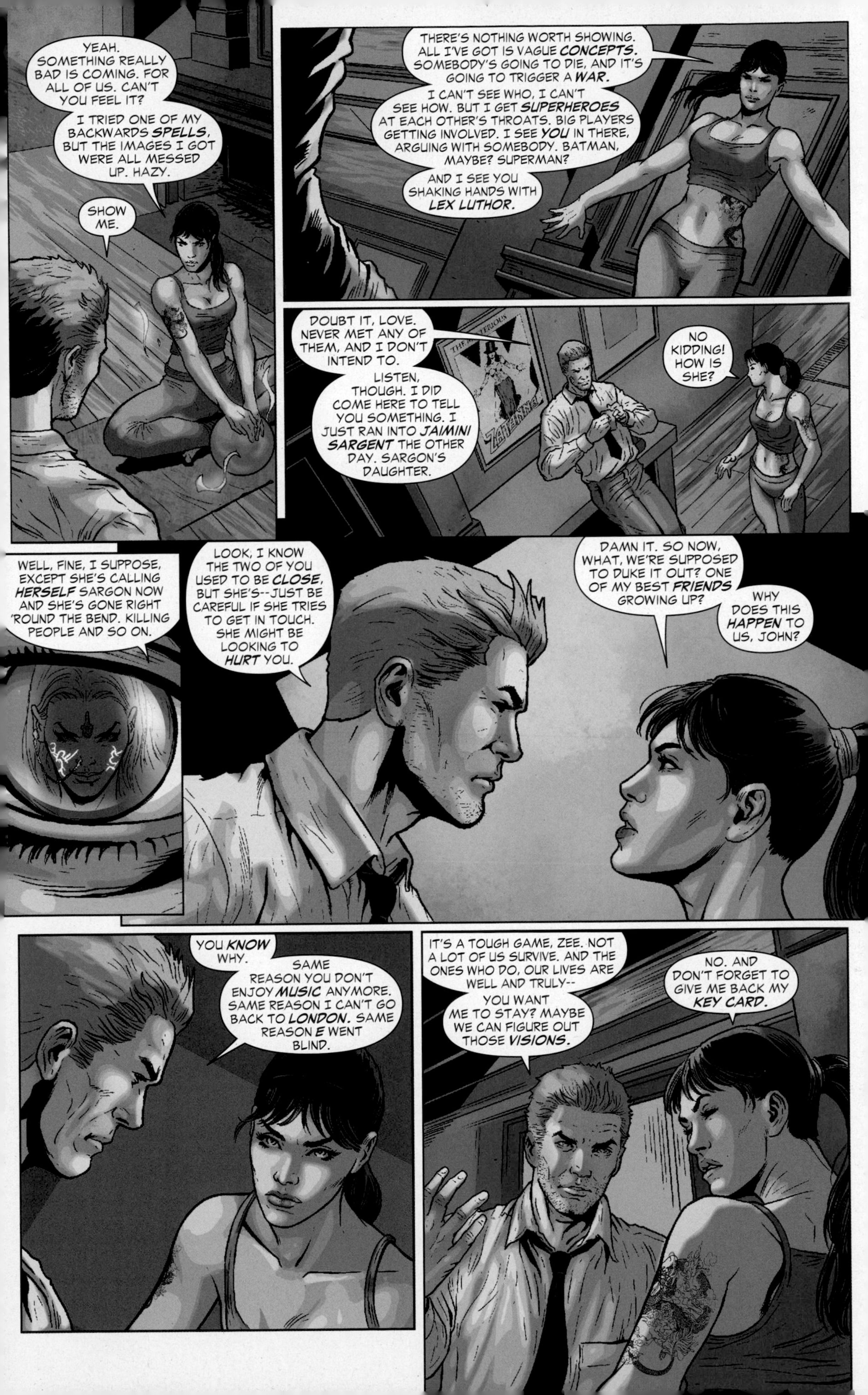
YEAH. SOMETHING REALLY BAD IS COMING. FOR ALL OF US. CAN'T YOU FEEL IT?
I TRIED ONE OF MY BACKWARDS SPELLS, BUT THE IMAGES I GOT WERE ALL MESSED UP. HAZY.
SHOW ME.
THERE'S NOTHING WORTH SHOWING. ALL I'VE GOT IS VAGUE CONCEPTS. SOMEBODY'S GOING TO DIE, AND IT'S GOING TO TRIGGER A WAR.
I CAN'T SEE WHO, I CAN'T SEE HOW. BUT I GET SUPERHEROES AT EACH OTHER'S THROATS. BIG PLAYERS GETTING INVOLVED. I SEE YOU IN THERE, ARGUING WITH SOMEBODY. BATMAN, MAYBE? SUPERMAN?
AND I SEE YOU SHAKING HANDS WITH LEX LUTHOR.
DOUBT IT, LOVE. NEVER MET ANY OF THEM, AND I DON'T INTEND TO.
LISTEN, THOUGH. I DID COME HERE TO TELL YOU SOMETHING. I JUST RAN INTO JAIMINI SARGENT THE OTHER DAY. SARGON'S DAUGHTER.
NO KIDDING! HOW IS SHE?
WELL, FINE, I SUPPOSE, EXCEPT SHE'S CALLING HERSELF SARGON NOW AND SHE'S GONE RIGHT 'ROUND THE BEND. KILLING PEOPLE AND SO ON.
LOOK, I KNOW THE TWO OF YOU USED TO BE CLOSE, BUT SHE'S--JUST BE CAREFUL IF SHE TRIES TO GET IN TOUCH. SHE MIGHT BE LOOKING TO HURT YOU.
DAMN IT. SO NOW, WHAT, WE'RE SUPPOSED TO DUKE IT OUT? ONE OF MY BEST FRIENDS GROWING UP?
WHY DOES THIS HAPPEN TO US, JOHN?
YOU KNOW WHY.
SAME REASON YOU DON'T ENJOY MUSIC ANYMORE. SAME REASON I CAN'T GO BACK TO LONDON. SAME REASON E WENT BLIND.
IT'S A TOUGH GAME, ZEE. NOT A LOT OF US SURVIVE. AND THE ONES WHO DO, OUR LIVES ARE WELL AND TRULY--
YOU WANT ME TO STAY? MAYBE WE CAN FIGURE OUT THOSE VISIONS.
NO. AND DON'T FORGET TO GIVE ME BACK MY KEY CARD.

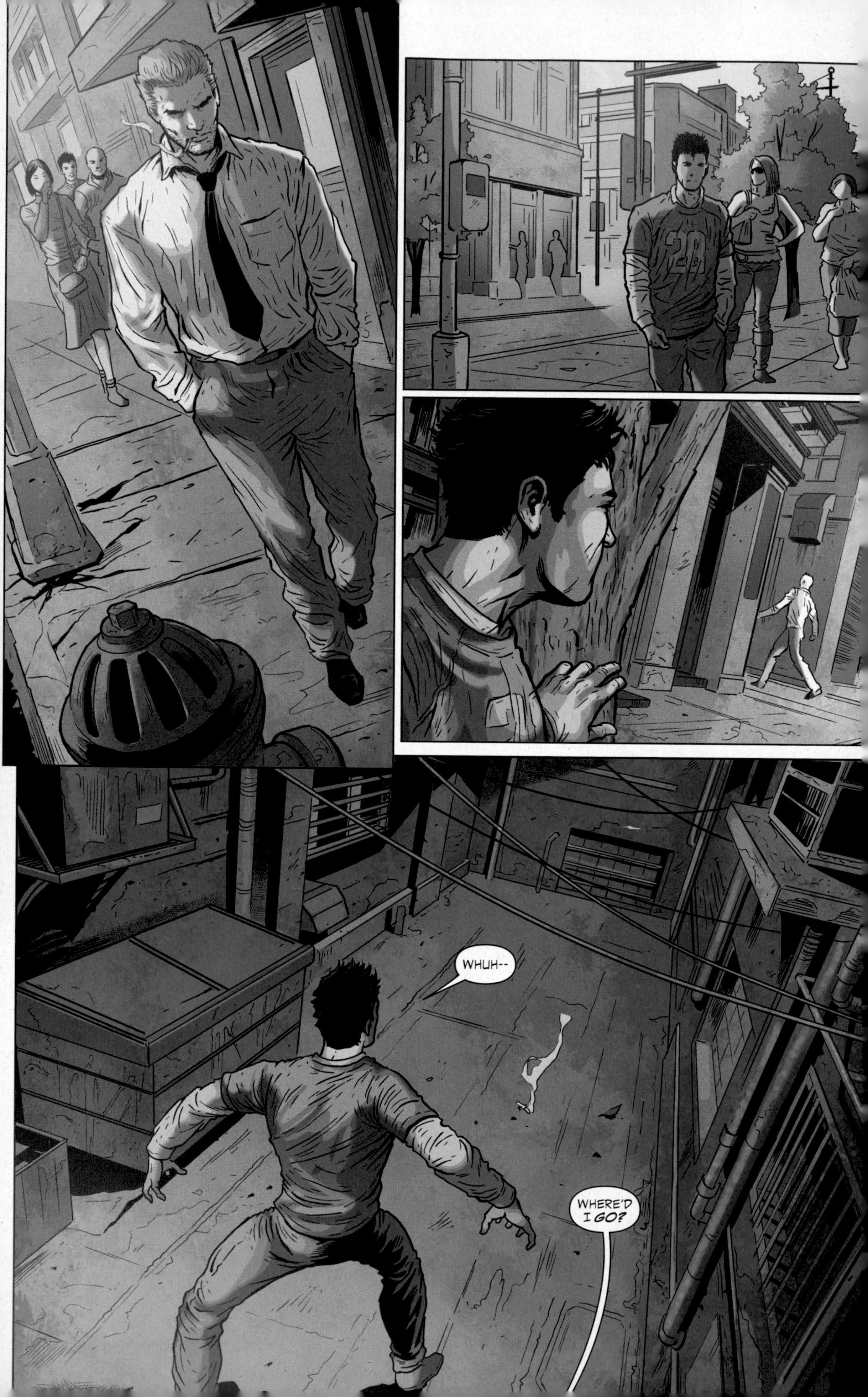
WHUH--
WHERE'D I GO?

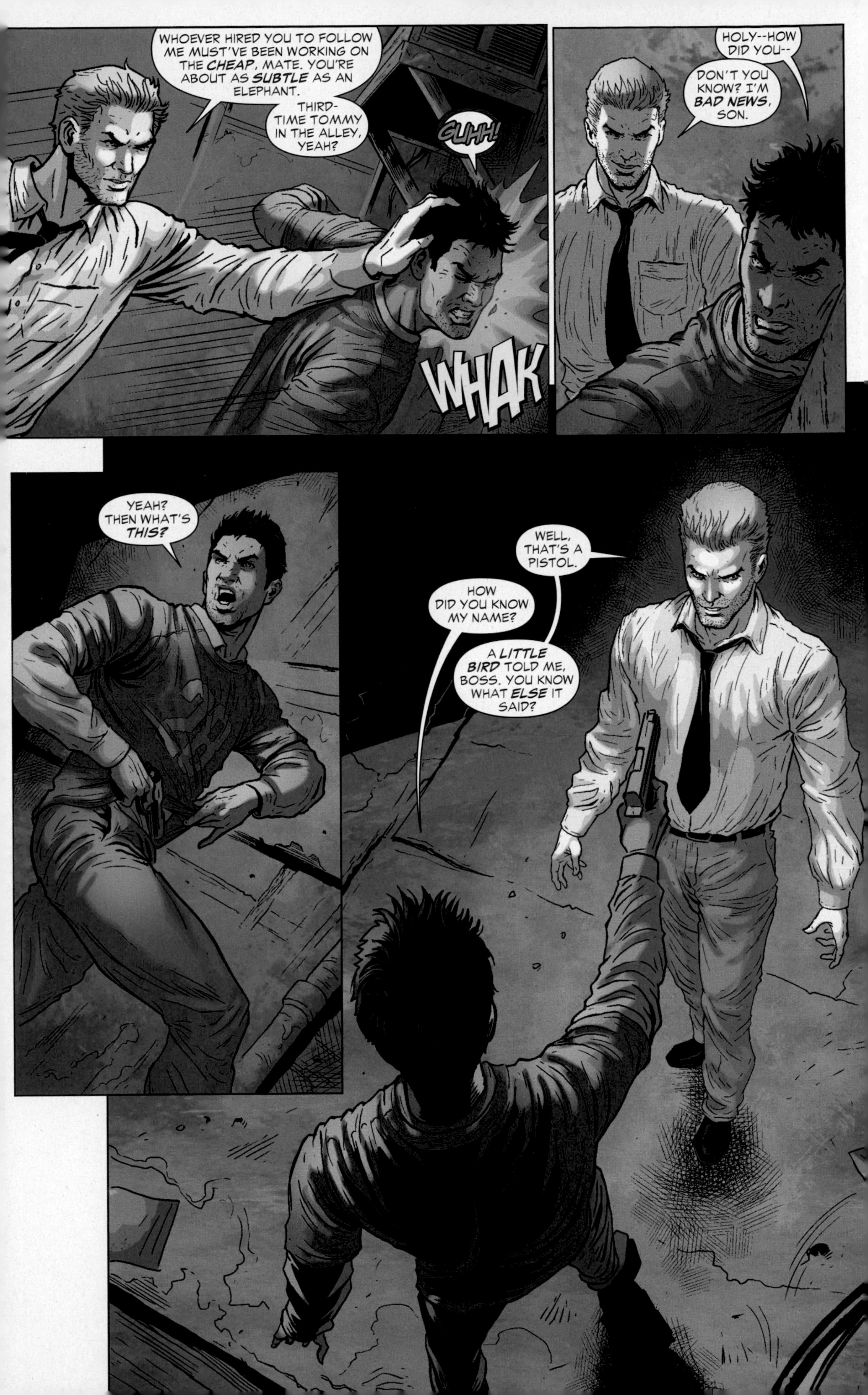
WHOEVER HIRED YOU TO FOLLOW ME MUST'VE BEEN WORKING ON THE CHEAP, MATE. YOU'RE ABOUT AS SUBTLE AS AN ELEPHANT.
THIRD-TIME TOMMY IN THE ALLEY, YEAH?
GUHH!
WHAK
HOLY--HOW DID YOU--
DON'T YOU KNOW? I'M BAD NEWS, SON.
YEAH? THEN WHAT'S THIS?
WELL, THAT'S A PISTOL.
HOW DID YOU KNOW MY NAME?
A LITTLE BIRD TOLD ME, BOSS. YOU KNOW WHAT ELSE IT SAID?

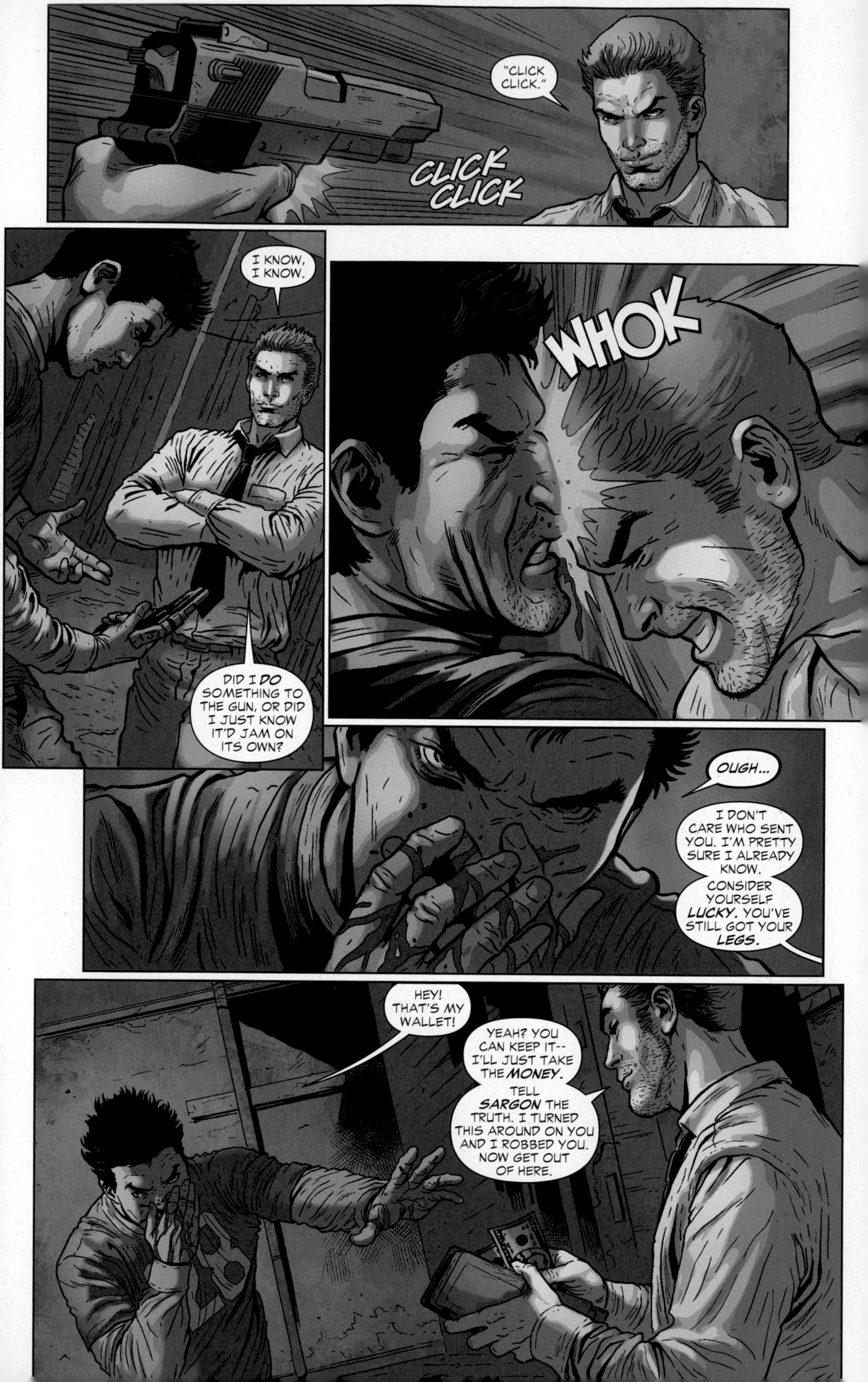
"CLICK CLICK."
CLICK CLICK
I KNOW, I KNOW.
WHOK
DID I DO SOMETHING TO THE GUN, OR DID I JUST KNOW IT'D JAM ON ITS OWN?
OUGH...
I DON'T CARE WHO SENT YOU. I'M PRETTY SURE I ALREADY KNOW.
CONSIDER YOURSELF LUCKY. YOU'VE STILL GOT YOUR LEGS.
HEY! THAT'S MY WALLET!
YEAH? YOU CAN KEEP IT-- I'LL JUST TAKE THE MONEY.
TELL SARGON THE TRUTH. I TURNED THIS AROUND ON YOU AND I ROBBED YOU. NOW GET OUT OF HERE.

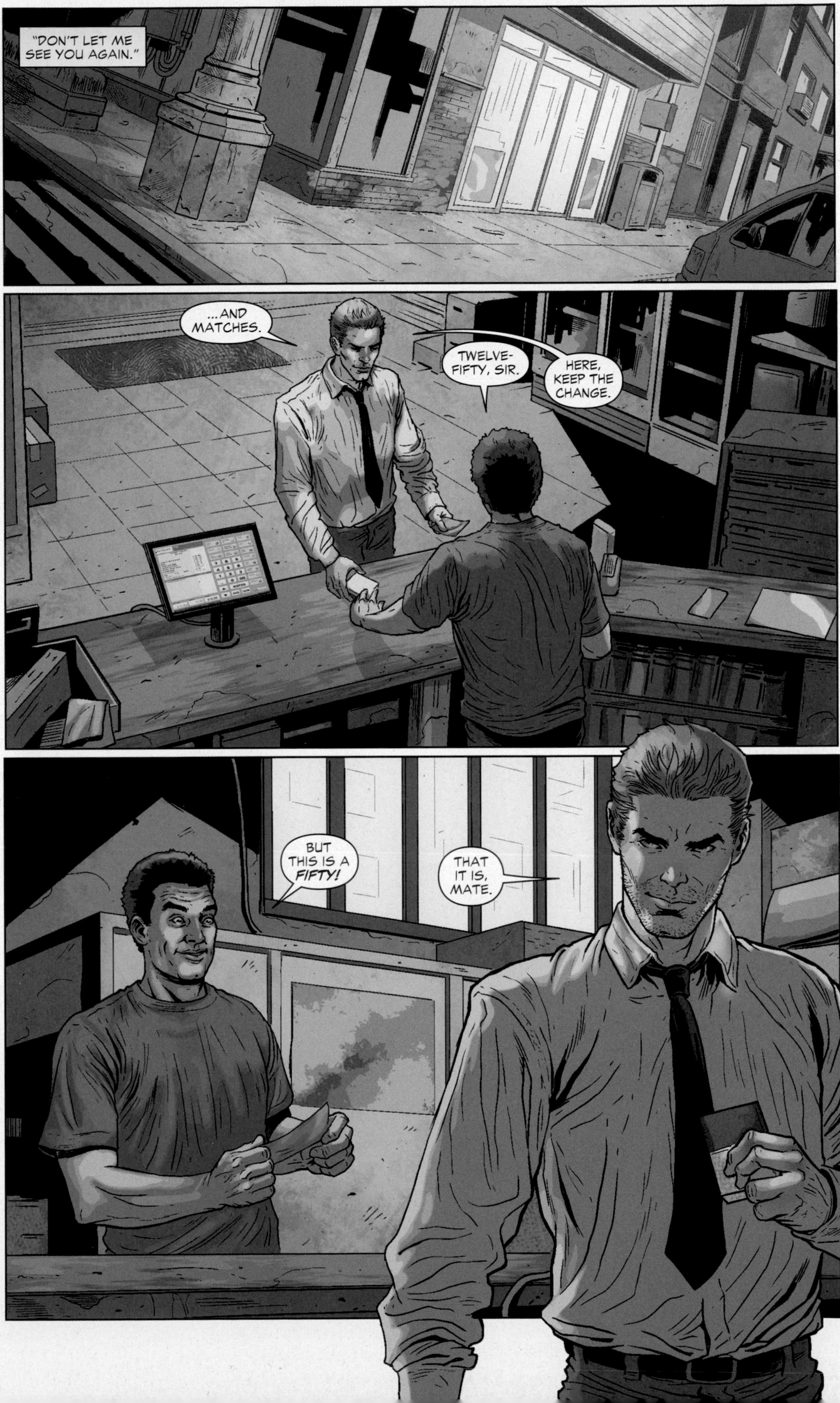
"DON'T LET ME SEE YOU AGAIN."
...AND MATCHES.
TWELVE-FIFTY, SIR.
HERE, KEEP THE CHANGE.
BUT THIS IS A *FIFTY!*
THAT IT IS, MATE.

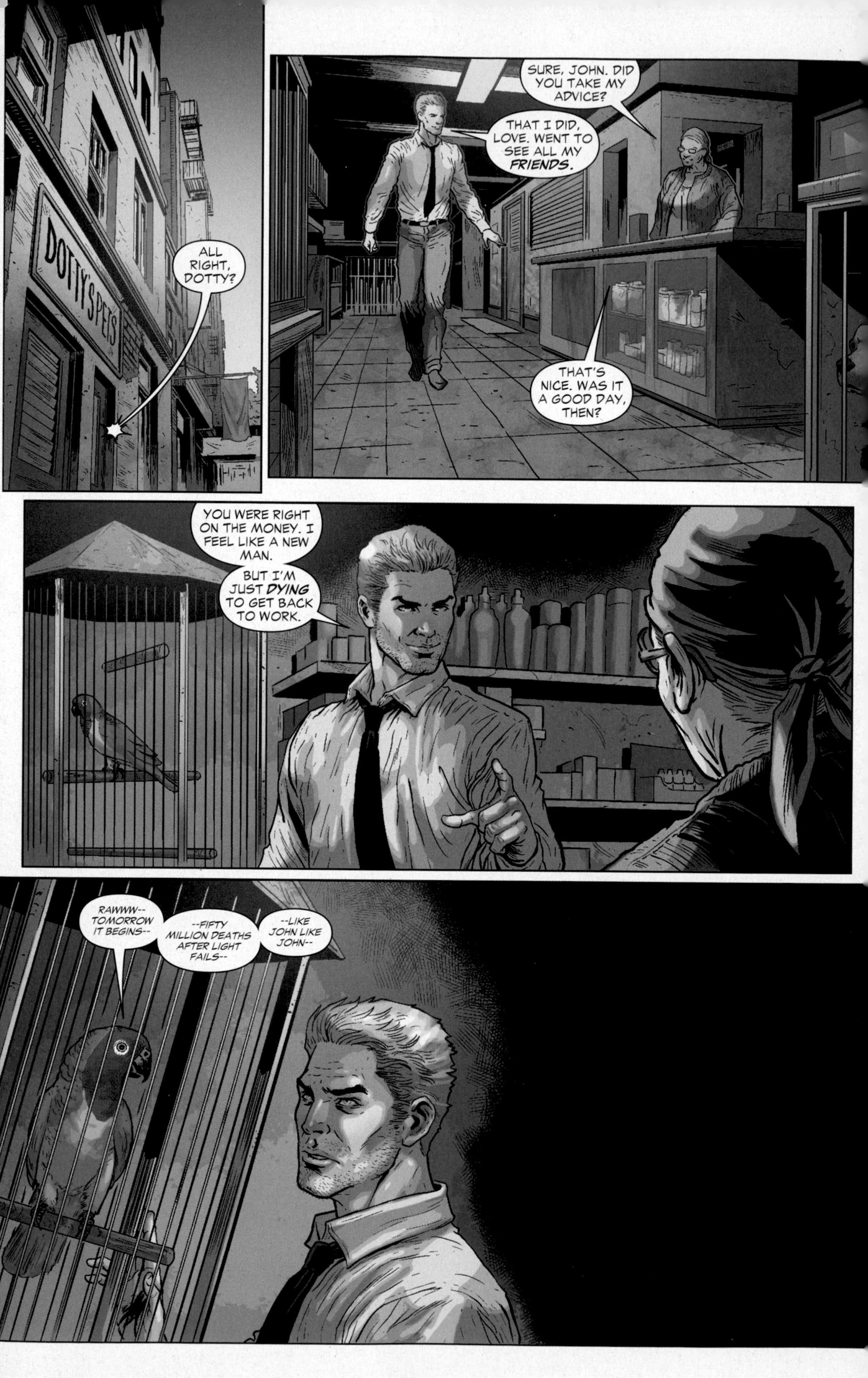
DOTTY'S PETS
ALL RIGHT, DOTTY?
SURE, JOHN. DID YOU TAKE MY ADVICE?
THAT I DID, LOVE. WENT TO SEE ALL MY FRIENDS.
THAT'S NICE. WAS IT A GOOD DAY, THEN?
YOU WERE RIGHT ON THE MONEY. I FEEL LIKE A NEW MAN.
BUT I'M JUST DYING TO GET BACK TO WORK.
RAWWW-- TOMORROW IT BEGINS--
--FIFTY MILLION DEATHS AFTER LIGHT FAILS--
--LIKE JOHN LIKE JOHN--

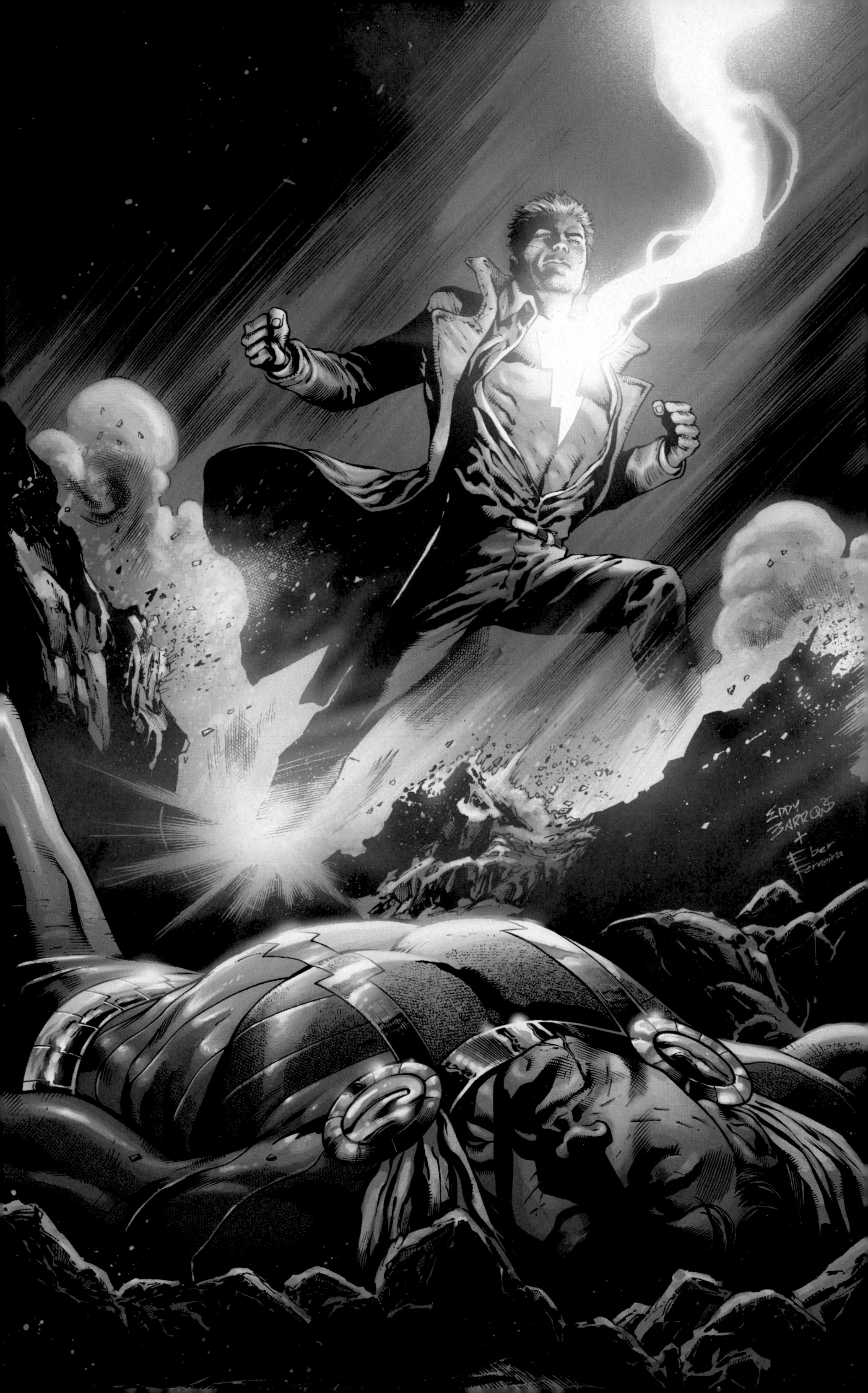
EDDY BARROWS
+
Eber Ferreira

STEALING THUNDER

RAY FAWKES writer **RENATO GUEDES** artist cover art by EDDY BARROWS, EBER FERREIRA and BRAD ANDERSON

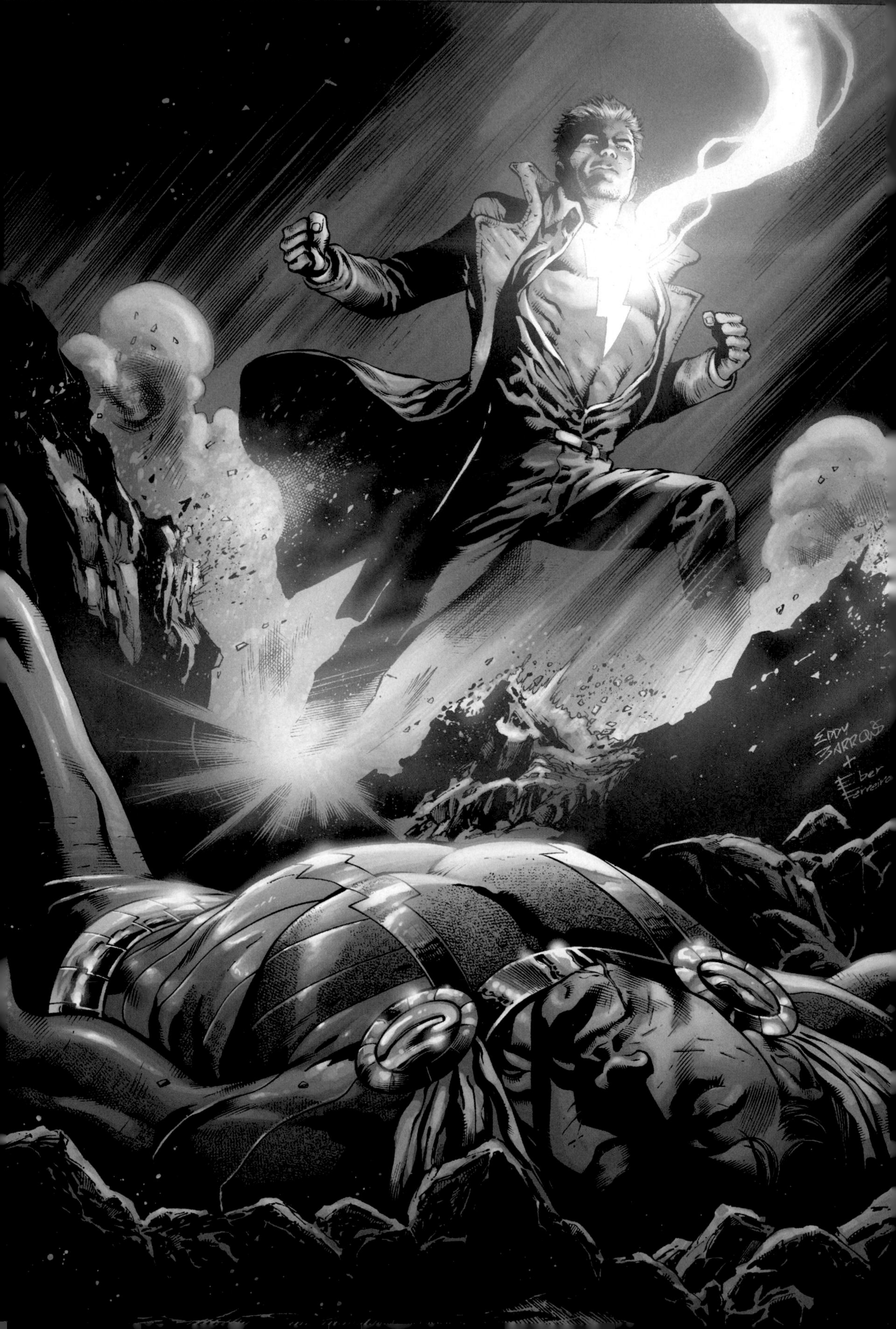

The Joint bar

The Joint

I *KNEW* TONIGHT WAS GOING TO BE A PAIN IN THE ASS.

LIKE, SOME NIGHTS JUST START OUT WRONG AND GET *WORSE*.

PUT CREAM IN MY COFFEE FIRST THING AND IT CAME OUT OF THE CARTON IN *LUMPS*. I SHOULDA GONE RIGHT BACK TO BED.

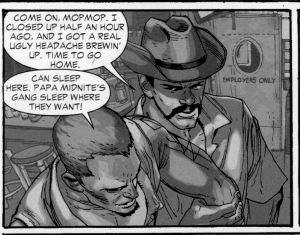

COME ON, MOPMOP. I CLOSED UP HALF AN HOUR AGO, AND I GOT A REAL UGLY HEADACHE BREWIN' UP. TIME TO GO HOME.

CAN SLEEP HERE. PAPA MIDNITE'S GANG SLEEP WHERE THEY WANT!

EMPLOYERS ONLY

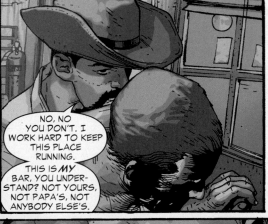

NO, NO YOU DON'T. I WORK HARD TO KEEP THIS PLACE RUNNING.

THIS IS *MY* BAR, YOU UNDER-STAND? NOT YOURS, NOT PAPA'S, NOT ANYBODY ELSE'S.

OI, LLOYD. LOCK IT UP.

GONNA NEED THE PLACE FOR A BIT.

EMPLOYERS ONLY

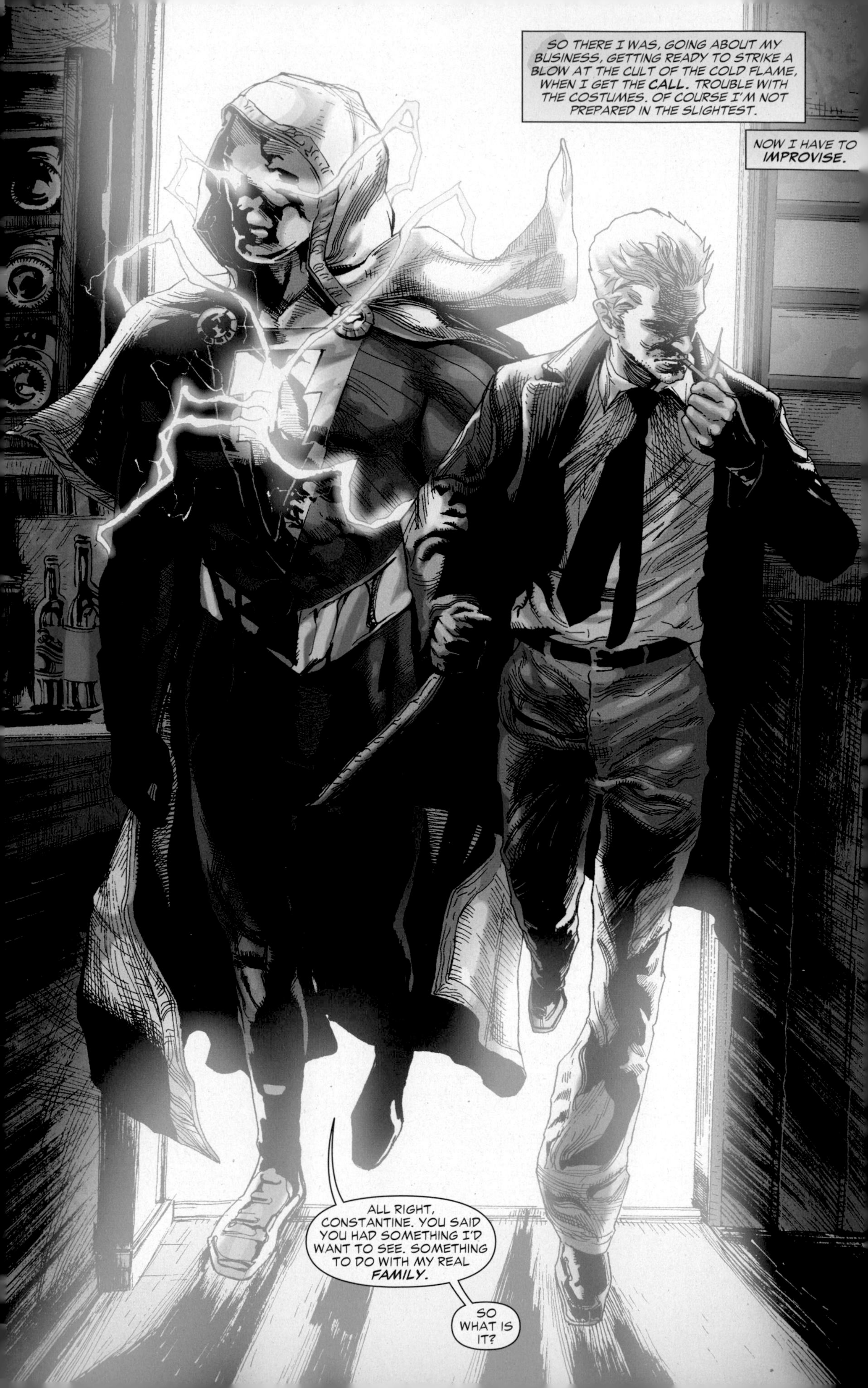
SO THERE I WAS, GOING ABOUT MY BUSINESS, GETTING READY TO STRIKE A BLOW AT THE CULT OF THE COLD FLAME, WHEN I GET THE CALL. TROUBLE WITH THE COSTUMES. OF COURSE I'M NOT PREPARED IN THE SLIGHTEST.
NOW I HAVE TO IMPROVISE.
ALL RIGHT, CONSTANTINE. YOU SAID YOU HAD SOMETHING I'D WANT TO SEE. SOMETHING TO DO WITH MY REAL FAMILY.
SO WHAT IS IT?

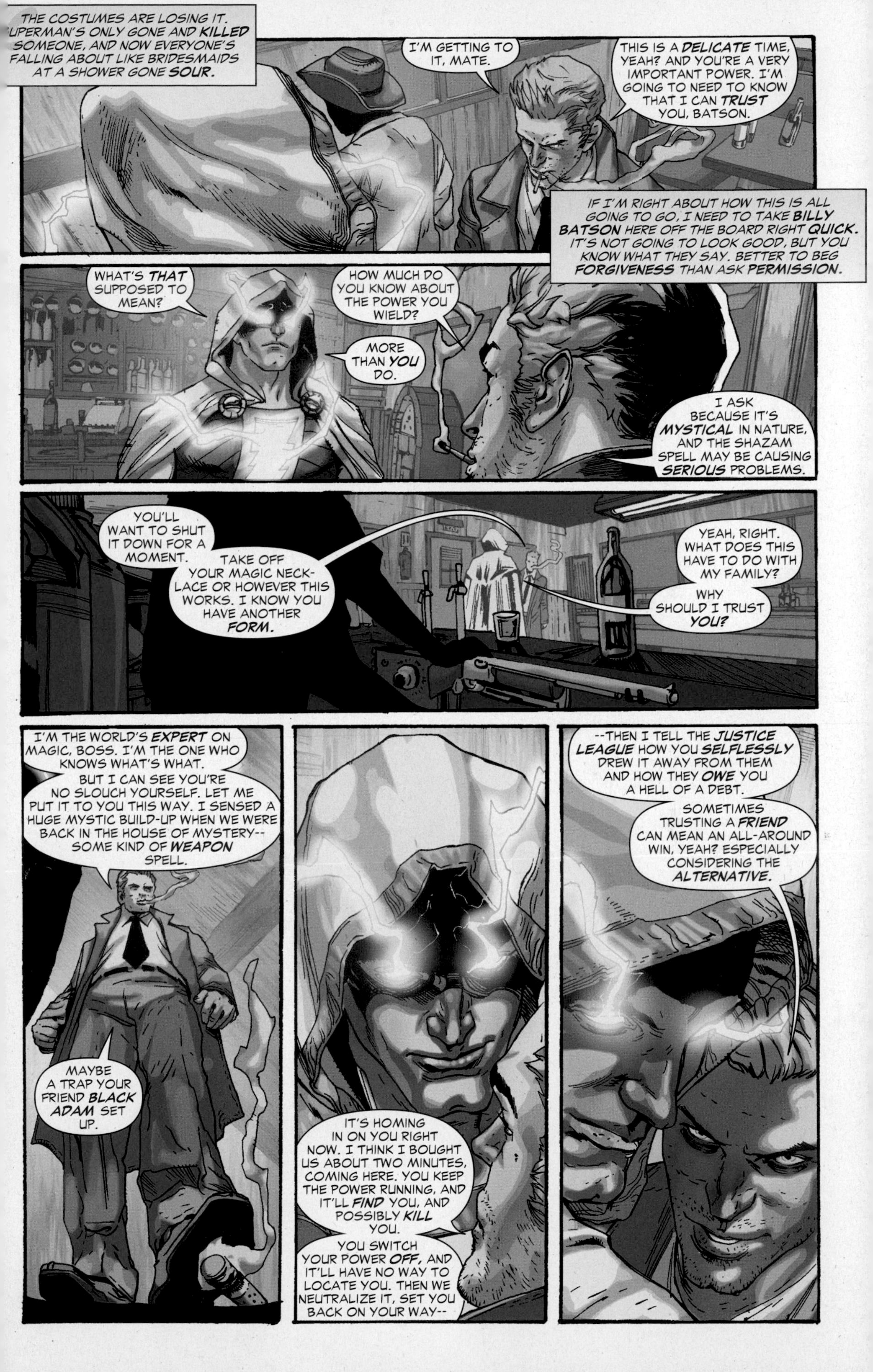
THE COSTUMES ARE LOSING IT. SUPERMAN'S ONLY GONE AND KILLED SOMEONE, AND NOW EVERYONE'S FALLING ABOUT LIKE BRIDESMAIDS AT A SHOWER GONE SOUR.
I'M GETTING TO IT, MATE.
THIS IS A DELICATE TIME, YEAH? AND YOU'RE A VERY IMPORTANT POWER. I'M GOING TO NEED TO KNOW THAT I CAN TRUST YOU, BATSON.
IF I'M RIGHT ABOUT HOW THIS IS ALL GOING TO GO, I NEED TO TAKE BILLY BATSON HERE OFF THE BOARD RIGHT QUICK. IT'S NOT GOING TO LOOK GOOD, BUT YOU KNOW WHAT THEY SAY. BETTER TO BEG FORGIVENESS THAN ASK PERMISSION.
WHAT'S THAT SUPPOSED TO MEAN?
HOW MUCH DO YOU KNOW ABOUT THE POWER YOU WIELD?
MORE THAN YOU DO.
I ASK BECAUSE IT'S MYSTICAL IN NATURE, AND THE SHAZAM SPELL MAY BE CAUSING SERIOUS PROBLEMS.
YOU'LL WANT TO SHUT IT DOWN FOR A MOMENT.
TAKE OFF YOUR MAGIC NECK-LACE OR HOWEVER THIS WORKS. I KNOW YOU HAVE ANOTHER FORM.
YEAH, RIGHT. WHAT DOES THIS HAVE TO DO WITH MY FAMILY?
WHY SHOULD I TRUST YOU?
I'M THE WORLD'S EXPERT ON MAGIC, BOSS. I'M THE ONE WHO KNOWS WHAT'S WHAT.
BUT I CAN SEE YOU'RE NO SLOUCH YOURSELF. LET ME PUT IT TO YOU THIS WAY. I SENSED A HUGE MYSTIC BUILD-UP WHEN WE WERE BACK IN THE HOUSE OF MYSTERY-- SOME KIND OF WEAPON SPELL.
MAYBE A TRAP YOUR FRIEND BLACK ADAM SET UP.
IT'S HOMING IN ON YOU RIGHT NOW. I THINK I BOUGHT US ABOUT TWO MINUTES, COMING HERE. YOU KEEP THE POWER RUNNING, AND IT'LL FIND YOU, AND POSSIBLY KILL YOU.
YOU SWITCH YOUR POWER OFF, AND IT'LL HAVE NO WAY TO LOCATE YOU. THEN WE NEUTRALIZE IT, SET YOU BACK ON YOUR WAY--
--THEN I TELL THE JUSTICE LEAGUE HOW YOU SELFLESSLY DREW IT AWAY FROM THEM AND HOW THEY OWE YOU A HELL OF A DEBT.
SOMETIMES TRUSTING A FRIEND CAN MEAN AN ALL-AROUND WIN, YEAH? ESPECIALLY CONSIDERING THE ALTERNATIVE.

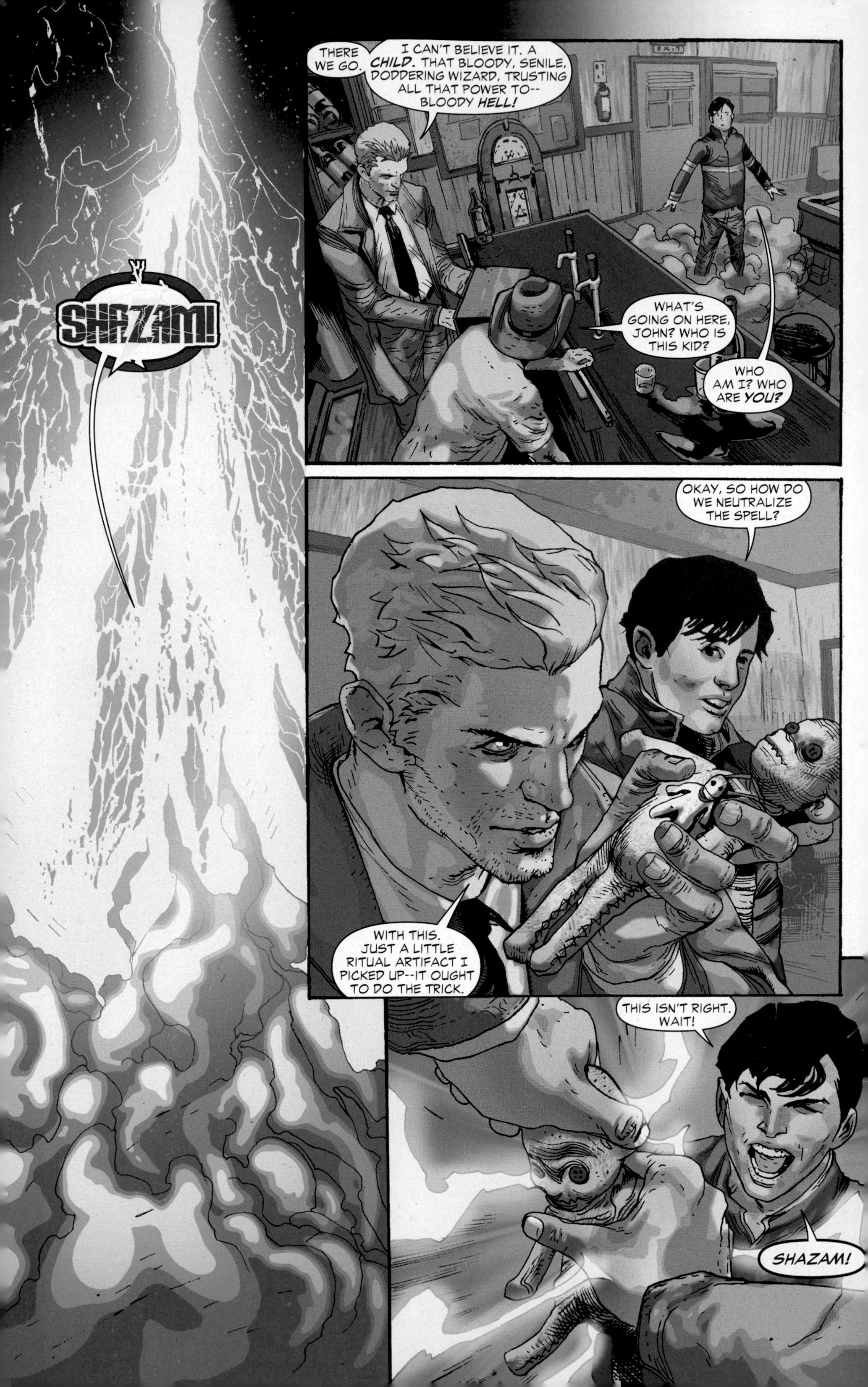
SHAZAM!
THERE WE GO.
I CAN'T BELIEVE IT. A CHILD. THAT BLOODY, SENILE, DODDERING WIZARD, TRUSTING ALL THAT POWER TO-- BLOODY HELL!
WHAT'S GOING ON HERE, JOHN? WHO IS THIS KID?
WHO AM I? WHO ARE YOU?
OKAY, SO HOW DO WE NEUTRALIZE THE SPELL?
WITH THIS. JUST A LITTLE RITUAL ARTIFACT I PICKED UP--IT OUGHT TO DO THE TRICK.
THIS ISN'T RIGHT. WAIT!
SHAZAM!

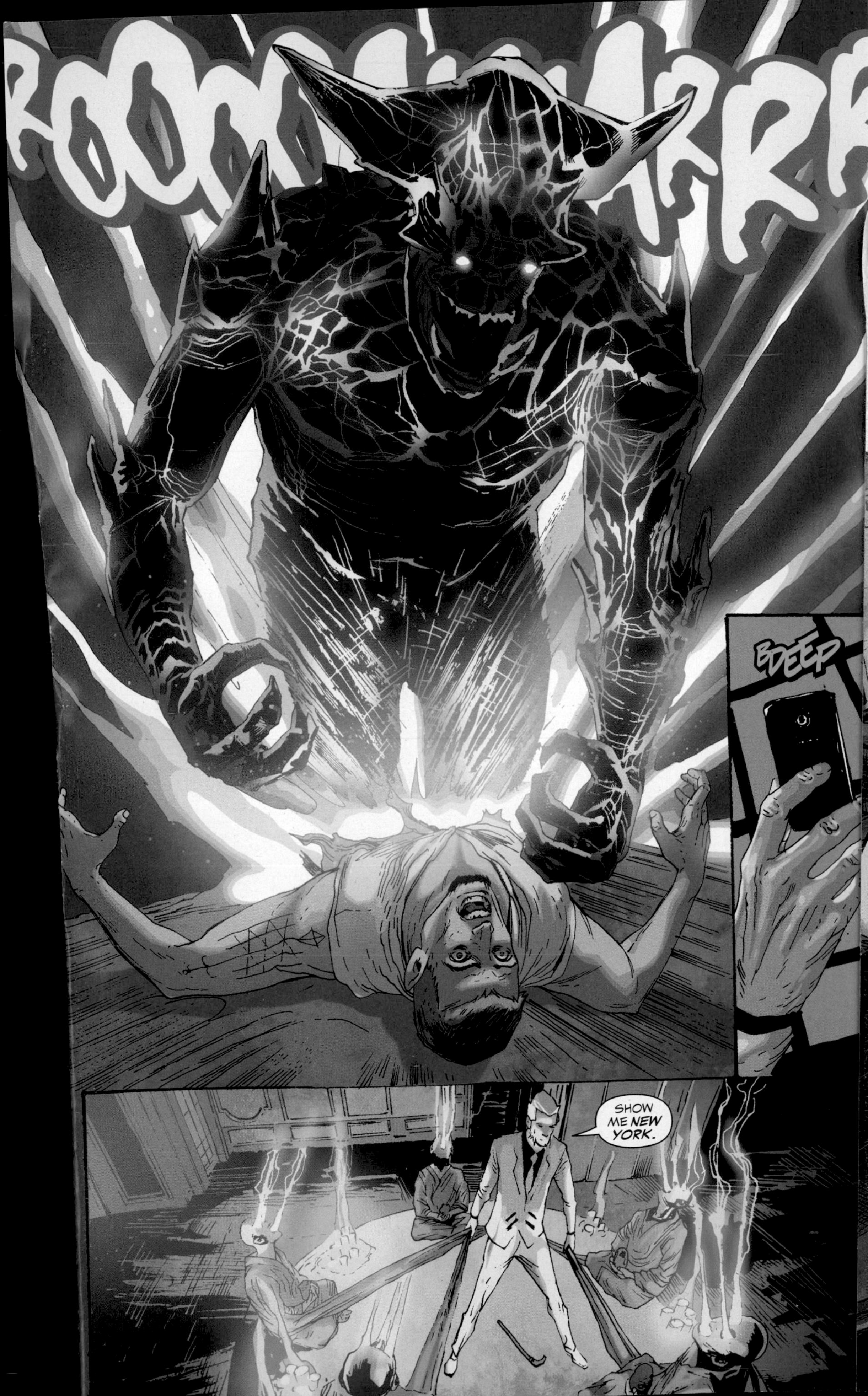
BDEEP
SHOW ME NEW YORK.

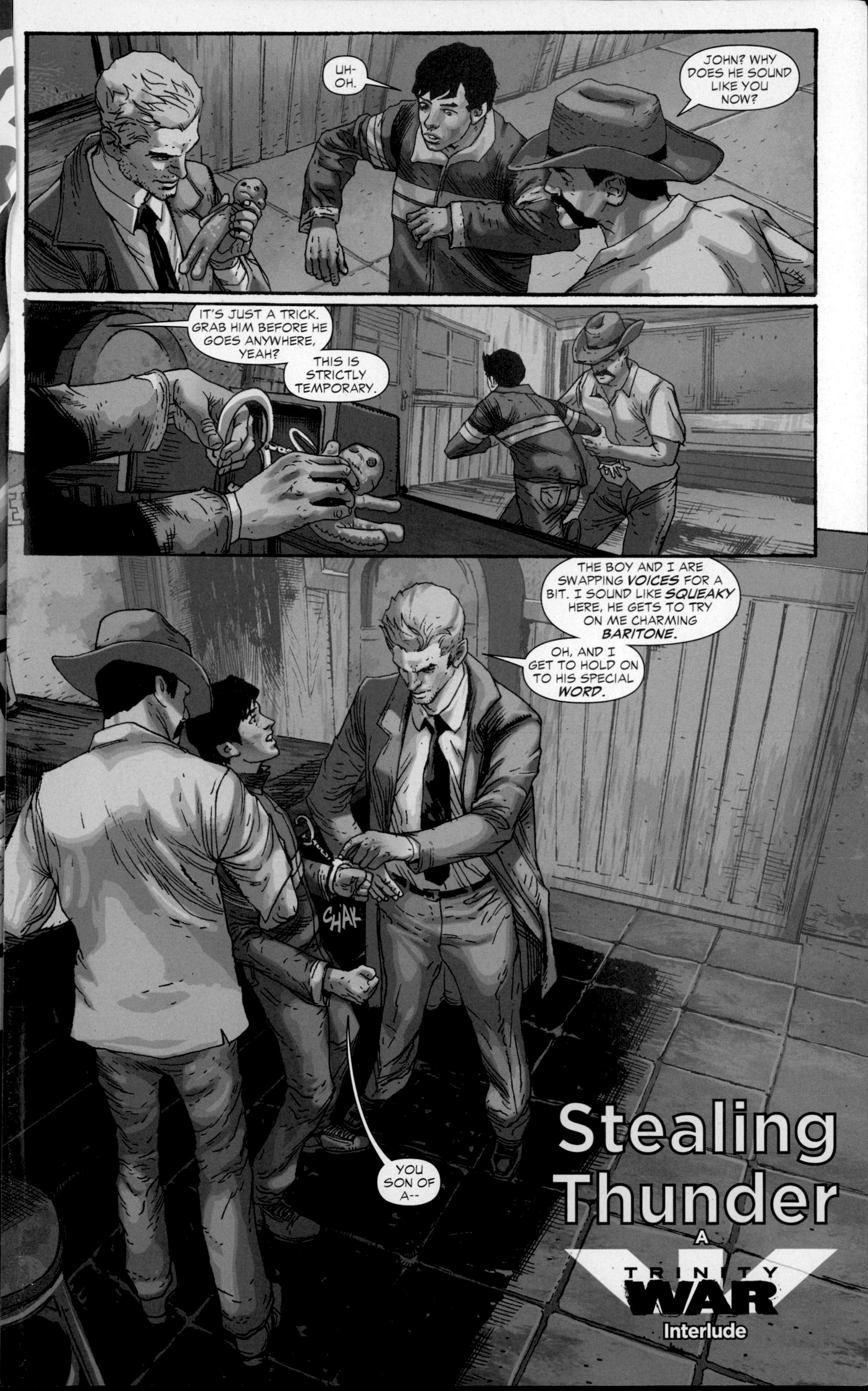
UH-OH.
JOHN? WHY DOES HE SOUND LIKE YOU NOW?
IT'S JUST A TRICK. GRAB HIM BEFORE HE GOES ANYWHERE, YEAH?
THIS IS STRICTLY TEMPORARY.
THE BOY AND I ARE SWAPPING VOICES FOR A BIT. I SOUND LIKE SQUEAKY HERE, HE GETS TO TRY ON ME CHARMING BARITONE.
OH, AND I GET TO HOLD ON TO HIS SPECIAL WORD.
CHAK
YOU SON OF A--
Stealing Thunder
A
TRINITY WAR
Interlude

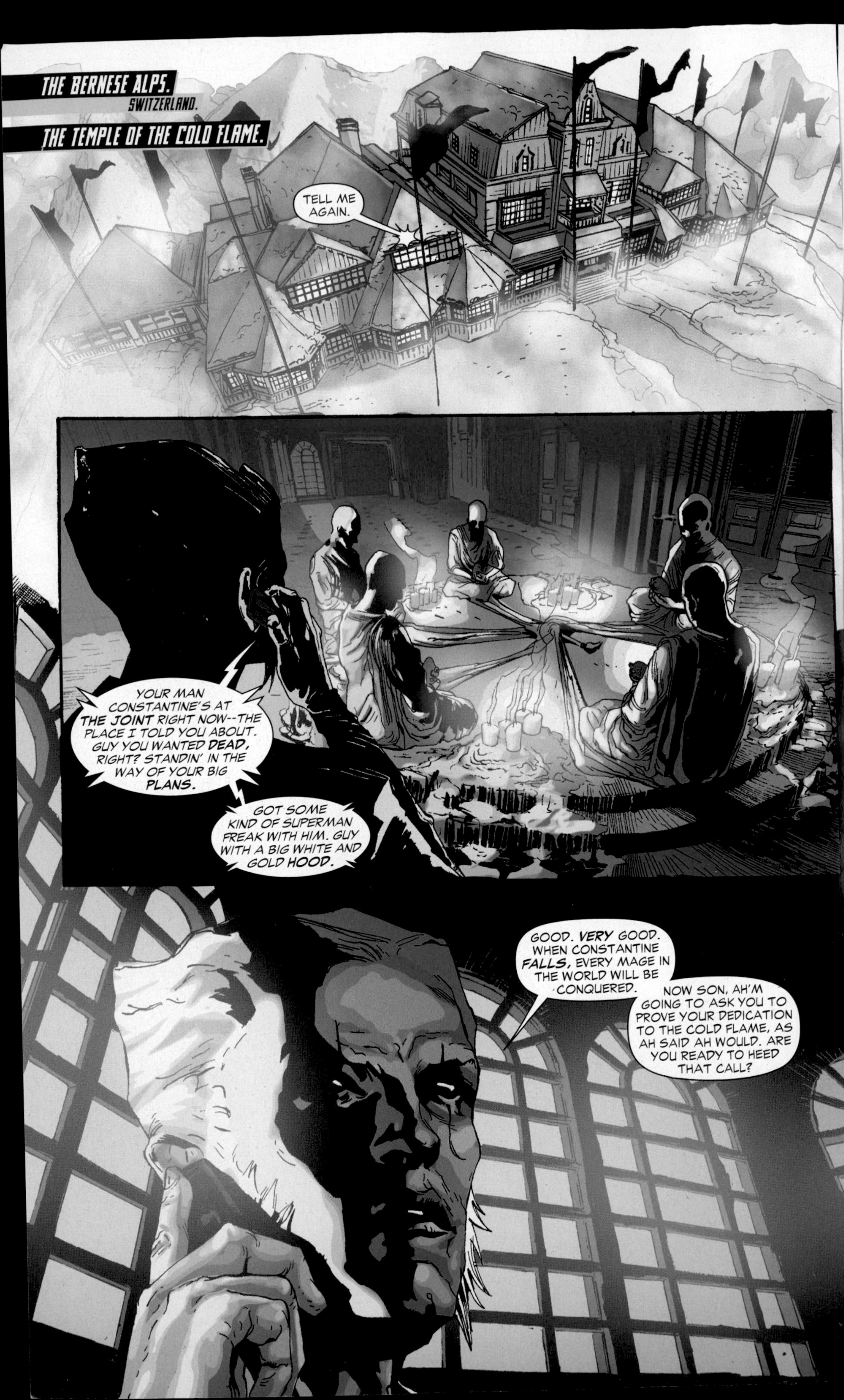
THE BERNESE ALPS.
SWITZERLAND.
THE TEMPLE OF THE COLD FLAME.
TELL ME AGAIN.
YOUR MAN CONSTANTINE'S AT THE JOINT RIGHT NOW--THE PLACE I TOLD YOU ABOUT. GUY YOU WANTED DEAD, RIGHT? STANDIN' IN THE WAY OF YOUR BIG PLANS.
GOT SOME KIND OF SUPERMAN FREAK WITH HIM. GUY WITH A BIG WHITE AND GOLD HOOD.
GOOD. VERY GOOD. WHEN CONSTANTINE FALLS, EVERY MAGE IN THE WORLD WILL BE CONQUERED.
NOW SON, AH'M GOING TO ASK YOU TO PROVE YOUR DEDICATION TO THE COLD FLAME, AS AH SAID AH WOULD. ARE YOU READY TO HEED THAT CALL?

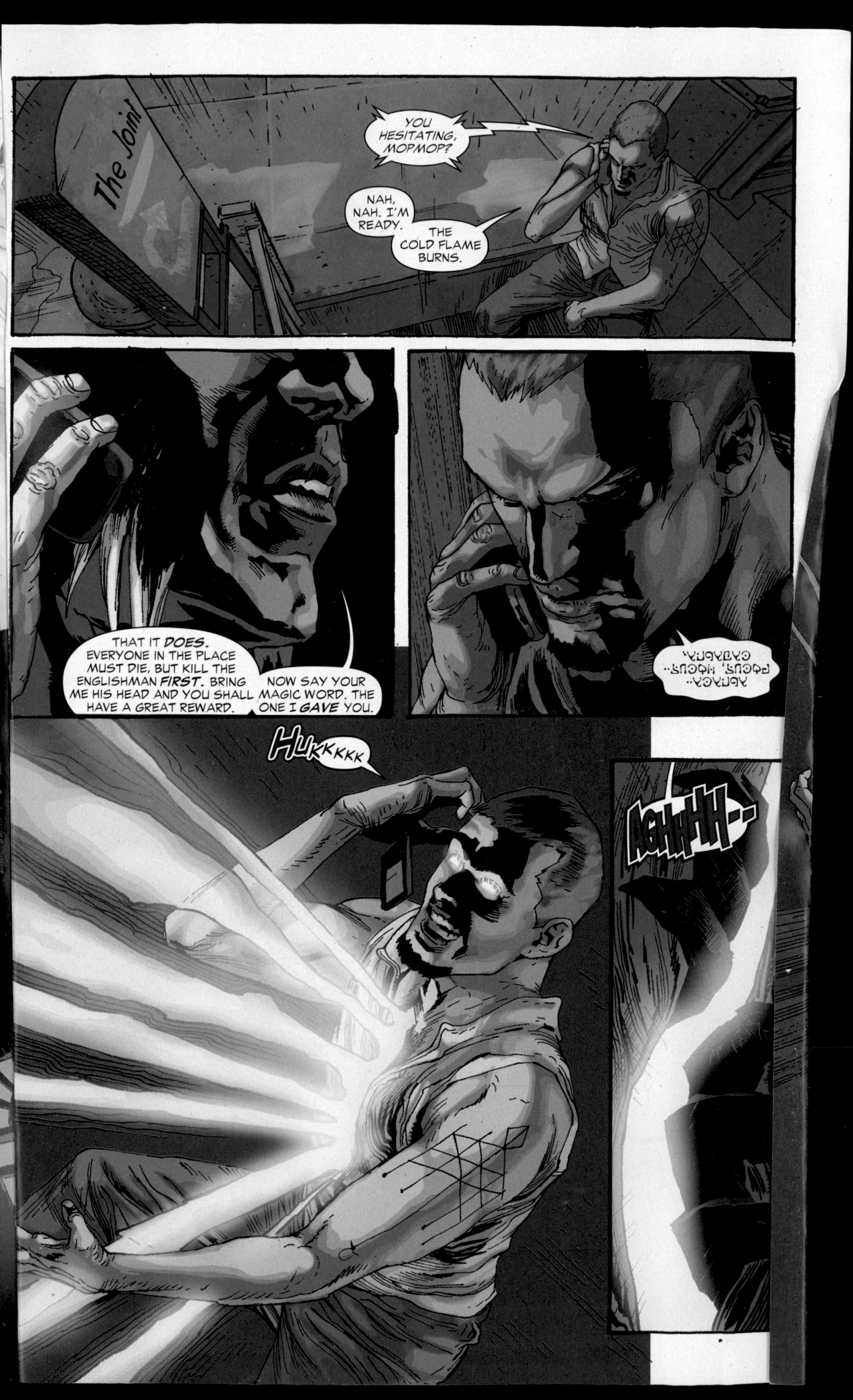
The Joint
YOU HESITATING, MOPMOP?
NAH, NAH. I'M READY.
THE COLD FLAME BURNS.
THAT IT DOES. EVERYONE IN THE PLACE MUST DIE, BUT KILL THE ENGLISHMAN FIRST. BRING ME HIS HEAD AND YOU SHALL HAVE A GREAT REWARD.
NOW SAY YOUR MAGIC WORD. THE ONE I GAVE YOU.
HUKKKKK
AGHHHH--

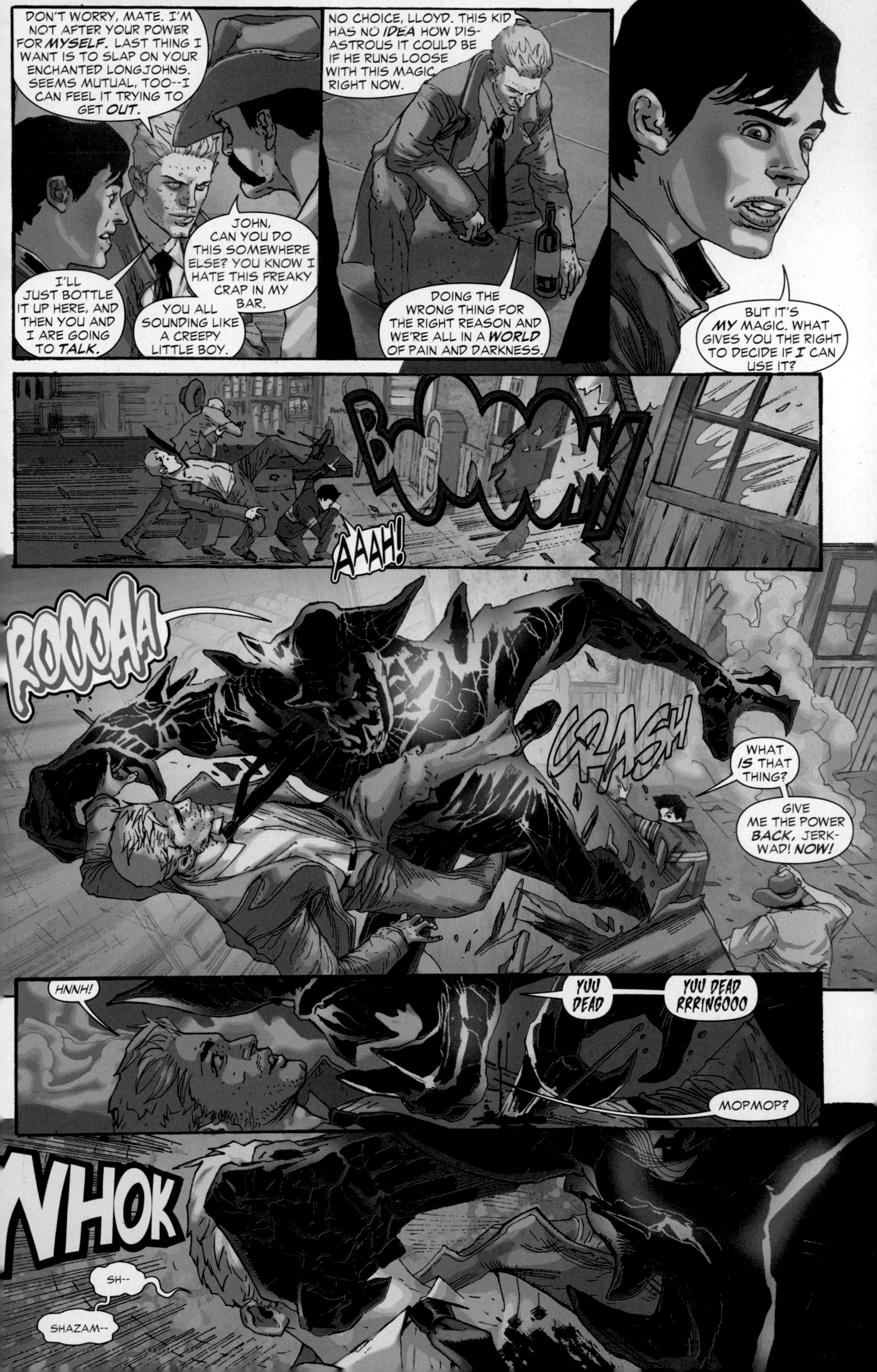
DON'T WORRY, MATE. I'M NOT AFTER YOUR POWER FOR MYSELF. LAST THING I WANT IS TO SLAP ON YOUR ENCHANTED LONGJOHNS. SEEMS MUTUAL, TOO--I CAN FEEL IT TRYING TO GET OUT.
I'LL JUST BOTTLE IT UP HERE, AND THEN YOU AND I ARE GOING TO TALK.
JOHN, CAN YOU DO THIS SOMEWHERE ELSE? YOU KNOW I HATE THIS FREAKY CRAP IN MY BAR.
YOU ALL SOUNDING LIKE A CREEPY LITTLE BOY.
NO CHOICE, LLOYD. THIS KID HAS NO IDEA HOW DISASTROUS IT COULD BE IF HE RUNS LOOSE WITH THIS MAGIC RIGHT NOW.
DOING THE WRONG THING FOR THE RIGHT REASON AND WE'RE ALL IN A WORLD OF PAIN AND DARKNESS.
BUT IT'S MY MAGIC. WHAT GIVES YOU THE RIGHT TO DECIDE IF I CAN USE IT?
BOOOM
AAAH!
ROOOAA
CRASH
WHAT IS THAT THING?
GIVE ME THE POWER BACK, JERK-WAD! NOW!
HNNH!
YUU DEAD
YUU DEAD RRRINGOOO
MOPMOP?
WHOK
SH--
SHAZAM--

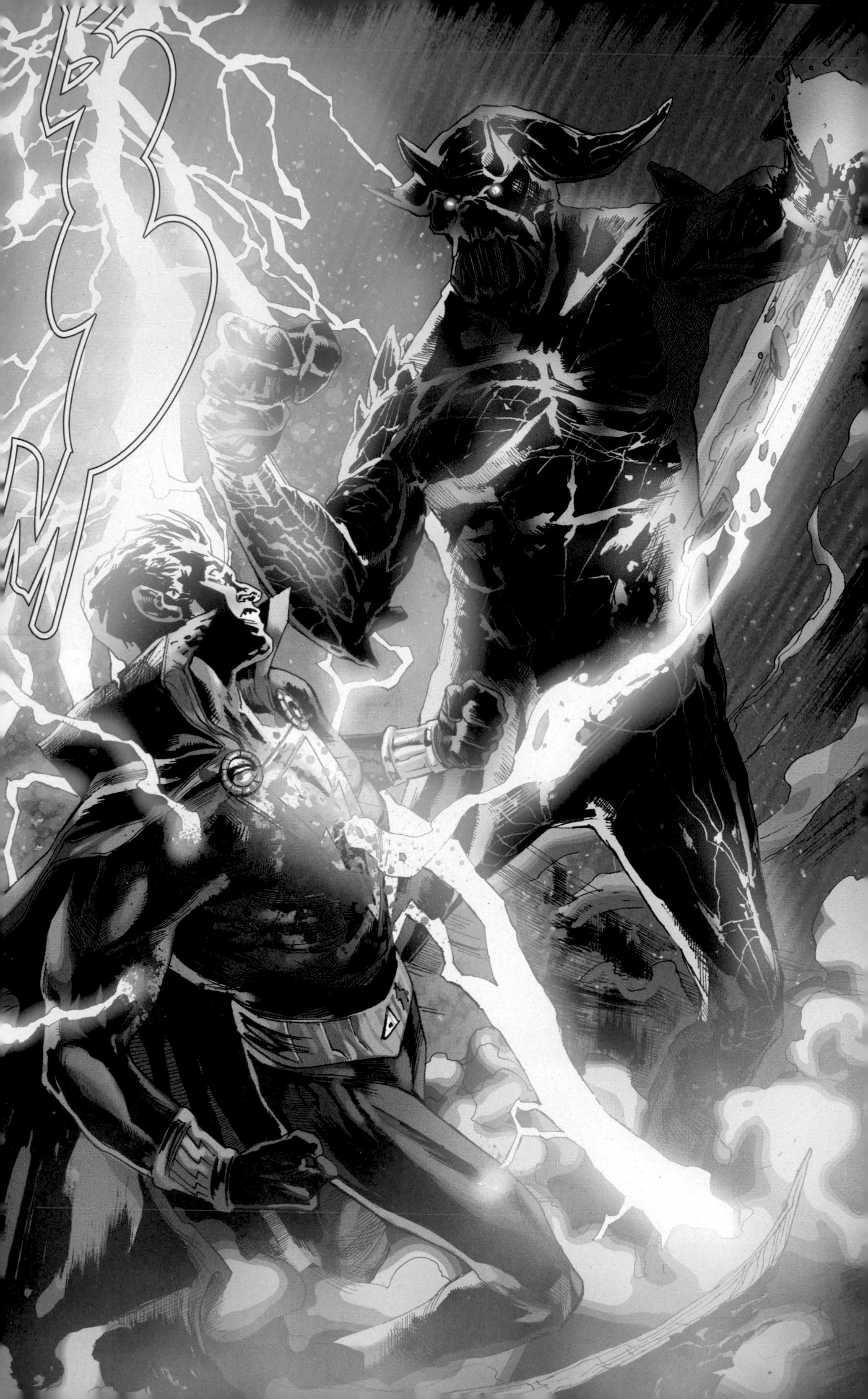

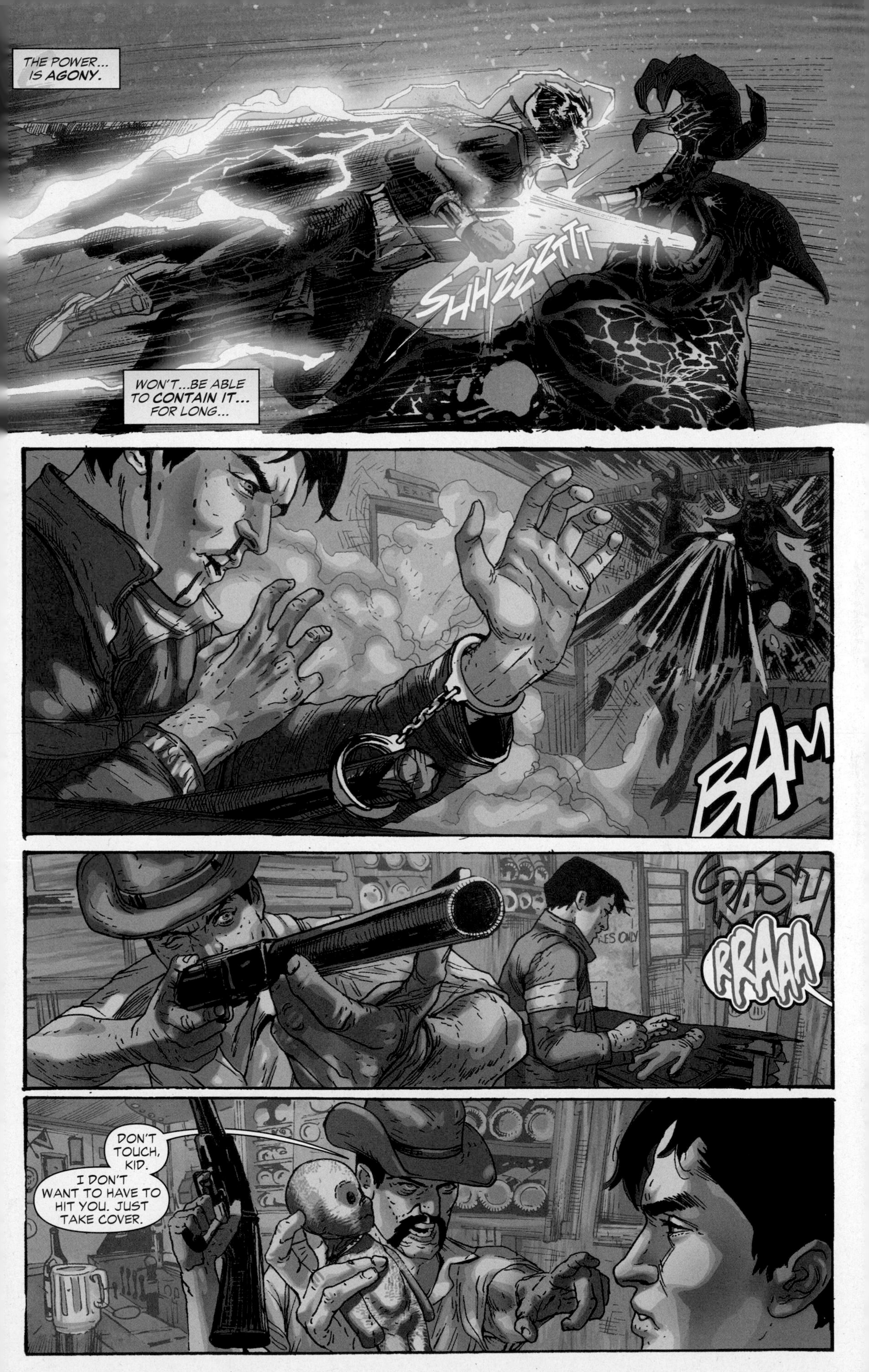
THE POWER... IS AGONY.
SHHZZZTTT
WON'T...BE ABLE TO CONTAIN IT... FOR LONG...
BAM
CRASH
BRAAA
DON'T TOUCH, KID.
I DON'T WANT TO HAVE TO HIT YOU. JUST TAKE COVER.

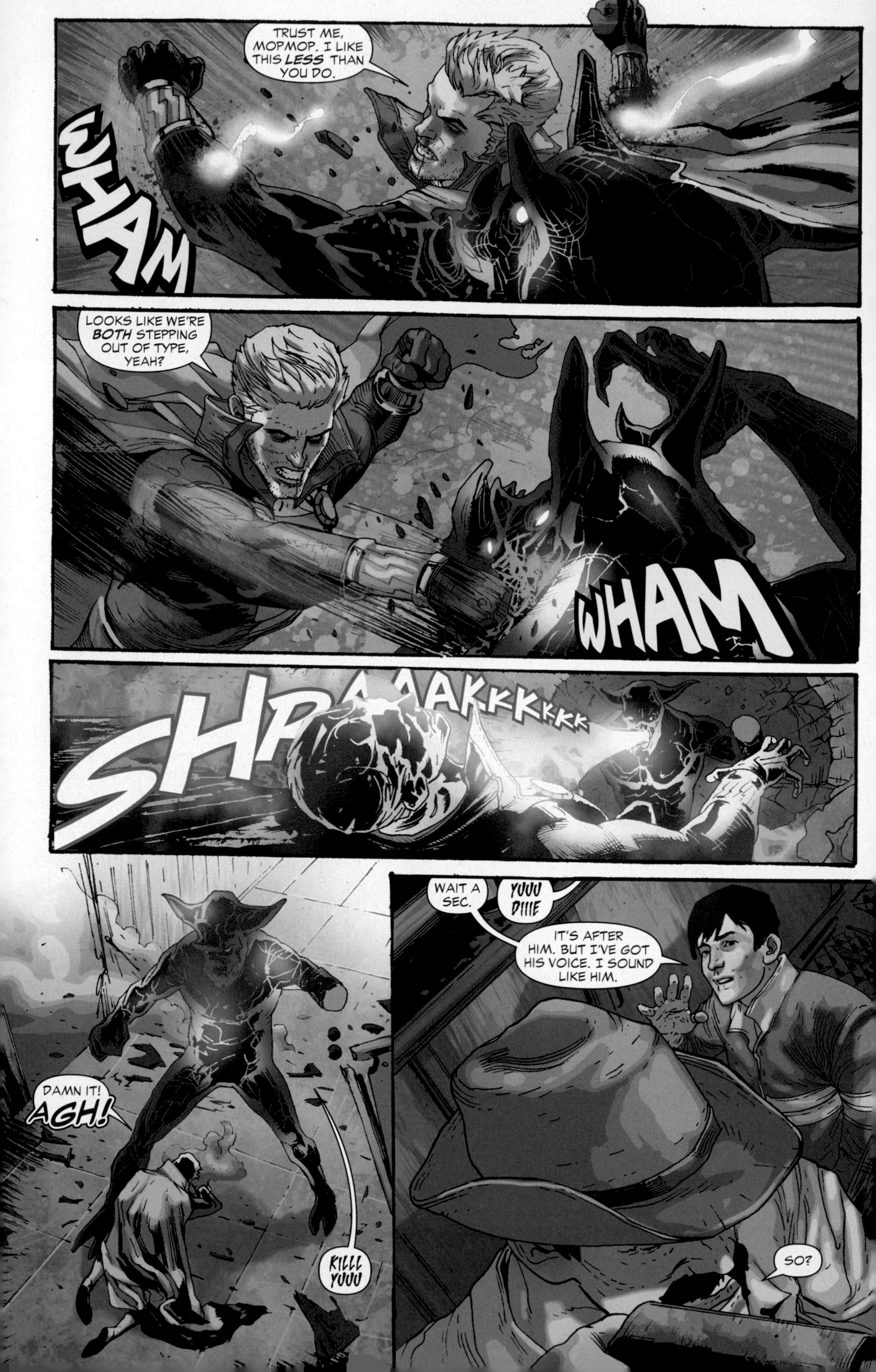
TRUST ME, MOPMOP. I LIKE THIS LESS THAN YOU DO.
WHAM
LOOKS LIKE WE'RE BOTH STEPPING OUT OF TYPE, YEAH?
WHAM
SHRAAAKKKKKK
DAMN IT! AGH!
KILLL YUUU
WAIT A SEC.
YUUU DIIIE
IT'S AFTER HIM. BUT I'VE GOT HIS VOICE. I SOUND LIKE HIM.
SO?

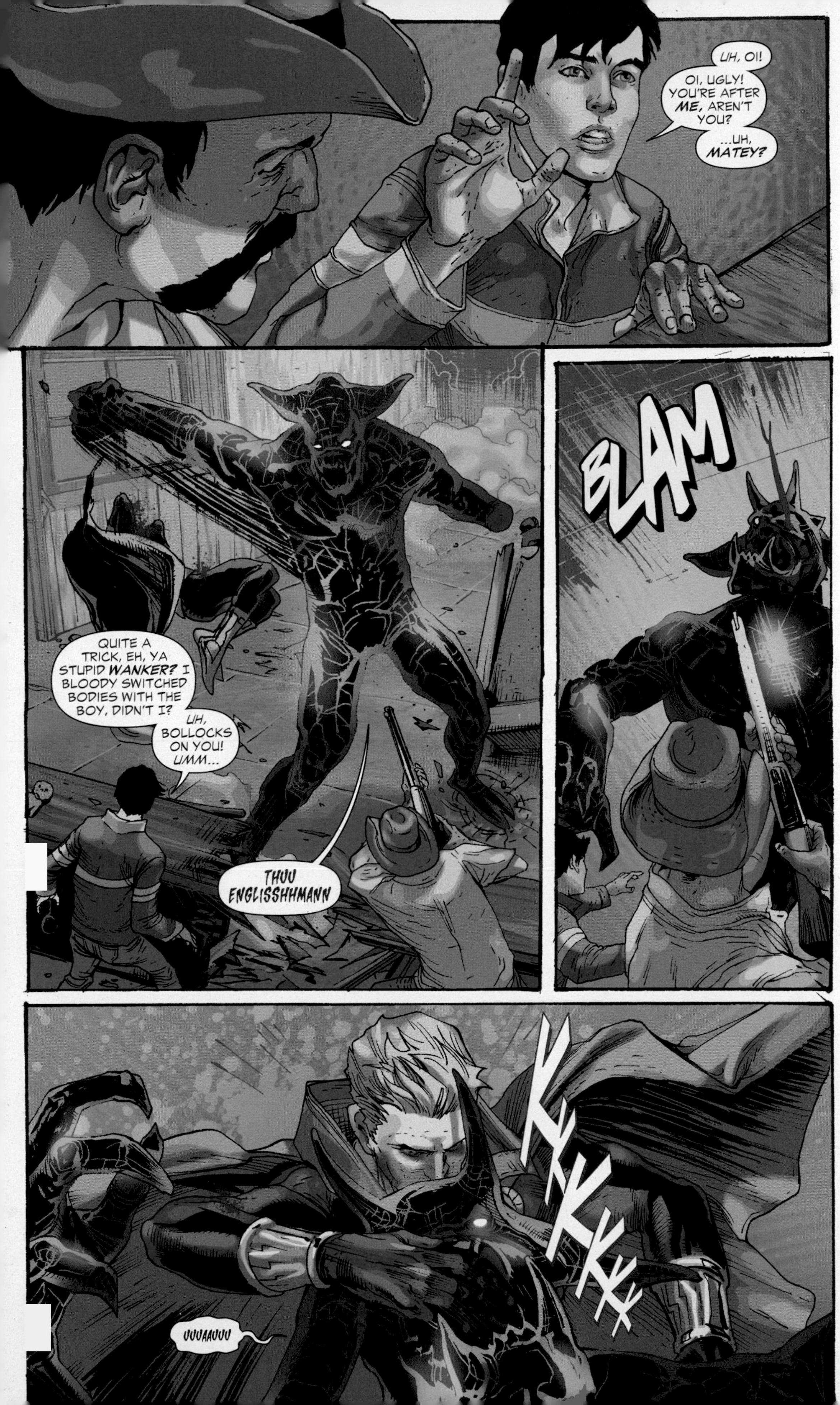
UH, OI!
OI, UGLY! YOU'RE AFTER ME, AREN'T YOU?
...UH, MATEY?
QUITE A TRICK, EH, YA STUPID WANKER? I BLOODY SWITCHED BODIES WITH THE BOY, DIDN'T I?
UH, BOLLOCKS ON YOU! UMM...
THUU ENGLISSHHMANN
BLAM
UUUAAUUU

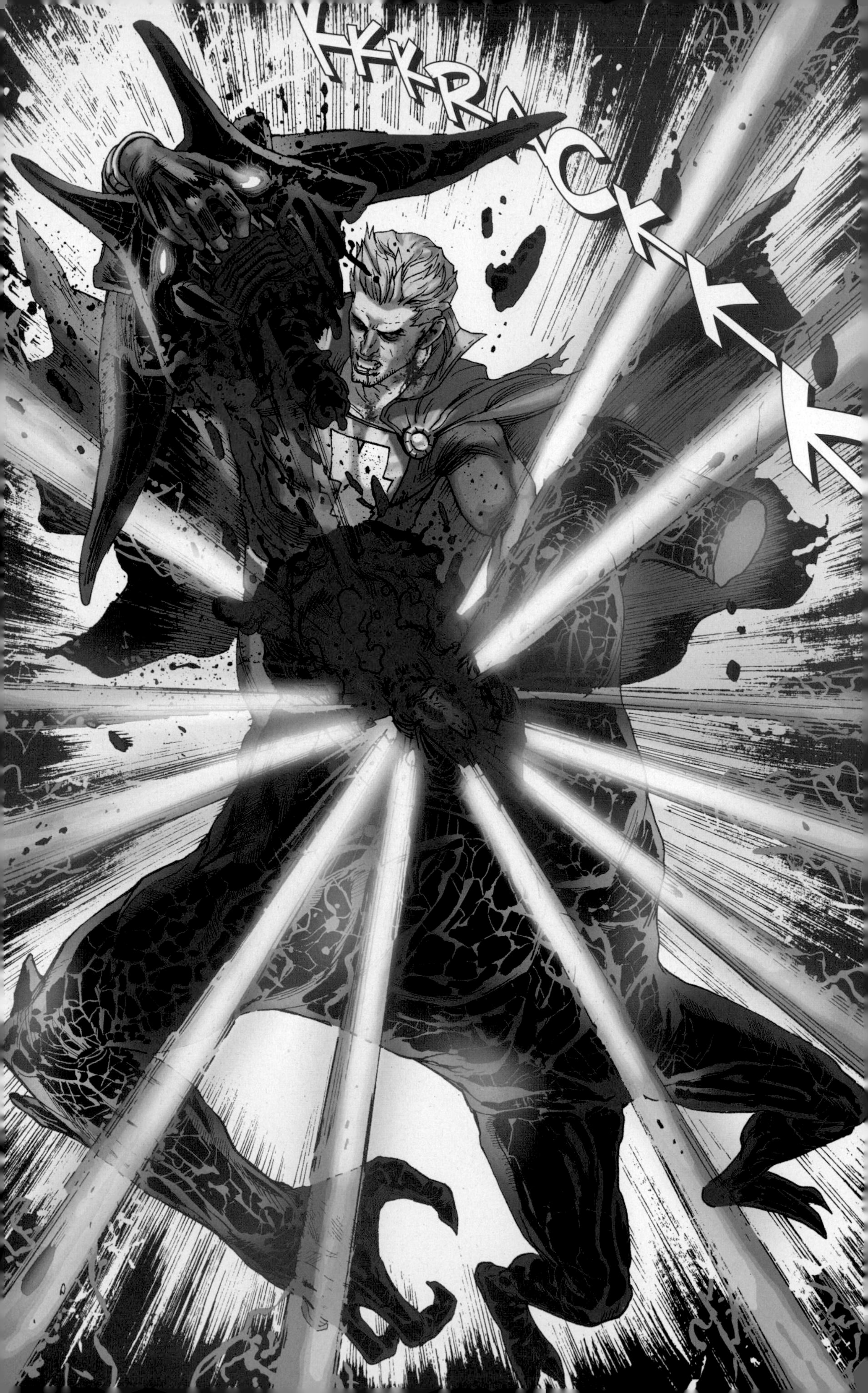

KKRACKKKK

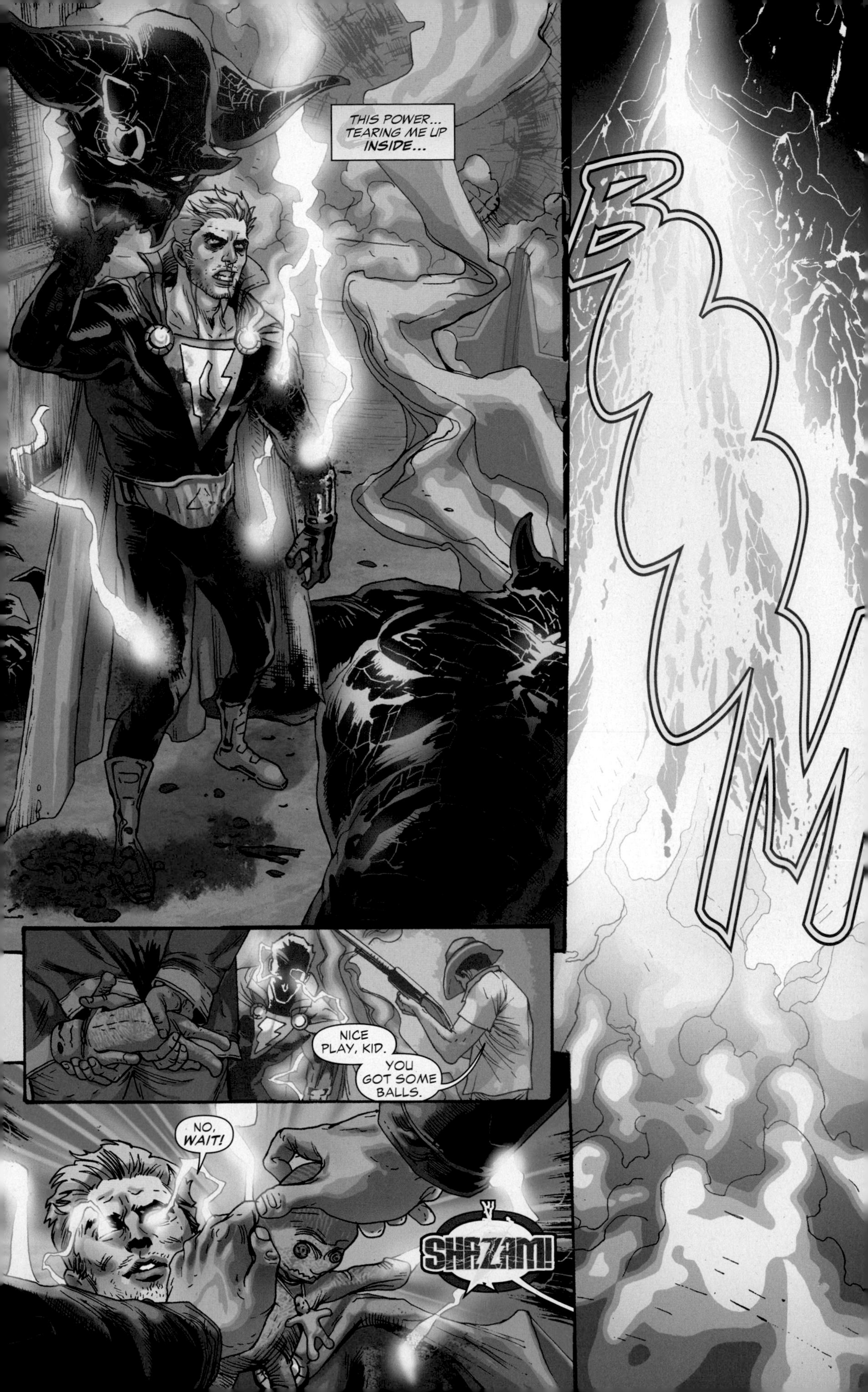
THIS POWER... TEARING ME UP INSIDE...
BLUMM
NICE PLAY, KID.
YOU GOT SOME BALLS.
NO, WAIT!
SHAZAM!

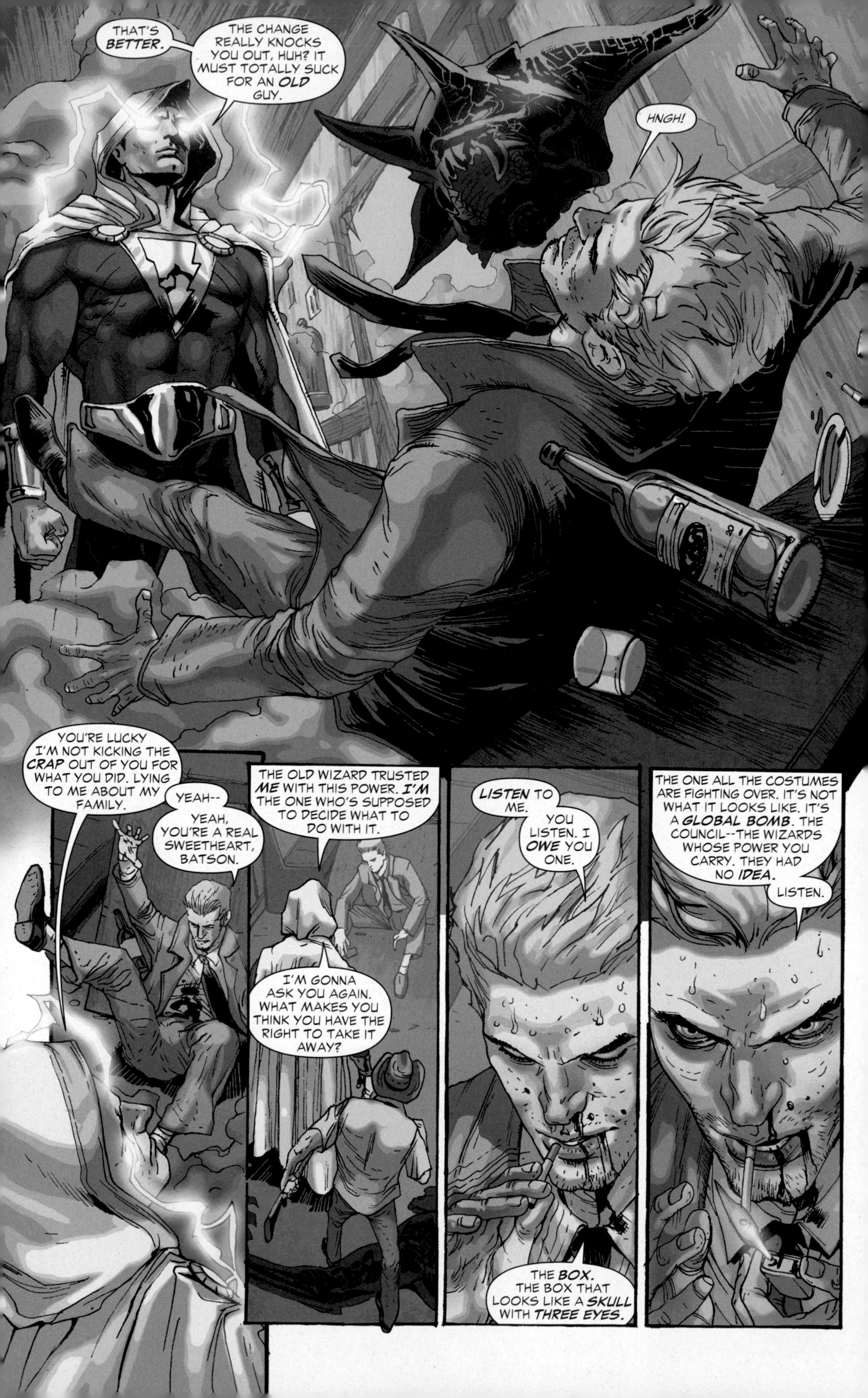
THAT'S BETTER.
THE CHANGE REALLY KNOCKS YOU OUT, HUH? IT MUST TOTALLY SUCK FOR AN OLD GUY.
HNGH!
YOU'RE LUCKY I'M NOT KICKING THE CRAP OUT OF YOU FOR WHAT YOU DID. LYING TO ME ABOUT MY FAMILY.
YEAH--
YEAH, YOU'RE A REAL SWEETHEART, BATSON.
THE OLD WIZARD TRUSTED ME WITH THIS POWER. I'M THE ONE WHO'S SUPPOSED TO DECIDE WHAT TO DO WITH IT.
I'M GONNA ASK YOU AGAIN. WHAT MAKES YOU THINK YOU HAVE THE RIGHT TO TAKE IT AWAY?
LISTEN TO ME.
YOU LISTEN. I OWE YOU ONE.
THE BOX. THE BOX THAT LOOKS LIKE A SKULL WITH THREE EYES.
THE ONE ALL THE COSTUMES ARE FIGHTING OVER. IT'S NOT WHAT IT LOOKS LIKE. IT'S A GLOBAL BOMB. THE COUNCIL--THE WIZARDS WHOSE POWER YOU CARRY. THEY HAD NO IDEA.
LISTEN.

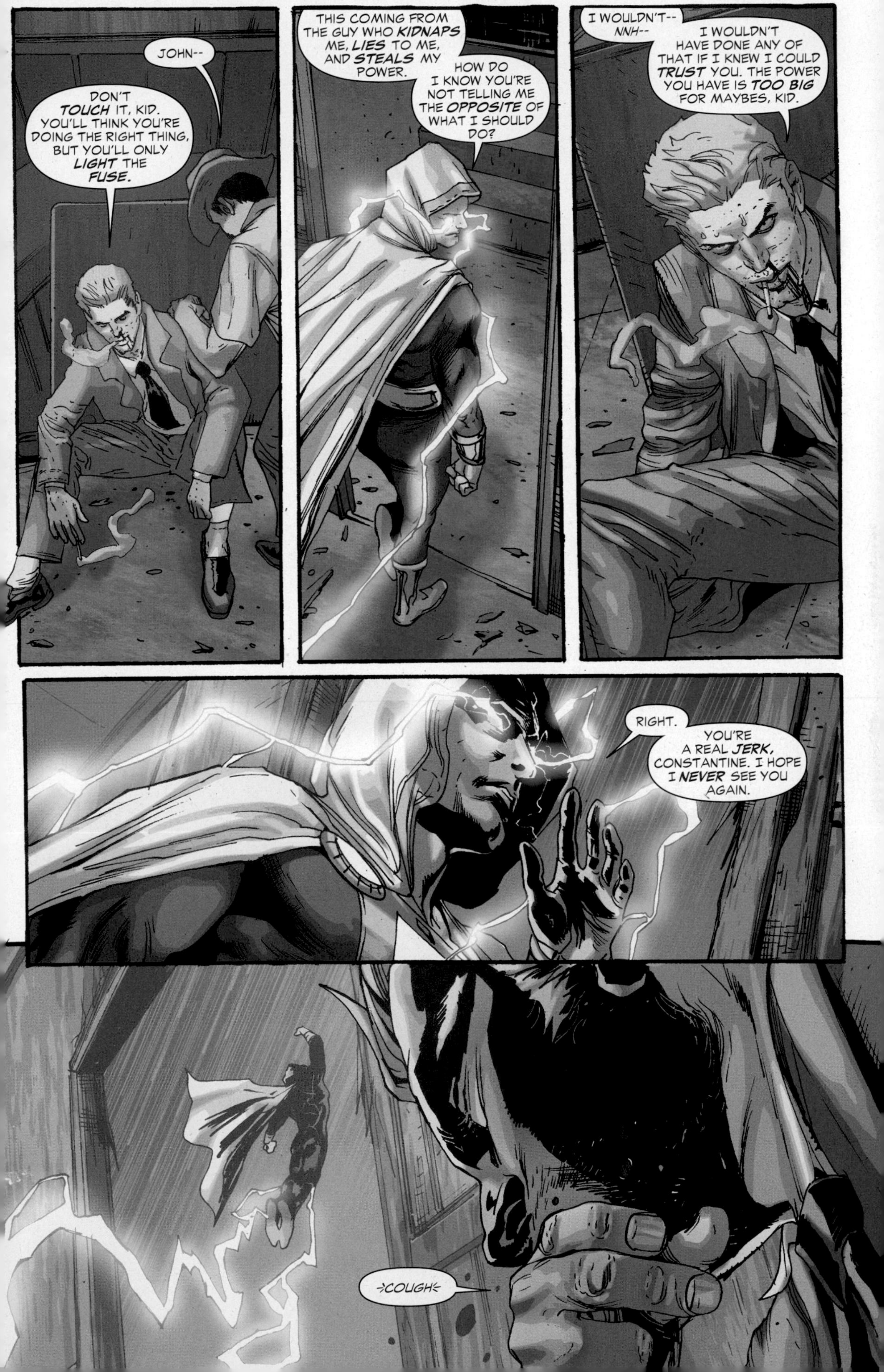
JOHN--
DON'T TOUCH IT, KID. YOU'LL THINK YOU'RE DOING THE RIGHT THING, BUT YOU'LL ONLY LIGHT THE FUSE.
THIS COMING FROM THE GUY WHO KIDNAPS ME, LIES TO ME, AND STEALS MY POWER.
HOW DO I KNOW YOU'RE NOT TELLING ME THE OPPOSITE OF WHAT I SHOULD DO?
I WOULDN'T-- NNH--
I WOULDN'T HAVE DONE ANY OF THAT IF I KNEW I COULD TRUST YOU. THE POWER YOU HAVE IS TOO BIG FOR MAYBES, KID.
RIGHT.
YOU'RE A REAL JERK, CONSTANTINE. I HOPE I NEVER SEE YOU AGAIN.
COUGH

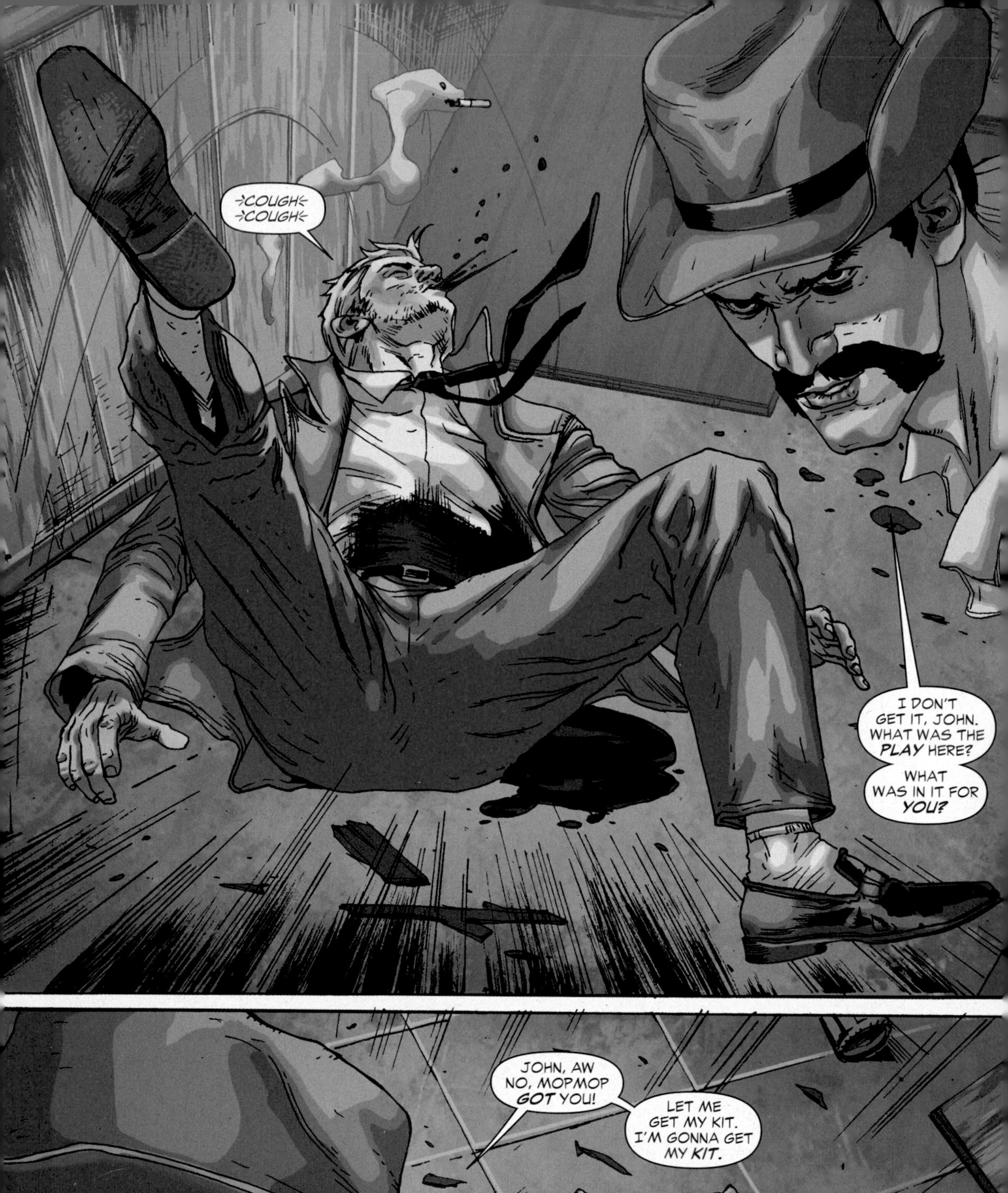

COUGH COUGH
I DON'T GET IT, JOHN. WHAT WAS THE PLAY HERE?
WHAT WAS IN IT FOR YOU?

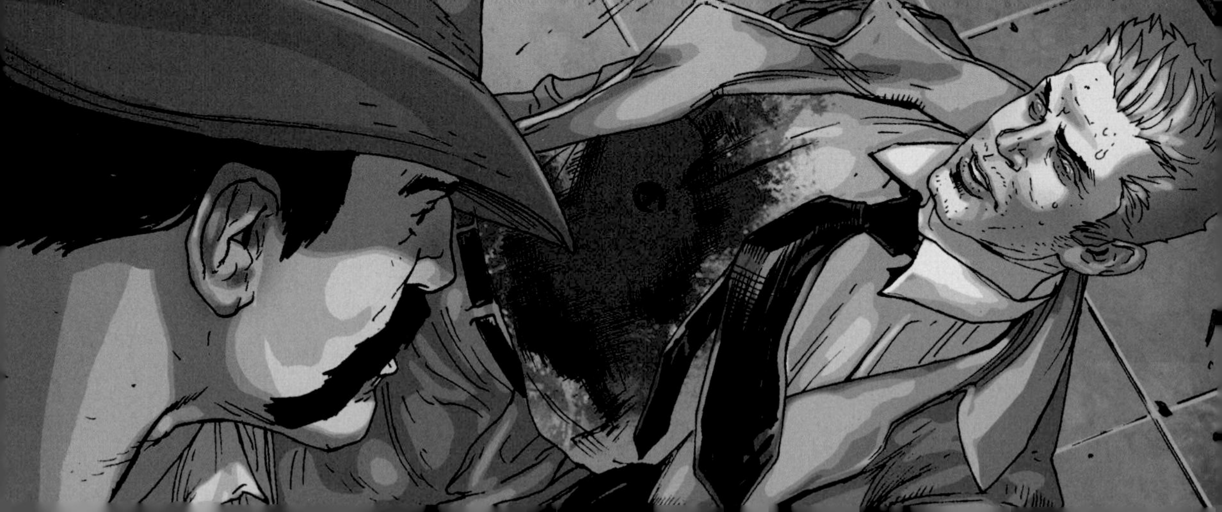

JOHN, AW NO, MOPMOP GOT YOU!
LET ME GET MY KIT. I'M GONNA GET MY KIT.

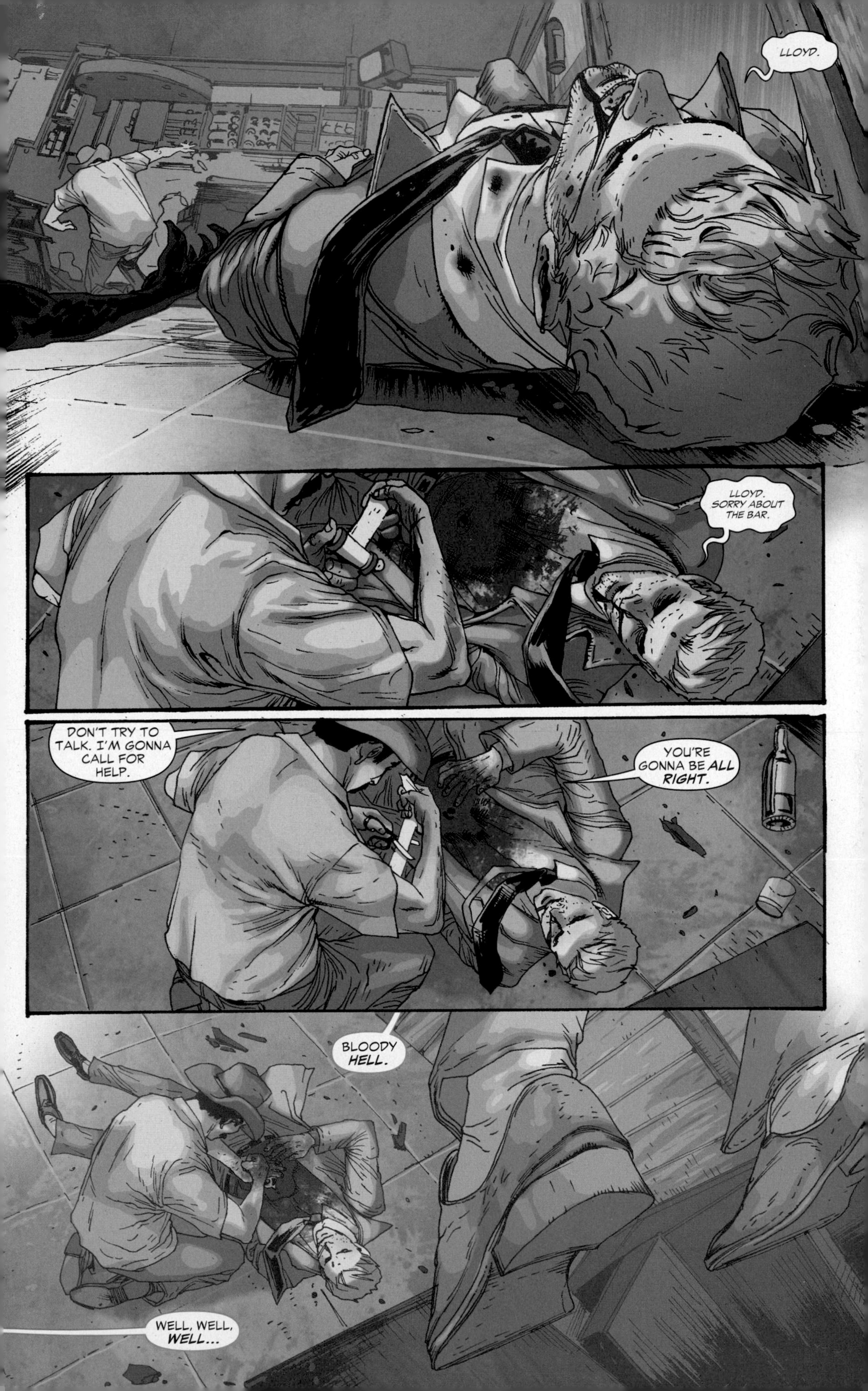
LLOYD.
LLOYD. SORRY ABOUT THE BAR.
DON'T TRY TO TALK. I'M GONNA CALL FOR HELP.
YOU'RE GONNA BE ALL RIGHT.
BLOODY HELL.
WELL, WELL, WELL...

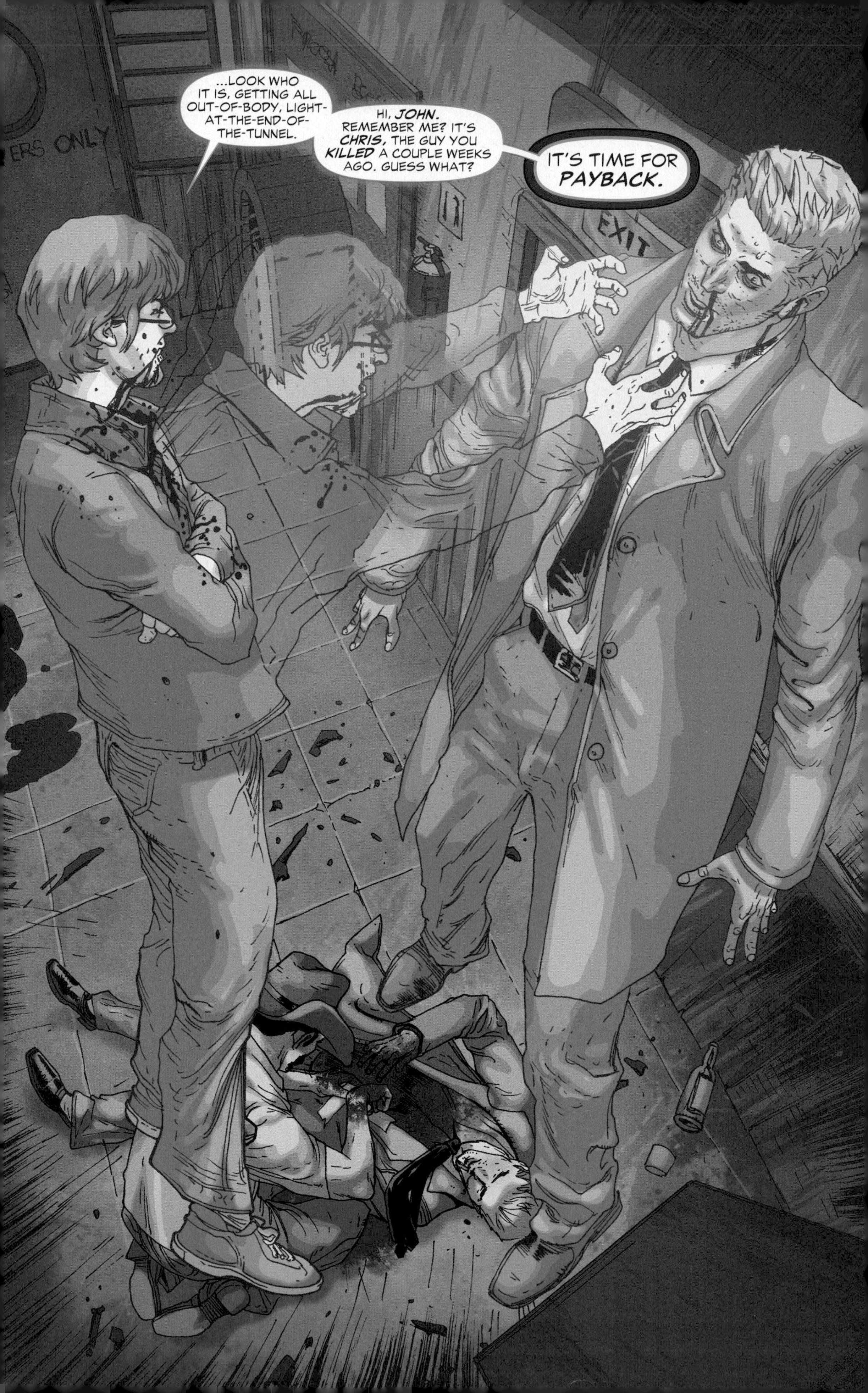

...LOOK WHO IT IS, GETTING ALL OUT-OF-BODY, LIGHT-AT-THE-END-OF-THE-TUNNEL.
HI, JOHN. REMEMBER ME? IT'S CHRIS, THE GUY YOU KILLED A COUPLE WEEKS AGO. GUESS WHAT?
IT'S TIME FOR PAYBACK.
ERS ONLY
EXIT

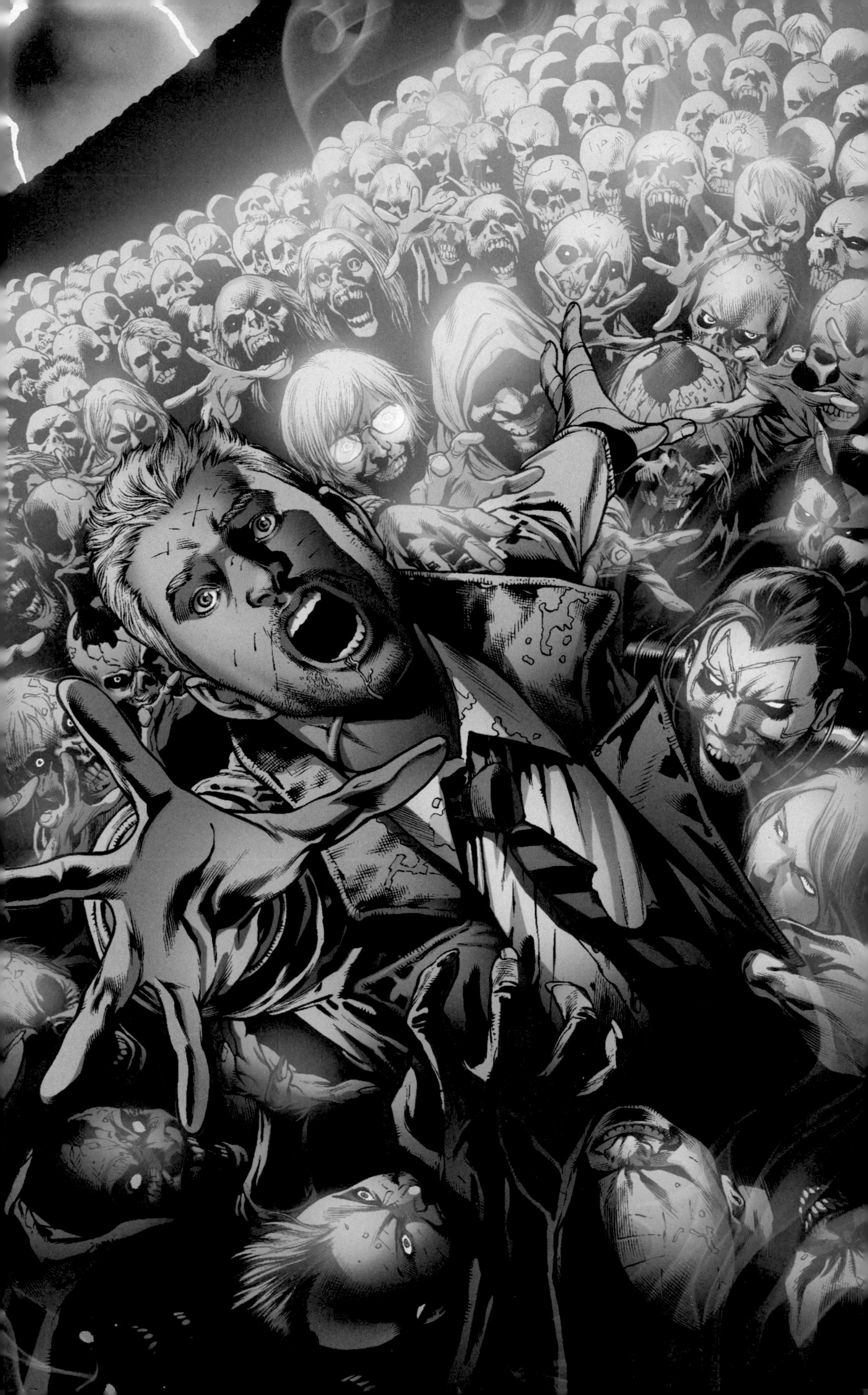

METAMORPHOSIS IN EXTREMIS

RAY FAWKES writer **RENATO GUEDES** artist cover art by EDDY BARROWS, EBER FERREIRA & WIL QUINTANA

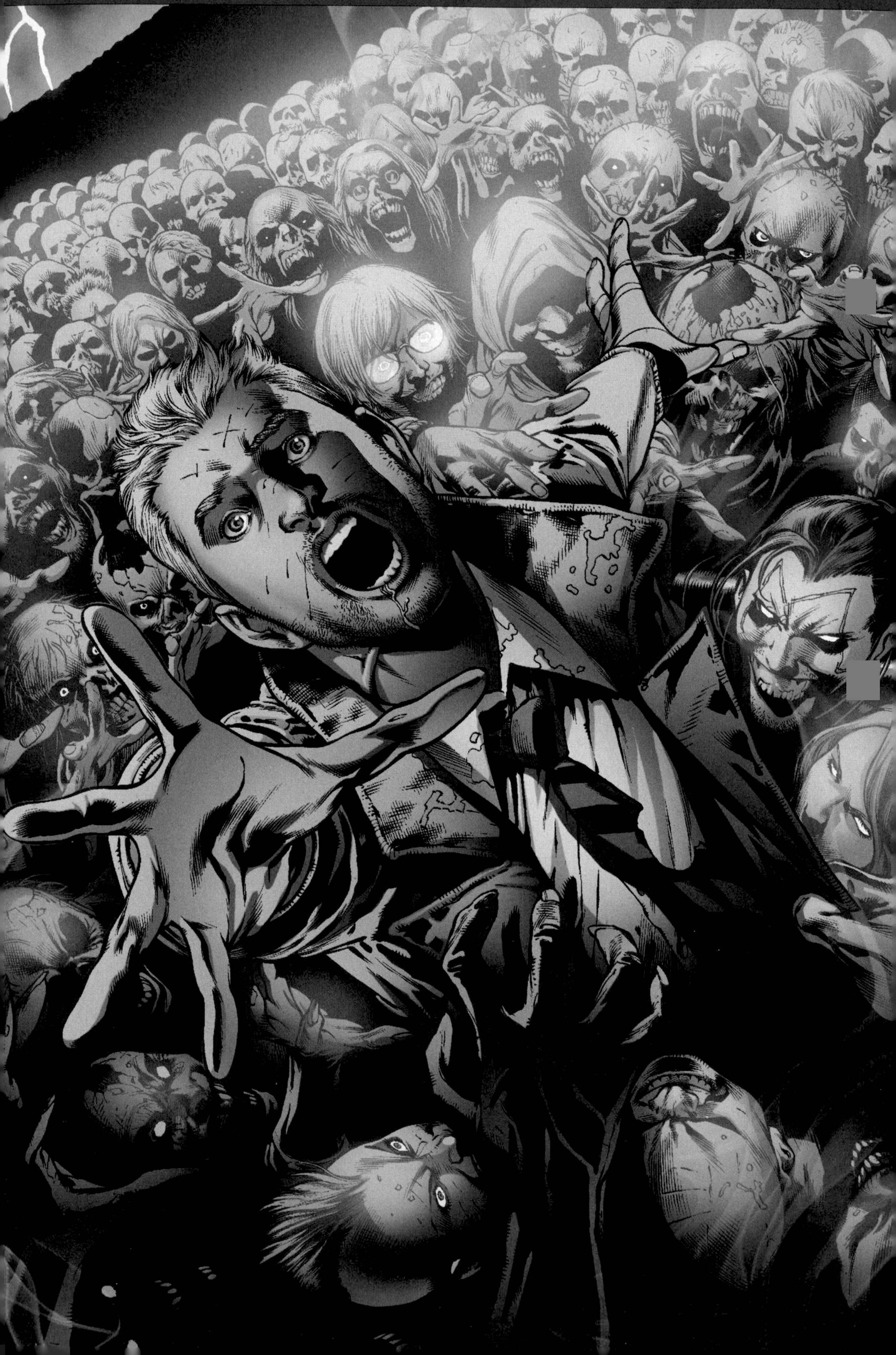

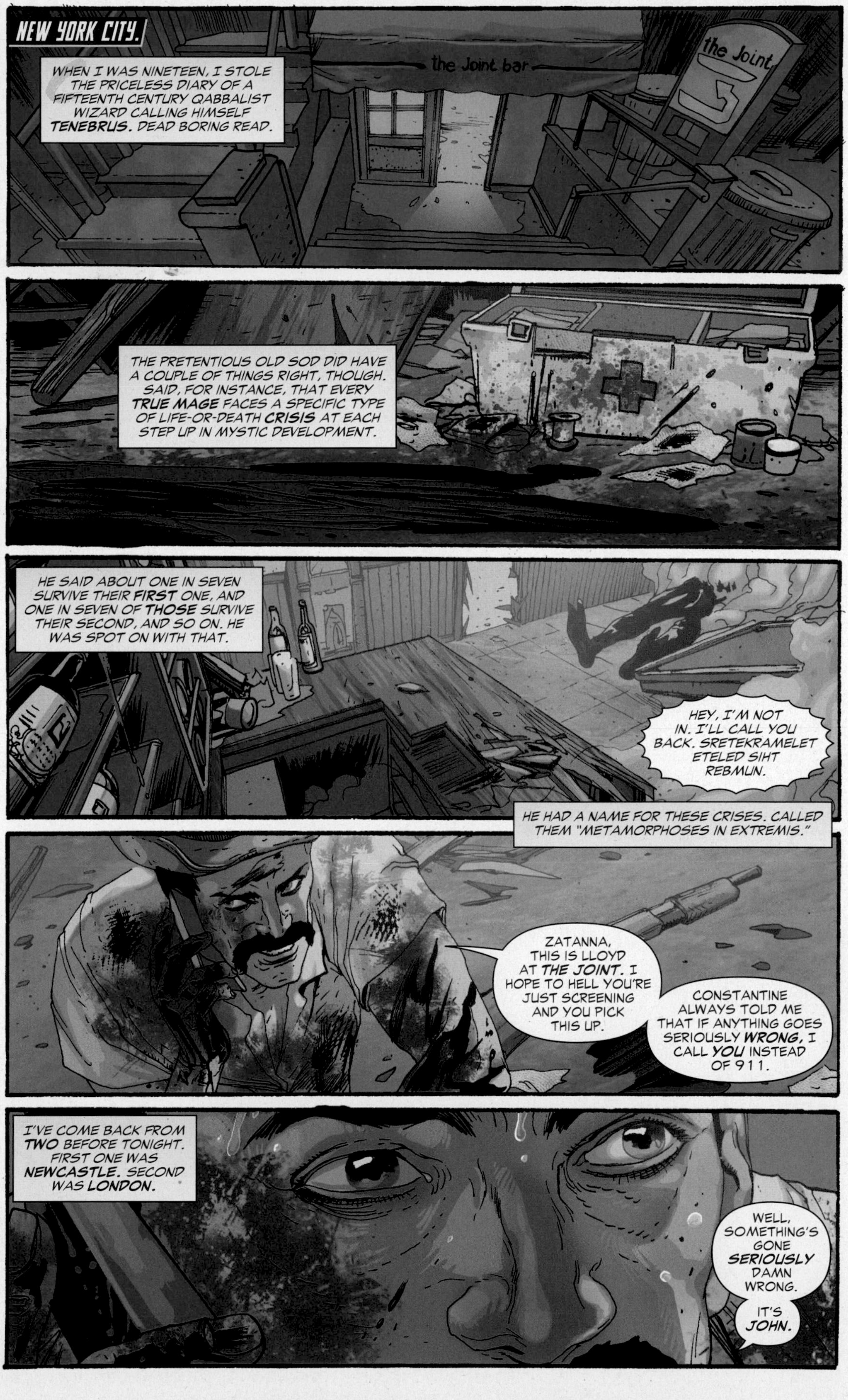
NEW YORK CITY.
WHEN I WAS NINETEEN, I STOLE THE PRICELESS DIARY OF A FIFTEENTH CENTURY QABBALIST WIZARD CALLING HIMSELF TENEBRUS. DEAD BORING READ.
the Joint bar
the Joint
THE PRETENTIOUS OLD SOD DID HAVE A COUPLE OF THINGS RIGHT, THOUGH. SAID, FOR INSTANCE, THAT EVERY TRUE MAGE FACES A SPECIFIC TYPE OF LIFE-OR-DEATH CRISIS AT EACH STEP UP IN MYSTIC DEVELOPMENT.
HE SAID ABOUT ONE IN SEVEN SURVIVE THEIR FIRST ONE, AND ONE IN SEVEN OF THOSE SURVIVE THEIR SECOND, AND SO ON. HE WAS SPOT ON WITH THAT.
HEY, I'M NOT IN. I'LL CALL YOU BACK. SRETEKRAMELET ETELED SIHT REBMUN.
HE HAD A NAME FOR THESE CRISES. CALLED THEM "METAMORPHOSES IN EXTREMIS."
ZATANNA, THIS IS LLOYD AT THE JOINT. I HOPE TO HELL YOU'RE JUST SCREENING AND YOU PICK THIS UP.
CONSTANTINE ALWAYS TOLD ME THAT IF ANYTHING GOES SERIOUSLY WRONG, I CALL YOU INSTEAD OF 911.
I'VE COME BACK FROM TWO BEFORE TONIGHT. FIRST ONE WAS NEWCASTLE. SECOND WAS LONDON.
WELL, SOMETHING'S GONE SERIOUSLY DAMN WRONG.
IT'S JOHN.

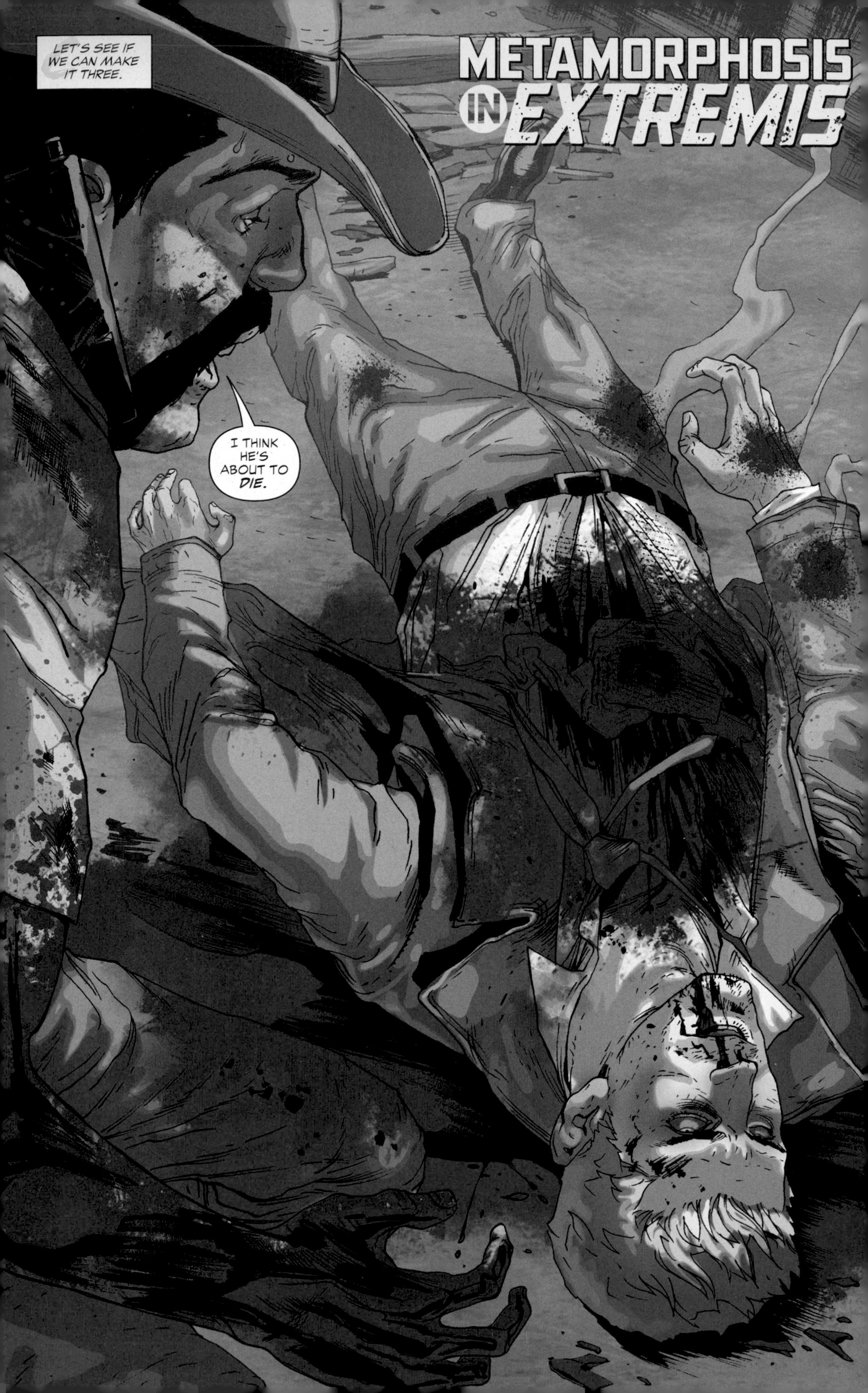
LET'S SEE IF WE CAN MAKE IT THREE.
METAMORPHOSIS IN EXTREMIS
I THINK HE'S ABOUT TO DIE.

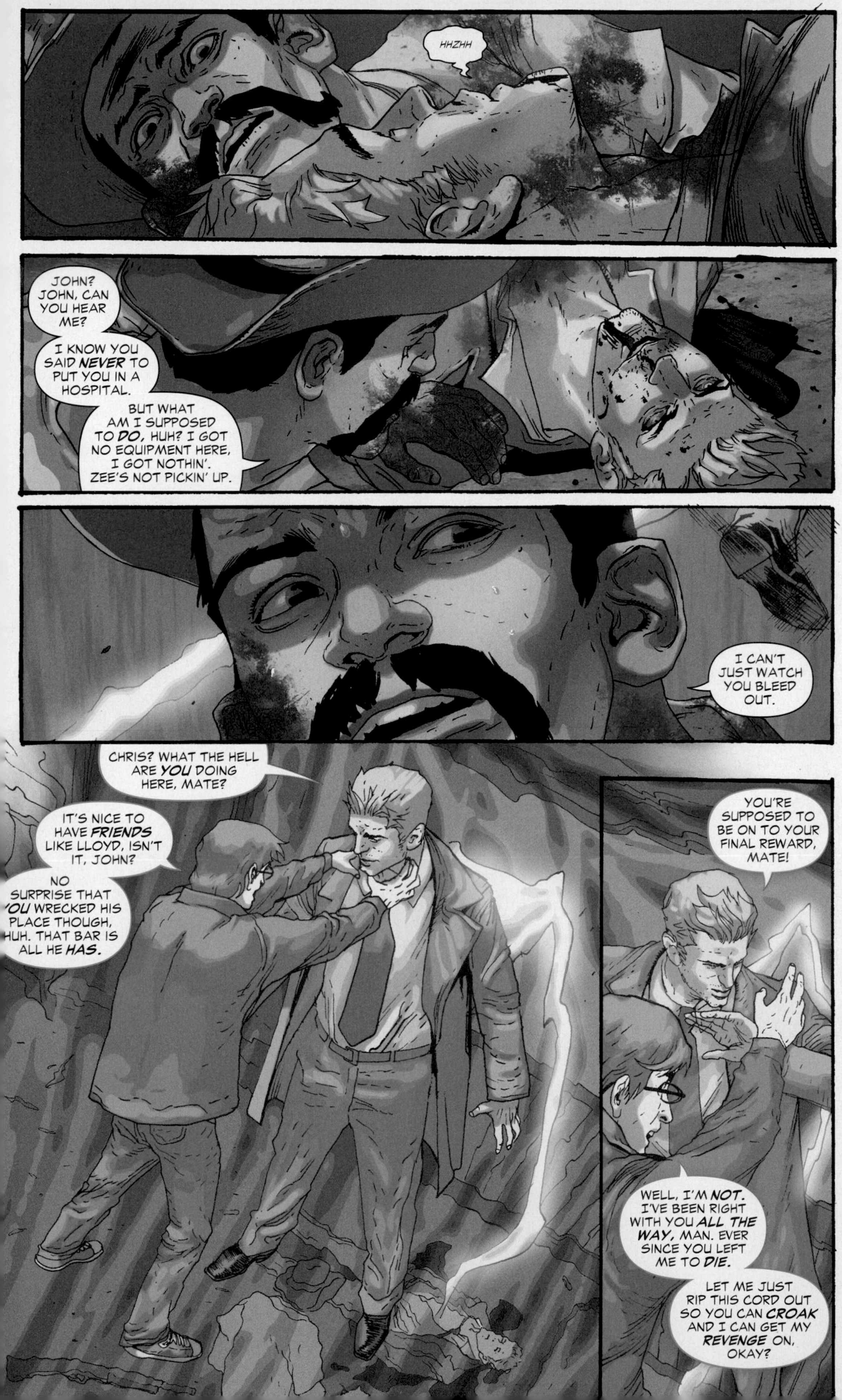
HHZHH
JOHN? JOHN, CAN YOU HEAR ME?
I KNOW YOU SAID NEVER TO PUT YOU IN A HOSPITAL.
BUT WHAT AM I SUPPOSED TO DO, HUH? I GOT NO EQUIPMENT HERE, I GOT NOTHIN'. ZEE'S NOT PICKIN' UP.
I CAN'T JUST WATCH YOU BLEED OUT.
CHRIS? WHAT THE HELL ARE YOU DOING HERE, MATE?
IT'S NICE TO HAVE FRIENDS LIKE LLOYD, ISN'T IT, JOHN?
NO SURPRISE THAT YOU WRECKED HIS PLACE THOUGH, HUH. THAT BAR IS ALL HE HAS.
YOU'RE SUPPOSED TO BE ON TO YOUR FINAL REWARD, MATE!
WELL, I'M NOT. I'VE BEEN RIGHT WITH YOU ALL THE WAY, MAN. EVER SINCE YOU LEFT ME TO DIE.
LET ME JUST RIP THIS CORD OUT SO YOU CAN CROAK AND I CAN GET MY REVENGE ON, OKAY?

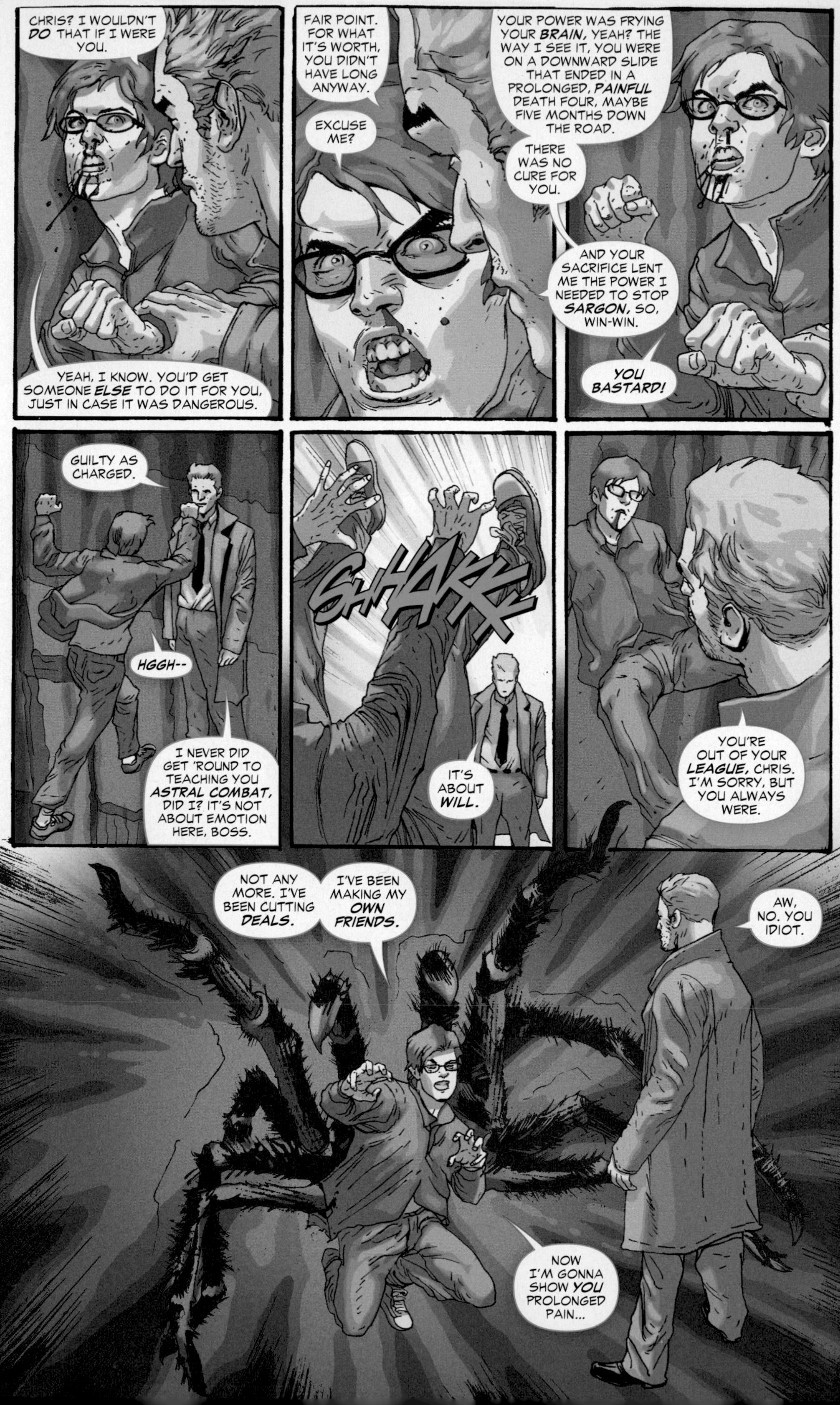
CHRIS? I WOULDN'T DO THAT IF I WERE YOU.
YEAH, I KNOW. YOU'D GET SOMEONE ELSE TO DO IT FOR YOU, JUST IN CASE IT WAS DANGEROUS.
FAIR POINT. FOR WHAT IT'S WORTH, YOU DIDN'T HAVE LONG ANYWAY.
EXCUSE ME?
YOUR POWER WAS FRYING YOUR BRAIN, YEAH? THE WAY I SEE IT, YOU WERE ON A DOWNWARD SLIDE THAT ENDED IN A PROLONGED, PAINFUL DEATH FOUR, MAYBE FIVE MONTHS DOWN THE ROAD.
THERE WAS NO CURE FOR YOU.
AND YOUR SACRIFICE LENT ME THE POWER I NEEDED TO STOP SARGON, SO, WIN-WIN.
YOU BASTARD!
GUILTY AS CHARGED.
HGGH--
I NEVER DID GET 'ROUND TO TEACHING YOU ASTRAL COMBAT, DID I? IT'S NOT ABOUT EMOTION HERE, BOSS.
SHHAKK
IT'S ABOUT WILL.
YOU'RE OUT OF YOUR LEAGUE, CHRIS. I'M SORRY, BUT YOU ALWAYS WERE.
NOT ANY MORE. I'VE BEEN CUTTING DEALS.
I'VE BEEN MAKING MY OWN FRIENDS.
AW, NO. YOU IDIOT.
NOW I'M GONNA SHOW YOU PROLONGED PAIN...

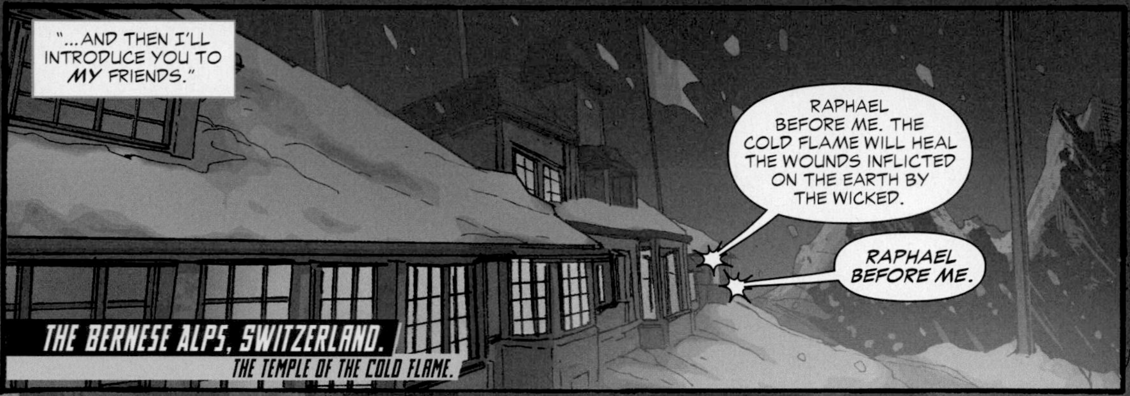
"...AND THEN I'LL INTRODUCE YOU TO MY FRIENDS."
RAPHAEL BEFORE ME. THE COLD FLAME WILL HEAL THE WOUNDS INFLICTED ON THE EARTH BY THE WICKED.
RAPHAEL BEFORE ME.
THE BERNESE ALPS, SWITZERLAND.
THE TEMPLE OF THE COLD FLAME.

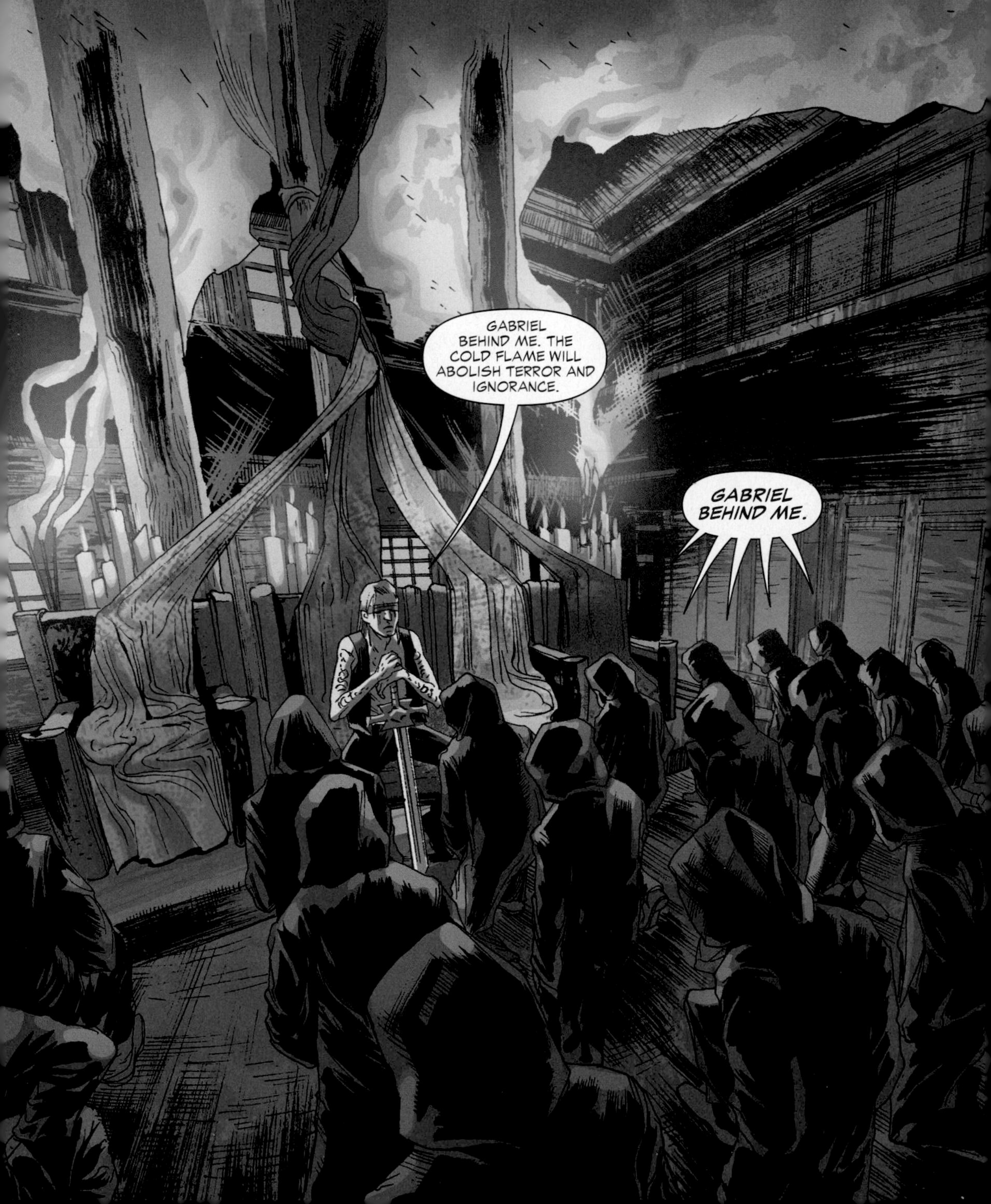
GABRIEL BEHIND ME. THE COLD FLAME WILL ABOLISH TERROR AND IGNORANCE.
GABRIEL BEHIND ME.

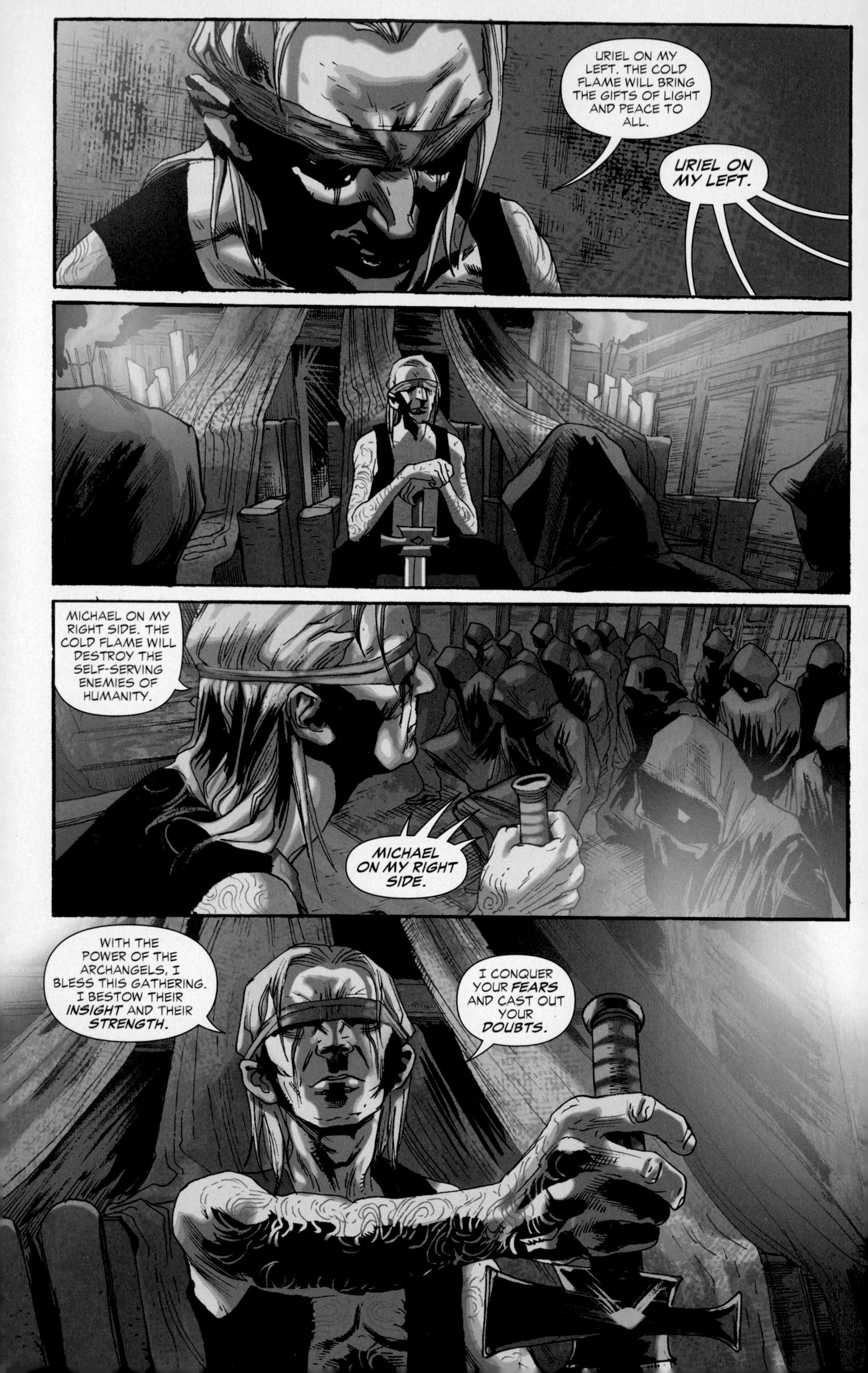

URIEL ON MY LEFT. THE COLD FLAME WILL BRING THE GIFTS OF LIGHT AND PEACE TO ALL.
URIEL ON MY LEFT.
MICHAEL ON MY RIGHT SIDE. THE COLD FLAME WILL DESTROY THE SELF-SERVING ENEMIES OF HUMANITY.
MICHAEL ON MY RIGHT SIDE.
WITH THE POWER OF THE ARCHANGELS, I BLESS THIS GATHERING. I BESTOW THEIR INSIGHT AND THEIR STRENGTH.
I CONQUER YOUR FEARS AND CAST OUT YOUR DOUBTS.

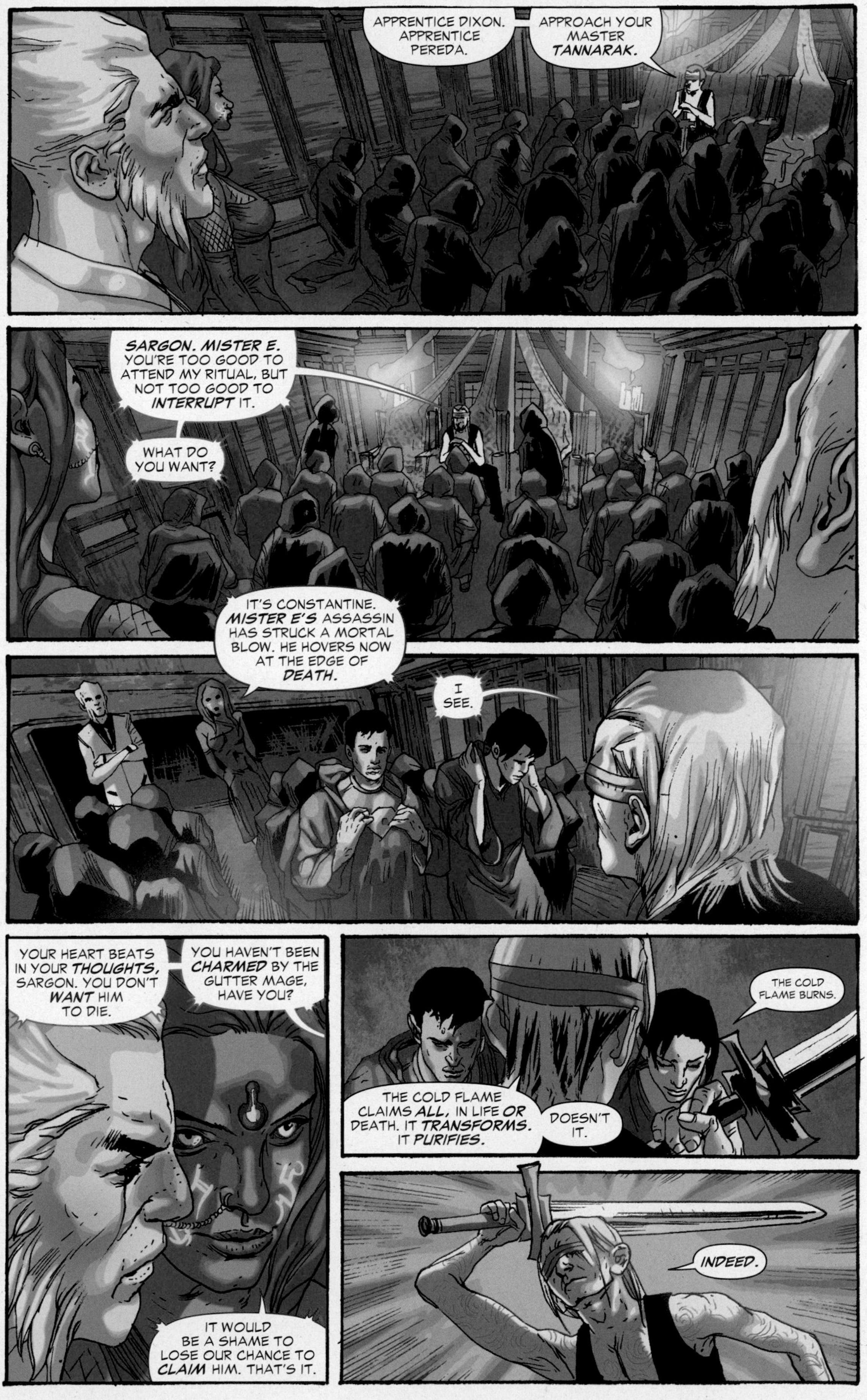
APPRENTICE DIXON. APPRENTICE PEREDA.
APPROACH YOUR MASTER TANNARAK.
SARGON. MISTER E. YOU'RE TOO GOOD TO ATTEND MY RITUAL, BUT NOT TOO GOOD TO INTERRUPT IT.
WHAT DO YOU WANT?
IT'S CONSTANTINE. MISTER E'S ASSASSIN HAS STRUCK A MORTAL BLOW. HE HOVERS NOW AT THE EDGE OF DEATH.
I SEE.
YOUR HEART BEATS IN YOUR THOUGHTS, SARGON. YOU DON'T WANT HIM TO DIE.
YOU HAVEN'T BEEN CHARMED BY THE GUTTER MAGE, HAVE YOU?
IT WOULD BE A SHAME TO LOSE OUR CHANCE TO CLAIM HIM. THAT'S IT.
THE COLD FLAME BURNS.
THE COLD FLAME CLAIMS ALL, IN LIFE OR DEATH. IT TRANSFORMS. IT PURIFIES.
DOESN'T IT.
INDEED.

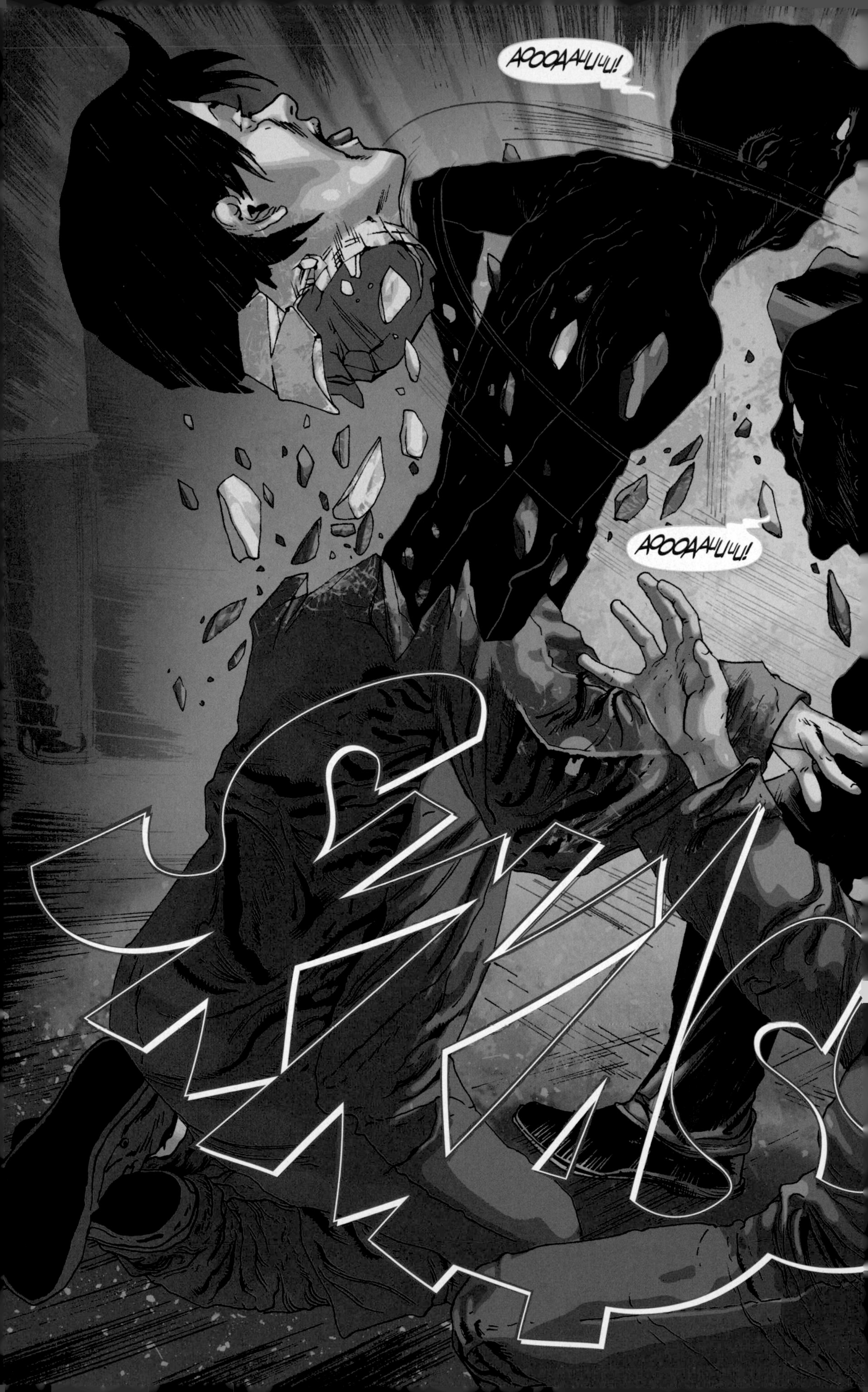
AOOOAAHUUU!
AOOOAAHUUU!

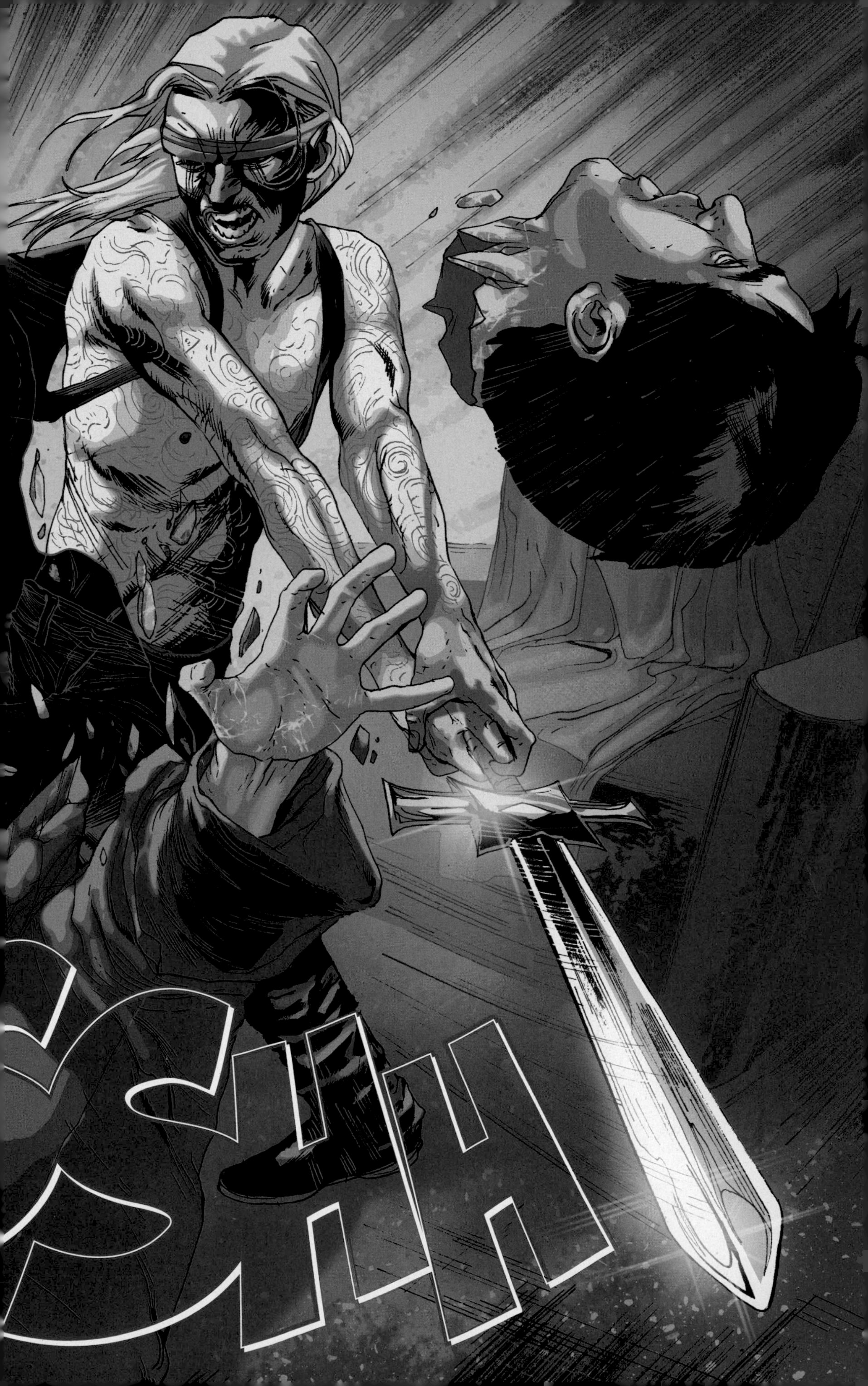
SHH

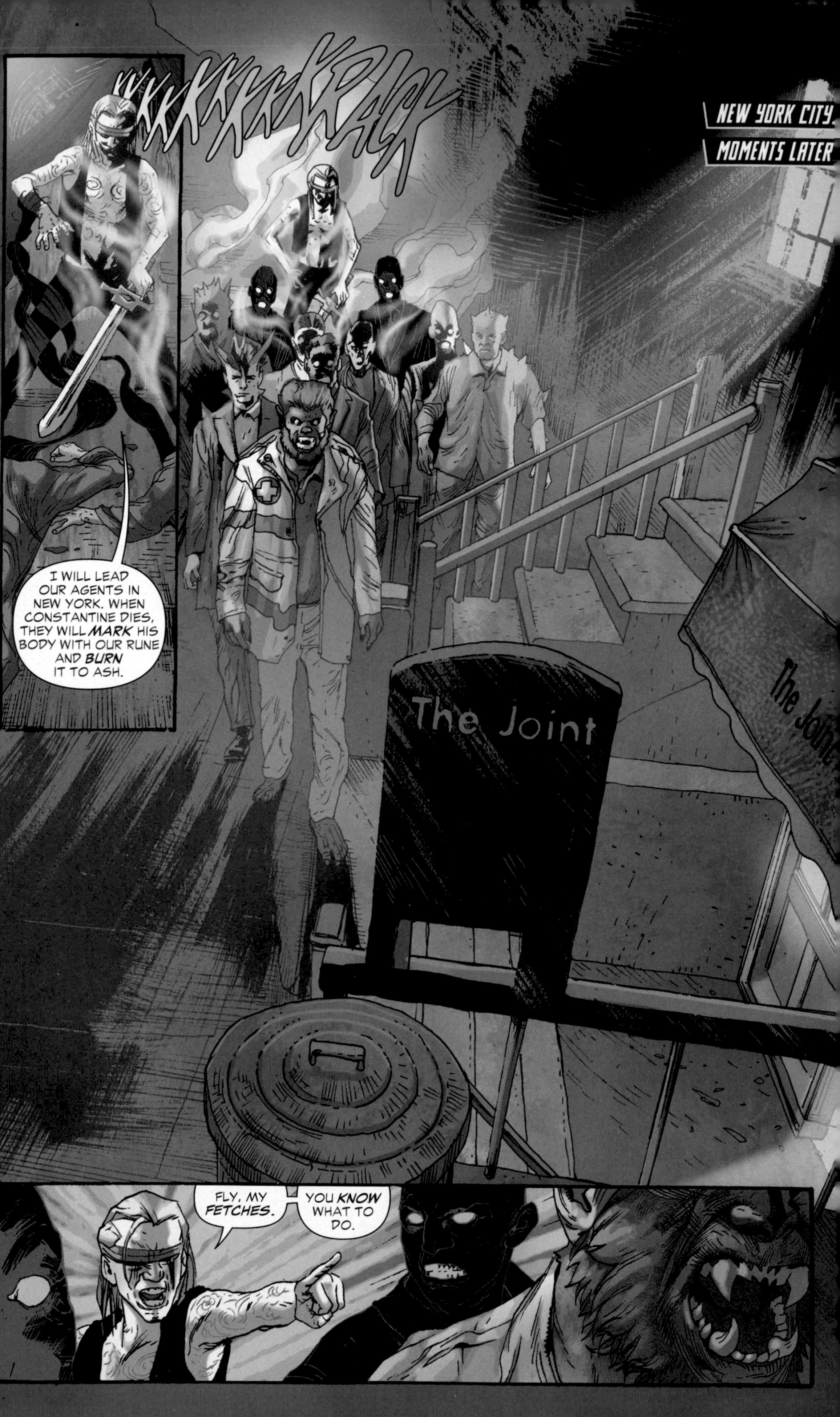

KKKKKKKKKRACK
NEW YORK CITY
MOMENTS LATER
I WILL LEAD OUR AGENTS IN NEW YORK. WHEN CONSTANTINE DIES, THEY WILL MARK HIS BODY WITH OUR RUNE AND BURN IT TO ASH.
The Joint
The Joint
FLY, MY FETCHES.
YOU KNOW WHAT TO DO.

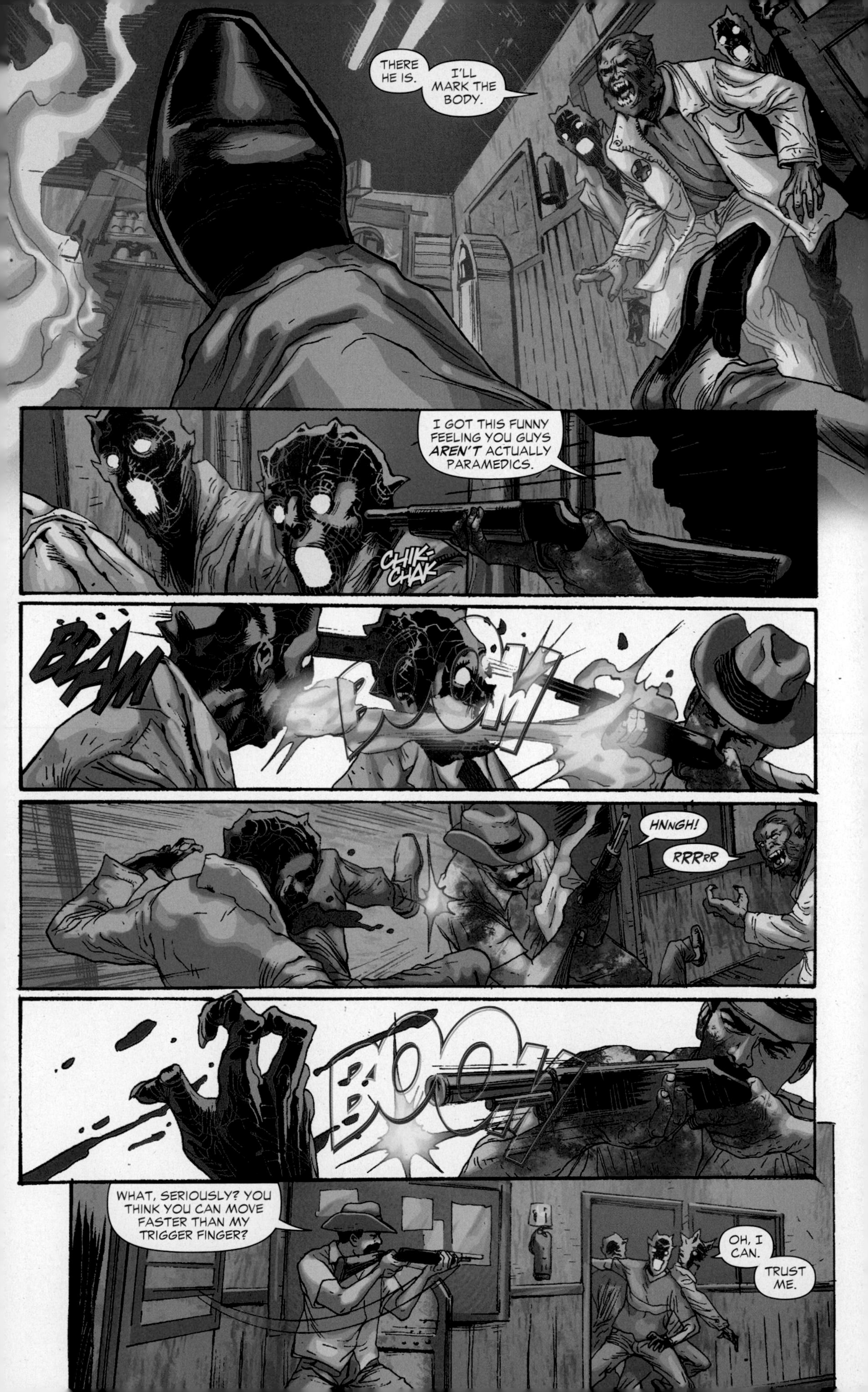
THERE HE IS.
I'LL MARK THE BODY.
I GOT THIS FUNNY FEELING YOU GUYS AREN'T ACTUALLY PARAMEDICS.
CHIK-CHAK
BLAM
BOOM
HNNGH!
RRRRR
BOOM
WHAT, SERIOUSLY? YOU THINK YOU CAN MOVE FASTER THAN MY TRIGGER FINGER?
OH, I CAN.
TRUST ME.

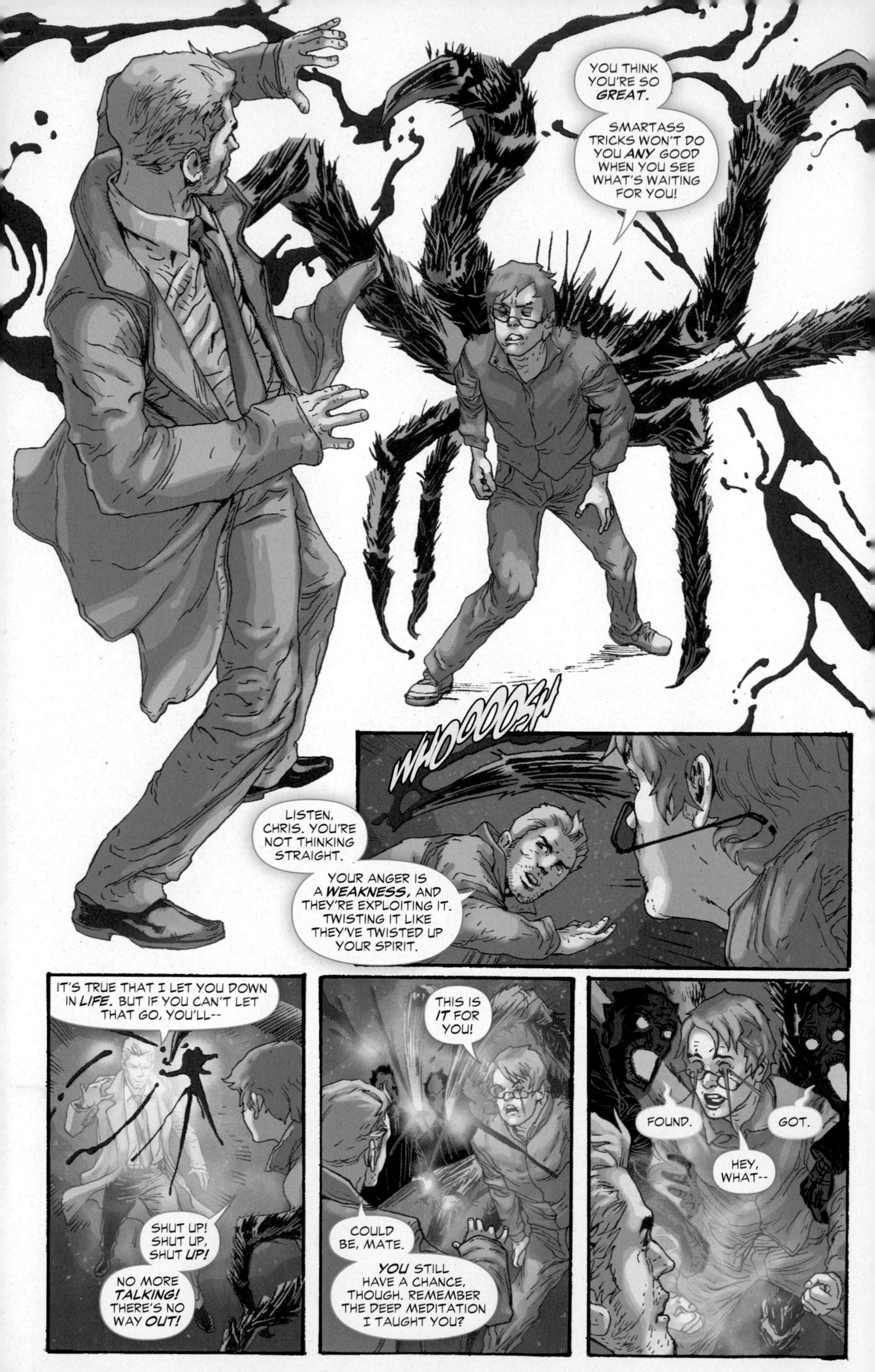
YOU THINK YOU'RE SO *GREAT*.
SMARTASS TRICKS WON'T DO YOU *ANY* GOOD WHEN YOU SEE WHAT'S WAITING FOR YOU!
WHOOOOOSH
LISTEN, CHRIS. YOU'RE NOT THINKING STRAIGHT.
YOUR ANGER IS A *WEAKNESS*, AND THEY'RE EXPLOITING IT. TWISTING IT LIKE THEY'VE TWISTED UP YOUR SPIRIT.
IT'S TRUE THAT I LET YOU DOWN IN *LIFE*. BUT IF YOU CAN'T LET THAT GO, YOU'LL--
SHUT UP! SHUT UP, SHUT *UP!*
NO MORE *TALKING!* THERE'S NO WAY *OUT!*
THIS IS *IT* FOR YOU!
COULD BE, MATE.
YOU STILL HAVE A CHANCE, THOUGH. REMEMBER THE DEEP MEDITATION I TAUGHT YOU?
FOUND.
GOT.
HEY, WHAT--

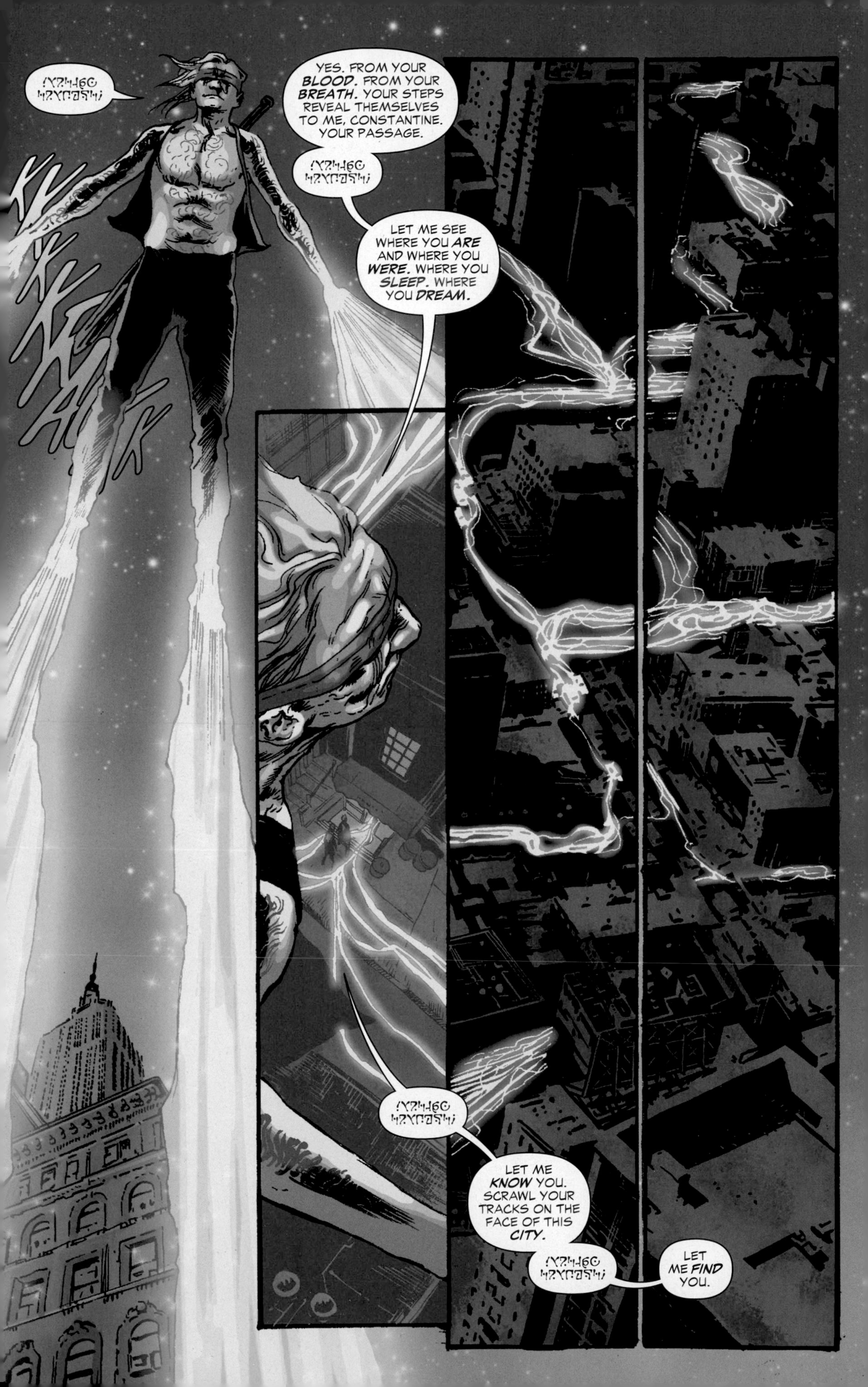
YES. FROM YOUR BLOOD. FROM YOUR BREATH. YOUR STEPS REVEAL THEMSELVES TO ME, CONSTANTINE. YOUR PASSAGE.
LET ME SEE WHERE YOU ARE AND WHERE YOU WERE. WHERE YOU SLEEP. WHERE YOU DREAM.
LET ME KNOW YOU. SCRAWL YOUR TRACKS ON THE FACE OF THIS CITY.
LET ME FIND YOU.

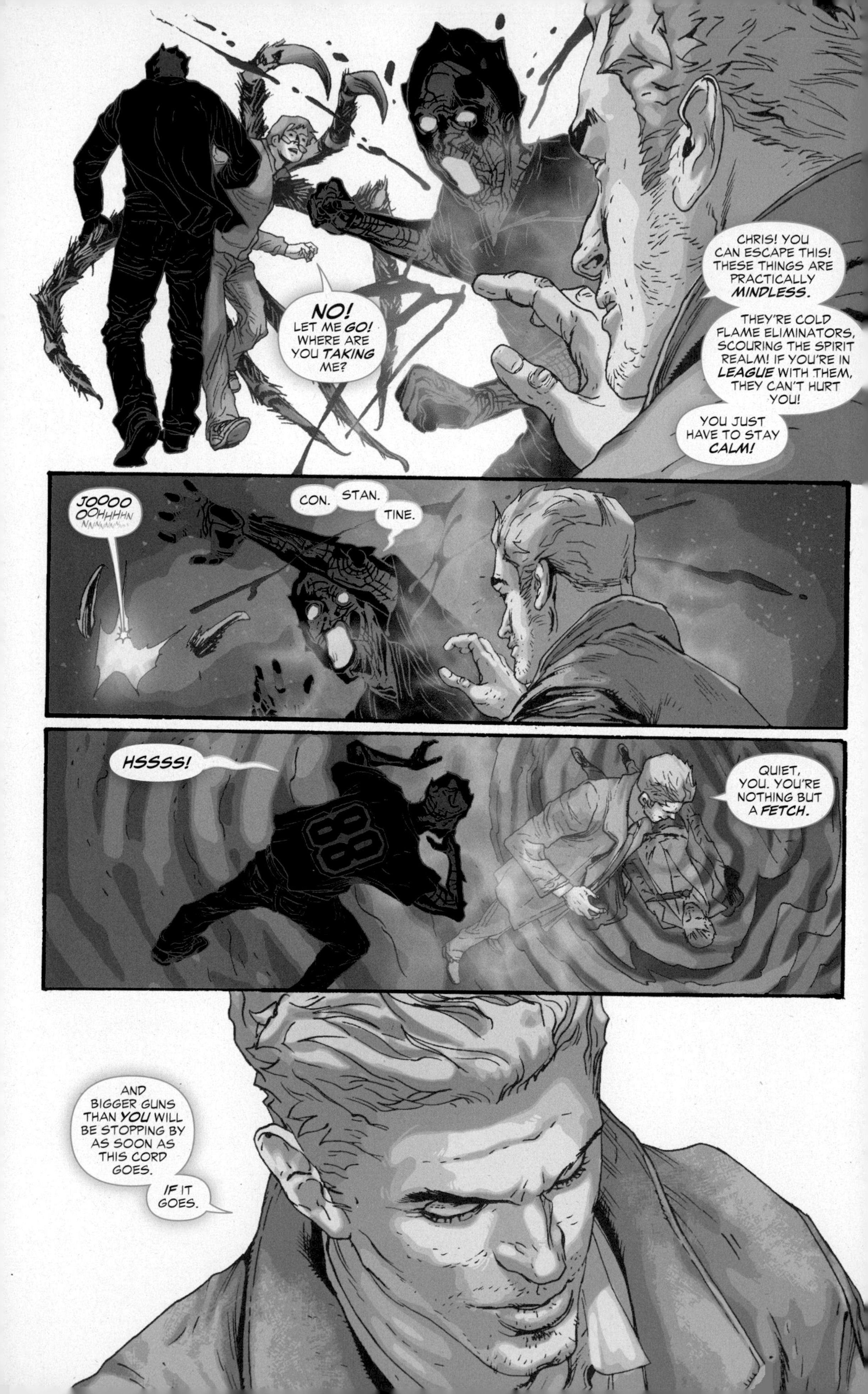
CHRIS! YOU CAN ESCAPE THIS! THESE THINGS ARE PRACTICALLY MINDLESS.
THEY'RE COLD FLAME ELIMINATORS, SCOURING THE SPIRIT REALM! IF YOU'RE IN LEAGUE WITH THEM, THEY CAN'T HURT YOU!
YOU JUST HAVE TO STAY CALM!
NO! LET ME GO! WHERE ARE YOU TAKING ME?
JOOOO OOHHHHN NNNNNNNNNss
CON.
STAN.
TINE.
HSSSS!
QUIET, YOU. YOU'RE NOTHING BUT A FETCH.
AND BIGGER GUNS THAN YOU WILL BE STOPPING BY AS SOON AS THIS CORD GOES.
IF IT GOES.

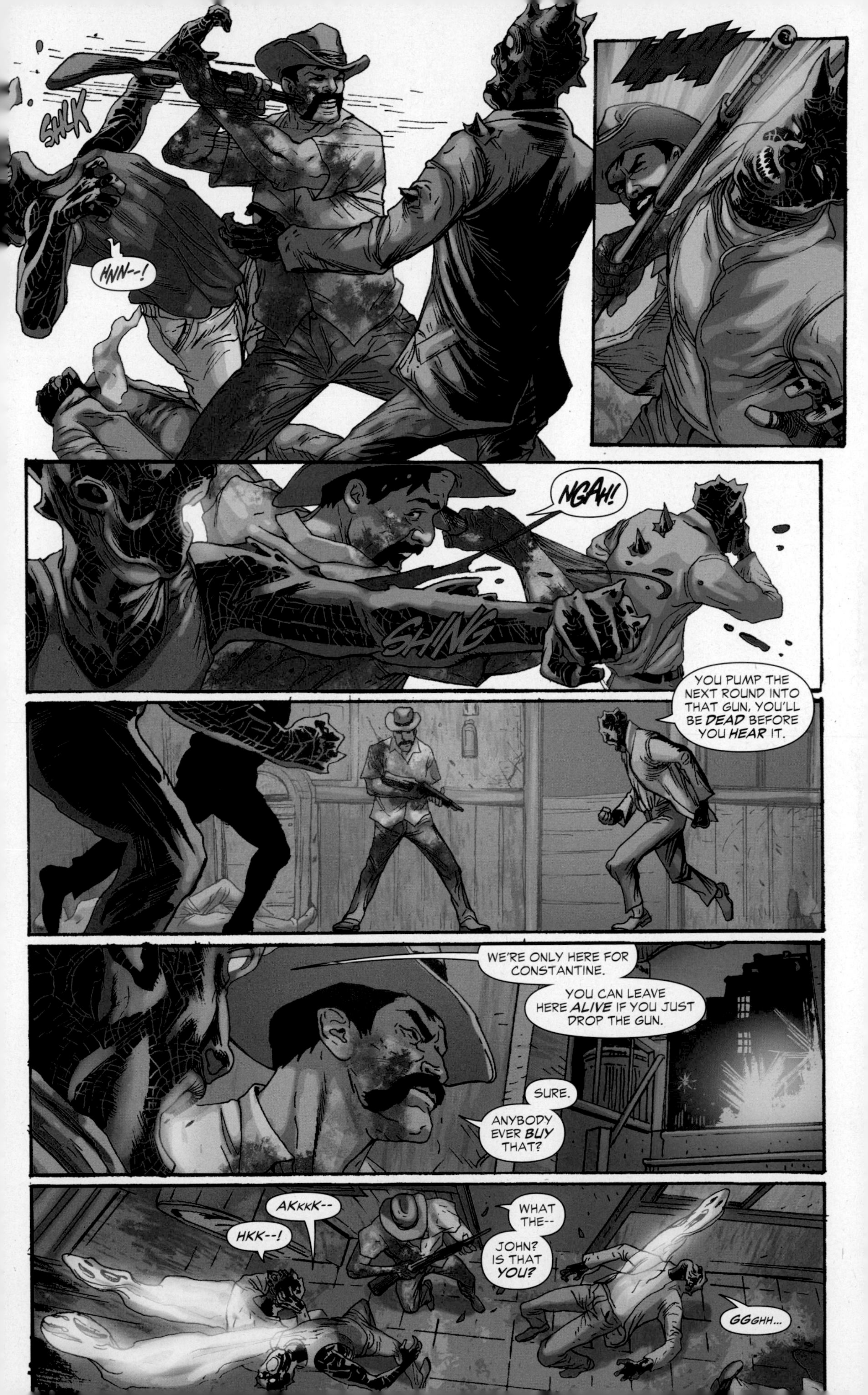
SHLK
HNN--!
NGAH!
SHING
YOU PUMP THE NEXT ROUND INTO THAT GUN, YOU'LL BE DEAD BEFORE YOU HEAR IT.
WE'RE ONLY HERE FOR CONSTANTINE.
YOU CAN LEAVE HERE ALIVE IF YOU JUST DROP THE GUN.
SURE.
ANYBODY EVER BUY THAT?
AKKKK--
HKK--!
WHAT THE--
JOHN? IS THAT YOU?
GGGHH...

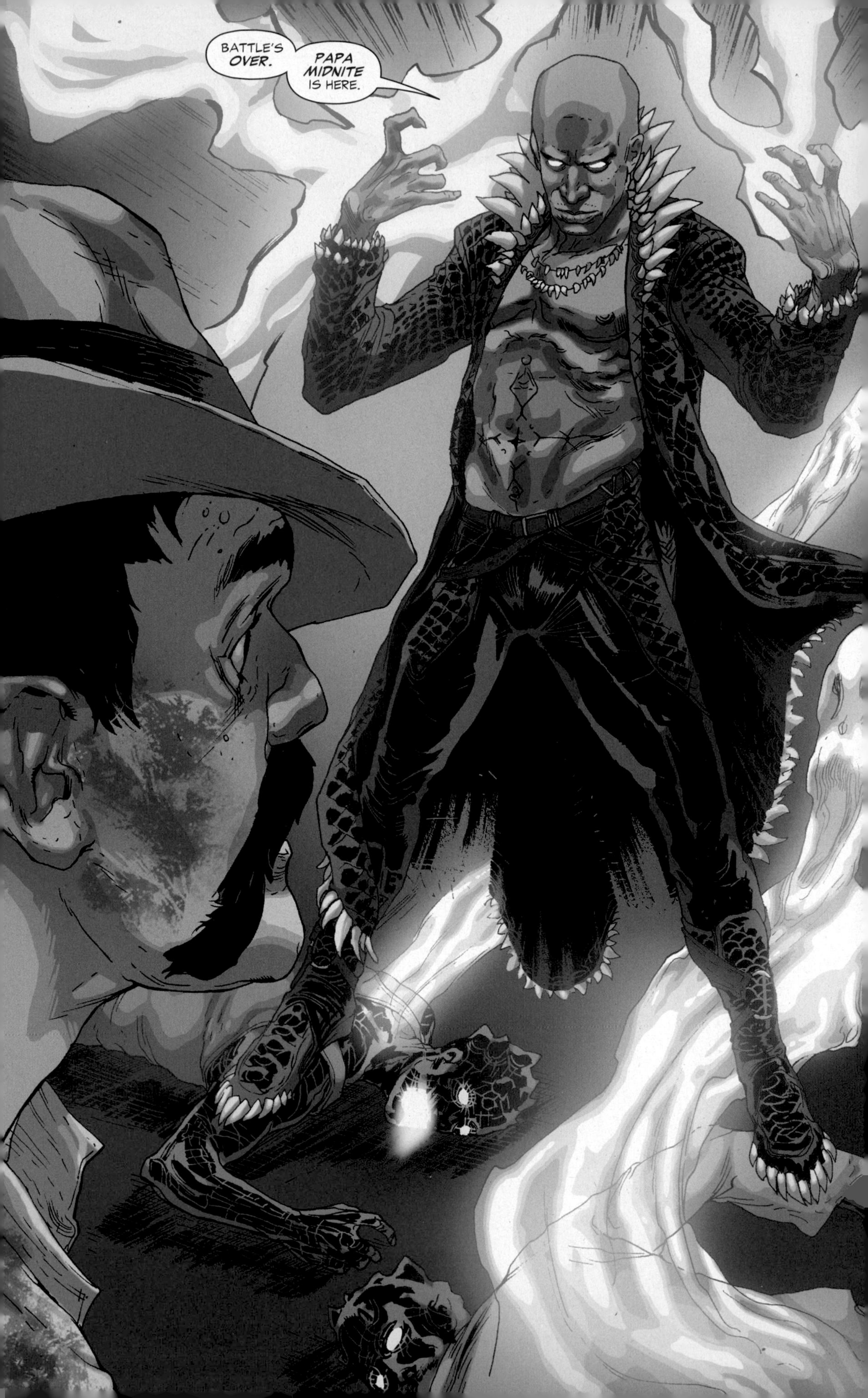
BATTLE'S OVER.
PAPA MIDNITE IS HERE.

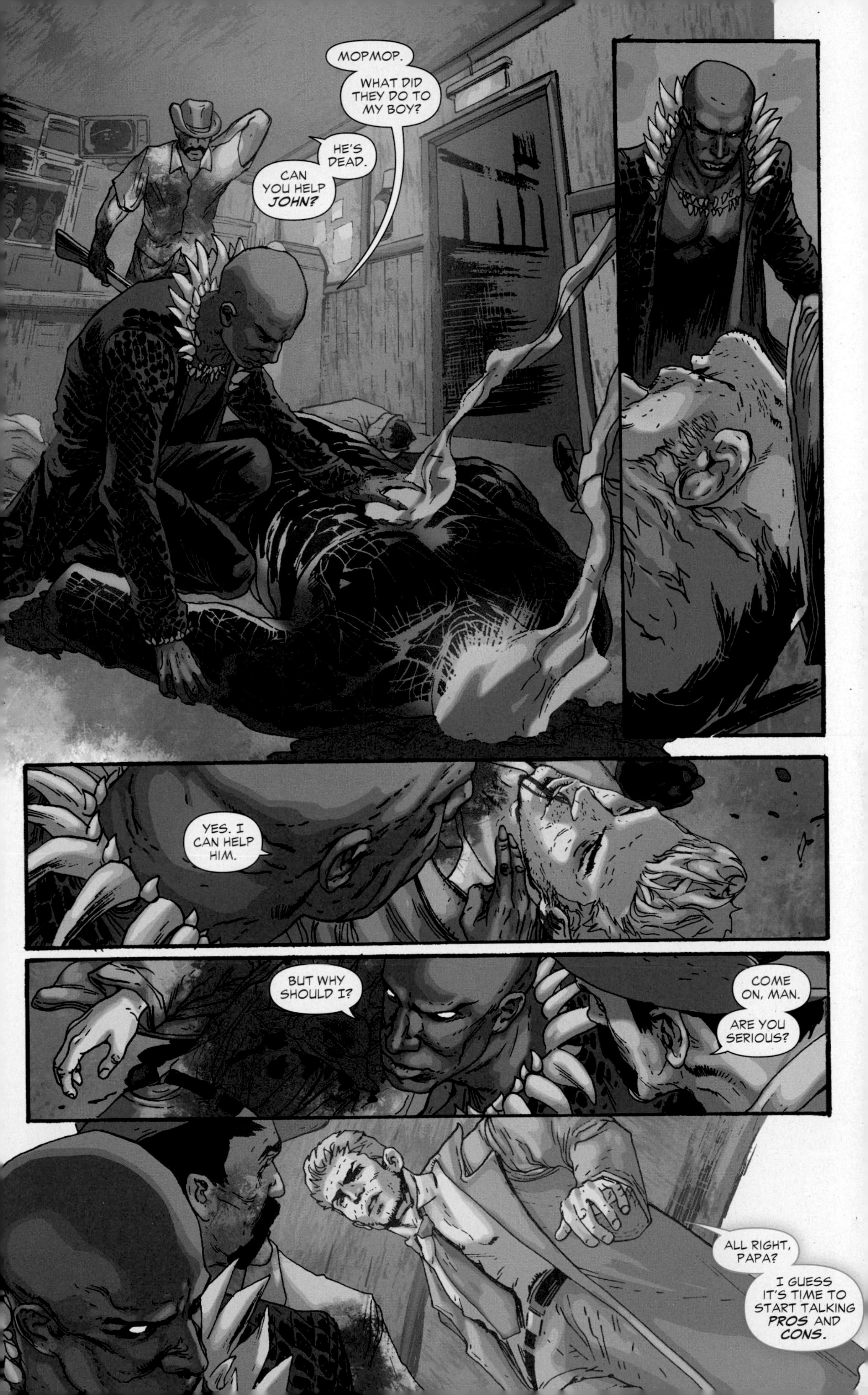
MOPMOP.
WHAT DID THEY DO TO MY BOY?
HE'S DEAD.
CAN YOU HELP JOHN?
YES. I CAN HELP HIM.
BUT WHY SHOULD I?
COME ON, MAN.
ARE YOU SERIOUS?
ALL RIGHT, PAPA?
I GUESS IT'S TIME TO START TALKING PROS AND CONS.

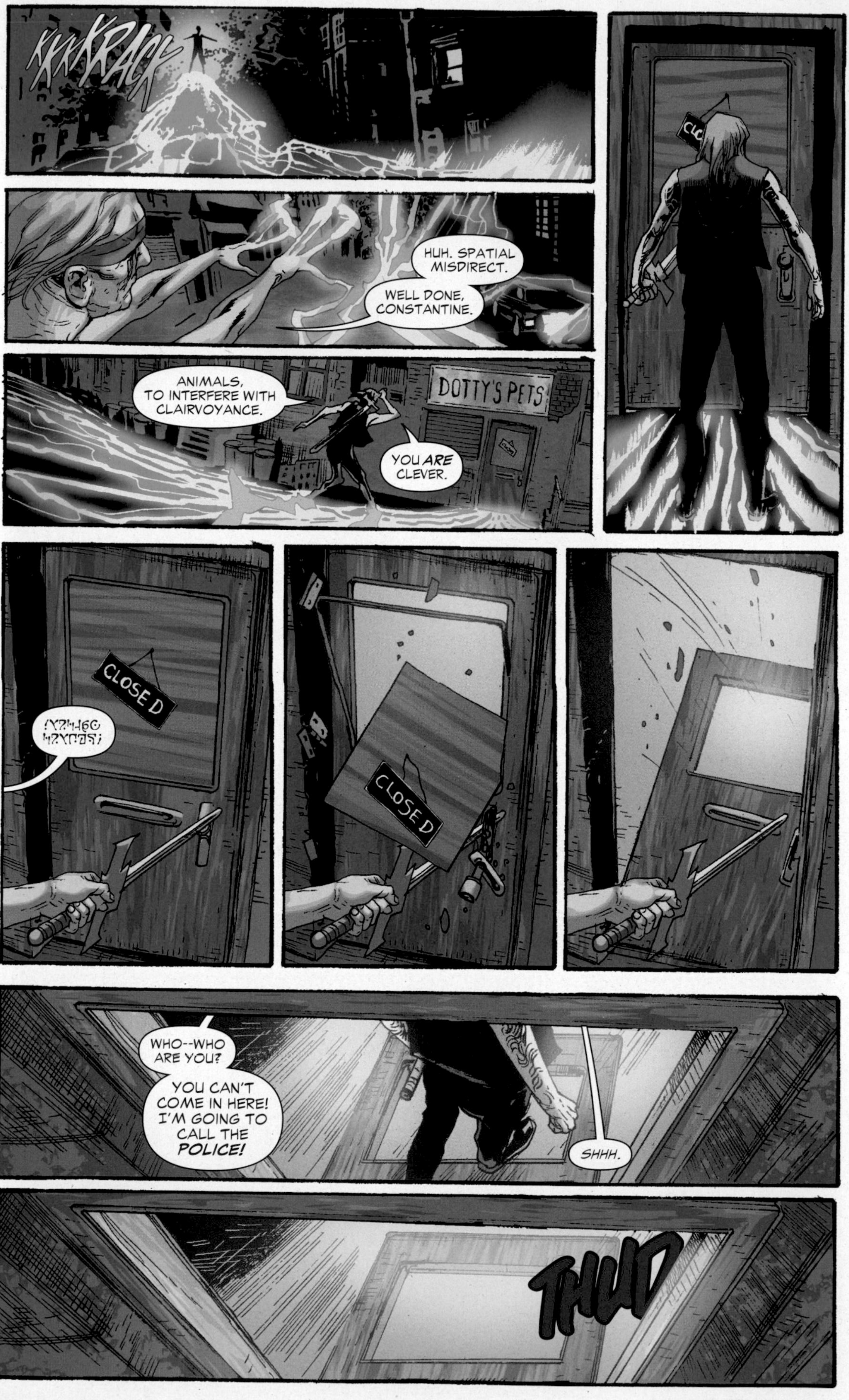
KKKKRACK
HUH. SPATIAL MISDIRECT.
WELL DONE, CONSTANTINE.
ANIMALS, TO INTERFERE WITH CLAIRVOYANCE.
DOTTY'S PETS
YOU ARE CLEVER.
CLOSED
CLOSED
WHO--WHO ARE YOU?
YOU CAN'T COME IN HERE! I'M GOING TO CALL THE POLICE!
SHHH.
THUD

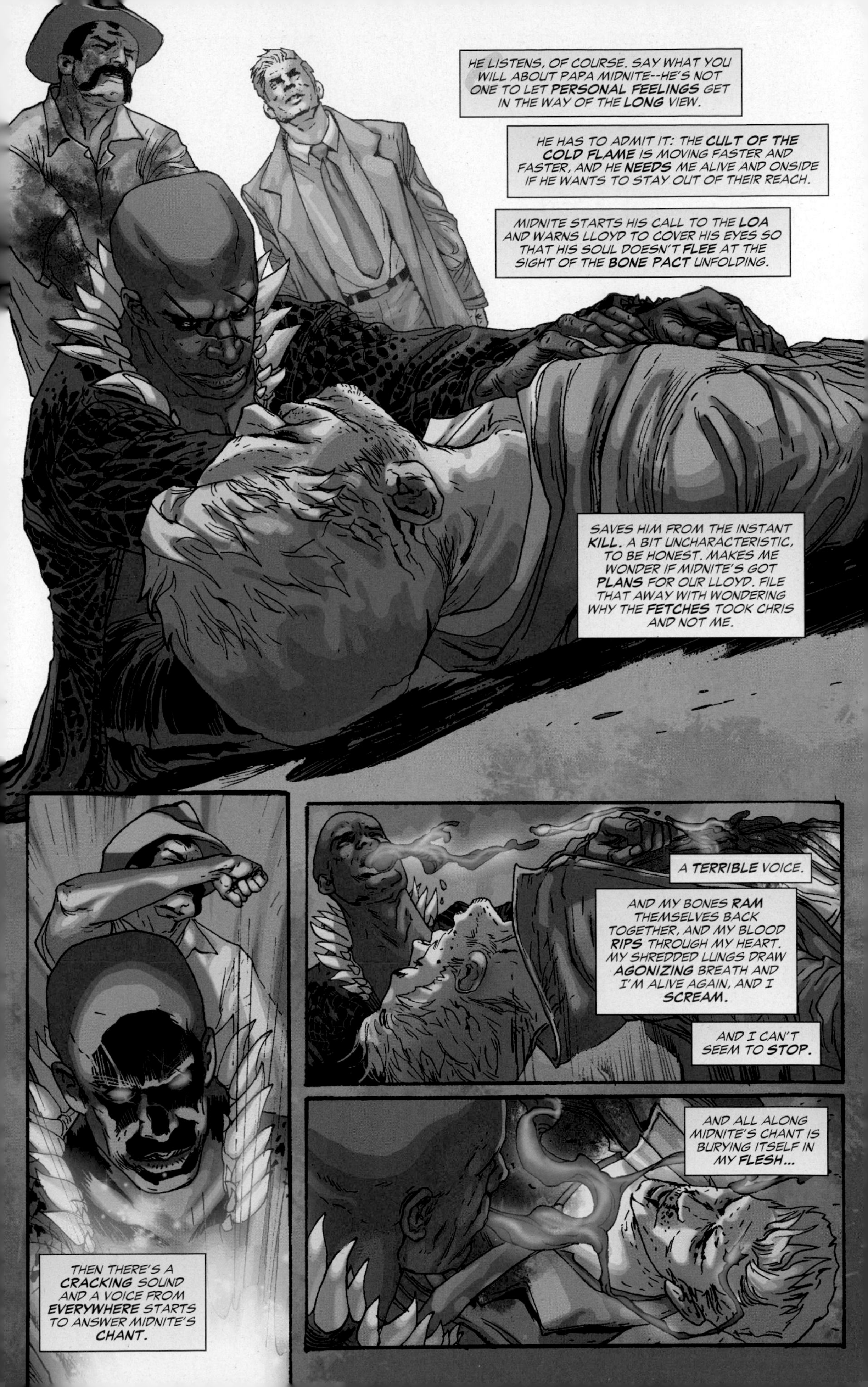

HE LISTENS, OF COURSE. SAY WHAT YOU WILL ABOUT PAPA MIDNITE--HE'S NOT ONE TO LET PERSONAL FEELINGS GET IN THE WAY OF THE LONG VIEW.
HE HAS TO ADMIT IT: THE CULT OF THE COLD FLAME IS MOVING FASTER AND FASTER, AND HE NEEDS ME ALIVE AND ONSIDE IF HE WANTS TO STAY OUT OF THEIR REACH.
MIDNITE STARTS HIS CALL TO THE LOA AND WARNS LLOYD TO COVER HIS EYES SO THAT HIS SOUL DOESN'T FLEE AT THE SIGHT OF THE BONE PACT UNFOLDING.
SAVES HIM FROM THE INSTANT KILL. A BIT UNCHARACTERISTIC, TO BE HONEST. MAKES ME WONDER IF MIDNITE'S GOT PLANS FOR OUR LLOYD. FILE THAT AWAY WITH WONDERING WHY THE FETCHES TOOK CHRIS AND NOT ME.
THEN THERE'S A CRACKING SOUND AND A VOICE FROM EVERYWHERE STARTS TO ANSWER MIDNITE'S CHANT.
A TERRIBLE VOICE.
AND MY BONES RAM THEMSELVES BACK TOGETHER, AND MY BLOOD RIPS THROUGH MY HEART. MY SHREDDED LUNGS DRAW AGONIZING BREATH AND I'M ALIVE AGAIN, AND I SCREAM.
AND I CAN'T SEEM TO STOP.
AND ALL ALONG MIDNITE'S CHANT IS BURYING ITSELF IN MY FLESH...

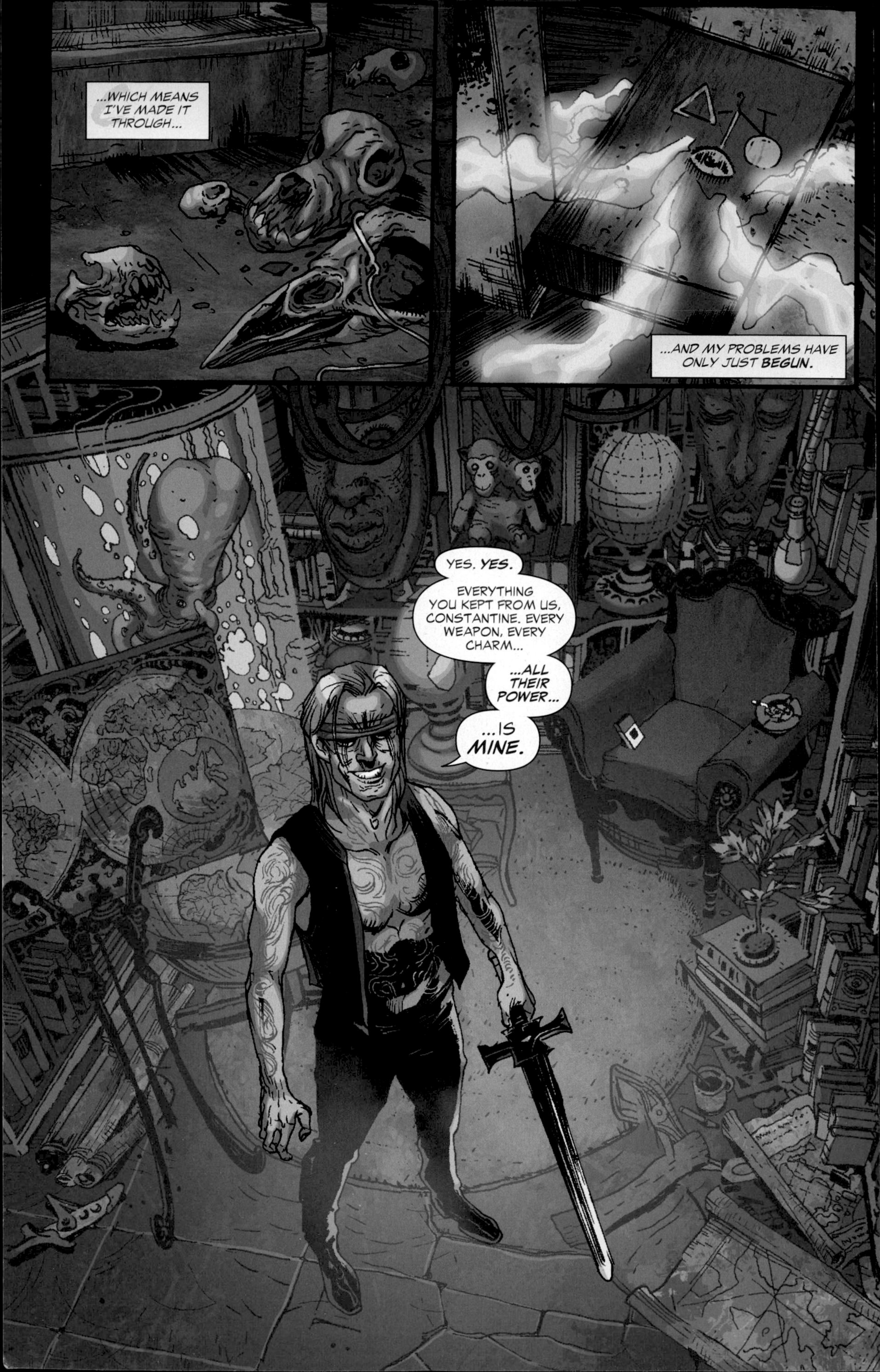
...WHICH MEANS I'VE MADE IT THROUGH...
...AND MY PROBLEMS HAVE ONLY JUST BEGUN.
YES. YES.
EVERYTHING YOU KEPT FROM US, CONSTANTINE. EVERY WEAPON, EVERY CHARM...
...ALL THEIR POWER...
...IS MINE.

Mr. E, Sargon Sr., Tannarak and Zatara designs by Jim Lee

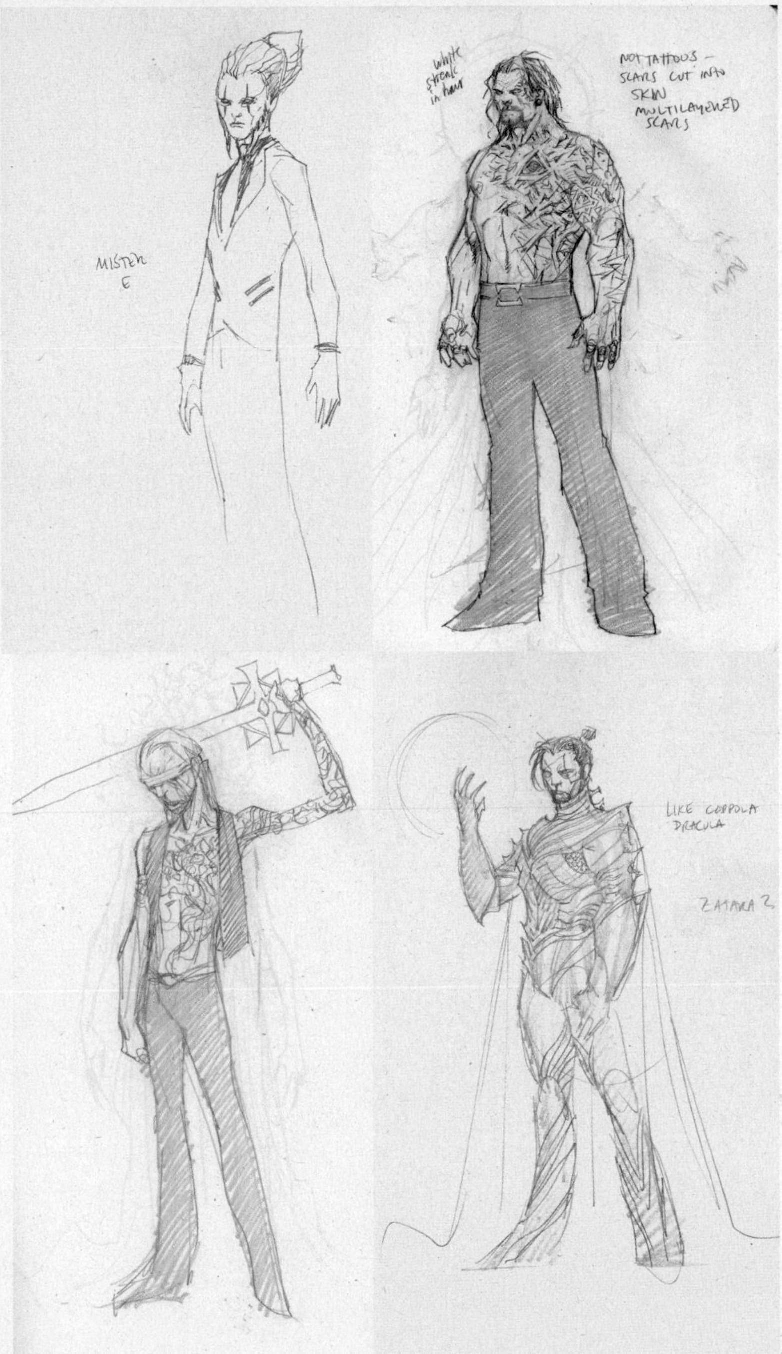

MISTER E
White streak in hair
NOT TATTOOS - SCARS CUT INTO SKIN MULTILAYERED SCARS
LIKE COPPOLA DRACULA
ZATARA ?

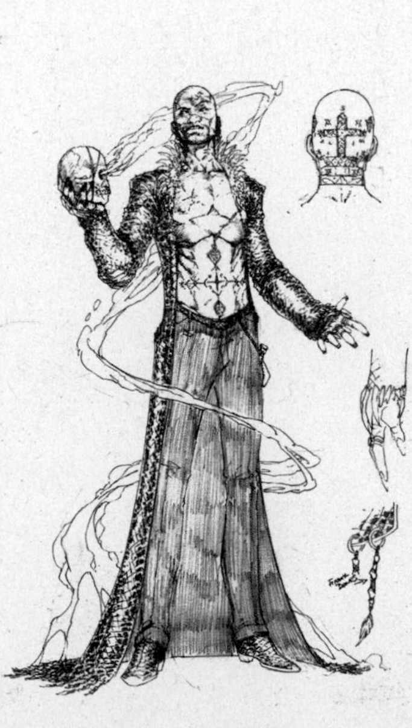

Papa Midnite design by Brett Booth

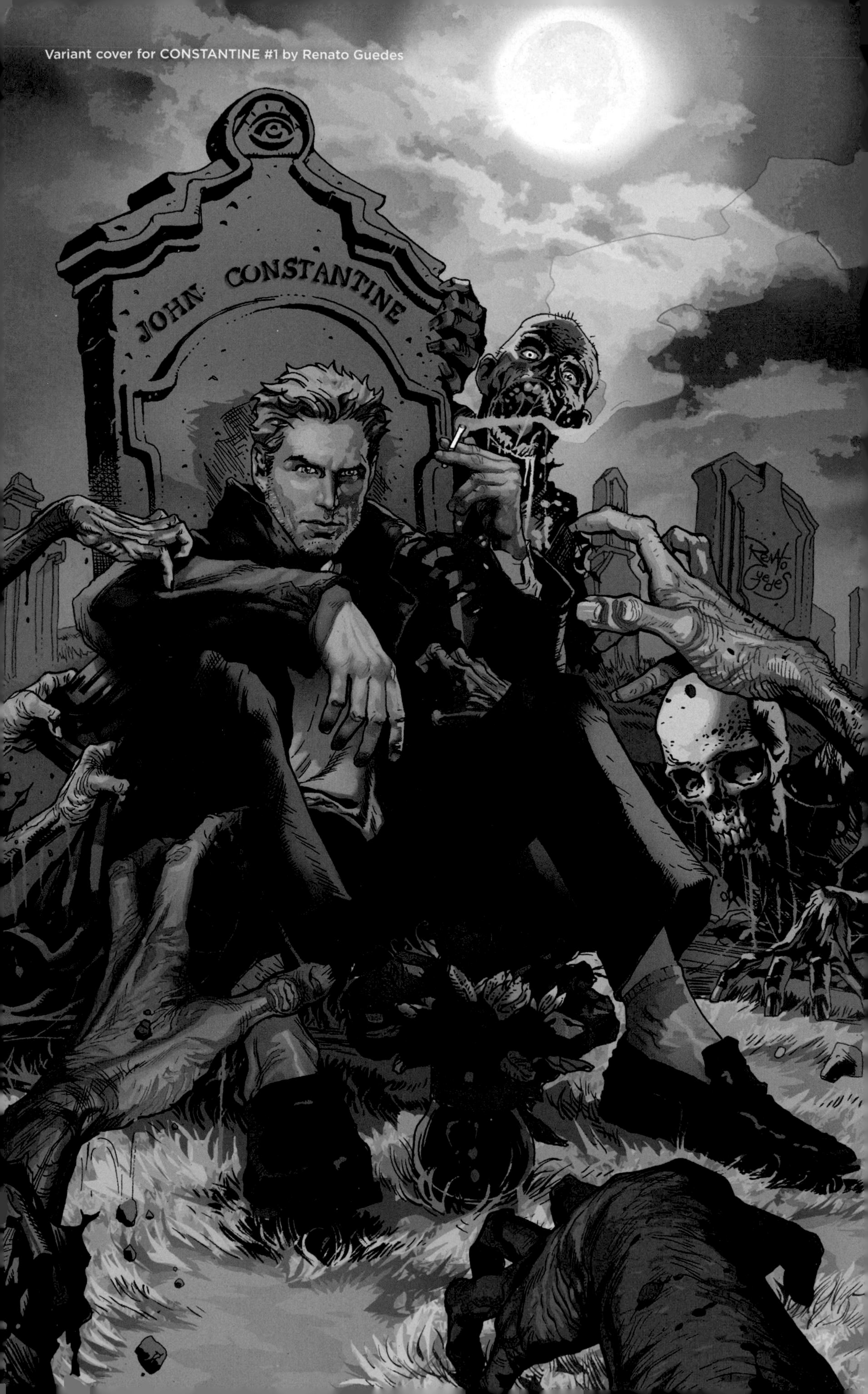
JOHN CONSTANTINE
Renato Guedes
Variant cover for CONSTANTINE #1 by Renato Guedes

Issue #3 cover sketch by Juan Jose Ryp

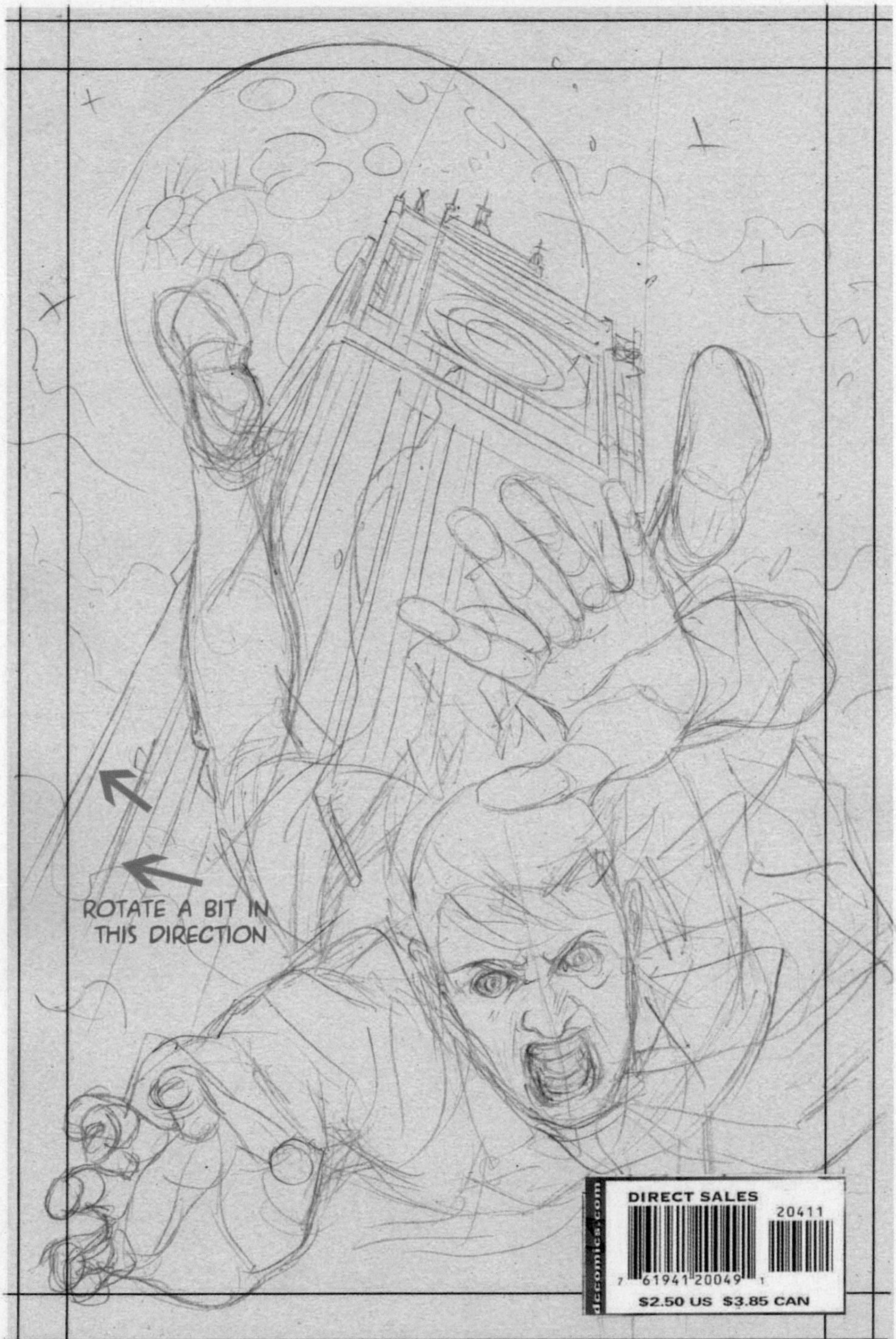
ROTATE A BIT IN
THIS DIRECTION
DIRECT SALES
20411
7 61941 20049 1
$2.50 US $3.85 CAN
dccomics.com

Issue #4 cover sketch by Eddy Barrows

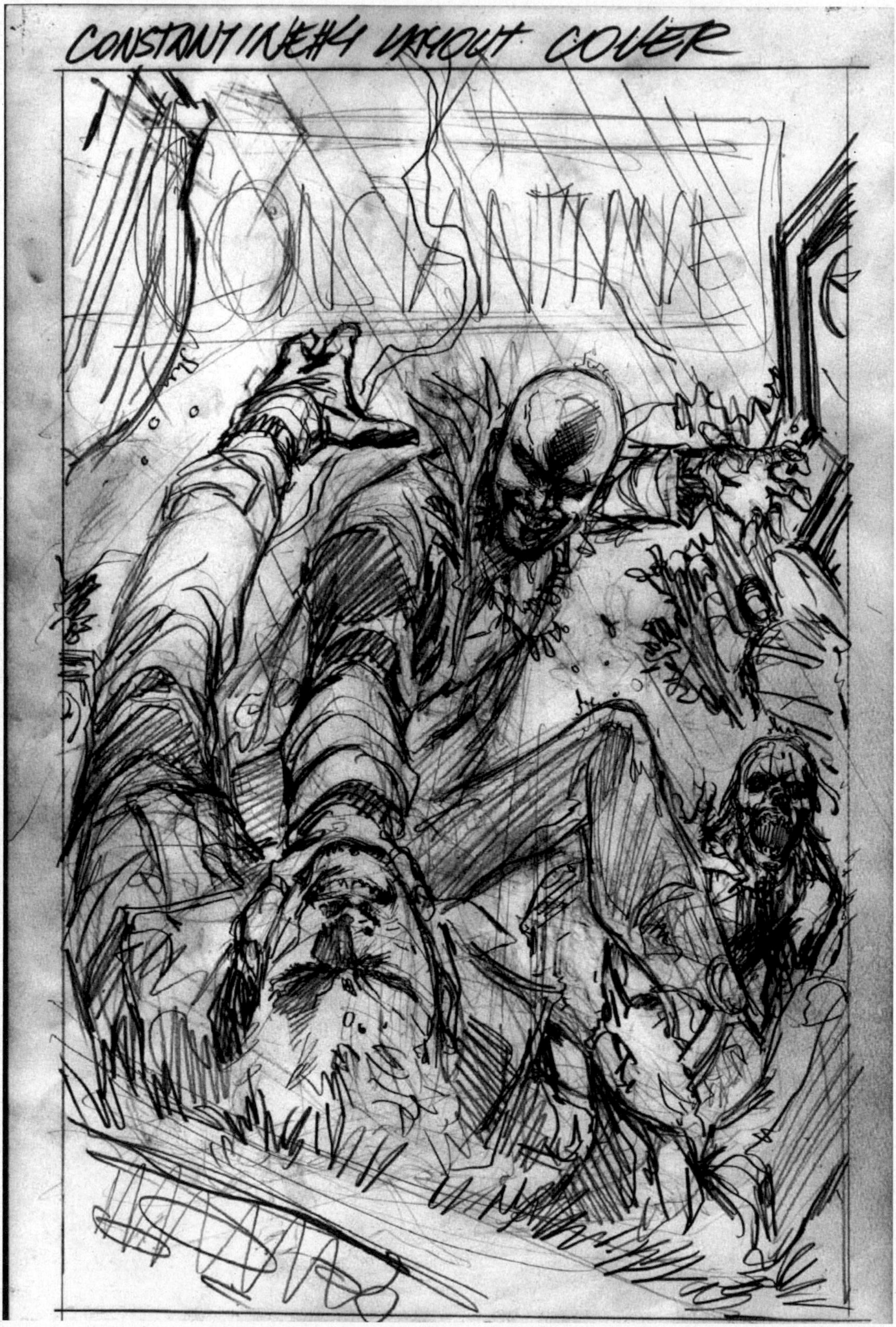
CONSTANTINE #4 LAYOUT COVER

Issue #5 cover sketch by Eddy Barrows

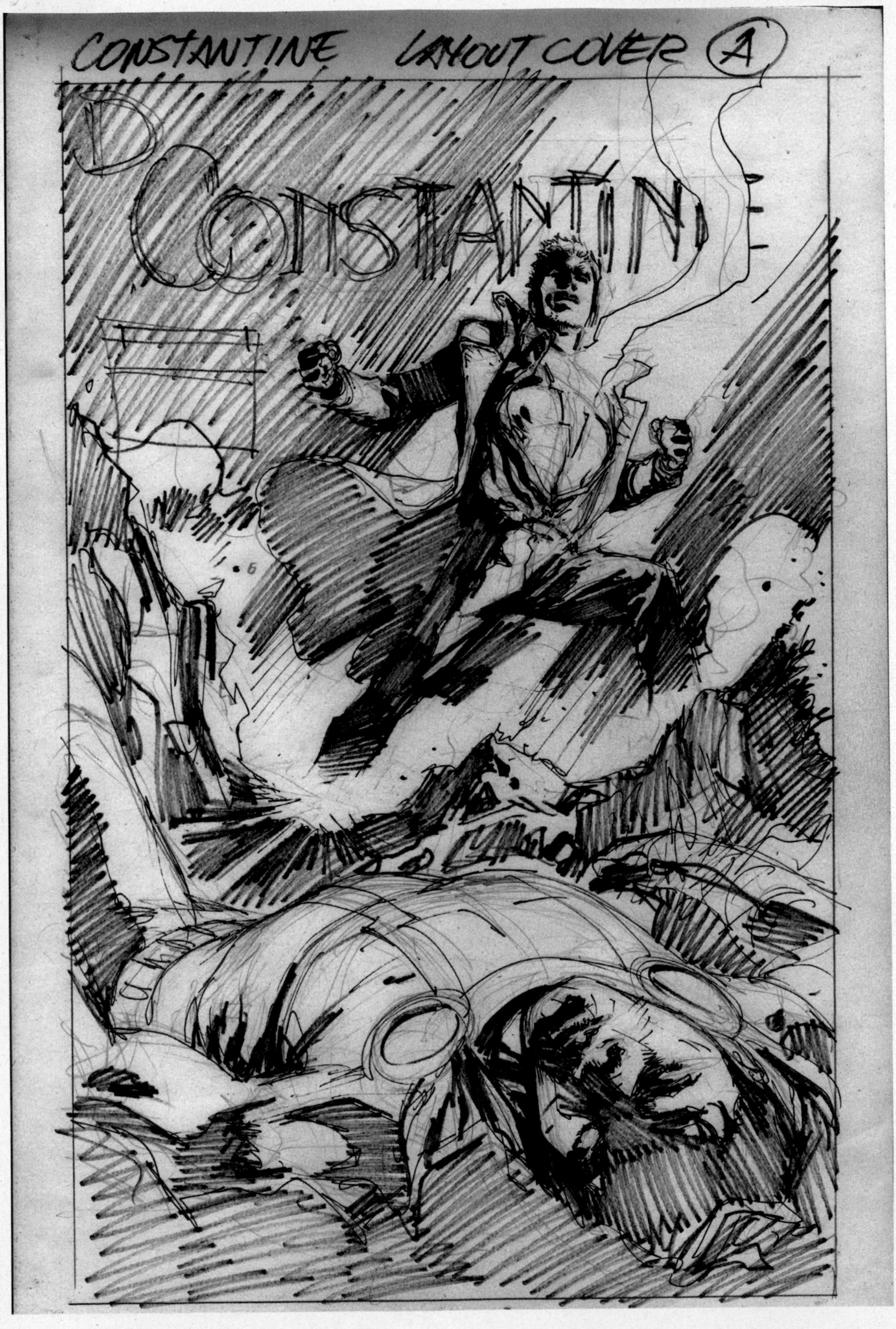
CONSTANTINE LAYOUT COVER A
CONSTANTINE

"If you don't love it from the very first page, you're not human."
—MTV GEEK

"ANIMAL MAN has the sensational Jeff Lemire at the helm."
—ENTERTAINMENT WEEKLY

START AT THE BEGINNING!

ANIMAL MAN
VOLUME 1: THE HUNT

JUSTICE LEAGUE DARK VOLUME 1: IN THE DARK

RESURRECTION MAN VOLUME 1: DEAD AGAIN

FRANKENSTEIN AGENT OF S.H.A.D.E. VOLUME 1: WAR OF THE MONSTERS

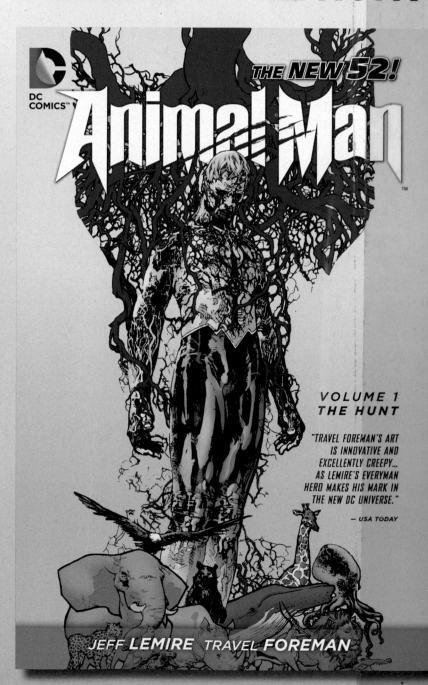

THE NEW 52!

DC COMICS™

Animal Man

VOLUME 1
THE HUNT

"TRAVEL FOREMAN'S ART IS INNOVATIVE AND EXCELLENTLY CREEPY... AS LEMIRE'S EVERYMAN HERO MAKES HIS MARK IN THE NEW DC UNIVERSE."
— USA TODAY

JEFF LEMIRE   TRAVEL FOREMAN